Institutions and Market Economies

Also by W. R. Garside

THE DURHAM MINERS, 1919–1960

THE MEASUREMENT OF UNEMPLOYMENT: Methods and Sources in Great Britain 1850–1979

AFTER THE SLUMP: Industry and Politics in 1930s Britain and Germany (*co-editor with C. Buchheim*)

BRITISH UNEMPLOYMENT, 1919–1939: A Study in Public Policy

CAPITALISM IN CRISIS: International Responses to the Great Depression

Institutions and Market Economies

The Political Economy of Growth and Development

Edited by

W. R. Garside

palgrave
macmillan

First published 2007 by
PALGRAVE MACMILLAN
Houndmills, Basingstoke, Hampshire RG21 6XS and
175 Fifth Avenue, New York, N.Y. 10010
Companies and representatives throughout the world

PALGRAVE MACMILLAN is the global academic imprint of the Palgrave Macmillan division of St. Martin's Press, LLC and of Palgrave Macmillan Ltd. Macmillan® is a registered trademark in the United States, United Kingdom and other countries. Palgrave is a registered trademark in the European Union and other countries.

ISBN-13: 978–1–4039–8758–7 hardback
ISBN-10: 1–4039–8758–0 hardback

This book is printed on paper suitable for recycling and made from fully managed and sustained forest sources. Logging, pulping and manufacturing processes are expected to conform to the environmental regulations of the country of origin.

A catalogue record for this book is available from the British Library.

A catalog record for this book is available from the Library of Congress.

10 9 8 7 6 5 4 3 2 1
16 15 14 13 12 11 10 09 08 07

Printed and bound in Great Britain by
Antony Rowe Ltd, Chippenham and Eastbourne

Contents

List of Figures

List of Tables

Preface

This book arises from a symposium on institutions and economic development held at the University of Otago, New Zealand. My thanks go to the University for financial support and to the academic and administrative staff who contributed to the success of the event. I am especially indebted to the authors included here, not only for their thoughtful chapters but also for their patience and cooperation during the preparation of this book. Chris Haig provided invaluable and timely assistance in preparing the material for publication, executing the task with consummate skill and good humour. I also acknowledge the help of Brenda Tustin. It was a pleasure to work with Alec Dubber and the production staff at Palgrave Macmillan. I thank them for their courtesy, guidance and expertise.

I have expressed thanks on previous occasions to my wife and family for their forbearance during my preoccupation with research and writing. That I do so again makes it no less sincere.

W. R. GARSIDE

Acknowledgments

The editor and publishers wish to thank the following for permission to reproduce copyright material:

Table 1.4 from D. Coates, *Models of Capitalism. Growth and Stagnation in the Modern Era* (Oxford: Blackwell, 2000).
Table 1 from Barry Eichengreen, 'Capitalizing on Globalization', *Asian Development Review*, 19(1), 2002.
Table 2.2 from Juro Teranishi, *Evolution of the Economic System in Japan* (Cheltenham, Edward Elgar, 2005).

Notes on Contributors

Aaron Batten is a PhD student studying at the Australian National University. He is carrying out research on the influences that foreign aid may have on the economic performance of recipient countries.

Gordon Boyce is Assistant Dean, Research and Director of the Institute of Organizational and Institutional Performance at the University of Newcastle, Australia. He is Vice-President of the Australia and New Zealand International Business Academy and serves on the Editorial Board of *Australian Economic History Review, Journal of Transport History* and *Enterprise & Society*. He has been a Visiting Fellow at the Australian National University, Duke University and the Centre for Business History. His recent publications include *How Organisations Connect* (with Simon Ville and Stuart MacIntyre), *Over Half a Million Careful Owners* and *Co-operative Structures in Global Business*. He has been the recipient of the Cass Prize, a Caird Fellowship and a British Commission for Transport History Prize.

Graham Brownlow has been Lecturer in Economics at the Queen's University of Belfast (QUB) since February 2007. He is a member of the Economic & Financial Institutions Research Group (EFIRG) at QUB. Prior to his current appointment, he lectured in Economics at Dublin City University, the University of East Anglia and Auckland University of Technology. His research has focused primarily on institutional and evolutionary economics and economic history. He has published papers on these topics in a range of outlets, including *Cambridge Journal of Economics* and *Economic History Review*.

Karl DeRouen Jr is Professor in the Political Science Department at the University of Alabama. His research focuses on conflict processes and international political economy. His work has appeared in *International Organization, British Journal of Political Science, International Studies Quarterly* and *Journal of Peace Research*, among others. He is currently working on two co-authored textbooks for Cambridge University Press.

W. R. Garside is currently Professor of Economic History in the Department of Economics at the University of Otago, New Zealand, having previously held the Chair of Economic History at the University of Birmingham, United Kingdom, from 1991 to 2001. He has written extensively on government economic policy in twentieth-century Britain with particular reference to industrial decline, unemployment and the political economy of structural change. He is currently completing a study of the political economy of growth and decline in Japan since 1945, building upon research first undertaken as Visiting Professor at the Institute of Economic Research, Hitotsubashi University, Tokyo. He is a Fellow of the Royal Historical Society and serves on the Editorial Board of *Australian Economic History Review.*

Shaun Goldfinch is Senior Lecturer in the Department of Political Studies, University of Otago, New Zealand, and Associate Professor of public administration at the American University of Sharjah. He is author of *Remaking New Zealand and Australian Economic Policy* (Washington D.C.: Georgetown University Press, 2000) and co-author of *Dangerous Enthusiasms: e-government, computer failure and information system development* (Dunedin: Otago University Press, 2006). Recent articles have appeared in *Governance, Australian Journal of Politics and History, Australian Journal of Political Science, Journal of Policy History* and *Journal of Peace Research.*

Michael Jones is an economic analyst in the Economics Department at the Reserve Bank of New Zealand. He graduated from the University of Otago in 2004 with an Honours degree in economics and worked as a policy analyst for the Ministry of Agriculture and Forestry before joining the Reserve Bank. His role in the forecasting team at the Reserve Bank has him heavily involved in the monetary policy process, primarily modelling short-term dynamics in the New Zealand economy.

Stefan Kesting PhD is Senior Lecturer in Economics at Auckland University of Technology (AUT). He holds a Diploma (MA) and a PhD in economics from the University of Bremen and has previously taught at the University of Bremen, Germany, and the University of Missouri, Kansas City. His main research interests are the interactive and linguistic turn in economic theory, ecological sustainability, gender, feminist and social and institutional economics.

Stephen Knowles is Associate Professor in Economics at the University of Otago, New Zealand. He holds a PhD from the University of Otago. He is an external research fellow of the Centre for Research on Economic Development and International Trade at the University of Nottingham, and has held visiting research fellowships at the Australian National University and Cambridge University. His main research is in the area of economic growth and development, especially the role of human capital, social capital, institutions and income inequality.

Alan Martina is Senior Lecturer at the Australian National University. He specializes in topics concerned with economic development. He has published on taxation theory, social welfare theory, the theory of poverty and famine policy, and the economics of demographic change. At present he is completing a book on the influences that the levels of health and economic institutions may have on the level of development of countries at the end of the twentieth century.

Philip Nel is Professor of Political Studies at the University of Otago, New Zealand, and Visiting Professor at the University of Stellenbosch, South Africa. He is one of the editors of *Foreign Policy Analysis*. His research interests include the comparative politics of economic inequality and the foreign policy of post-apartheid South Africa. His book on the politics of economic inequality in developing countries is to be published by Palgrave Macmillan in 2008.

P. Dorian Owen is Professor of Economics at the University of Otago, New Zealand. He holds MSc and PhD degrees from the University of Wales. He has previously taught at the University of Reading (UK) and the University of Canterbury (NZ) and has been editor of *New Zealand Economic Papers*. His research interests include empirical modelling of economic growth and development, applied econometrics and sports economics.

Barry Supple was Professor of Economic History at the University of Cambridge and Master of St Catherine's College until 1993. Subsequently, he served as Director of the Leverhulme Trust between 1993 and 2001. Since 2001 he has been Academic Adviser to Arcadia, a grant-giving foundation. His academic interests have extended to economic fluctuations in early modern England, nineteenth-century American economic development and business history, British industrial and company history with special reference to the coal and insurance industries, and the performance and management of the British economy. The books he has published include *Commercial Crisis and Change in England, 1600–42* (Cambridge, 1959); *Boston Capitalists and Western Railroads* (Harvard, 1967, co-author with Arthur M Johnson); *The Royal Exchange Assurance: A History of British Insurance, 1720–1970* (Cambridge, 1970); and *The History of the British Coalmining Industry, Vol IV, 1913–46: The Political Economy of Decline* (Oxford, 1987).

Elizabeth Thurbon is Senior Lecturer in the School of Social Sciences and International Studies at the University of New South Wales, Australia. She specializes in researching and teaching the international political economy of trade, finance and industrial development, with a focus on Northeast Asia, Australia and the United States. She has published numerous journal articles in this area, and is the co-author of *How to Kill a Country* (Allen & Unwin, 2004), which deals with the Free Trade Agreement between Australia and the United States, and *National Insecurity* (Allen & Unwin, 2007), which documents and explains the Howard Government's systematic undermining of Australia's military and economic interests during its decade of leadership.

Simon Ville is Professor and Head in the School of Economics, University of Wollongong, specializing in the teaching and research of the economic and business history of Britain, Europe, Australia and New Zealand. He is a Fellow of the Academy of Social Sciences in Australia and President of the Economic History Society of Australia and New Zealand. He has written extensively for the leading international journals in economic and business history including *Journal of Economic History, Economic History Review* and *Business History Review*. His book *The Rural Entrepreneurs: A History of the Stock and Station Agent Industry in Australia and New Zealand* (Cambridge University Press, 2000), won the Bruce McComish prize for Economic History.

Robert H. Wade is Professor of Political Economy at the London School of Economics. After studying economics at the University of Otago and Victoria University, he took a PhD in social anthropology at the University of Sussex. He subsequently worked at the Institute of Development Studies, Sussex University, the World Bank, the US Congress' Office of Technology Assessment, Princeton University, MIT and Brown University. He has conducted field research in Pitcairn Is., southern Tuscany, India, South Korea, Taiwan and inside the World

Bank. He is the author of *Irrigation and Agricultural Politics in South Korea* (1982), *Village Republics: Economic Conditions of Collective Action in South India* (1988, 1994) and *Governing the Market: Economic Theory and the Role of Government in East Asia's Industrialization* (1990, 2004). His more recent work has dealt with world income distribution, global economic governance and the validity or otherwise of neoliberal policy prescriptions, with particular reference to East Asia, the United States and the United Kingdom.

Clayton R. Weatherston is currently a research fellow in the Department of Economics at the University of Otago, New Zealand. His recently completed PhD thesis explores the fundamental determinants of long-run economic development, and specifically the relative roles of man-made institutions and geography in determining the wide distribution of development outcomes across the world today. His other research interest is in the economics of sport with a particular focus on Rugby Union in New Zealand. Before returning to Otago to undertake his doctorate he worked as a policy analyst in the education team at the New Zealand Treasury.

1

Introduction: Economic Growth and Development – An Institutional Perspective

W. R. Garside

In recent decades, the study of the nature and role of institutions has become a central concern of economists and other social scientists. In part this reflects a preoccupation to establish the fundamental determinants of capital accumulation and innovation, and thereby long-term growth and development. The time has long passed when explanations of economic progress could focus only on inputs into the production process. The aggregate production function approach which stressed the need to raise the ratio of investment to income as the means of quickening the pace of self-sustained growth has been found wanting. Although both physical and human capital accumulation are important, there is ample evidence of countries enjoying only modest economic growth despite having high rates of physical capital accumulation, and of others gaining little or no growth even when education has expanded rapidly (Clague, 1997: 13).

Williamson and Coase have stressed the structural determinants of the firm as an institution, while North puts institutions at the centre of a discussion on the historical development of modern capitalism (Coase, 1937, 1960; Williamson, 1975, 1981, 1985; North, 1990). Such studies have in turn spawned 'institutionalist' movements within the disciplines of economics, sociology and politics, to name but three. As Hodgson has noted, political science has examined the contributions of states and democratic governance to economic performance; economic sociology and organization science have expanded perspectives on the nature and evolution of markets and firms; geographers have emphasized the spatial characteristics of institutions and networks; while historians and anthropologists have renewed their long-standing interest in the evolution of institutions in their temporal and cultural setting (Hodgson, 2005: i–ii).

Institutions are established and accepted ways of getting things done in society, and include sets of norms, rules and procedures that define social practice and influence interactions. There is now general agreement among proponents of new institutional economics[1] that institutions which embrace all the conventions, both formal and informal, that shape society's political, social and economic behaviour are major determinants of the incentive structure and the direction of economic growth (North, 1990, 1991).[2] Empirical evidence suggests that the quality of institutions, through their influence upon the levels of investment and the regulatory, economic and financial environment in which firms operate, affects the level and growth of GDP per capita and the volatility of growth (Hall and Jones, 1999; Easterly and Levine, 2003; Frances, 2004; Rodrik *et al.*, 2004).

Societies with weak institutions tend to grow more slowly in the long run (Acemoglu *et al.*, 2003). But although it is readily accepted that well-performing institutions are associated with economic growth, there is keen debate over whether they are always or necessarily the prime movers. Easterly and Levine (2003) suggest that geography/endowments have played a determining factor in influencing the quality of land, labour and production technologies, and explain cross-country differences in economic development through their impact upon institutions. Colonists, for example, tended to settle in countries with hospitable climates (as measured by mortality rates) and brought their attendant institutions to bear, whilst less hospitable countries suffered 'extractive' institutions that encouraged the removal of economic resources to a colonial power (Acemoglu *et al.*, 2001; Engerman and Sokoloff, 2003; Sachs, 2003; Frances, 2004: 2). This suggests that the quality of a country's institutions was directly affected by how European colonists saw a country as a place of settlement. But that does not mean that geography, as distinct from the quality of institutions themselves, was necessarily the most important factor affecting economic growth (Rodrik *et al.*, 2004).

Nor can we be any more determinant when we consider the many underlying social, political and economic institutions that affect how economic agents act and interact within a country. If we limit ourselves first to those institutions that potentially shape the economic activity of firms, the range is formidable enough. They include social conventions such as customs, norms and social networks; formal institutions including the judiciary and bureaucracy; the rules relating to property rights; institutions that affect resource allocation and employment within firms; and institutions affecting governance and transactions between firms. Together these formal and informal institutions shape the environment in which economic activity takes place and govern the activities of firms as they operate within the market and engage in transactions with others (Williamson, 2000; Frances, 2004: 3–4).

It is clear, for example, that levels of trust and social networks affect attitudes towards risk and uncertainty, individual aspirations towards education and training, the diffusion of new knowledge, and the capacity for conflict resolution, all critical to innovation and the accumulation and quality of human capital (Granovetter, 1985; Offer, 1997; Rodrik, 1999).

Firms face transaction costs when they are uncertain whether they will receive an expected outcome from an exchange. Institutions matter in this context because the rules surrounding the protection of assets held by a firm (including protection from expropriation by the state) and contract enforcement reduce such costs by encouraging investment in human and physical capital and by increasing the likelihood of expected outcomes (Coase, 1960; North, 1994; Aron, 2000). At the more formal level, therefore, institutions which affect the context within which firms operate, such as the constitution and the rule of law which protect private property rights and prevent corruption, can be regarded as 'market creating' since they safeguard potential returns on investment and influence the scope for rent-seeking (Rodrik, 2003).

The introduction and viability of such enabling institutions frequently depends upon the distribution of political power within a country. As Frances puts it:

> The role of political institutions in the creation of economic institutions means that economic institutions will not always be designed in ways that aim to maximize economic growth. However, the distribution of political power can change over time as the political and economic environment change and create an appetite for efficiency-enhancing change in economic institutions (2004: 8).

Institutions such as democracy, for example, shape the political process that produces laws and regulations which ultimately affect the quality of economic institutions. But much depends upon the political balance of power. The International Monetary Fund found that countries settled by Europeans sustained greater economic development than those which empowered local elite bent on maintaining their own power and wealth (IMF, 2003). The causal links between political and economic institutions and economic growth are not entirely clear. While the political power structure can affect economic growth by shaping a country's economic institutions, these in turn shape political power through their effect upon the distribution of resources (Acemoglu *et al.*, 2004).

It is not necessarily the case, therefore, that political institutions cause economic growth. Insofar as investment in human and social capital leads to economic growth, this can in turn foster greater political stability and with it greater security of property rights for investment and economic activity. But those outcomes can conceivably emerge from dictatorships as well as democracy (Glaeser *et al.*, 2004).

It is with such considerations in mind that economists, economic historians and political scientists met in conference in New Zealand to examine the complex issue of institutions, markets and economic development. Differing methodologies and approaches were brought to bear to emphasize how eclectic an approach must be if we are to understand more fully those 'deeper' determinants of long-run growth.

Although economic theory has recently turned its attention to the respective role of institutions and markets in economic development, economic historians have invariably taken it for granted that institutions (including attitudes) have played a vital role in economic processes. Nevertheless, there is disagreement still as to where the balance lies as between institutions shaping economic activity (that is, playing an exogenous role) and those being shaped by economic imperatives (that is, playing an endogenous role). To illuminate this, Supple provides a survey of a number of controversies and debates in economic history which touch on the general issue of the importance of institutions in the course of economic change and development since the sixteenth century. In the final analysis, it is most unlikely that institutions are purely either exogenous or endogenous. Circumstance, the historical evolution and adaptability of institutions themselves, and the role of political economy all affect the influence of institutions in differing societies and periods of history. 'Context and function', writes Supple, 'are as important as character and form'.

Economic historians have also recently joined the debate on the supposed links between democratic political institutions and economic development. Lindert (2003) has noted that previous studies of the topic written by economists have failed to use adequate historical evidence, have mistaken nominally democratic electoral systems for true voice and have failed to note that the institutional channels linking voice and growth have altered over time, concluding that 'The average democracy has been better for economic growth than the average autocracy' (Lindert, 2003: 344).

However, given the existence of electorally important ethno-religious cleavages around the world, and the associated existence of institutionalized discrimination and segmentation, locating a clear distinction between 'average democracies' and 'average autocracies' seems more problematic than Lindert assumed. In the context of Irish history, ethno-religious division, political division and economic instability have all been closely intertwined. Such inter-linkages make the study of the relationship between economy and polity especially difficult for economic historians of institutions. Brownlow examines how the nexus of political and economic institutions in Northern Ireland shaped the region's economic and political development. By doing so he emphasizes that economic history has a vital role to play in any analysis of the links between political institutions and economic development.

Historical specificity is at the heart of Garside's discussion of Japan's developmental state during the period of high post-war growth and immediately beyond. It focuses upon a feature of recent development historiography, namely the oft-repeated assertion that Japan's relative economic success down to the 1990s was less the result of a government-inspired and bureaucratically engineered growth strategy than the fervent application of readily available and cheap factors of production, destined to be of limited long-term advantage because of diminishing returns. The corollary frequently suggested is that the country currently needs a fundamental reappraisal of the respective roles of the state and the market in order to achieve sustainable economic growth, the former to be denigrated and the latter elevated. His chapter accepts the problems Japan brought upon itself by failing to adapt its institutional structures and practices in the years before the crises of the 1990s, but challenges the premise that earlier state-led developmental policies were merely the harbinger of future decline and by default of limited value to any future reform programme. It suggests that criticisms of developmentalism have often been ill-informed and overdrawn.

Any analysis of Japan's immediate future can only be based on a clearer perception of what needs to be retained and discarded from past practice. In that regard, the overriding presumption that Japan is beyond developmentalism needs to be based on a clearer analysis of the role played by institutions within post-war Japan and of the precise importance of the embeddedness of the state in fostering economic change. The vacuous debate of whether the state or the market was at the heart of Japan's rise and fall since 1945 disguises the more nuanced relations that existed between the principal economic agents. The symbiotic links between the state and the market provide the context within which to appreciate the mainsprings of non-Anglo-American growth in Japan at a time when, wrought by defeat, the country was forced to establish very different ways in which to gain a competitive edge over the West.

A 'developmental logic' similarly drove liberalization in pre-crisis Taiwan. Thurbon challenges the widely held view that developmental states, not least after the Asian crisis of 1997–98, demonstrate the incompatibility of trying to govern the market whilst retaining financial openness. She argues that financial liberalization was, by contrast, a key constituent element of the Taiwanese state's developmental strategy. Selective industrial development and upgrading were linked directly to financial arrangements institutionalized through the Taiwan Central Bank. To appreciate the significance of financial liberalization in Taiwan, therefore, it is necessary to recognize the institutional framework (seen in terms of the ideational and organizational environment) in which liberalization was planned and implemented. Her analysis of the Taiwanese experience reflects the importance of domestic institutions in shaping approaches and responses to external economic and political pressures. It emphasizes, moreover, how global interpretations of change which focus almost exclusively upon external market pressures can ignore the developmental motives that shape liberalization. The two forces need not, and should not, be seen as mutually exclusive.

In asking how political institutions affect inequality, Nel looks at the comparative experience of OECD and developing countries with respect to the effect of democratization on redistribution. Contrary to the expectation of the median-voter hypothesis, namely that the median voter will use the vote to redistribute in her favour in societies where the median income is below the mean, redistribution is not very extensive in high-income OECD countries, while in developing countries democratization is often accompanied by a further concentration of wealth, not redistribution. Recent quality data on the dynamics of income distribution in a large number of developing countries allow us to explain this incongruence. Using time series data on Estimated Household Income Inequality trends as prepared by the University of Texas Inequality Project and controlling for prominent political and economic features of developing countries, Nel develops and tests an explanation for the counter-intuitive effects of democratization on developing countries. He suggests that our political-economic models of redistribution are insensitive to the impact that control over power resources has on the ability of the poor and middle class in developing countries to redistribute in their favour, especially under conditions of economic openness.

So far as the 'deep' determinants of economic development are concerned, Owen and Weatherston summarize the various mechanisms by which the main contenders (geography, institutions, the extent of a country's 'openness' and integration with world markets, and macroeconomic policy) might affect development. They provide a critical review of the relevant empirical literature and of the statistical exercises that posit the relative strength of causal relationships. Such exercises often produce conflicting conclusions between those who claim that geography matters only insofar as it impacts upon institutions, and those who support a more direct link between geography and levels of GDP per capita. One of their principal contentions is that the lack of definite conclusions in this field of enquiry stems largely from a failure in modelling methodology. They provide some new results based upon what they consider to be a more appropriate testing methodology.

In a similar vein, Jones, Knowles and Owen note that early contributions to the debate within development economics as to whether institutions or geography is the more important fundamental (or 'deep') determinant of economic development claimed that institutions were more important than geography in explaining different levels of economic development. Although geographic conditions affect development, it was argued, they did so only through their impact on the development of different types of institutions; after controlling for institutional quality, geography appeared to have little direct effect on income. However, more recent studies have challenged this view on the primacy of institutions, emphasizing instead the importance of geographic and pre-historic biogeography in explaining cross-country variation in levels of income per capita. The authors offer cross-country regressions to test the statistical significance of institutions and geography in explaining economic development, as conventionally proxied by income per capita. They go further by recognizing that income per capita is only one dimension of development. The widely used Human Development Index, for example, includes measures of health and education, as well as income. Their chapter analyses the effect of institutions and geography on different measures of health status (life expectancy, infant mortality rate and child mortality rate) to test whether the results from previous studies are as robust when an alternative indicator of economic development is used as the dependent variable.

Batten and Martina ask whether the risk of contracting virulent infectious diseases has been of importance relative to the role of economic institutions in explaining the variation in the level of development across countries in the late twentieth century. At an intuitive level, they are sceptical of the broad conclusion derived from Acemoglu *et al.* (2001) and Rodrik *et al.* (2004) that the quality of economic institutions directed at property rights and the rule of law is the dominant factor in determining the distribution of per capita GDP across countries. A casual perusal of economic/demographic/epidemiological history indicates that one of the consequences of a widespread virulent disease being present within a community is that economic development is severely impeded. This tends to be so even if economic institutions of a comparatively high quality are in place in the community at the time chronic disease is prevalent. Severe outbreaks of bubonic plague, for example, severely limited economic activity in Europe in the mid-fourteenth century and on subsequent occasions. Yellow fever prevented attempts to complete the building of the Panama Canal in the 1880s and 1890s. HIV/AIDS and potent forms of malaria continue to impose considerable economic costs on the countries of sub-Saharan Africa. These observations mirror some of those found in Sachs (2003) who also emphasized the need to consider malaria transmission in any discussion of the determinants of economic development. In extending the empirical analysis to be found in Sachs (2003), Batten and Martina's regression results suggest that institutions are a dominant factor in explaining the level of economic development across countries when the disease variable is omitted from the specification of the regression equation. This ceases to be so once disease is included as a regressor; disease then becomes the dominant variable. Batten and Martina discuss the implications of their empirical results for the design of effective public policy in developing countries.

The broad scope of the institutions/development debate is illustrated in the more eclectic themes of other contributors. Ville traces the origins and development of institutions that have had a significant influence upon innovation as one of the key drivers of the economic growth of Australia since White Settlement over two centuries ago. Although it is generally recognized that innovation systems help us to appreciate the way in which countries receive and adapt new forms of technology, our understanding of what determines the nature of a national innovation system is limited. Ville contends that understanding the bases of national innovation systems requires an analysis of a nation's institutions. Australia historically has clustered its economic activity in natural resource and related industries (primary production, mining, energy, shipping and mercantile trade). It traditionally drew upon domestically generated new technology in its traditional clusters but moved to heavy reliance upon imported technology to develop a broad manufacturing base. This required a new national innovation system that drew upon more diverse sources of knowledge. The adaptiveness of Australian institutions over two centuries suggests to Ville a structure receptive to the opportunities presented by innovation. Moreover, it is one which has set distinctive ground rules of critical importance to innovative activity in the twenty-first century, including a capacity to surmount the problems of geographical distance and to harness the benefits of social cohesion, networking skills, foreign direct investment and the richness of natural resources.

Boyce explores the rise and proliferation of professional groups that have contributed to economic development. As conspicuous features of an emerging modern society, such groups have contributed to economic development by providing an institutional construct that facilitates the creation and wider application of specialized human capital. Boyce examines professions as systems that support transactions involving knowledge. Historically, the organizing influence of professional organizations was limited to the jurisdiction controlled by the state that delegated to them the authority to set accreditation standards, control entry and self-regulate. Thus, being based on authority structures and institutional frameworks, the operation of professional bodies has been confined to national and provincial boundaries. While these associations have long used international networks for exchanging subsets of their knowledge, today they are being pressurized to reduce their control within regional or national jurisdictions in favour of a measure of globalization in the provision of professional services. Boyce discusses the nature and origins of those tensions that currently beset professional groups.

Kesting pursues the theme that the path-dependent processes which construct and change institutional arrangements not only incur costs but also produce transaction benefits. A fully developed cost–benefit analysis of institutional change, he argues, requires both categories. He traces the literature of authors who tend to restrict their analysis to an enquiry of transaction cost only but then moves to examine more recent attempts to broaden the institutional analysis, including work on mental models as a means of recognizing transaction benefits, on image, on the formation of preferences and on trust. Transaction benefits, he maintains, are based on the fundamental social institution of language. They are derived from those collective communicative processes embedded in economic transactions. Such transactions affect and alter ideas in the minds of participants. This can lead to the construction and transformation of reassuring and stabilizing institutions. Kesting urges a change in the assumptions underlying the motives of economic actors and a general progression in theory from rational choice towards a pragmatic and discursive conception of human action.

It has long been recognized that even if there is a relationship between the protection of property rights and growth, there are other features of political systems, such as their stability, that also effect growth. Neither, however, should be confused with democracy (Haggard, 1987: 121). Scholars have been keen to establish systematic cross-national evidence in order to assess the effects that democratic institutions might have upon economic policy. Goldfinch and DeRouen take up the issue of democracy but with a rather different slant. Civil and international conflict causes misery and poverty to millions, disrupts economies and undermines often years of development. The reduction of international conflict, therefore, has direct relevance to any study of economic development. These authors investigate international crises from 1918 to 1994 to examine the role of democratic institutions in preventing conflict. As they demonstrate, institutionalized democracy produces humans that are less likely to escalate to the use of violence in international crisis, but be more likely to use negotiation and non-violent means of dispute resolution. One of the best ways of reducing international and civil conflicts, they argue, is to encourage the building of democracies across the world.

Few debates on institutional development and economic change in general can escape the analytical framework of globalization. Neoliberalism, Wade reminds us, has not been successful in reviving long-term economic growth in much of the world. The widening gap between the rhetoric (benefits for all) and the reality (hugely disproportionate benefit for small elites), combined with macroeconomic imbalances and financial instability, has created conditions for crisis on a world scale. His initial focus is on the crisis of the 1970s, when economic elites in most of the OECD world, and especially in the United States and the United Kingdom, felt their position threatened. Under the banner of restoring economic growth by widening market freedom and shrinking the state, governments promoted three meta-policies which – to the satisfaction of economic elites – had the effect of redistributing income, wealth and power upwards, both within nations and also internationally from poorer to richer countries. His chapter identifies these meta-policies as 'commodification' (or horizontal and vertical enclosure of private property), 'financialization' (policies which promote the organizational and normative dominance of the financial sector) and 'the anchorless economy' (the removal of price anchors or stabilizers in the labour market and in financial markets). It discusses these policy trends both in the aggregate and with 'grass roots' cases to illustrate the capillary processes through which the neoliberal project has been advanced and the sinews of the informal American empire strengthened. The chapter concludes with a discussion of several steps which may check the neoliberal project and allow markets to be subject to social controls decided through a political process.

There are many explanations in the literature as to why some countries grow rich and others do not. They include among others geography, the Protestant ethic, technology and, of course, institutions broadly defined as the formal laws and unwritten rules that govern society. Such institutions tend on the whole to function better in rich economies than in poor ones. We are now ready to concede that capitalism is realized in different ways in different countries and that it tends to reflect the prevailing 'logic' of specific institutional structures (Beeson, 2002: 17). The volume of literature on 'varieties of capitalism' is, however, stronger on descriptions of various capitalist institutions than it is on empirical or historical evidence. Much the same can be said of North's most recent conceptual discussion of the process of economic change (North, 2005). It is difficult to 'prove' that good institutions are a cause rather than a by-product of economic progress. Moreover, the design and reform of institutions are never easy processes. Nonetheless, the contribution that institutions, both formal and informal, make to economic growth is now rarely disputed in principle. The specific nature of that contribution remains complex and disputatious as the chapters of this book demonstrate. They do not attempt to resolve the contemporary debate. They enrich it, however, by providing a mixture of conceptual, empirical, historical and methodological approaches.

Notes

1. Space does not permit a full discussion of the literature surrounding new institutional economics. For informative guides see Vromen (1995), Clague (1997), Touffut (2003) and Hodgson (2003).
2. This chapter draws upon the excellent review of relevant literature in Frances, 2004.

References

Acemoglu, D., Johnson, S. and Robinson, J. 'The Colonial Origins of Comparative Development: An Empirical Investigation.' *American Economic Review*, 91 (5) (2001): 1369–401.

Acemoglu, D., Johnson, S. and Robinson, J. *Institutions as the Fundamental Cause of Long-run Growth*. Cambridge MA, National Bureau of Economic Research, Working Paper No, 10481 (2004).

Acemoglu, D., Johnson, S., Robinson, J. and Thaicharoen, Y. 'Institutional Causes, Macroeconomic Symptoms: Volatility, Crises and Growth'. *Journal of Monetary Economics*, 50 (1) (2003): 49–123.

Aron, J. 'Growth and Institutions: A Review of the Evidence'. *World Bank Research Observer*, 15 (1) (2000): 99–135.

Beeson, M. (ed.), *Reconfiguring East Asia. Regional Institutions and Organisations After the Crisis* (London: Routledge Curzon, 2002).

Clague, C. (ed.), *Institutions and Economic Development, Growth and Governance in Less-Developed and Post-Socialist Countries* (Baltimore: The Johns Hopkins University Press, 1997).

Coase, R. H. 'The Nature of the Firm', *Economica*, 4 (16) (1937): 386–405.

Coase, R. H. 'The Problem of Social Cost', *Journal of Law and Economics*, 3 (1960): 1–44.

Easterly, W. and Levine, R. 'Tropics, Germs, and Crops: How Endowments Influence Economic Development', *Journal of Monetary Economics*, 50 (1) (2003): 3–9.

Engerman, S. L. and Sokoloff, K. L. *Institutional and Non-institutional Explanations of Economic Differences*. Cambridge MA, National Bureau of Economic Research, Working Paper No. 9989 (2003).

Frances, J. 'Institutions, Firms and Economic Growth', New Zealand Treasury Working Paper 04/19 (2004): 1–36.

Glaeser, E. L., La Porta, R., Lopez-de-Silane, F. and Shleifer, A. 'Do Institutions Cause Growth?', *Journal of Economic Growth*, 9 (2004): 271–303.

Granovetter, M. 'Economic Action and Social Structure: The Problem of Embeddedness', *American Journal of Sociology*, 91 (3) (1985): 481–510.

Haggard, S. 'Democratic Institutions, Economic Policy, and Development', in G. Clague (ed.), *Institutions and Economic Development, Growth and Governance in Less-Developed and Post-Socialist Countries* (Baltimore: The Johns Hopkins University Press, 1997): 121–49.

Hall, R. and Jones, C. 'Why Do Some Countries Produce So Much More Output Per Worker than Others?', *Quarterly Journal of Economics*, 114 (1) (1999): 83–116.

Hodgson, G. (ed.), *Recent Developments in Institutional Economics* (Cheltenham: Edward Elgar, 2003).

Hodgson, G. 'Introduction', *Journal of Institutional Economics*, 1 (2005): i–ii.

IMF. *World Economic Outlook: Growth and Institutions*, Washington DC, International Monetary Fund (2003) http://www.imf.org/external/pubs/ft/weo/2003/01/.

Lindert, P. 'Voice and Growth: Was Churchill Right?', *Journal of Economic History*, 63 (2) (2003): 315–50.

North, D. C. *Institutions, Institutional Change and Economic Performance* (Cambridge: Cambridge University Press, 1990).

North, D. C. 'Institutions', *Journal of Economic Perspectives*, 5 (1) (1991): 97–112.
North, D. C. 'Economic Performance Through Time', *American Economic* Review, 84 (3) (1994): 359–68.
North, D. C. *Understanding the Process of Economic Change* (Princeton and Oxford: Princeton University Press, 2005).
Offer, A. 'Between the Gift and the Market: The Economy of Regard', *Economic History Review*, 50 (3) (1997): 450–76.
Rodrik, D. 'Where Did All the Growth Go? External Shocks, Social Conflict, and Growth Collapses', *Journal of Economic Growth*, 4 (4) (1999): 385–412.
Rodrik, D. *Growth Strategies*, Cambridge MA., National Bureau of Economic Research, Working Paper No. 10050 (2003).
Rodrik, D., Subramanian, A. and Trebbi, F. 'Institutions Rule: The Primacy of Institutions over Geography and Integration in Economic Development', *Journal of Economic Growth*, 9 (2) (2004): 131–65.
Sachs, J. *Institutions Don't Rule: Direct Effects of Geography on Per Capita Income*, Cambridge MA, National Bureau of Economic Research, Working Paper No. 9490 (2003).
Touffut, J. P. (ed.), *Institutions, Innovation and Growth* (Cheltenham: Edward Elgar, 2003).
Vromen, J. *Economic Evolution: An Enquiry into the Foundations of New Institutional Economics* (London: Routledge, 1995).
Williamson, O. E. *Markets and Hierarchies: Analysis and Antitrust Implications* (New York: Free Press, 1975).
Williamson, O. E. 'The Modern Corporation: Origins, Evolution, Attributes', *Journal of Economic Literature*, 19 (1981): 1537–68.
Williamson, O. E. *The Economic Institutions of Capitalism* (New York: Free Press 1985): 3–4.
Williamson, O. E. 'The New Institutional Economics: Taking Stock, Looking Ahead', *Journal of Economic Literature*, 38 (3) (2000): 595–613.

2

Institutions and Economic Development: Economic History and Human Arrangement

Barry Supple

This chapter is essentially a survey of a number of controversies and debates in economic history touching on the general issue of the importance of institutions in the course of economic change and development since the sixteenth century. Its context is, of course, the general theme of this book: the respective role of institutions and markets in economic development, a topic recently revived as a central theme of economic theory. But since my perspective is that of the economic historian rather than the economist, it is perhaps worthwhile emphasizing that, although economic historians have always and invariably taken it for granted that institutions (including, of course, attitudes) have played a vital role in economic processes, they very rarely deploy the sort of systematic, analytical approach which now characterizes so much of the approach of modern economics. Nevertheless, the fact remains that much debate in economic history is, at bottom, driven by disagreement as to where the balance lies between institutions shaping economic activity (that is, playing an exogenous role) or being shaped by economic imperatives (that is, playing an endogenous role). At the same time, the fact remains that economic historians have rarely challenged the significance of institutions. Indeed, that is what the subject's critics often say: that economic history is too atheoretical, descriptive and narrative.

This is not an unjustified criticism, even though ironically one of the exceptions (Douglass North) has earned a Nobel Prize for his pioneering work on institutions and economic development (North, 1981). In practice, most economic historians take the role of institutions for granted. As a result, they appear to deal in a rather breezy way with a fiendishly complicated subject matter. This fact explains, even if it does not entirely justify, the surprise that most of us felt when we learned that economists had decided to reopen the black box of norms and institutions.

Of course, economists have always accepted that the black box exists. There was a time, well before statistical analysis came on the scene, when they rummaged around in it fairly actively. That was certainly the case when the discipline was born. In spite of its apparent novelties, the new institutional economics or the new political economy has deep roots in the very origins of the subject. After all, it is impossible to read Adam Smith without being aware that his preoccupation with markets did not exclude (indeed, it presupposed) a dynamic role for institutions, public policy and cultural norms in determining the wealth of nations. He was, after all, the originator of a theory of moral sentiments as well as the analyst of the wealth of nations, and was quite explicit in drawing his readers' attention to the problem of externalities and the consequent need for institutional intervention by the state. As he wrote, an 'important duty of the sovereign or commonwealth is that of erecting and maintaining those public institutions and those public works which, though they may be in the highest degree advantageous to a great society, are, however, of such a nature that the profit could never repay the expense to any individual or small number of individuals, and which it therefore cannot be expected that any individual or small number of individuals should erect or maintain' (Smith, 1776).

Indeed, even the more arid classical economists took account of the real world – either positively or negatively. At the minimum they explained economic change against the benchmarks of their assumptions by the presence or absence of particular sorts of institution. Most frequently, even in a presumed regime of *laissez-faire*, this opened the way for an acceptance of the need for the state to shape the institutions which shaped the market. This was the case with David Ricardo. He argued that the evils of backward countries with abundant land but indolent populations 'proceeds from bad government, from the insecurity of property, and from a want of education in all ranks of the people. To be made happier they require only to be better governed and instructed' (Ricardo, 1821: chapter V). This is easier said than done, of course. But good government and instruction are reasonable first approximations to the beneficial institutions that we assume are prerequisites of development.

Quite apart from the state's role, even when the classical economists did appear to assume that some institution or behavioural norm was an unchangeable parameter of economic processes, they were rarely able to demonstrate the point beyond criticism. Here, Malthus is a good example. In the less subtle version of his essay on population, he appears to assume that, while the soil's fertility was limited, the human urge to reproduce was boundless, and moral restraint unlikely. This enabled him to argue that the natural tendency to population growth would lead to vice and misery and thereby impose a severe check on material progress. From his viewpoint, therefore, the institutional reform that was a prerequisite of development was a harsh regime of social services: the withdrawal of welfare. The state had to become a wicked fairy rather than a good angel. In this 'model' such an unavoidable policy would obviously erode the beneficial potential of national wealth for large numbers of people.

But, as William Hazlitt pointed out in his swingeing critique of Malthus, 'sexual passion', and with it population growth, can be and is 'subject to control from personal feelings and character, from public opinion and the institutions of society'. More generally, Hazlitt argued, Malthus's appeal to the laws of nature and of God are 'no other than a limited fertility and a limited earth. Within those bounds the rest is regulated by the laws of man. The division of the produce of the soil, the price of labour, the relief accorded to the poor [he argued crucially], are matters of human arrangement' (Hazlitt, 1824–25: 171, 175).

In fact, the concept of what Hazlitt called 'human arrangement' is central to our discussions. We can elaborate his statement in more modern terminology: in effect, he was arguing that the scope for economic growth is fashioned by malleable institutions and norms, which are capable of adapting themselves to circumstances. Put in contemporary jargon, Hazlitt subscribed to the endogenous school of thought on institutions and economic development. Not only this, but he was aware of the welfare implications of development, since he argued that 'human arrangement' can directly amend Malthus's presumed 'grinding law of necessity for the poor'. He offered as provocative evidence the fact that 'a labouring man is not allowed to knock down a hare or a partridge that spoils his garden: a country-squire keeps a pack of hounds: a lady of quality rides out with a footman behind her on two sleek, well-fed horses' (Hazlitt, 1824–25: 175). In other words, the wealth of nations is distributed in part as the result of the institutions that determine the division of social and political power: a point central to economic history and, of course, to the argument of some modern economists. As we shall see, this is particularly relevant when we consider the thesis that inequality determines institutions, or at least the longevity of institutions.

Obviously, this sort of criticism of the unreal assumptions of neoclassical economics begs a number of questions. The core issue is not so much whether institutions are important for economic development (all commentators seem to agree that they are), but rather how far they can adapt to circumstances: whether, to use more fashionable concepts, they are endogenous or exogenous to economic processes; whether and to what degree they are susceptible to change; and (most crucially) whether development is dependent on specific institutional forms and attitudes or on processes and functions that can be shaped in a number of forms (and can themselves be stimulated by market pressures and incentives). Put another way, as modern economic historians (Engerman and Sokoloff, 2003) have summarized it, accepting that institutions are important, the question is, where do they come from and how do they evolve?

What follows does not pretend to offer any more satisfactory and convincing answers to such sweeping questions than those already in professional circulation. Rather, it describes a few of the empirical issues involving institutions and development that have agitated economic historians.

At the outset it is worth emphasizing that the very origins of modern economic history were embedded in just such a topic. Of course, going to the discipline's prehistory, Adam Smith was himself an economic historian. But the modern version of the subject was born in the second half of the nineteenth century, as scholars attempted to delineate and understand the history of institutions judged to be (or to have been) involved in progress or stagnation. As a result, they turned their attention to tribal property and the rival cultures of custom and contract; the evolution of legal systems; the organization and function of medieval manor and trade gild; the imposition of taxes and the control of currency; the peculiarities of agricultural tenure and common lands or shared property rights; the regulation of industry; and public policy seeking to attain national self-sufficiency and protect vested interests. All these were represented in the late-nineteenth-century scholarship that spawned the modern discipline of economic history.

Much of this early scholarship was, of course, piecemeal in approach and unsystematic in conclusion. But there was an implicit unity because the ultimate concern was with the interaction between these institutional arrangements and what we would now describe as economic performance, whether in terms of productivity or national development. It was not long before these implicit characteristics became explicit, and spilled over into the debates of economists. Heavily influenced by German scholarship, historical economics attempted to understand economic processes not with the aid of deductive argument but through a descriptive and therefore empirical study of the changing institutional relationships. From this perspective, economic development was primarily understood as the evolution of institutional forms, albeit an evolution which had teleological elements insofar as it was assumed that each form was more permissive of economic growth than the last, and that the hierarchy of economic processes pointed inexorably towards the then modern economic system and the high level of contemporary development.

The classic example of this inductive methodology was of course the 'Stage Theory' of development (or, more relevantly, of Western-European development). Much more a European continental than an Anglo-Saxon approach, Stage Theory (at least as a model) proved to be something of a dead end in its purely descriptive form. But some of its influence survived when analytical models were deployed, which was the case, of course, with one of its pioneers, Karl Marx. In practice, however, very few people remain much interested in stage-theory methodology, at least in its classic form. In one respect (and unavoidably) it tended to oscillate between institutional determinism and institutional dependence, just as some recent attempts to incorporate institutions into our understanding of macroeconomic processes oscillate between an exogenous and an endogenous view of social and political structures and norms.

It is more instructive for our purpose to deal not with such generalities but with a handful of the empirical controversies which have moved economic historians in the twentieth century (and will no doubt continue to do in the twenty-first), and to do so by deploying what its critics rather cruelly call the 'casual empiricism' of traditional economic history. Those controversies concern religion and capitalism, the origins of the British Industrial Revolution, the diffusion of industrialism, the nature of decline, and new states as laboratories for research into the dynamics of institutions and development.

2.1 Religion and the rise of capitalism

The first issue is in some ways the most fundamental, although also one of the most elusive. It is that old chestnut of the relationship between religion and the rise of capitalism. Although it appears to present a relatively straightforward case study, it actually raises most of the conceptual issues that concern us.

The 'core' institution in the argument is, of course, Protestantism (or more accurately the Protestant outlook); that is, a particular religious ideology, which was assumed to place a pre-eminent emphasis on a work ethic, on individual aspirations and responsibility, and on the postponement of gratification. In this way its presumed rationalism was thought to disrupt tradition and traditional behaviour. Its significance for economic history was assumed to be mediated through its secular impact: rational accounting and organization, dedication to work, profit-seeking investment and individual motivation. In essence, the controversy is about the effect of one institution (the Protestant mindset) on another (market-based entrepreneurship), leading to 'capitalism as we know it'. Note, however, that even in this formulation, the debate involves the primary causal conundrum. As with the rather more transcendental controversy about the existence and activity of God, but now in the more prosaic arena of economic change, it raised the question of whether Protestantism was a prime mover. Or, to put it another way, where did the Protestant Ethic come from? Can we analyse economic development as if this institutional norm was a given (like God, an uncaused cause, or at least determined by non-economic phenomena)? Or was it itself the product of contextual changes in society and the economy (perhaps even of the economic development that it is adduced to explain)?

Apart from this fairly fundamental issue, there are tautological aspects to the argument that a religious ethic could 'give rise' to a 'capitalist spirit'. After all, Max Weber defined or specified Protestantism in terms which converged fairly closely with a definition of capitalist behaviour, hence the title of his monograph: *The Protestant Ethic and the Spirit of Capitalism* (1904 edition). In other words, once it was assumed that the vital, endogenous element in economic change was a change in outlook, there must have been a strong temptation to postulate a causal relationship between what may have been merely the two sides (the religious and the secular) of one emerging phenomenon (the pursuit of individualism, non-hierarchical rationality in behaviour, and a work ethic).

In its original formulation, the Weber hypothesis saw religious norms as setting the pace for changes in secular/behavioural norms, from which it could be assumed without contention that there emerged a capitalist system (that is, a set of rational market and commercial-financial institutions, themselves integrally leading to economic growth).

But it was not long before the dangers of circular reasoning and misidentified causality became apparent. On the one hand, while it was true that the most successful capitalist societies in the early-modern period tended to be Protestant, it was obvious that this did not necessarily mean that their success rested on their religious evolution. It might equally have been the case that their religious evolution rested on their economic experience: the thrust towards capitalism and away from traditional activity may have predisposed societies to pursue secular nonconformity and religious individualism.

So far, therefore, and very crudely put, we have two options: Protestantism stimulated capitalism, or capitalism stimulated Protestantism. But (quite apart from the remote possibility that the changes in religion and economic behaviour were entirely independent) there is also a third and very obvious possibility, namely that the location of the first capitalist and Protestant nations along or around the North-west coast of Europe may have been an even more significant fact, for both their religion and their economic outlook and achievement. That location, and its consequent history, had all sorts of potential implications for any explanatory model: trade expansion and the exchange of ideas that came with trade; temperate climate and the challenges and possibilities that were associated with it; the accident of factor endowments favourable to growth and markets (which also encouraged that growth); imperial primacy; relatively 'open' societies which encouraged both freer thought and more individualistic economic behaviour; and in general a prior history of sophisticated national development producing more liberal and flexible institutions and outlooks. And once those implications were unfolded, religious as well as secular ideologies may have been transformed to suit.

None of this is surprising or new. Historians (as with many economists today) have long acknowledged the potential significance of economic geography for both institutions and performance. When we come to other periods and problems, the same issue – essentially the relationship between geography, outlooks and institutions – inevitably arises. But before we leave this particular example, let us note another possible twist to the argument. This relates to the fact that the central focus of the debate about religion and capitalism lies in a specific period: the early-modern world of the sixteenth and seventeenth centuries. As its name implies, that world appeared to anticipate the modernity which was still to come: changes in exploration (itself not a Protestant monopoly, even in the sixteenth century); shifts in trade and prices and population; upheavals in economic activity generally which created opportunities as well as decline. All this raises two chronological questions.

First, even if the sixteenth and seventeenth centuries were the breeding ground for modern capitalism as a system, they did not invent the outlook which we associate with it. Thirteenth- and fourteenth-century bankers and merchants, fourteenth- and fifteenth-century wool producers (even monastic wool producers), and cloth manufacturers and mining entrepreneurs throughout the period could be every bit as enterprising, hard-working and investment-orientated as their sixteenth- and seventeenth-century successors, even if they did not invent as many new institutions. Before the sixteenth century we are obviously not dealing with Protestantism in its formalized meaning. Rather, insofar as a 'spirit' was involved, we are probably dealing with a similar ethic in the minds of Catholics, even in the minds of the pious inhabitants of great sheep-farming monasteries. In effect, then, Protestants may not have had a monopoly on the institution that we call the 'Protestant ethic'.

Secondly, even if capitalist activity existed before capitalism, economic development came some time after the institutions that are supposed to have caused it. Weber identified the capitalist spirit with the sixteenth century, but the evidence of contemporary or coincidental development in the modern sense is pretty weak. Of course, we may choose to see the decisive origins of modern attitudes and techniques in the sixteenth and seventeenth centuries. But we have to fast forward at least another century or so before seeing the presumed outcomes in terms of rapid development and fundamental macroeconomic change. In other words, at best, we should have to accept that what we observe in the early-modern period is an embryonic capitalism, the stirrings of new norms and 'human arrangement': not an indication but an anticipation of macroeconomic change, and an anticipation by some 150–200 years. That is an awfully long time for a cause to produce an effect. In the course of that long haul, there were so many other pressures, incentives and transformations that it would be hard to give an exclusive or even necessarily a pre-eminent causal role to one particular outlook embedded in the evolution of religious ideology a century or more before.

In fact, it is only when we move forward in time to that extent that we can get our teeth into a controversy where institutions interrelate with economic development in a more direct, modern and familiar sense.

2.2 The British Industrial Revolution

The British Industrial Revolution provides the classic case of an historical controversy about the role of institutions in economic development. Indeed, that controversy provides an echo of a definition of 'development' which is concerned, in the main, with what caused industrialization in Britain, how its use of natural and human capital was sustained, and what its effects were in terms of equitable distribution of wealth, particularly the standard of living of the relatively poor.

Of course, the distinction between the 'causes' of industrial development and the reasons for its being 'sustained' is pretty empty – even silly – since unless it were sustained there would be no Industrial Revolution to explain, no causes to identify! But there *is* a possible reason why historians of the Industrial Revolution have occasionally maintained such a distinction. This is (or was) the view that pioneering growth of this sort is a two-stage process: first comes a spurt (or what used to be called a 'critical minimum effort'); and this is followed by a period of reinforcement and prolonged development.

This presumed discontinuity was a vital element in Walt Rostow's 1950s model, which he called (with a nod of acknowledgement to the earlier historical economists) 'the stages of economic growth' (Rostow, 1960). That model was based on the hypothesis that industrialization (generally, as well as in Britain) began with a 'take-off'. This was assumed to be a functional prerequisite, on the analogy of an airplane's need to reach an escape velocity. Insofar as that was accepted, then it was logical to consider the processes by which sustained flight was subsequently attained, since, in principle at least, it might be possible to have an abortive take-off with no follow-through. (Alexander Gerschenkron, whose ideas are considered later, and who took exception to much of Rostow's argument, did in fact argue that some 'spurts', as he called them, failed.)

This may well have been one more example of intellectuals falling victims to metaphors, for we are all tempted to assume that metaphors describe reality in a literal sense. In the event however, Rostow's concepts have fallen into disuse as historians have come to recognize that the presumed drama of British industrialization (or, at least, the industrialization of the British economy as a whole) was a modest and incremental process. In statistical terms the macroeconomic curve from before to after the presumed Industrial Revolution was fairly smooth and the incline shallow. On the other hand, however, sharp accelerations could and did take place in individual industries (possibly even in the manufacturing sector as a whole). This point is relevant to the contemporaneous observation of events in Britain (when people were struck by dramatic transformations in the cotton or engineering industries), and to the process of diffusion in other countries.

In practice, however, although historians are frequently tempted to seek a presumed *original* 'cause' or stimulus to British industrialization–perhaps in a sharp movement in export markets, in shifts in the rate of interest or agricultural productivity, in population pressure or a virtually spontaneous up-rush of technical innovations – they tend in practice to focus on the forces that facilitated and sustained it, that made development qualitatively different from earlier examples. In fact, the rate of growth during the Industrial Revolution was fairly modest: say 1.5–2.5% per annum, or what we think of as the characteristic 'British rate of growth'. But in this respect we should bear in mind that in the absence of earlier examples of decisive industrialization, even a modest, if unprecedented, rate of change over a long period might be historically very significant, whether it produced or resulted from far-reaching changes in institutions and perceptions.

Accepting, then, that an historically significant process began somewhere in the middle decades of the eighteenth century, what might have provoked it, or at least made it possible? Obviously, the shopping list of the forces that could have stimulated and sustained contemporary industrial development is potentially endless. It can be summarized in three categories.

At one level, as has already been anticipated, there is favourable economic geography: Britain's compact size and structure and the disposition of its resources, which blessed it with low transport costs and the ability to combine resources easily; its island position on the corner of a developing continent, which gave it relatively low-cost access to global trade, raw materials and markets; and its own abundant raw materials for what proved to be crucial leading sectors (notably iron and coal and engineering).

At another level, since success breeds success, Britain had enjoyed a distinctive history on which sophisticated industrialism could be built: imperial control of raw materials and markets; prolonged (if not dramatic) expansion in earlier centuries which generated marketing, financial and entrepreneurial skills and an appetite for risk-taking; embryonic home-based industries, which generated manufacturing and technical skills and a fairly well qualified and moderately mobile labour force; and agricultural and financial 'revolutions' (as they used to be called) which fed the population, provided raw materials for processing industries, and facilitated large-scale, safe and continuous investment. (Economic historians appreciate that all this is circular in character, but it demonstrates the strong likelihood that growth is a long and cumulative process with a good deal of path dependence.)

Thirdly, and more relevant to us, is the fact that industrial development could not have happened without the emergence and reinforcement of favourable 'institutions'. These included, on the one hand, innovative, entrepreneurial and risk-taking attitudes and, on the other, institutional arrangements dependent not only on earlier capitalist-type activity, but (as Smith and Ricardo pointed out at the time) on a reasonably strong central state. Such a state could overcome the excesses and fragmentations of rent-seeking vested interests. It could also establish a framework of taxation and financial and commercial law supportive of capital accumulation and investment, and enforce the secure bases of property rights conducive to invention and investment. In this respect, the market could only work well if buttressed by 'human arrangement' that could only really be shaped and enforced by the sovereign power. We can go further than this to take account of the distribution of social power: Britain benefited from the fact that although that power resided in governing classes based on land ownership and, in the main, inheritance, they were broadly sympathetic to, and indeed representative of, the commercial and financial interests which helped transform the British economy. 'Gentlemanly capitalism' (Cain and Hopkins, 2001) it may have been, but capitalism nevertheless.

Clearly, then, as with the relationship between religious and secular outlooks, or the economic pre-history of the Industrial Revolution, we are dealing with a symbiotic and evolving process, not a dramatic and exogenous intervention by 'non-economic' forces. The eighteenth-century British state and legal system, like the eighteenth-century British economy, was itself the product of history: war and empire generated a need for efficient tax gathering; and an efficient tax system both bolstered the power of the state and could be manipulated in favour of entrepreneurial classes. The distribution of social power could determine a particular distribution and protection of property rights and patent laws that favoured development while they benefited particular classes. A powerful and unitary state, an easily defended island status, a rich empire, a predominant military and naval power, a self-confident ruling class, a devotion to orderly legal relationships – the public institutional bases for development are not far to seek.

Here, however, it is worth emphasizing two points. First, insofar as the state was important to British industrialization, its role was permissive and contextual rather than self-conscious, direct and interventionist (as it was to become in the case of the later development of less-advanced economies). Second, since this is an historical process, it would be absurd to stipulate that institutional forces were exogenous to the Britain's economic history. For example, even the distribution of power, or the pursuit of national domination, were integral aspects of the inherited economic dynamic. Socio-political institutions and financial and economic development came to exemplify an inextricable symbiotic relationship.

British history suggests that (at least in Britain's case) institutions are not like economic geography (even if they are influenced by it). They are neither givens nor predominantly economic in character and effect. We are dealing with a set of historical interactions. Economic development is, after all, a dynamic system of some complexity. Over time and at any one period the variables seem to interact in ways that exceed the power of our empirical knowledge and statistical analysis to unravel with any great precision.

In fact, as with the controversy about religion and capitalism, the argument about industrialization and institutions has an element of tautology about it. Institutions favourable to economic development were themselves the products of economic development. What appears to be an exogenous influence at one period may well assume an endogenous character at another, and vice versa! Perhaps above all we should emphasize that historical processes are cumulative: the interaction between institutions and performance can be dramatically reinforcing, in either virtuous or vicious circles. Sceptics may therefore conclude that (in the absence of extreme external shocks) economic development occurs because it occurs; sophisticates will phrase it differently and say that economic development is a function of path dependence and that feedback can be either positive or negative. The trick is to be pointing in the right direction and to be able to adjust the distribution of power in the right way.

2.3 Diffusion

The general arguments that arise from a discussion of the British Industrial Revolution can be given a sharper focus if we ask a broader question about the diffusion of industrialism.

However successfully we manage to disentangle the threads that shaped the British Industrial Revolution, there can be no doubt that it was the pioneer example of 'modern' economic development. This means that for economic historians interested in the broader canvas the next question must be, 'how did Britain's achievement spread? By what mechanisms was industrial growth diffused into other parts of the (mainly Western) world in the nineteenth century?'

Of course, in asking the question in this way there is a danger of sidestepping one of the central issues of world history, namely why, over the millennia, some countries or societies benefited from economic development, while others were left far behind? So it may be worth emphasizing that although no one could neglect the original role of environment, climate and the distribution of natural resources in the long-run divergence of the poor from the rich, it is hardly conceivable that we could explain the subsequent uneven distribution of industrialism and wealth throughout the world without taking account of the pre-eminent role of institutions in their cultural and political senses: ideologies, cultural and behavioural norms, social power, the flexibility of social structures, and imperial dominance or subservience.

However, in what follows we want to touch on a less overarching issue: given that in the course of the nineteenth century a number of Western (and one or two Eastern) societies underwent fairly significant (if uneven) processes of industrial development, what, if anything, linked the multinational experience of the developed or developing countries? And was that process of diffusion the outcome primarily of market forces or of institutional change?

A useful, if not the only, starting point for this discussion is obviously the direct influence of the British Industrial Revolution itself. Whether or not we accept the institutional or the market-based explanation of the diffusion of industrial development, it would be difficult to argue that other industrial revolutions were independent of the British example. The first industrial nation, as it has been called, was influential in two possible ways.

One was presumably market-driven: the economic prospects of other societies could have been transformed by the British Industrial Revolution's contribution to technical knowledge, by the consequent availability and lower cost of capital equipment and by drastic and beneficial changes in factor prices and the supply of and markets for raw materials and consumer goods. The other possible British influence was more self-conscious: Britain's example, by offering a vision of the private and public rewards of industrial growth, could have stimulated parallel developments elsewhere as other societies moved to imitate the norms of economic behaviour and the institutional arrangements that seemed to characterize Britain's success, or which fulfilled the same developmental functions in different circumstances.

The starting point of this discussion must be that for most followers or latecomers (and excluding fairly sophisticated economies like the Dutch) pre-industrial institutions were not on the whole conducive to modern economic development. If that is so, then we can also assume that whether market pressure or self-conscious responses were prime movers in the nineteenth century, institutional change must have played a role. In other words, there had to be a change in the rules of the game. On the one hand, the stimulation of market forces and opportunities encouraged and enforced adaptations of outlooks and institutions. On the other hand, the desire to follow Britain's example (that is, the perceived advantages of economic change) persuaded or enticed those in positions of influence and authority to adopt changes in norms and expectations, policies and behaviour, economic systems and even class relationships.

On balance, the consensus appears to be that some vital institutional changes were indeed exogenous; that is, the markets for factors of production, goods and services were modernized and expanded as the result of purposeful changes in the way people thought and the human arrangements they adopted.

This was the implicit theme of Gerschenkron's seminal contribution to comparative economic history (Gerschenkron, 1962). At the core of his argument was the concept of economic backwardness or a profoundly low level of economic development. He defined this in terms of low incomes, primitive or archaic economic structures, and widespread unadventurous and unenterprising attitudes. He argued that backwardness could have three implications.

First, by offering a contrast between what was (that is, the existing level of development and the existing obstacles to further development) and what might be (the achievements of developed economies and the available technologies), it established a tension which could stimulate action to close the gap. The greater the technological backlog, the greater the promise of development. At the same time, however, Gerschenkron was careful to point out that the opportunities for industrialization varied with the country's endowment of natural resources and that 'no industrialization seemed possible, and hence no "tension" existed, as long as certain formidable institutional obstacles (such as serfdom ... or the far-reaching absence of political unification) remained' (Gerschenkron, 1962: 8). The removal of such profound obstacles was unavoidably a function of the state and, therefore, depended on the location and deployment of social and political power.

Second, the more backward an economy (and here Gerschenkron was really defining backwardness in terms of institutional arrangements), the more likely it was that economic success would have to be pursued by institutional innovations, but institutional innovations that had directly economic effects; that is, there had to be arrangements that were drastic substitutes for the mechanisms that had been successful in more fortunate economies. Such institutional innovations tended to be concentrated in the marshalling and investment of capital funds.

A significant feature of Gerschenkron's argument was that such institutional innovations only depended on the state in circumstances of extreme backwardness. In France and Germany, for example, investment was encouraged by banking mergers and industrial cartelization, whereas in Russia (he argued) capital was in such short supply and the banking system and standards of business honesty so low that the state was needed to marshal capital and ensure its application to a rail network and heavy industry, albeit only after it had reformed serfdom and begun the transformation of the labour market.

The third aspect of Gerschenkron's model was that backward countries needed a rapid reinforcement through an economic spurt, if development was to maintain momentum. Such reinforcement was important not only because of the economic rationale but for psychological reasons: development imposes strains, and produces a backlash unless it succeeds in bringing rewards fairly quickly. Futhermore, backward economies were more likely to be able to attain such an acceleration since they could borrow from a backlog of innovation created by the technologies and investment lessons of the pioneers of development. In fact, they could leapfrog the earlier stages of less sophisticated technology and organizational structures that had characterized pioneer economies. Hence, according to this view, the experience of latecomers to development (France in one corner; Russia in another; perhaps Japan in a third, although Gerschenkron did not write much about Asia) was of institutional novelty to fulfil familiar functions, and dramatic speed of growth (at least as far as a limited number of sectors were concerned). A spurt therefore relied on heavy industry, interrelated change and, in Gerschenkron's words, 'the acceptance of specific industrialization ideologies' (Gerschenkron, 1962: 11).

Gerschenkron held that there were four distinctive levels at which industrialization in backward countries, compared with the process in advanced societies, could be considered: first, in terms of a faster rate of industrial growth and its productive and organizational structures; second, through the 'application of institutional instruments for which there was little or no counterpart in an established industrial country'; third, in 'the intellectual climate within which industrialization proceeded, its "spirit" or "ideology" '; and fourth, in the fact that the extent to which these attributes occurred varied directly with the degree of backwardness and the natural industrial potentialities of the countries concerned. Admittedly, since Gerschenkron formulated his ingenious and influential theories, more searching tests of his correlations have suggested that they are not bombproof. Nevertheless, even if the concept of economic backwardness and its Gerschenkronian implications have their defects, they remind us of some vital general lessons about development on the world scene.

First, the shape and pace of development are determined in part by the availability of increasingly more 'advanced' technologies and modes of organization. Second, the development of latecomers is achieved through institutions, not markets alone: development does not take place in a psychological, let alone an institutional, vacuum. Third, development is increasingly associated with perceptions of its advantages, with self-conscious attitudes, and with the willingness to transform institutions. Finally, and from the present viewpoint the most important lesson, there is no unique set of prerequisites, let alone institutional prerequisites. Gerschenkron's great contribution was to demonstrate that institutions are not timeless. He urged the significance of substitutions and related the gradations of substitutions to the degree of backwardness. Indeed, he went out of his way to say that even capital accumulation was not a vital prerequisite where credit creation is made possible by other means. The paradoxical result of course is that Gerschenkron's argument, even while pointing out that no particular set of institutions is necessary for development, confirmed the importance and centrality of their role and existence.

In summary, while much of discussion of diffusion centres on the global economy and the power of market forces, behind such pressures lurk institutional assumptions: the need to introduce market institutions and reliability of contracts and the ownership or control of property; an orderly state mechanism and financial system; ease of technology transfer. The balance between these two perspectives depends, no doubt, on which side of the globalization divide one stands. Where controversy fades is probably where Gerschenkron based his case; that is, when it is a question of backwardness, so that the nature of society means that market forces and history are not particularly propitious. Here, it is inconceivable that development can take place without a degree of exogenous institutional change; without, in other words, a powerful injection of political economy. The greater the obstacles, the greater the need for changes in 'human arrangement'.

2.4 Decline

The argument now turns from the sunny uplands of economic development to the swamps of economic decline, using Britain as an example of how economic historians approach the subject. This is useful because Britain's pre-eminence as a pioneer of industrialization also means that it is frequently offered as a pre-eminent example of a society fallen from economic grace.

Theories of unambiguous and pathological decline have little appeal (Supple, 1994). In fact, over the long run the British economy has maintained a fairly consistent if not spectacular growth rate (the 'British growth rate' referred to earlier). Even after the breast-beating of the later twentieth century, its level of development (that is, its per capita national income and the quality at least of its leading sectors) is up there among the favoured few nations. Admittedly, there have been periods when Britain's relative performance, and certainly its lagging industrial productivity, have induced profound pessimism in political and economic circles. This is particularly true of erstwhile heroic industries now diminished or long gone. But as others have emphasized, looking at the economy as a whole, the gap between America's rates of income and productivity growth and those of Europe, for example, is probably a much more interesting issue than the relatively more minor differences between the late-twentieth-century growth rates in Britain and the rest of Western Europe.

Still, we cannot deny the fact that there is something to explain, not merely in terms of perceptions, but also in performance, relative to either the achievement of other economies or the potentialities of the economy. The subtext here is the presumed failure to build on Britain's early start, suggesting (as we shall discuss below) that there might be disadvantages as well as advantages in early achievements.

Many interpretations of Britain's presumed decline are not directly relevant to our current discussion. They concern attitudes, appetites and the geopolitics of global power. Indeed, a good deal of this 'decline' is a matter of perception: a *feeling* of decline rather than the reality. It embodies not enfeeblement or frailty, but insecurity and shame at the loss of empire and supreme global standing; resentment at the advance of presumed lesser nations (many will recall the incredulity when Italy's per capita GDP appeared to approach Britain's); and perhaps above all frustration because Britain's non-American national income was seen as inadequate to sustain what popular culture hungers after in terms of American standards of private consumption and public affluence.

But the sense of decline is not rooted only in free-standing psychological perceptions. It is also intimately related to the view that modern Britain has fallen below some presumed measure of its potential. Insofar as this is the case, it is hardly possible to avoid an institutional explanation of performance. Indeed, given the influence of global markets, and the fact that other societies with comparable geographies have seemed to do better, institutional explanations must almost invariably be predominant: either global institutions or the institutions of rival economies impacting on Britain's prospects, or (more likely in Britain's case) its own institutions and outlook reshaping its potential.

Put another way, if we are concerned to explain differential change between countries, then in the global context both development and decline must be strongly influenced by institutions. We can fairly easily adduce market explanations for global boom and slump. But this type of explanation is far more problematic when we consider national departures from global averages. To explain these we have to seek *institutional* hypotheses: outlooks, structures and policies.

In fact in Britain's case there is a long history, extending back over at least a century, of theorizing about how an early lead was lost, what went wrong, how the economy was overtaken by upstarts, how in competitive terms it was its own worst enemy. Clearly, this culture of complaint has had some rationale since the later nineteenth century, when development on the continent and in the United States began to push Britain down the industrial league table. But it is significant that jeremiads were not unknown even when Britain was assuming the pioneering industrial role. Indeed, at the very outset of modern economics, it was left to Adam Smith to reassure the pessimists: 'Be assured, my young friend', he wrote to an anxious correspondent almost two hundred years ago, 'there is a great deal of ruin in a nation' (Smith, cited in Sinclair, 1831: I, 390–1).

Still, we gain a better perspective on the problem if we return to more recent history, when relative performance became more obviously unsatisfactory. Against this background, as we have pointed out, institutional explanations reign supreme and, broadly speaking, the institutions and norms that are said to be responsible for lagging growth are most commonly those rooted in history. In the gloomy historiography of this subject, the central explanations of Britain's apparently disappointing performance revolve around cultural outlook and institutional rigidity, conceivably reinforced by commitments to domestic and foreign policies based on earlier experience.

We are perhaps sated by detailed discussions of the usual socio-cultural suspects. As the academic world knows, they include a lack of (or, perhaps more accurately, a decline in) entrepreneurial spirit; a cultural denigration of industry and the more prosaic aspects of commercial endeavour; a neglect of the level and type of education appropriate to the twentieth-century economic needs; rigidity through the growth of vested interests in financial, commercial and labour organizations; and the diversion of what might have been investment resources into protecting the overvalued pound or sustaining an expensive welfare system or maintaining imperial and global commitments derived from a glorious past.

Historians have dealt with this range of presumed experience in a variety of mostly casual or dogmatic ways. On the other hand, even before the recent flowering of the new institutional economics, some economists tried to tackle them more systematically. This was obviously the case with Joseph Schumpeter in the mid-twentieth century (Schumpeter, 1942). However, his fears that the intellectual freedoms of capitalism threatened its survival through the encouragement of critical anti-capitalist ideologies were general rather than specific to Britain. More pertinently, Mancur Olson (1982) provided perhaps the most elaborate and systematic theory of institution-based decline with his arguments concerning the rigidities and inefficiencies spawned by collusive distributional coalitions which were the product of stability and time. The industrial economy of Britain was certainly abundantly endowed with both these.

Unfortunately, systematic analysis of such 'decline' has been fairly rare. Yet, irrespective of the origins of the myriad arguments about institutions and norms, they all fall into a limited number of general categories. Indeed, there are probably no more than two related types of explanation: ossification through the rise of vested interests and political pressures; and ossification through negative feedback from attitudes, institutions and policies which were appropriate to or innocuous in earlier periods of economic success, but which have proved inimical to subsequent needs.

A few general points about this division merit consideration. First, both sorts of argument are really part of a single metaview, namely that the present institutional and attitudinal frameworks are outcomes of past experience. Path dependence rules in institutional no less than in technological history. Second, and certainly in the case of Britain's twentieth-century economic performance, the distinction between institutions and attitudes is generally irrelevant, and cannot always be perceived. If there is a vicious circle of rigidifying institutions (in education, in cartels, in the distribution of social power, in the maintenance of imperial or welfare expenditures), they are indissolubly linked with the inhibiting attitudes and cultural norms that are their symptoms. Institutions generate and are supported by attitudes; and attitudes sustain institutions. 'Gentlemanly capitalism', if it importantly exists, not only awards kudos to finance and international trade, and biases government policy, but is also embodied in educational institutions and banking and commercial structures. The collusive power of trade unions gives rise to welfare expenditures, and welfare expenditures establish vested interests. The leading sectors of financial and commercial capitalism give priority to global and imperial investments and commitments, and these reinforce the authority of the institutions that embody that economic system. So it can go on; but does it? In fact, all this is probably too neat to be believed easily, and a number of important doubts arise.

The first problem concerns the general character of these presumed theories. Unless the development path of all economies follows a logistic curve, we still need an explanation of individual cases, including Britain's. There are no doubt models which imply a general theory, and Olson's, for example, seemed to do just that. But very few researchers are willing to go that far. Even Olson accepted the possibility of far-reaching change through a political willingness to mount an assault on coalitions: a willingness which, if it exists, would not be equally powerful in all societies.

But if the impact of institutions (even institutions which inhibit growth) is not uniform, we are left with the possibility that even if we take the situation at a particular period, institutions and attitudes are not parameters. This means that even if we accept the cultural/institutional explanation of Britain's (relative) decline, we are still left with question of why those inhibitions were not overcome? What keeps (or kept) Britain so constrained by the past? Nor will it do to say that its institutions and outlooks have been slow to change, for that is obviously too circular an argument. Indeed, a further chink in the conventional argument is opened wider by the no-doubt controversial observation that recent experience suggests that institutions and attitudes can change, or, rather, be changed. The political economy of the 1980s and 1990s, and not only in Britain, suggested that a combination of global market pressure and determined governments could, indeed, shift the balance between competitive forces and established interest groups and state commitments, between the official and the market allocation of resources. In this respect it is worth remembering that Olson, like the 1970s governments throughout the world, was heavily influenced by the experience of stagflation. The pendulum of political economy began to swing when the disruptions of stagflation had bitten deeply enough.

Nor is this problem solely a matter of inherited commitments to purely economic ways of doing and organizing things. Political economy in its older sense also comes into play. Whether or not there really is a trade-off between wealth on the one hand and welfare provision or political commitments overseas on the other, an influential and powerful body of opinion came to believe that there was, and to act accordingly by reforming domestic welfare systems and withdrawing from foreign entanglements. These are not easy goals: democracy on the one hand and pride on the other certainly make them difficult. But the fact that the effort was made (and is still being made) is a measure of the institutional influence on performance.

Clearly, when we come to consider economic decline, or at least disappointing economic performance, we have to acknowledge that institutions and attitudes must bear the brunt of any explanation. This is so whether they are considered as general phenomena or because there are institutional, political-economy reasons specific to individual societies which shape and reshape the adaptations that are the prerequisite of economic satisfaction.

2.5 The development of the Americas: Land versus institutions

So far, much of the perspective of this chapter has been the conventional preoccupation of historians. But there is another sort of case, which is quite different from the circumstances of Britain's presumed decline. This is the experience of the Americas, which for economists and a few historians has been used as a virtual laboratory in which the role of institutions can be more systematically appraised.

In particular, the American experience has enabled researchers to focus more precisely on the question of the association of institutions with development, and whether they are exogenous or endogenous to that process. This is in principle possible, of course, because Europeans, having pushed aside indigenous populations, developed North and South America as if they were entirely new lands. What this meant was that settlement by people from Western Europe injected similar institutions and cultures into different societies and regions, and differing institutions and cultures into similar societies and regions. So, at least in principle, causal links can be identified and cross-compared.

Conventionally (and generally among historians) the assumption has been that both the nature of institutional evolution and the course of economic growth were heavily influenced by the origins and institutions of the first successful settlers: Spanish or English, landed classes or yeomen farmers, Puritans or Catholics, democrats or aristocrats.

But the most persuasive studies in this field (those by Engerman and Sokoloff, 2002, 2003) concluded that neither the course of development nor the nature of institutions was explained by the national or even social origins of settlers, that is by the original institutions and attitudes that they brought with them to North or South America. Rather, the modern institutions associated with particular regions developed over time, and that development, as with the evolving institutions themselves, was primarily determined by inequalities in wealth, human capital and political power. Moreover, and perhaps most important to their argument, these inequalities developed from within the realities of the Americas, rather than being imported across the ocean. But once established, they tended to perpetuate themselves and their influences. That is, the roots of the inequalities are to be found in differences in initial factor endowment (the fertility of the land, the specificity of crops and the organization and labour systems appropriate to their cultivation), all going back to the initial period of European colonization.

Engerman and Sokoloff document their thesis by studying the evolution of suffrage and of policies for the distribution of public land and for education. In effect, they argue, where economic geography, factor endowment and labour supply created units of production which promoted large inequalities, those inequalities led to the creation of institutional structures which greatly advantaged members of the elite classes, in terms of the influence on politics (that is, policy) and access to economic opportunities and the shaping of institutions. By the same token, they had differing effects on the rate and direction of economic growth.

In other words, differences between the economic and the political institutions of different areas were very important. However, they were determined not by the social and national origins of the settlers, but by the character and imperatives of the lands they settled. This in turn implies that the founding realities of the land shaped institutions, rather than institutions shaping the course of development, even if those institutions outlived their origins to help determine later phases of economic development.

On the other side, however, Engerman and Sokoloff also acknowledge that while the institutions that embody Hazlitt's 'human arrangement' naturally influence development, they are not embodied in unique forms. That is, they emphasize that, just as institutions emerge from factor endowments and labour supply (from the conditions of the economy and polity), so no specific set of institutions nor any particular form of an institution is essential for development: 'function', not 'form', is the keyword. Institutions adapt. In other words, we are back with Gerschenkron and the substitutability of institutional arrangements.

This is obviously an attractive, even seductive, approach, bolstered by an unusually lucid presentation. Interestingly, economic historians have been in this sort of place before: six decades ago and more, Harold Innis, probably the most distinguished of Canadian economic historians, examined the history of new lands, resource exploitation and moving frontiers. Among social scientists he is perhaps best known for his more ambitious work on the history of communications, which he argued were the key to economic history and to social evolution throughout the world, but he also articulated a more bread-and-butter approach to the history of Canada, which is of relevance here (Innis's, 1956).

This was the staple theory of growth. From this perspective, the potential and challenges of Western development, and particularly the commercial attractiveness of large-scale production of staple products in a new and expansive setting (grain, meat, dairy produce; timber, minerals, oil) led to adaptations of European institutions and infrastructures. Traditional institutions (transport mechanisms, business enterprise and organization, intermediate infrastructures) were stimulated into existence by the need to insert staple production into world trade. The resulting staple economy thereby generated externalities which supported and extended processing and diversification (including secondary industries) so that development became general. In other words, the flexibility of the founding institutions established bases for other economic activities and more widespread growth. The pressure to extend across space so as to realize the potential of staple production produced what has been called a 'a grand space-binding economic and social system, founded on powerful media of transportation and communication' (Innis, 1956: 7). In a way, this is a sort of mirror image of the frontier thesis. The frontier thesis held that the opportunities of westward expansion transformed inherited institutions and replaced them with new approaches which came to typify an 'American system'. Innis's staple theory placed more emphasis on the adaptability of European institutions to transforming the space that was the frontier, and incidentally created the basis for continental-level development.

All this is heady stuff, even as a version of the economic-geographical interpretation of development. But it is necessary to introduce another cautionary note. The problem (as with the Engerman–Sokoloff view of the role of institutions in American development) is that it tends to sidestep the role of history itself. After all, Africa, Asia and Russia also had staples and extensive factor endowments. Yet in these cases the deadweight of inherited and entrenched institutions as well as imperialism could prevent the proliferation of tangible and intangible infrastructure which in Canada's case generated such booming externalities. Once again, we see that institutions have their own history, and it is that history which helps determine their flexibility and influence.

2.6 Conclusion

The contributions of most historians to the complex debate about institutions and economic development have been different, and less rigorously systematic, than economists would have liked and have themselves attempted. On the one hand, historians have neglected the statistical approaches, and especially regression analysis, that are generally so persuasive in economic argument. On the other hand, however, taking the importance of institutions as a given, they have undertaken far more research into the nature and operations of institutions and attitudes. Yet in the end it may well be that this approach is complementary to, rather than divergent from, the statistical and econometric. All agree that institutions play, and must play, a crucial role in development, especially if we define that role generously to include their absence as well as presence. After all, in North's phrase, they determine the rules of the game. What they are, and who controls them, are vital elements in economic performance and the distribution of its fruits.

We all also feel that there is a useful distinction to be drawn between the presumed endogenous and the exogenous roles of institutions. But in the final analysis most would agree that it is inconceivable that institutions are purely one or the other. Historical experience confirms that there are many ways to skin a cat: that positive 'human arrangement' is vital for economic growth, but that there is no highly specific form (as distinct from function) that it must take in order to play a beneficial role. Different circumstances, different societies, different periods of history – each will have their own imperatives. Overarching these, establishing a counterpoint to the protean flexibility that characterizes the history of institutions, is the opposite fact that, since they have their own history, they may exercise a less than beneficial influence on development as their inhibiting influences are perpetuated by their own inertia. Indeed, more than this, as we see in the case of Britain, institutions appropriate to one phase of economic history may turn out to be restrictive at another, or at least evolve in ways that prove restrictive as economies evolve. Nor is this an economic phenomenon: once we introduce the concept of political economy we must acknowledge the influence of power and its exercise both institutionally and as a determinant of economic policy and performance, and of the equity with which the fruits of development are made available.

In history, nothing interesting is unique or uniquely influential, and in economic development as in so many other spheres, what works depends on the necessities of the situation as well as on the intrinsic character of the institutions which interact with that situation. Context and function are as important as character and form.

References

Cain, P. J. and Hopkins, A. G. *British Imperialism, 1688–2000*, second edition (London: Longmans, 2001).

Engerman, S. and Sokoloff, K. 'Factor Endowments, Inequality, and Paths of Development Among New World Economies'. Cambridge, MA, National Bureau of Economic Research, Working Paper No. 9259 (2002).

Engerman, S. and Sokoloff, K. 'Institutional and Non-Institutional Explanations of Economic Differences'. Cambridge, MA, National Bureau of Economic Research, Working Paper No. 9989 (2003).

Gerschenkron, A. *Economic Backwardness in Historical Perspective* (Cambridge, MA.: Harvard University Press, 1962).

Hazlitt, W. *The Spirit of the Age* (1824-25; Collins: London, 1969).

Innis, H. *Essays in Canadian Economic History* (Toronto: Toronto University Press 1956).

North, D. C. *Structure and Change in Economic History* (New York: W. W. Norton, 1981).

Olson, M. *The Rise and Decline of Nations* (New Haven and London: Yale University Press, 1982).

Ricardo, D. *The Principles of Political Economy and Taxation*, third edition (1821; London, Everyman edition, 1911).

Rostow, W. W. *The Stages of Economic Growth* (Cambridge: Cambridge University Press, 1960).

Schumpeter, J. A. *Capitalism, Socialism and Democracy* (New York: Allen and Unwin, 1942).

The Correspondence of Sir John Sinclair, Bt. (London, 1831), I: 390–1.

Smith, A. *The Wealth of Nations* (1776), Book V, Chapter I, Part III.

Supple, B. 'Fear of Failing: Economic History and the Decline of Britain', *Economic History Review*, XLVII (3) (1994): 441–58.

Weber, M. *The Protestant Ethic and the Spirit of Capitalism* (London: Allen and Unwin, 1968).

3
A 'Tiresome Complexity'? Rent-seeking, Devolution and Economic Performance in Northern Ireland, 1945–72

Graham Brownlow

3.1 Introduction: Geography, institutions and economic history

Institutional structures are viewed by many contemporary economic historians, following the pioneering work of Douglass North, as being the ultimate determinant of economic growth (North, 1990, 2005). Baumol's work on the relationship between institutions and entrepreneurship has provided further theoretical support for North's position (Baumol, 1990). According to Baumol, the study of economic history suggests that it is institutional structures that determine what projects entrepreneurs pursue. It is the balance between these different types of entrepreneurship that contribute to determining growth and development. Baumol's analysis of institutions and entrepreneurship can be summarized by his three key propositions: (1) The rules of the game that determine the relative payoffs to different entrepreneurial activities *do* change dramatically from one time and place to another; (2) 'Entrepreneurial behaviour changes direction from one economy to another in a manner that corresponds to the variation in the rules of the game' (Baumol, 1990: 899); (3) 'The allocation of entrepreneurship between productive and unproductive activities, though by no means the only pertinent influence, can have a profound effect on the innovativeness of the economy and the degree of dissemination of its technological discoveries' (Baumol, 1990: 909).

The contemporary economics profession still contains many who are suspicious of this institutionalist line of argument. Often these institutional (and the closely related historical) sceptics argue that geographical rather than institutional factors tend to explain divergences in the wealth of nations (Sachs, 2001). Some geographers, moreover, purport to provide supporting evidence for this position (Diamond, 1997). This rival 'geographical school' suggests that geography is a key determinant of climate, endowment of natural resources, disease burden, transport costs and the diffusion of knowledge and technology from advanced countries. Geography thus exerts a strong influence on agricultural product ivity and the quality of human resources that tend to stimulate growth (Rodrik *et al.*, 2002: 1).

Winters and Martins' recent empirical study outlines, for example, that because of the additional costs of peripheral location, associated with remoteness and smallness, micro-states face formidable barriers to industrialization (Winters and Martins, 2004). Winters and Martin propose that in addition to subventions, micro-states should attain scale economies by combining government functions with each other (Winters and Martins, 2004: 159). It is a moot point, however, if it is indeed not the 'smallness' rather than the 'remoteness' that is the real 'geographical' barrier to economic development identified by Winters and Martins. The kind of problems identified with the geographical line of argument in large part explains the emergence of a recent, but highly influential, empirical branch of research that supports the claim that institutions are the ultimate source of growth (Acemoglu *et al.*, 2001; Rodrik *et al.*, 2002).

Some cautionary notes must be placed, however, in this account of the relationship between institutions and growth. First, the recent empirical literature on the relationship between institutions and growth unfortunately does not integrate the idea of entrepreneurship into its discussion. Moreover, the use of detailed archival evidence by economists on both sides of the 'geography versus institutions' debate has been conspicuous by its absence; indeed, both 'schools' have instead constructed highly stylized accounts based on secondary sources.[1] Secondly, Engerman and Sokoloff have suggested that the institutional school of thought has misrepresented the place of institutions in the development process. Engerman and Sokoloff propose that an examination of the historical record demonstrates that the institutional structure appropriate for promoting growth in one environment may be inappropriate in another (Engerman and Sokoloff, 2005).

Engerman and Sokoloff's analysis implies that the propensity with which beneficial institutional changes are innovated and/or diffused in response to political and economic changes is crucial to understanding and classifying the nexus between growth and institutions.

When institutions adjust positively, it can be said that the institutional framework is 'flexible' and growth-promoting. In contrast, when institutional inertia or 'inflexibility' exists, institutions will not respond constructively to take advantage of new opportunities. The potential for growth will be correspondingly reduced. Their analysis indicates that factors influencing the rate and direction of institutional change should be the focus of research rather than an empirical search for a 'menu' of institutional structures that will promote growth in all contexts of space and time (Engerman and Sokoloff, 2005: 662).

This chapter follows a structure that considers the rate and direction of institutional change. In Section 3.2, the geographical interpretation of Northern Irish economic underperformance between 1945 and 1972 is outlined and critiqued in the light of institutional economic history. Section 3.3 considers some insights from the economics of conflicts of interest and devolution. In Section 3.4, historical evidence is used to outline how the structure of political institutions created a situation detrimental to the interests of productive entrepreneurship. Sections 3.5–3.7 develop historical perspectives further, demonstrating that while Prime Minister O'Neill's modernizing settlement represented a new institutional perspective in the area of industrial development and one more consistent with the pursuit of economic growth, its political foundations were much less secure. The concluding section demonstrates that the specific findings on political economy presented here can thus be viewed as contributing more general insights on the respective weights that can be placed on geography, institutions and economic history in the study of growth.

3.2 Northern Ireland's poor economic performance: Geography or institutions?

At first glance, the relative backwardness that Northern Ireland experienced between 1945 and 1972 may be thought to reinforce further the geographical school's interpretation of development (albeit at the regional rather than the national level). Indeed, since the publication of Isles and Cuthbert's seminal study, *An Economic Survey of Northern Ireland* in 1957, it has been a conventional wisdom that a peripheral geographical location has been the root cause of the region's poor economic record since partition. In the *Economic Survey*, the alleged 'hard' additional costs of access to markets, caused by higher transport costs, were highlighted as providing a barrier to growth (Isles and Cuthbert, 1957: 48). In recent decades this geographical interpretation has been refined somewhat. The geographical problem is now presented as being one of 'peripherality'. Remoteness from the core is suggested to have caused barriers in the form of 'soft' factors to emerge. It is argued for instance that inadequate access to information has been one such 'soft' barrier to growth in the region's economy (Begg and Mayes, 1994).

However, neither the 'soft' nor the 'hard' versions of the peripherality thesis have much support in explaining the contemporary economic performance of the province. In a world of the Internet and the 'weightless economy', and the Celtic Tiger just across the border, it is implausible to focus on remoteness-based explanations for contemporary growth rates. The peripherality thesis, moreover, does not account for the fact that Ulster experienced rapid development in the late nineteenth and early twentieth century (Kennedy and Ollerenshaw, 1985). In any case, the precise origins of the peripherality thesis are particularly murky.[2] Over the course of this chapter the reasons for the eagerness of the Unionists to bolster a peripherality interpretation will become clear.

The archival evidence, interpreted in the light of rent-seeking theory presented in this chapter, suggests a revisionist interpretation. This new interpretation is more in line with the contemporary institutional economic history literature. The thesis can be summarized in the following four arguments:

1. The institutional structure of governance in Northern Ireland lacked conflict of interest controls between 1945 and 1963. In other words, there was an overlap between those benefiting from the allocation of grants and those awarding them. Some Ulster Unionist Party (UUP) politicians objected to the endemic conflicts of interest that existed.
2. The situation described by (1) tended to impede creation of an industrial policy that would have more easily encouraged the reallocation of resources from the old industries to the new. It also ensured that politically well-connected enterprises received grants rather than more efficient firms.
3. In 1963, with the emergence of O'Neill as prime minister, those opposed to these conflicts of interest managed to instigate institutional reforms in the area of industrial policy.
4. On balance, it seems plausible to suggest that situation (2) hindered the pursuit of economic efficiency. Conflicts of interest within the formulation of industrial policy tended to impede the operation of beneficial economic adjustments. In turn, these barriers to adjustment towards a more efficient allocation of resources must

have restrained economic development. It therefore seems plausible to suggest that the institutional reforms initiated in 1963 must have encouraged the pursuit of policies that tended to stimulate productivity improvements (Brownlow, 2007).

3.3 Some theoretical perspectives

This chapter's analysis of the province's political economy during the 'golden age' draws upon two issues of political economy: economics of conflicts of interest and of devolution and federalism. Stigler's analysis of conflicts of interest, stretching back to four decades, is important to the story told; likewise Weingast's much more recent survey of the economics of devolution and federalism also provides important insights (Stigler, 1967; Weingast, 2005). Stigler's thesis starts from the premise that conflicts of interest arise because of the existence of principal–agent relationships. Public officials and business people, acting as agents of the voters, and shareholders additionally (in the case of some firms) may act opportunistically relative to these principals' best interests: 'Conflicts of interest arise wherever one man is an agent for another; the agent does not bear the full consequences of his actions' (Stigler, 1967: 101). Stigler did not use the framework of three different kinds of entrepreneurship discussed in the introduction; yet a clear implication of Stigler's analysis, using Baumol's terminology, is that there is a danger that incentives may be skewed in such a way that conflicts of interest give rise to a relative increase in unproductive and destructive forms of entrepreneurship. Stigler gave some guidance on the kinds of institutional structures that would lead to these socially unproductive and rent-seeking forms of entrepreneurship.

First, Stigler observed that for publicly quoted firms, featuring large market capitalizations, the risk of detection for engaging in a conflict of interest would be high, relative to the possible returns that an opportunistic actor would get from promoting such unproductive activities. Conflicts of interest harmful to principals' interests would thus be restrained (Stigler, 1967: 100). Conflicts of interest would be much more likely to emerge in the case of privately owned firms, and/or publicly quoted firms with small market capitalizations. In such cases, the opportunistic investor could take a large stake. Because such enterprises offer a risk-return profile in which conflicts of interest that are harmful to principals are less likely to be detected or punished, the likelihood of unproductive or destructive forms of entrepreneurship being promoted would be correspondingly increased (Stigler, 1967: 100).

Second, Stigler claimed that the marginal effects of policies surrounding taxation and subsidies would be far more likely to create conflicts of interest harmful to principals. Taxation and subsidy-induced rent-seeking has a higher probability of leading to socially unproductive forms of ownership than in cases of marginal additions to revenue gained through government purchases. Tax and subsidy benefits are more valuable than government purchases because a tax dollar (or pound) conferred is a dollar received by a business in the form of profit. In contrast, a tax dollar of purchases based on procurement represents only a fraction of that amount in profits.

Northern Ireland's economy was, relative to Britain, dominated by privately owned firms, which involved a minimal diffusion of share ownership. The ratio of paid-up capital in private to public linen companies was around two to one as late as the 1950s (Ollerenshaw, 1991: 65).[3] Furthermore, as will be developed throughout this chapter, the conflicts of interest emerged in areas of industrial policy connected to subsidy rather than areas connected to government purchases. Stigler's predictions, therefore, seem to be borne out by the historical evidence presented in this chapter.

Weingast's (2005) survey of the economics of federalism outlines how the modern literature treats the issue. Modern economists have shown how the performance of a federal devolved system of government depends on the institutional arrangements underpinning the federal system. The modern theoretical literature is pessimistic compared to the earlier literature because the assumption of benevolent governmental actors is relaxed and principal–agent relationships are studied (Weingast, 2005: 150). Weingast summarizes the contemporary research on devolution as follows:

> As the Federalist observed more than 200 years ago, 'if men were angels' we would not have to worry about structuring incentives through the appropriate design of political designs; but as they observed, because men are not angels, we must be concerned with creating political institutions that provide government officials with appropriate incentives
>
> (Weingast, 2005: 156).

In contemporary public choice research, for instance, it is recognized that different institutional arrangements affect the incentives of various levels of government and hence affect their performance (Weingast, 2005: 151). The modern theoretical literature thus views it as being important to design constitutional settlements under which principal–agent issues do not arise between officials (agents) and the electorate (principals). The case developed here is very clearly one in which there was a high scope for opportunism until the O'Neillite reforms of the 1960s.

3.4 Causes of rent-seeking: Features of political institutions, 1945–72

Contemporaries within Northern Ireland suggested that the existence of devolved political institutions had a positive impact on the functioning of the regional economy. Charles Carter, the distinguished economist, writing in 1954, explicitly highlighted the structure and autonomy of the region's devolved political institutions as offering commercial advantages to potential investors:

> [Within Northern Ireland it is] easier to offer special inducements to attract new industry-inducements greater than are available in the Development Areas of Great Britain. Furthermore, the machinery of government is much less ponderous. Things which would take months to settle within Whitehall can be settled in a day by driving out to Stormont and talking to the people concerned. Some industrialists are believed to have been glad to escape from the tiresome complexity of getting things done in Britain to a land where enterprise is made officially welcome.
>
> (Carter, 1954: 3).

Yet far from being the greatest strength of Northern Ireland's governmental system, the lack of 'ponderous' rules was actually one of the major reasons why 'unproductive' forms of entrepreneurship influenced industrial policy until the 1960s. The Stormont government's patronage powers on disbursing grants faced minimal oversight from either Whitehall or Westminster. Much of the modern theoretical economics literature is concerned that the autonomy of devolved governments will be inadequate. It is predicted that a national government will intervene too much in the devolved levels of business; in the historical example presented here, perhaps the problem was too much rather than too little autonomy.

The relatively high level of autonomy exercised within Northern Ireland added to the government's patronage power; it also reinforced the overlap that existed between the region's political (patronage-giving) and business (patronage-receiving) leaders. It is not difficult to cite examples of how the structure of political institutions, with the attendant lobbying and principal–agent issues, shaped the formulation of economic institutions in the region in ways that made the attainment of economic efficiency less, not more, likely. By way of illustration, the Safeguarding of Employment Act (Northern Ireland) 1947 made it illegal for workers in non-exempt categories from outside Northern Ireland, including from Britain, to be employed in the province without special permission. Such a regulation was hardly consistent with what one would expect of a government committed to inward investment (Brownlow, 2002: 103–104). This quasi-protectionist approach even extended to the awarding of government contracts (Brownlow, 2002: 104). A combination of inability and unwillingness to introduce efficiency-raising measures at Shorts and Harland encouraged the Stormont government to lobby (unsuccessfully) for a new, second British government–owned aerospace producer. Again the politically popular option (of not reforming a publicly owned firm) was detrimental to regional economic performance (Brownlow, 2002: 115–16).

The economic and political interests of Unionist politicians also led them to consider radical deviations from British legal practice. For instance, in 1964, Brian Faulkner, the commerce minister, was forced to examine the legal possibilities of Northern Ireland opting out of the repeal of Resale Price Maintenance (RPM) (Brownlow, 2002: 287). Eventually, it was found to be politically easier to get RPM abolished by recourse to Westminster rather than local legislation. This course of action protected O'Neill, the reformist prime minister, from the UUP's influential shopkeepers' lobby (Brownlow, 2002: 287). It is in addition notable that an attempt by the Northern Ireland Labour Party (NILP) in 1960 to get the Unionist government to agree to British rules on members' interests was defeated by 26 votes to 4.[4] Cronyism, with its attendant principal–agent issues, was most famously apparent in the 'Seenozip affair'. The Unionist Westminster MP for West Belfast, Patricia McLaughlin, was influential in attracting the Seenozip firm into the province. However, she also acted as a shareholder and company director. This situation eventually led to her resignation due to 'ill health'.[5]

This scandal was just the tip of the iceberg. Stigler's insights discussed earlier are useful for trying to understand the political economy that existed in the province. Before 1963, politicians acting in their public capacity as grant dispensers (or patrons) and those individuals acting as grant recipients (or clients) were all too often one and the same; these distorted incentives had predictable results for the allocation of resources. It should also be recalled that since the creation of the Stormont parliamentary system in 1920, the electorate had never entertained any realistic prospect of voting in an alternative government. The agents were less than fully accountable to the principals at the ballot box. Formal legal/constitutional (or alternatively, informal cultural) restraints were needed to bring the incentives of the agents into line with the needs of the principals. There was little in the way of sustained and viable electoral competition to reduce the potential for opportunistic behaviour that gave rise to relatively unproductive forms of entrepreneurship.[6]

Terence O'Neill became prime minister of Northern Ireland on Monday 25 March 1963. Mulholland, in a highly persuasive historical account, has explained O'Neill's rise to power in terms of the changes in the province's political economy that occurred during the 1950s. Mulholland has observed that the growth of the 'golden age' improved the province's living standards relative to the Republic of Ireland (Mulholland, 2000: x). Such a state of affairs, Mulholland contends, reinforced partition. Furthermore, political stability created an atmosphere in which an assimilatory Ulster unionism, ambitious to include Catholics in the political process, could rise to leadership in the province. Mulholland maintains that from the 1950s it was likely that Brookeborough's successor as prime minister would come from a more liberal political generation that had not been politically active in the 1920s. O'Neill was, in Mulholland's account, the main beneficiary of this growing liberalism and had a desire for reform (Mulholland, 2000: x). It is important to observe that O'Neill's modernizing impulses, and those like-minded advisors who surrounded him, were based on a belief in the ability of devolution to deliver (Gordon, 1989: 10). It did not take long for new institutional structures to emerge that would affect the conduct of industrial policy in ways that tended to promote more productive forms of entrepreneurship.

3.5 Consequences of rent-seeking: The economic record, 1945–72

A combination of supply- and demand-side factors specific to Northern Ireland contributed to sluggish growth. The high unemployment ratios recorded in Table 3.1 were the result of its population growth being high relative to other regions (a supply-side factor) combined with the

Table 3.1 Unemployment as a proportion of the civil labour force (expressed as a multiple of the average UK ratio)

	Northern Ireland	Scotland	Wales
1947	3.9	2.0	3.2
1950	3.4	2.1	2.2
1955	5.3	2.1	1.4
1960	3.6	2.2	1.4
1965	3.7	2.0	1.6
1970	2.5	1.6	1.3
1975	1.9	1.3	1.3
Average 1947–75	3.47	1.80	1.77

Notes: Derived from *British Labour Statistics, 1886–1968* and later editions of the *Department of Employment Gazette*.
Source: Simpson (1983: 82).

continuous decline of employment opportunities in its staple sectors such as agriculture, shipbuilding, textiles and clothing (a situation with both supply- and demand-side elements). Measured in terms of its regional GDP per capita relative to the UK average, it also consistently remained the poorest region. From Table 3.1 it can be seen that the economy clearly deteriorated in the 1950s and the relative improvement in the region's figures only came with the growth slowdown of the early 1970s.[7]

Crafts has observed that even allowing for the region's large share of government consumption, the annual growth rate was 0.81 per cent lower than might have been expected had it grown in line with other European economies (Crafts, 1995: 10–12). Of course, while these differences in the predicted growth record may not seem large on an annual basis, the cumulative impact would have been profound over the duration of the 'golden age'. In a region already characterized by supply- and demand-side impediments to improving manufacturing efficiency, the allocation of industrial grants would have profound implications for the relative success or failure of attempts to restructure the region's manufacturing sector.

Table 3.2 demonstrates that during the 1950s and early 1960s the economy expanded at much the same rate as the (exogenously determined) national average. Nonetheless, in the mid-1960s the region's economic growth diverged from Great Britain's. Economic growth in the province accelerated in the period 1963–68 compared to the growth record of the previous 6 years, while it slowed down in

Table 3.2 Average annual percentage increases in GDP (at constant prices)

Period	United Kingdom	Northern Ireland
1950–58	2.0	1.9
1958–63 (a)	3.7	4.1
1963–68	3.3	4.3
1968–73	3.5	3.4
1973–79	1.1	1.7

Note: (a) 1958–62 for Northern Ireland.
Source: McClements (1981: 103).

Britain after 1963. This divergence suggests that there were some endogenous (region-specific) factors determining relative performance. The performance of Northern Ireland compared to other UK regions, and in particular Scotland, will be studied in the concluding section.

The variation in growth rates was largely caused by variation in the quantity and quality of capital available to industry. The annual average expenditure on industrial policy increased from £12.27 million in the period between 1945 and 1957 to double that in the last 6 years of Brookeborough's premiership.[8] The increased budget ensured that between 1958 and 1968 foreign investment increased markedly in the province; after 1968, as civil unrest grew, the rate of expansion was necessarily more modest.[9] Table 3.3 shows that, while between 1945 and 1965 Northern Ireland accounted for far fewer new jobs in the United Kingdom than Scotland, the proportion of new jobs accounted for by Northern Ireland between 1952–59 and 1960–65 grew faster. Inward investment was an important determinant of this observed pattern.

The changes in country of origin were in part the result of American multinationals redistributing their stock around Europe, while at the

Table 3.3 Proportion of new jobs coming to NI and Scotland compared

	Northern Ireland	Scotland
1945–1951	3.8	13.0
1952–1959	2.6	7.3
1960–1965	8.0	15.4
1945–1965	4.6	11.9
% of UK industrial employment in 1966	2.1	8.2

Source: Simpson, (1983: 87).

same time the overall number of European multinationals grew (Teague, 1987: 162). The fact that foreign investors chose to locate in the province, rather than elsewhere in the United Kingdom, can be explained by the more efficiency-orientated approach to inward investment that occurred in the period after 1963. It was such shift, as well as wider changes in firm organization, that was instrumental in raising the stock of inward investment (Teague, 1987: 162). The region's ability to attract productive enterprise grew after 1963; this growth was despite Britain's regional policy becoming simultaneously more generous. A first impact of the change in the budget and direction of industrial policy was that the size distribution of employment came to resemble more closely the rest of the United Kingdom.[10] This reflects the fact that multinationals were seeking to exploit economies of scale (Teague, 1987: 164). Table 3.4 demonstrates that the inward investment plant tended to be larger than indigenous factories. The increased attraction of inward investment hence tended to promote cost competitiveness, which stimulated the ability to export. This export potential in turn stimulated job creation; as will be demonstrated in Section 3.5, this employment growth in turn particularly affected the economic prospects of women.

Another piece of empirical evidence which supports the earlier view that reforms initiated in 1963 encouraged the pursuit of policies that stimulated productivity is that the more vigorous pursuit of inward investment, made possible by institutional and policy shifts after that date, tended to promote a convergence of the productivity level relative to Britain's. As the industrial policy strategy favoured relatively efficient newer sectors, and the economy's underlying structural shifts wiped out the less efficient staple industries, so productivity growth was stimulated despite the decline of indigenous firms in the staple industries. Manufacturing productivity grew faster between 1958 and 1970 than was the case between 1948 and 1958. The timing of changes in the region's productivity record is all the more notable because it was the opposite of that experienced in Scotland and the North of England (Brownlow, 2002: 107).

It is apparent that the convergence of productivity levels (and the associated divergence of growth rates shown in Table 3.2) were the result of improvements in productivity in the old sector (as the numbers of workers employed in the staples declined) as well as the expansion of new sectors benefiting from the expansion of inward investment that occurred in the 1960s. Yet the evidence of rapid structural changes presented in Tables 3.2 and 3.5 reinforce the idea that productivity

Table 3.4 Industrial development assisted industry with origins outside Northern Ireland, 1968

Establishment size (number of workers)	Number of establishments (a)	% (a)	Employment (a)	% (a)	Number of establishments (b)	% (b)	Employment (b)	% (b)
1–10	6	3.8	41	0.1	480	32.5	2,281	2.0
11–24	6	3.8	103	0.2	295	20.0	5,558	4.8
25–99	44	27.8	2,544	5.0	422	28.6	20,730	18.0
100–499	74	46.8	16,080	31.5	259	17.5	50,546	43.8
500–999	16	10.2	9,885	19.5	10	0.7	8,806	7.6
1000–1499	7	4.4	8,384	16.5	4	0.3	4,896	4.2
1500	5	3.2	13,803	27.2	6	0.4	22,483	19.6
Total	158	100.0	50,810	100.0	1,476	100.0	115,300	100.0

Note: (a) Inward moves
(b) Total less inward moves

Source: PRONI COM/101/1/6 'Size Comparisons – UK and Northern Ireland Industry', Memorandum by Ministry of Commerce, 13 March 1973.

Table 3.5 Northern Ireland net output per head, 1949–73 (NI/GB, GB = 100)

	Numbers employed in sector in June 1949	Numbers employed in sector in June 1966	1949	1958	1963–73 Average
Total manufacturing	207,350	192,590	71	68	84
Food, drink and tobacco	20,980	30,630	80	87	106
Chemicals	1,610	2880	88	n.a.	121
Metals	1,220	470	n.a.	41	72
Mechanical engineering	14,180	30,080	65	77	89
Instrument engineering	–	–	91	89	76
Electrical engineering	–	–	75	83	79
Shipbuilding	19,560	9,530	n.a.	n.a.	59
Aerospace	14,900	4,350	n.a.	n.a.	70
Metal goods	1,980	3080	n.a	91	89
Textiles	52,250	55,170	67	71	73
Man-made fibres	20,910	–	n.a.	n.a.	138
Clothing & footwear	31,240	27,310	70	71	71
Bricks, pottery, glass & cement	–	4080	93	91	95
Timber & furniture	–	5080	73	95	80
Paper & printing	5,900	6930	73	75	79
Other manufacturing	–	–	n.a.	60	80

Notes: In order to make the Census of Production figures consistent with the *Census of Production* series, a number of calculations were performed: in Ulster Yearbook 1950 there is only an entry for 'Other Engineering and Electrical Goods' and instead of Aerospace there is 'Vehicles (excluding ships)' in both 1950 and 1966/68 yearbooks; for textiles we include a combination of the Ulster Yearbook's categories of 'Flax processing and scrutching', 'Flax spinning and thread manufacture' and 'linen weaving'. For man-made fibres we include 'other textiles' and categories for 'Metal manufacture' and 'metal goods not elsewhere defined' in both 1950 and 1966/68 yearbooks. In Ulster Yearbook 1966/68 the relavant entries were restricted to the broad categories of 'Engineering and electrical goods' and 'Textiles'.
Sources: Ulster Yearbooks 1950 and 1966/68, Census of Production (Birnie and Hitchens, 2001: 5).

convergence was mostly due to the supply-side inflow of multinational enterprises rather than being the inevitable result of a much more persistent demand-driven decline in the staple sector's output levels. Factors linking the operation of devolved political institutions to the region's pool of technology and organizations are thus vital to understanding the province's convergence process. The productivity record is thus compatible with the interpretation presented earlier in this chapter.

Industries in which multinationals played a vital role acted as motors for convergence. In four sectors, Food, Drink and Tobacco, Chemicals,

Paper and Printing, and Mechanical Engineering, shown in Table 3.5, the figures show an increase in employment between 1949 and 1966 as well as a sustained convergence of productivity with British levels of productivity. It is equally noticeable that in only one sector (synthetic fibres) was the region's output per worker record between 1963 and 1973 substantially better than the rest of the United Kingdom. The convergence of productivity, which occurred in the 1960s, must in a large measure be attributed to the attraction of inward investment by synthetic fibre firms being made easier by the new institutional environment. In contrast, politically powerful staples like aerospace, shipbuilding and textiles had much lower levels of labour productivity than their British peer groups in the period 1963–73. Conflicts of interest in the area of industrial policy tended to blunt the effectiveness of regional industrial policy because it discouraged diversification and restructuring that tended to stimulate productivity increases.

3.6 Institutional stability and the linen lobby: Northern Ireland's political economy, 1945–63

It was the stated government view in the 1940s and 1950s to support inward investment. Furthermore, by the time of the publication of the Hall Report in 1962, the need to attract inward investment was seen as the key for stabilizing the politically charged unemployment situation. This shift in economic strategy has been taken for granted as being inevitable (Harris, 1991). But that perspective ignores the delicate economic and political balance which existed within the Stormont government and which eventually led to the Commerce ministry changing its emphasis. The linen industry was the province's biggest manufacturing employer for most of the 'golden age' of economic growth. It was also a successful special interest group: the term 'linen lobby' was actually used by contemporary politicians and civil servants to refer privately to the continuous and vocal calls for government support for the linen industry.[11]

Northern Ireland's economic and social strategy under devolution is of interest to economic historians of Scotland. Clear contrasts can be discerned, as immediately following the war inward investment was seen as an essential part of reducing unemployment in the province. By way of illustration, legislation was rushed through (the Industries Development Act (Northern Ireland) 1945) enabling the province to benefit from the need for industrial capacity after demobilization. Rather than use the land and resources for public housing, it was industry that immediately benefited. Industrial expansion, rather than an immediate focus on social equity, was a vital objective for policy-makers. The growth of new employment opportunities for women was not at the forefront of policy-makers' concerns either; this gender element is a topic that will be developed later in this section.

The strategy pursued by the Stormont government stood in stark contrast to the one pursued by the Scottish Office. From 1945, the Scottish Office pursued a regional economic policy that focused on the provision of public housing rather than industrial plant. The political economy in Scotland was shaped by the fact that the dominant Scottish Labour Party found it beneficial in electoral terms to offset low wages by keeping public sector rents well below levels necessary to balance the public accounts (Lee, 2005: 226–8). The New Town Act of 1946 further added to the need for public sector house building in Scotland (Lee, 1995: 165). Only in the 1960s did Northern Ireland, with the creation of Craigavon, copy the Scottish 'new town' model. In the Scottish case, it was buoyant regional growth that was relied upon during the 'golden age' to generate greater employment prospects, especially amongst women (Lee, 2005: 217–19). Table 3.6 demonstrates that the Scottish growth record was superior during the 'golden age'. Political economy considerations ensured that neither Scotland's growth performance nor the increasingly important economic contribution of women was replicated by the province during the early decades of the 'golden age'. In the concluding section, the Scottish–Northern Ireland comparison will be developed more fully.

As early as 1953, the *Belfast Telegraph* was worried about the political feasibility of redirecting subsidies away from the old staples to new industries. The Belfast linen industry operated a virtual monopsony in

Table 3.6 Annual average percentage growth of manufacturing net output, 1948–70, in certain regions

Region	1948–51	1951–54	1954–58	1948–58	1958–70
N. Ireland	6.0	0.6	1.7	1.7	2.3
Northern	5.3	4.6	5.5	5.5	5.2
Scotland	3.4	1.2	3.1	3.1	2.6
Wales	9.1	6.3	3.0	3.0	5.8
United Kingdom	4.4	2.6	3.2	3.2	3.4

Note: N. Ireland data for 1949 (1948 not available).
Sources: Calculated from *Census of Production*, and Harris (1991: 16, 52).

substantial segments of the female labour market.[12] By 1954 the Ministry of Commerce was privately critical of the ability of local employers to keep pace with the need for job creation. Still, the Ministry was already aware that local employers were complaining that competition for scarce skilled labour from new entrants was reducing the cost competitiveness of local industry.[13] The empirical evidence, however, does not suggest that new entrants should be held responsible for any reduction in regional cost competitiveness.[14]

During the 1940s, in a forerunner of Isles and Cuthbert's analysis regarding attitudes in local industry, linen producers constantly voiced concern at 'cut throat price competition' (Beacham, 1944: 114). The industry's favoured 'solutions' to the 'problem' of price competition were a combination of import controls and export subsidies. However, neither of these 'solutions' could address the overriding issue of domestic overcapacity. The proposal of such 'solutions' is entirely compatible with an interpretation of industrial development in which rent-seeking played an important part (Brownlow, 2007). In a 1944 study, Beacham identified the managers of family-owned firms in the linen industry as being the source of the long tail of under-performing firms in the industry, a finding that Isles and Cuthbert were to repeat 13 years later (Beacham, 1944: 205; Isles and Cuthbert, 1957: 289). This was a problem for the economy, as family ownership remained dominant in the industry. Realizing that voluntary attempts to restructure the linen complex were doomed to failure, the government instead chose to subsidize investment. The Re-equipment of Industry Act (1951) enabled well-established local producers across all sectors to modernize their technology and plant through grant aid (Ollerenshaw, 1991: 77). The offer of re-equipment grants was seized by the industry. By 1954 half of all the applicants were linen producers (Ollerenshaw, 1991: 77). Given that the stated objective was to subsidize new industry, this persistence of staples receiving a disproportionate share of the subsidy requires a *political economy* rather than a pure *efficiency* explanation. A series of increasingly generous capital grant acts in 1954, 1957 and 1959 made industrial policy increasingly an area of importance to regional economic development (Bew *et al.*, 1995: 123).

The need for inward investment was conventional wisdom within the Ministry of Commerce before the appointment of J. L. O. Andrews as commerce minister in 1961. Between 1945 and 1961 every commerce minister had supported inward investment as the basis of future development rather than supporting the linen complex.[15] Lord Glentoran (Andrews' predecessor) was an enthusiastic supporter. He served as a director of Cyril Lord Ltd, the Donaghadee carpet firm, at the same time as serving as commerce minister.[16] Such a position highlights once again lax conflict of interest regulations, and the vital importance which political economy considerations played in the formulation of industrial policy.[17]

Such considerations became apparent during the early 1960s. During a Cabinet discussion in June 1962 on the provision of advance factories for new firms, Andrews repeated his opposition to new industries on the grounds that such factories would compete for labour with linen and would drive up labour costs.[18] Andrews also invoked conservative social attitudes in his preference for using taxpayer funds to create male as opposed to female jobs.[19] A political and economic tension existed between a diversification strategy, involving an increase in the range of job opportunities available to women, and the protection of politically well-connected staple industries. Indeed, it is notable that O'Neill's more positive approach to inward investment corresponded with a more diverse set of job opportunities becoming available for women. In part, this was a consequence of the decline of linen. Between 1956 and 1971, female linen and textile employment contracted from 42,430 to 20,150, yet total female employment grew from 176,000 to 196,880 during the same period. It is especially notable that most of this growth was concentrated between 1960 and 1966, when total female employment grew from 177,000 to 194,000. The timing of this change again seems consistent with O'Neill's shift away from support of the (previously politically powerful) linen lobby.

3.7 Institutions and economy at the crossroads: Northern Ireland's political economy, 1963–72

The introduction of a Cabinet code of conduct in May 1963 was economically an important change, especially in the light of Stigler's observations. The new situation permitted ministers to hold commercial directorships only if they avoided a clear conflict of interest. The institutional change brought Stormont more into line with the British (Churchill) code of conduct, which dated from 1952. The new code replaced the much more lax set of rules that dated from Craigavon's guidelines in the 1930s.[20] O'Neill's desire to respond to public opinion was the explanation proffered by the modest coverage of the local newspapers.[21] The contents of the letters pages of the *Belfast Telegraph*, *Newsletter* and *Irish News* during the Glentoran crisis of 1963 do not, however, provide supporting evidence for this explanation (Brownlow, 2007).[22]

O'Neill's willingness in 1967 to dismiss Harry West, his minister of agriculture, over a breach of the code of conduct added to the growing political opposition to O'Neill. O'Neill's political liberalism, combined with his attack on the privileges that politicians had enjoyed, must have made his tenure less secure.[23] Mulholland has plausibly argued that O'Neill's decision directly strengthened the organized forces arrayed against him and it put his leadership in considerable doubt (Mulholland, 2000: 121–2). Mulholland's interpretation of the political ramifications of enforcing the O'Neill code is convincing. Mulholland nevertheless downplayed the fact that O'Neill's rule change also had important implications for the conduct of industrial policy and the implicit changes in principal–agent relationships that this involved. O'Neill's reforms, by placing more emphasis on housing conditions and reducing the conflicts of interest problems, brought the region's political economy marginally closer to Scotland's. Economically, these reforms tended to be beneficial in terms of their potential impact on equity and efficiency (Brownlow, 2007).

The 'political economy' aspect of the situation becomes even clearer if we accept Mulholland's claim that the NILP was, by the 1960s, an increasingly serious threat to Unionism's electoral dominance (Mulholland, 2004). If we accept this highly controversial claim, then not only were rents increasingly difficult to obtain once elected, but even getting elected in the first place was increasingly being made difficult by the political shifts initiated by O'Neillism. In such a situation it is no wonder that O'Neill and Chichester-Clarke could not retain the support of substantial elements of their own party. The reformist leaderships had presided over a transition towards productive entrepreneurship that, while being socially and economically beneficial overall, was damaging to the political and commercial interests of a long-established patron–client network. The combination of political liberalism and economic reformism thus were not leadership features guaranteed to provide job security. It is also notable that when O'Neill, against the backdrop of rising civil unrest, was replaced by James Chichester-Clark in May 1969, the new prime minister reiterated the O'Neill code.[24] This was a bold decision from a political economy perspective, for the same reasons that O'Neill's 1963 reforms were bold.

Despite high grant levels, it would soon prove to be difficult to attract innovative firms against the backdrop of civil unrest (Scott, 2004: 339). Of course, by maintaining the strict code, and being ideologically similar, Chichester-Clark found himself subject to similar political hostility as his predecessor and like O'Neill he eventually resigned in 1971. It has been noted that O'Neill's reforming approach to traditional power blocs within unionism – local government, Belfast corporation, the West and farmers – served to alienate the powerful constituencies within the UUP (Mulholland, 2000: 199). To this list must be added those political interests with electoral and/or business interests in the old staple industries.

O'Neillism was undermined by the eruption of civil unrest, which gave its political opponents within unionism the opportunity to try and place the brakes on reform, while Catholics increasingly became frustrated by what they understood to be the slow pace of reform (Mulholland, 2000: 201). Eventually O'Neill's political support within the UUP disintegrated, forcing his resignation. This was not, however, the end of O'Neillism. Chichester-Clark continued the modernization, but his primary problem was that, like his predecessor, his attempt to extend O'Neill's reforms further ran into vociferous political opposition from those within the UUP opposed to the social, political and economic implications of the modernization strategy. Against the backdrop of growing political violence, the hardliners could more easily ferment opposition to Chichester-Clark's leadership, and again a leader was forced from power.

The British government, after decades of inactivity and lack of interest, now became involved in the day-to-day running of the devolved government (Scoular, 2000: 115). Eventually, in 1972, it took over the running of the government of Northern Ireland, but as Mulholland, writing in 2000, stated, 'The irony was that, in destroying O'Neill, Ulster unionism opened an era, uninterrupted since, of *de facto* administration of Northern Ireland by the very liberal establishment they had so resented' (Mulholland, 2000: 203). Hence, the erosion of autonomy caused by the replacement of direct rule with devolution altered the region's political economy even further away from the 1920 settlement.[25]

3.8 Conclusions: Rent-seeking and economic history

There are both specific and general lessons to be drawn from the evidence presented here. First, specifically, Northern Ireland's poor industrial performance during the 'golden age' is informed more by institutional economics than by remoteness. This conforms to the findings of economic historians interested in earlier periods of Ulster's economic history. Institutional factors, moreover, were generally important as determinants of regional economic performance. Political economy is crucial to understanding Irish economic history, regardless of period (Brownlow, 2005a: 46). An interpretation of the material presented here, along the lines suggested by Engerman and Sokoloff's theoretical analysis as presented in the Introduction, is that O'Neillism represented an attempt at increasing the institutional flexibility of Northern Ireland. O'Neillism was an attempt to increase the rate of institutional change and to move institutional forms in a more efficient and equitable direction. However, this attempt at institutional modernization had profound implications for the balance between different entrepreneurial forms in the province.

Second, the conclusion that institutional factors are important for understanding regional economic performance is in line with recent work on Scottish economic history (Lee, 1995, 2005: 228; Peden, 2005: 234). As has been demonstrated here, while Northern Ireland shared many of the same social and economic problems as Scotland, it was unable to emulate the Scottish path because its institutional structures did not permit it to do so until the 1960s. Table 3.6 shows that, except in the earliest post-war period (1948–51), Northern Ireland's growth rate languished relative to the other UK regions. The more detailed comparison with Scotland shows that between 1958 and 1970, despite the economic improvements initiated by O'Neill, Scotland's growth rate outpaced performance in the province. Scotland's faster growth rate allowed its economy and society to support measures aimed at further raising efficiency and equity.

Third, this chapter has illustrated that institutional factors were embedded in the unusual constitutional settlement that the province had after its creation in 1920. The evidence presented here on rent-seeking is thus of interest to scholars considering the application of constitutional political economy beyond the domain of the American model. The need for such an extension has been a recent feature of the public choice literature (Shughart and Tollison, 2005). Weingast's account, discussed in Section 3.2 of this chapter, indicates the importance of public choice thinking in understanding the operation of devolved political institutions (Weingast, 2005). Public choice theorists have, however, feared a national government acting as a Leviathan in its relationship with devolved entities. In the case of Northern Ireland, British governments between the 1920s and the 1960s acted as anything but a Leviathan. Indeed, one message to come from the historical material is that the autonomy was arguably excessive in practice, if not in theory.

It is notable that a more recent official report has shown that under direct rule a conflict of interests emerged as part of the loan and venture capital awarding powers connected to the operation of the Local Enterprise Development Unit (LEDU) in Northern Ireland (NIAO, 2006). A similar finding emerged from an analysis of the De Lorean affair.[26] The scale of the sums involved in the LEDU case, however, was much smaller than in the 1950s and 1960s, but the re-emergence of conflicts of interest demonstrates that in a small society such institutional dangers must be guarded against continually. Tentatively, it may be suggested that perhaps it is the size of a society, rather than its geographical remoteness, that is the most salient factor where geography enters into considerations of economic development. In the case of Northern Ireland, arguably its remoteness has been exaggerated; and in any case as part of the United Kingdom, it should not have suffered from the problem of a small domestic market.

A fourth and final implication that emerges is that it is far easier to construct an historical account of economic development which provides a key role for entrepreneurship when institutions are placed at the centre of the developmental story than is the case with those accounts that focus narrowly on location aspects of geographical economics. Geographical, unlike institutional, accounts provide no clear theoretical role for entrepreneurship in helping or hindering economic growth. While some economists may not mind such a lack of realism, many others will object.

The economic history literature suggests that it is more realistic to acknowledge that it is often through entrepreneurship that institutions have influenced economic development. In the case considered here, an important by-product of the transition to a different economic and institutional environment was related to gender rather than location. Inward investment increased female job opportunities. Such gender consequences of economic change are an important facet of the study of economic history, if not the 'new' economic geography. Economists from both the institutional and the geographical schools should, in the manner advocated by North, therefore pay more heed to the abundant insights that economic history provides in considering the ultimate determinants of growth.

Notes

1. The geographical perspective ignores, for instance, the long-standing focus in historical literature on how institutional factors found at the regional rather

than the national level have shaped industrialization and development since the British Industrial Revolution (Pollard, 1981).

2. Isles and Cuthbert's focus on geography in the final version of their report, and the 'spin' that has been placed on it since, were in large part the result of political manipulation (Brownlow, 2002: 119–26).
3. Whereas 63 per cent of all paid-up capital in the United Kingdom was held in public companies, the figure for Northern Ireland overall was only 39 per cent and it was a mere 34 per cent in the Northern Irish linen industry (Ollerenshaw, 1991: 65).
4. PRONI CAB/4/1147, 'Labour Party's Motion on Public and Private Business', Memorandum by Prime Minister, 17 November 1960.
5. *Belfast Telegraph*, 13 January 1964. For more details see Brownlow, 2002.
6. However, it has been claimed by Mulholland that this electoral monopoly disappeared in the 1960s (Mulholland, 2004).
7. Between 1951 and 1958 Northern Ireland's relative income per head actually slipped (from 65 to 61 per cent of the national average), and it was only between 1962 and 1966–73 that its income per capita converged from 63 to 71.1 per cent of the national average (Scott, 2004: 338).
8. PRONI CAB/4/1227/5, 'Report of the Official Employment Committee', Memorandum from the Economic Advisory Office, 21 March 1963.
9. Simpson reports that studies repeatedly show, relative to Britain, that the mid-1960s was the most successful period for the attraction of inward investment. The proportion of new jobs relative to the level of existing employment was much better than for other regions. The results were some 50 per cent better than for Scotland, the next highest region (Simpson, 1983). It is worth noting that it was only between the 1960s and the 1980s that Scotland started actively to pursue the relocation of plants from other UK regions. It seems no coincidence that in terms of income per capita this period coincided with considerable catch-up growth (Lee, 2005: 221).
10. PRONI COM/101/1/6, 'Size Comparisons-UK and Northern Ireland Industry', Memorandum by Ministry of Commerce, 13 March 1973.
11. PRONI CAB/4/1190, 'Conclusions of a Cabinet Meeting', 7 March 1962.
12. *Belfast Telegraph*, 28 April 1953.
13. PRONI CAB/4/944/3, 'Industrial Development', Memorandum by Minister of Commerce, 9 June 1954.
14. In terms of wage costs per unit of industrial output between 1956 and 1973, Northern Ireland's relative position improved slightly, increasing by 69 per cent compared to a national average increase of 88 per cent (Simpson, 1983: 91).
15. PRONI CAB/4/1148, 'Conclusions of a Cabinet Meeting', 13 December 1960.
16. *Belfast Telegraph*, 24 November 1960.
17. The overlap is especially clear when one considers that Cyril Lord Ltd received a major grant, while Lord Glentoran was simultaneously both a company director and the relevant government minister. The contents of the official minutes for a Cabinet meeting in March 1962 outlines Andrews' hostility to Glentoran's earlier strategy of attracting inward investment. It states, 'He [Commerce Minister Andrews] thought it would be disastrous to existing employment in trade if new firms were allowed to settle where

they liked and compete for the labour already engaged in linen production' (PRONI CAB/4/1190, 'Conclusions of a Cabinet Meeting').
18. PRONI CAB/4/1195, 'Conclusions of a Cabinet Meeting', 19 June 1962.
19. PRONI CAB/4/1195/2, 'Establishment of New Industries Requiring Females', Memorandum by Minister of Commerce, May 1962.
20. PRONI CAB 1453/8 'Private Interests of Ministers', Memorandum by the Prime Minister, 7 July 1969.
21. *Newsletter*, 5 July 1963.
22. Finding the real reasons behind the change is also difficult because the surviving primary sources on this topic are few and far between. In addition, the secondary sources are vague (Brownlow, 2007). O'Neill's reform in this area met enduring political opposition from within his own party ranks. O'Neill's autobiography, for instance, notes that as late as 1966 the new ministerial code was still opposed by a substantial section of the UUP (O'Neill, 1972: 87). Mulholland suggests that O'Neill's stance on the code signalled that O'Neill would monitor closely the activities of his ministers and that he would not tolerate the discontent on the issue that marred the final days of Brookeborough's premiership (Mulholland, 2000: 24).
23. The dismissal of West, who had been involved in the purchase of land that he knew was to be the location of an airport, was unprecedented in the life of the Stormont Parliament (*Newsletter*, 27 April 1967; *Belfast Telegraph*, 27 April 1967).
24. PRONI CAB 4/1453/8, 'Private Interests of Ministers'.
25. The institutional economics of direct rule are considered elsewhere (Brownlow, 2002: 160–257; Brownlow, 2005b).
26. *Belfast Telegraph*, 14 February 2006.

References

Primary sources

Cabinet Secretariat papers (CAB) held at the Public Record Office for Northern Ireland (PRONI)

Ministry of Commerce papers (COM) held at the Public Record Office for Northern Ireland (PRONI)

Ulster Year Books (Various)

Northern Ireland Accounts Office (NIAO), *Governance Issues in the Development of Enterprise, Trade and Investment's Former Local Enterprise Development Unit, In Relation to the Establishment and Oversight of the Emerging Business Trust Loan and Venture Funds*, Report by the Comptroller and Auditor General (Belfast, 2006)

Belfast Telegraph

Irish News

Newsletter

The Statist

Secondary sources

Acemoglu, D., Johnson, S. and Robinson, J. 'The Colonial Origins of Comparative Development: An Empirical Investigation', *American Economic Review*, 91 (5) (2001): 1369–401.

Baumol, W. 'Entrepreneurship: Productive, Unproductive and Destructive', *Journal of Political Economy*, 98 (1990): 893–921.

Beacham, A. 'The Ulster Linen Industry', *Economica*, 11 (1944): 199–209.

Begg, I. and Mayes, D. 'Peripherality and Northern Ireland', *National Institute Economic Review*, 150 (1994): 90–9.

Bew, P., Gibbon, P. and Patterson, H. *Northern Ireland 1921–1994: Political Forces and Social Classes* (London: Serif, 1995).

Birnie, E. and Hitchens, D. 'Chasing the Wind? Half a Century of Economic Strategy Documents in Northern Ireland', *Irish Political Studies*, 16 (2001): 1–27.

Brownlow, G. 'Institutional Change and the Two Irelands 1945–1990: An Application of North's Institutional Economics', unpublished PhD thesis, Queen's University, Belfast (2002).

Brownlow, G. 'The Political Economy of the Ulster Crisis: Historiography, Social Capability and Globalisation', in D. G. Boyce and A. O Day (eds), *The Ulster Crisis: 1885–1921* (Basingstoke: Palgrave, 2005a): 27–46.

Brownlow, G. 'Democratic Deficits, Fiscal Subventions and the Inter-related Strategy: Northern Ireland, 1969–1990', unpublished Paper (2005b).

Brownlow, G. 'The Causes and Consequences of Rent-Seeking in Northern Ireland 1945–72', *Economic History Review*, 60 (1) (2007): 70–96.

Carter, C. 'A Chance of Prosperity', *The Statist*, November (1954): 3.

Crafts, N. 'The Golden Age of Economic Growth in Post-war Europe: Why Did Northern Ireland Miss Out?', *Irish Economic and Social History*, XXII (1995): 5–25.

Diamond, J. *Guns, Germs and Steel* (New York: W. W. Norton, 1997).

Engerman, S. L. and. Sokoloff, K. L. 'Institutional and Non-Institutional Explanations of Economic Differences', in C. Menard and M. M. Shirley (eds), *Handbook of New Institutional Economics* (Berlin: Springer, 2005): 639–67.

Gordon, D. *The O'Neill Years: Unionist Politics 1963–1969* (Belfast: Athol, 1989).

Harris, R. *Regional Economic Policy in Northern Ireland 1945–1988* (Aldershot: Ashgate, 1991).

Isles, K. and Cuthbert, N. *An Economic Survey of Northern Ireland* (Belfast: HMSO, 1957).

Kennedy, L. and Ollerenshaw, P. (eds), *An Economic History of Ulster, 1820–1939* (Manchester: Manchester University Press, 1985).

Lee, C. H. *Scotland and the United Kingdom: The Economy and the Union in the Twentieth Century* (Manchester: Manchester University Press, 1995).

Lee, C. H. 'Unbalanced Growth: Prosperity and Deprivation', in T. M. Devine, C. H. Lee and G. C. Peden (eds), *The Transformation of Scotland: The Economy Since 1700* (Edinburgh: Edinburgh University Press, 2005): 208–32.

McClements, L. 'Economic Constraints', in D. Watt (ed.), *The Constitution of Northern Ireland: Problems and Prospects* (London: Heinemann, 1981): 100–21.

Mulholland, M. *Northern Ireland at the Crossroads: Ulster Unionism in the O'Neill Years 1960–9* (Basingstoke: Macmillan, 2000).

Mulholland, M. 'Why Did Unionists Discriminate?', in S. Wichert (ed.), *From the United Irishmen to Twentieth-century Unionism: a Festschrift for A.T.Q. Stewart* (Dublin: Four Courts, 2004): 187–206.

North, D. C. *Institutions, Institutional Change and Economic Performance* (New York: Cambridge University Press, 1990).

North, D. C. *Understanding the Process of Economic Change* (Princeton: Princeton University Press, 2005).

Ollerenshaw, P. 'Textiles and Regional Economic Decline: Northern Ireland, 1914–70', in C. Holmes and A. Booth (eds), *Economy and Society: European Industrialisation and its Social Consequences* (Leicester: Leicester University Press, 1991): 58–83.

O'Neill, T. *The Autobiography of Terence O'Neill: Prime Minister of Northern Ireland 1963–1969* (London: Rupert Hart-Davis, 1972).

Peden, G. C. 'The Managed Economy: Scotland, 1919–2000', in T. M. Devine, C. H. Lee and G. C. Peden (eds), *The Transformation of Scotland: The Economy Since 1700* (Edinburgh: Edinburgh University Press, 2005): 233–65.

Pollard, S. *Peaceful Conquest: The Industrialization of Europe 1760–1970* (Oxford: Oxford University Press, 1981).

Rodrik, D., Subramanian, A. and Trebbi, F. 'Institutions Rule: The Primacy of Institutions Over Geography and Integration in Economic Development', unpublished paper, Harvard University (2002).

Sachs, J. 'Tropical Underdevelopment'. Cambridge, MA, National Bureau for Economic Research, Working Paper No. w8119 (2001).

Scott, P. 'Regional Development and Policy', in R. Floud and P. Johnson (eds), *The Cambridge Economic History of Modern Britain Volume 3: Structural Change and Growth* (Cambridge: Cambridge University Press, 2004): 332–68.

Scoular, C. *James Chichester-Clark: Prime Minister of Northern Ireland* (Killyleagh: Clive Scoular, 2000).

Shughart, W. F. and Tollison, R. D. 'The Unfinished Business of Public Choice', *Public Choice*, 124 (2005): 237–47.

Simpson, J. 'Economic Development: Cause or Effect in the Northern Irish Conflict', in J. Darby (ed.), *Northern Ireland: The Background to the Conflict* (Belfast: Appletree, 1983): 79–110.

Stigler, G. 'The Economics of Conflict of Interest', *Journal of Political Economy*, 75 (1967): 100–101.

Teague, P. 'Multinational Companies in the Northern Ireland Economy: An Outmoded Model of Industrial Development', *Beyond the Rhetoric: Politics, the Economy and Social Policy in Northern Ireland* (London: Lawrence and Wishart, 1987): 160–83.

Weingast, B. R. 'The Performance and Stability of Federalism: An Institutional Perspective', in C. Menard and M. M. Shirley (eds), *Handbook of New Institutional Economics* (Berlin: Springer, 2005): 149–75.

Winters, L. A. and Martins, P. G. *Beautiful but Costly: Business Costs in Small Remote Economies* (London: Commonwealth Secretariat, 2004).

4

Institutional Capacity and Social Capability: Japan's 'Deviant' Capitalism in the High-growth Period and Beyond

W. R. Garside

It is a commonplace of the post-1945 period that Japan, wrought by wartime defeat, transformed itself in a relatively short period of time into a dominant player on the world's economic stage. The central role of government in strategic planning, 'picking winners' in sectors or firms, orchestrating cartels and protecting or subsidizing industry stood in stark contrast to the practice of more mature industrialized nations such as Great Britain. In Japan, the government protected sunrise industries in their infancy through quotas and high tariffs. Firms were encouraged to compete and to adapt foreign technology in order to spur increased production and returns to scale, thereby lowering production costs. The Japanese state was far more embedded within the political economy of the nation (Evans, 1995). It provided distinctive coordinating mechanisms that produced 'constellations of power and interest' (Beeson, 2002:19) which for many years were regarded as fundamental to the country's economic success.

Those aspects of Japan's economic past are well established in the literature. But the nature of the debate over Japan's post-1945 economic experience and its lessons for the future has altered noticeably over recent years. The contrast with Britain provides one contextual example. With the coexistence since the 1990s of relative British prosperity and the denouement of the Japanese economy, a revised liturgy has appeared on the horizon. Many observers have become convinced that the sources of Japan's previous economic success must have been ephemeral or at least suspect if the nation was singularly unable either to predict or cope with the economic hubris of recent decades. Whatever the sources of the 'British disease' before the 1980s, the Thatcherite neoliberal embrace of the free market and the removal of the clammy hand of the state were hailed as the source of Britain's 'economic renaissance'. By contrast it was the over-dependence of Japan on state-led developmentalism that was its ultimate undoing. Collusion and collaboration had spawned corruption, 'crony capitalism' and stagnation (Masina, 2002).

4.1 Enter the critics

Not only are the certainties of past writings on Japan's post-war economic development now much more fluid, but the criticisms of the 'developmental state' are deepening. It is not merely that the system soured. It was, critics argue, always deeply flawed. Moreover, most economists they assert and historians, they assert, have been living with a delusion created in part by Japan itself to cover the nakedness of its self-interest. Salvation from current woes will come only when the country embraces neoliberal Anglo-Saxon capitalism. We are now told for instance that the developmental state of Japan's high-growth period was a fable; that the keiretsu was a figment of academics' imagination; that Japan grew merely because of the neoclassical application of factor inputs; that the country was always wedded to political vote-chasing with economic policy fashioned accordingly; that the supposed virtues of the 'Japanese system' such as consensus, nationalism and trust were but the harbingers of future decline; that the much lauded bank-centred financial system was merely a vehicle for featherbedding, over lending and inbred uncompetitiveness; and that academics, especially in the West, have been judging a 'Japan that never was' (Miwa and Ramseyer, 2002; Beason and Patterson, 2004; Lin, 2005).

By the 1980s, Japan had to face some of the consequences of its previous spectacular, if unexpected, economic growth. We are now more aware of the chequered history of that experience, and retrospective analyses of the 'Japanese miracle' are now the staple diet of revisionist economists and historians. They have a case. Chalmers Johnson's classic description of a powerful and sophisticated bureaucracy judiciously deploying incentives and administrative guidance to steer the economy (Johnson, 1982) has spawned counter studies of a divided, ineffective and at times counterproductive political and bureaucratic apparatus: Calder (1988), Friedman (1988), Okimoto (1989), Samuels (1987) and Tolliday (2001), to list only a few from a burgeoning literature.

State 'management' of the economy has certainly lost much of its former appeal as countries such as Japan remain stuck in recession while other nations apparently bask in the economic good fortune delivered by neoclassical deregulation, privatization and retrenchment of state spending. While it is acknowledged, for example, that during the early phases of its post-war modernization the Japanese government provided essential costly and scarce information to firms through indicative planning and offered through a highly developed consultative processes a 'vision' to guide private sector investment, the fact that there were clear divergences between private and public sector interests at the peak of the Ministry of International Trade and Industry (MITI)'s influence in the early 1960s, sufficient to encourage some firms to defy state directives, raises the question of whether the private sector was ever a passive follower of government. MITI both tried and failed to restructure shipbuilding, machine tools, the car industry in the 1960s and petrochemicals (Friedman 1988; Okimoto, 1989; Krauss, 1992; Abe and Gourvish, 1997). At the same time it subsidized declining sectors such as coal and textiles under the pressure of intense lobbying (Coates, 2000; Garside, 2005). And although historians are ready to accept that the Japanese economy required considerable state intervention in the 1950s in order to correct previous distortions of interventionist policy during the 1930s and 1940s primarily because of military preoccupations, recent critics have asserted that the Japanese state, far from being an integrated entity capable of orchestrating spectacular growth through its flexibility, coordinating abilities, professionalism and trustworthiness, was in reality far weaker than conventionally assumed (Callon, 1995; Boyd and Ngo, 2005). What was critical, it is argued, was the favourable international economic environment in which Japan operated, underpinned by the hegemony of US liberal capitalism during the years of high growth, the willingness of it and other industrialized nations to comply with Japan's highly protectionist strategies and the competitive benefits Japan enjoyed from a favourable and fixed exchange rate during the period 1950–71. There was, moreover, the steely determination of Japanese politicians, preoccupied with politics and power, to ensure that official economic policy was fashioned for the benefit of those groups most likely to render caucus support (Beason and Patterson, 2004).

In addition, while no one dismisses the effectiveness of Japan's corporate structures and complex inter-firm networks in fostering research and development cooperation, skill formation and competition, the influence of local-level lobbying and other interest-based associations acting as mediators and coordinators of inter-business and state–business relations was probably of greater significance than has customarily been acknowledged. Moreover, as evidence mounts, on the one hand, of proactive managerial efforts down to the 1990s to experiment, to take risks and to encourage other entrepreneurs to follow suit for the sake of growth and, on the other, of the state's connivance with the very questionable corporate inter-financial links that ultimately gave rise to deception and bankruptcies on an unprecedented scale, the benign view of the Japanese 'developmental state' has taken a further battering. And once the low-interest regime of the 1980s gave way to a speculative borrowing binge, to an outpouring of loans for public works constructions of greater political than economic value, and the protection of a banking structure whose regulatory regime was opaque, to say the least, the neoclassical chorus of 'we told you so' began to take on a vibrant echo.

To this have been added the cool reappraisals of academic economists. Few cast doubt upon Japan's high-growth experience. As Table 4.1 shows, the country's annual growth rate exceeded that of the OECD during the period 1950–90, even though the 'miracle' years were over by 1973. Both the United States and the British economies performed less well throughout.

However, reductionist claims and counterclaims over which agency or set of circumstances was at the heart of Japan's growth experience down to the 1990s have so polarized commentary that much of the country's pragmatic, faltering, but essentially holistic approach to economic betterment is often difficult to discern (Huang, 2005).

Table 4.1 Real GDP growth, 1950–90 (average annual percentage change)[a]

	1950–60	1960–73	1973–80	1980–90
US	3.3	4.0	2.1	3.0
UK	2.8	3.1	0.9	2.7
Germany	8.2	4.4	2.2	1.9
Sweden	3.4	4.6	1.7[b]	1.7
Japan	8.8	9.6	3.7	4.2
South Korea[c]	1.3	6.5	7.4	6.8

[a] OECD rates: 1950–73, 4.7%; 1973–87, 2.4%.
[b] the Swedish figure is an average for 1970–92.
[c] the South Korean figures are GDP per head.
Source: Coates, 2000: 5.

Growth-accounting methods, for example, decompose the growth experience of Japan and other Asian countries into factor accumulation and productivity components and have led pessimists to conclude that Japan's growth, though exceptional, leaves little to be explained. Krugman (1994) has pointed to the country's 'astonishing mobilization of resources', especially capital and labour. As Table 4.2 indicates, the percentage contribution of total factor productivity in Japan during the period 1957–90 was lower and its output elasticity of capital higher than in France, Germany, the United Kingdom and the United States during roughly comparable periods. As a late developer, in other words, Japan simply relied more than most upon factor accumulation and rather less than most upon increases in the efficiency with which those inputs were used. 'The neoclassical model', write Beason and Patterson, 'more than adequately accounts for Japan's post-war economic trajectory' (Beason and Patterson, 2004: 8).

It has been demonstrated, too, that for all the emphasis put upon industrial targeting the greatest beneficiaries of developmental tariffs and quotas, subsidies, low-interest government loans and sectoral corporate tax breaks in Japan between 1955 and 1990 were the poorest-performing sectors in terms of growth rates, such as mining and textiles. The former was the biggest winner in terms of Japan Development Bank loans, net subsidies and tax relief (Beason and Weinstein, 1996). Moreover, as industrial policies were pursued over the post-war period, connections between the regulators and the regulated in Japan became more intimate. Leading firms became more able to influence policy at the same time as the bureaucrat's ability to monitor the performance of enterprises grew more difficult (Eichengreen, 2002). In addition, as Japan moved towards the technological frontier from the 1980s it had to rely more on indigenous technical change and innovation rather than imported know-how. This called for the preferences of large firms to be removed and for government command over resources and its bureaucratic efforts to control their allocation to be reduced (Callon, 1995).

Miwa has even claimed that, after the closest scrutiny, the roles and activities of the Ministry of International Trade and Industry and the Ministry of Finance, Japan's elite bureaucratic agencies, were 'all just an illusion'. The state's less than successful intervention in agriculture, finance, distribution and the small business sector, together with its particularly 'incompetent' role in the crucial machine tool industry both during wartime and in the high-growth period, undermines in his view the notion that an elite bureaucracy made effective a 'plan rational'

Table 4.2 Growth rates of labour productivity and total factor productivity in newly industrializing economies (NIEs) and developed industrial economies

	Output elasticity of capital β	Average growth rate per year (%)			Percentage contribution of total factor productivity $(G(A)/G(Y/L))$
		Labour productivity $G(Y/L)$	Capital-labour ratio $G(K/L)$	Total factor productivity $G(A)$	
NIEs					
Korea 1960–90	0.45	5.1	8.9	1.1	21
Taiwan 1953–90	0.49	6.2	9.6	1.5	24
Hong Kong 1966–90	0.40	5.2	6.1	2.8	54
Singapore 1964–90	0.44	4.5	6.6	1.6	36
Average	0.45	5.3	7.8	1.8	34
Developed economies					
France 1957–90	0.28	3.8	4.7	2.5	66
Germany (FR) 1960–90	0.25	3.6	4.9	2.4	67
UK 1957–90	0.27	2.3	3.0	1.5	65
USA 1948–90	0.23	1.5	1.6	1.2	80
Japan 1957–90	0.30	6.0	9.7	3.1	52
Average	0.27	3.4	4.8	2.1	66

Notes: B: Average estimates using the translog production function.
Y: Real GDP per work hour.
K: Reproducible capital (excluding residential buildings) adjusted for utilization rates.
L: Work hours.

Source: Eichengreen, 2002: 18, citing Kim and Lau, 1994, Tables 3–1, 6–3 and 7–1.

developmental state capable of overseeing the long-term growth and structure of the economy. On the contrary, he writes:

> Observers have drawn causal conclusions from toy facts. Nobody has ever tested either the competence of the Japanese state or its active intervention and its contribution to development. [The state] was not competent enough to do such a job and actually did not even try. Ultimately it was the market which played by far the greater role in the achievement. The notion that the Japanese government fostered economic growth through its intervention is instead a fable, a story we collectively tell and retell because we so badly wish it were true.
>
> (Miwa, 2004: xxiii)

Porter, Takeuchi and Sakakibara postulate in a similar vein:

> Conventional wisdom attributes the lion's share of Japan's post-war competitive success to the actions of its government; to the set of economic policies so prominently associated with Japan that they are universally known as the Japanese government model. But conventional wisdom is wrong.
>
> (Porter *et al.*, 2000: 18)

Even when we turn to the much lauded institutional framework embedded in bank-centred finance, conventionally held responsible for the capacity of Japanese industry to eschew short-term profit-taking for longer-term strategic development, all does not appear to be as we thought. During the high-growth period, keiretsu firms were supposedly bound to one another in a web of obligation that, together with the support of their main bank, assured mutual financial assistance for the sake of growth and stability. But as Table 4.3 shows, the Mitsui Bank in 1965 made only 31 per cent of its loans to Mitsui group borrowers, and the Mitsui Trust Bank only 25 per cent to the group. Mitsui firms in turn borrowed only just over 14 per cent of their debt from the Mitsui Bank and just over 9 per cent from the Mitsui Trust Bank. Keiretsu members, in other words, appear to have had a much broader diversification of borrowings than conventional analysis presumes, and borrowed only a small portion of the loans they needed from the keiretsu bank (Miwa and Ramseyer, 2002: 176–9).

Another favoured 'institutional' bedrock of post-war Japanese economic success down to the 1990s – its 'employment system'– emphasized

Table 4.3 Keiretsu loans, 1965–85

Keiretsu	Year	Number of Firms	Borrowings (million yen)	Loans as percentage of								
				financial-institution lending				nonfinancial-firm borrowing				
				Bank	Trust Bank	Life Insurance	Marine & Fire Ins.	Bank	Trust Bank	Life Insurance	Marine & Fire Ins.	Total
Mitsui	1965	71	1,224,259	31.0	24.5	33.3	18.9	14.3	9.3	1.5	0.1	25.2
	1970	71	2,476,819	26.6	20.4	32.7	26.4	11.3	9.1	2.1	0.2	22.7
	1975	95	5,769,301	20.9	18.1	29.3	2.6	10.9	8.2	2.1	0.0	21.2
	1980	104	9,649,457	15.2	15.0	21.5	14.4	8.2	6.4	2.0	0.2	16.8
	1985	104	9,649,457	9.9	9.2	13.1	11.2	8.4	5.9	1.5	0.2	16.1

Source: Adapted from Miwa and Ramseyer (2002: 177).

loyalty, consensus, cooperation, harmony and productive efficiency to such an extent that Western manufacturers were constantly urged – and some even tried – to 'learn from Japan'. The industrial relations harmony that outsiders found so alluring was, however, hard-won. The post-war rise of labour militancy in Japan did not disappear because of a sudden purge by Occupation forces or because of managerial reaction. In steel and coal in particular, battles over wage setting and working conditions continued throughout the 1950s. The shift from the struggle for control of the workplace to a 'hegemony of corporate values' resulted from managers in key industries (steel is a good example) forging new personnel policies with segments of the trade union movement which promised a share of the benefits of company growth in return for the embrace of workers by the company. But it involved a much narrower concept of democracy in the workplace. A series of defeats of the Japanese trade union movement in the early 1950s paved the way for the creation of enterprise unions which, through practices such as 'lifetime employment' (enjoyed in reality by around only one worker in four), seniority promotion and group bonuses, created a culture of social unity 'designed to keep Japanese labour weak or contained during the long boom that followed' (Tabb, 1995; Gordon, 1998; Coates, 2000: 132–3).

4.2 State versus market: A vacuous debate?

The revisionist perspectives briefly outlined above suggest that Japan's post-war developmental state was both more ineffective and perhaps ultimately more damaging than is conventionally assumed. But such revisionism is frequently based upon stylized presumptions about the roles of the state and the market in fostering economic growth. The capitalist system is made up of a range of institutions, including, but not only, markets. Institutional and evolutionary economists emphasize that the invisible hand of the market can only work well when the visible hand of state bureaucracy works equally well through a complex system of institutions (North, 1990; Burlamaqui *et al.*, 2000). This comes as no surprise to economic historians who have repeatedly shown that markets came late in capitalist development and almost always as a result of state activity. To quote Karl Polanyi:

> The road to the free-market was opened and kept open by an enormous increase in continuous, centrally organised and controlled interventionism ... Witness the complexity of the provisions in the innumerable enclosure laws; the amount of bureaucratic control

> involved in the administration of the New Poor Laws which for the first time since Queen Elizabeth's reign were effectively supervised by central authority; or the increase in governmental administration entailed in the meritorious task of municipal reform.
>
> (Polanyi, 1957: 140, cited in Chang, 2000: 15)

What authors such as Evans and Block have emphasized is that both states and markets are limited in their ability to produce desirable results when they operate according to their own logic. What is required is a combination of their different logics to produce positive outcomes. This exercise, in what Block calls 'disorderly coordination', requires policies to undergo continuous adjustment, which in turn requires strong and effective central government. This is not a call for capitalism to be overcome by the force of the state but a recognition that since the capitalist system is not coherent but actually made up of multiple interlocking markets, each of which has itself been shaped by state action, the state can have a significant effect on how those markets work, even by exercising a small amount of leverage. Such leverage comes from governments interacting with the choices made by those operating within markets, that is the interaction between state action and individual decision-makers. From this perspective, the state can act as a network builder and strategist, exchanging information with private sector firms to assist cooperative structures within a competitive environment. And this the more so since market signals can be a notoriously imperfect means of providing entrepreneurs with the information needed to determine, say, human resource management or choice of technology (Evans, 1995; Block, 2000; Chang, 2002).

Much of this, of course, offends the deterministic and highly abstract axioms of general equilibrium analysis which emphasize the self-correcting powers of the market. But such mechanistic approaches can only take us so far. Far too often in mainstream economic theory, Geoffrey Hodgson reminds us, 'explanation is no longer the goal, and reality is no longer the object of reference' (Hodgson, 2000: 110). Arguably, therefore, institutions 'beyond market rationality' are needed to coordinate selective policies orchestrated by the state in cooperation with private sector agencies to cope with uncertainty, learning, structural transformation and instability. The market, as one observer has put it, is a good servant but a bad master (Burlamaqui, 2000: 47).

4.3 Catch-up and institutional capacity

With these thoughts in mind let us return to the characterization outlined earlier of the economic performance of Japan down to the 1990s. To argue that Japan merely engaged in an exercise of catch-up and convergence overlooks rather too quickly the fact that it did catch up when other countries with an opportunity to do so did not and that in doing so Japan achieved spectacular success. Membership of the post-war convergence club was not automatic and it is too simplistic to view catch-up simply as a process of mobilizing hitherto under-utilized economic resources. As Coates has pithily observed, mapping convergence is one thing; explaining it is another (Coates, 2000: 154–7).

Economic growth is the result of more than the simple decomposition of factor inputs. From a technical point of view, growth-accounting models may have underestimated the combined effect of innovation (shifts in technology) and technical efficiency (the extent to which known technologies were applied to actual production). There is evidence to suggest that the latter was important for countries imitating the frontier technologies of developed countries and that models which ignore such catching-up influences may have yielded estimates of productivity growth that were biased towards developed countries (Kim and Lee, 2006). More fundamentally, although North identified the important roles of property rights, efficient market structures and democratic and decentralized decision-making, he also acknowledged that we do not know what actually creates efficient markets. Insofar as they reveal low transaction costs, incentives to compete on price and quality, they also require institutions to effect such outcomes. As he puts it, 'With economies bent on "catching up" by borrowing technology and organizational knowledge there is ample opportunity to accelerate the process by deliberately attempting to structure markets to achieve such results.' Path dependence will have an influence on the pattern of a country's development depending on cultural heritage ('frugality, industry, honesty and fidelity' in the case of Japan) and also upon how adaptive is the institutional structure (North, 1998: 552–60).

Abramovitz's focus on a nation's 'social capability' is relevant in this context. It is based on a somewhat vague and immeasurable term but one which none the less embraces:

> personal attributes, notably levels of education . . . but . . . also competitiveness, the ability to cooperate in joint ventures, honesty . . .

> trust... [and]... a variety of political and economic institutions. It includes the stability of governments and their effectiveness in enforcing the rules of economic life and in supporting growth.
>
> (Abramovitz, 1994: 88)

The components of growth, in other words, extend beyond resource endowments of capital, labour and technology. They incorporate institutional practices rooted in social systems of production, ideology, socio-economic pressure groups, the international economic order, historical accident and opportunity, external shocks, national economic policy and the competence of firms. How such influences interact over time is critical in determining whether economies forge ahead, fall behind or remain on a distinct growth trajectory (Kitson, 2005). At best, growth accounting can only indicate the proximate rather than the ultimate causes of growth (Maddison, 1995: 103).

Impelled for the sake of survival to meet competition in world markets from first-comers such as the United Kingdom and the United States, Japan evolved a series of institutional forms that fitted it with the capacity to accelerate technical change and the growth of productivity in the interest of lower costs – in particular, by constituting close relationships between manufacturing corporations and banks as well as by participating in various forms of vertical and horizontal networks to foster inter-firm coordination and cooperation. With funds allocated to domestic manufacturing rather than to domestic consumption or international lending, the mercantilist state was able to provide 'the protection and subsidies required to enhance the capacity of domestic business to conquer world export markets', an effort buttressed by the determination of the United States to strengthen a potential rival economically as a means of protecting both it and the post-war capitalist system from the threat of communism (Brenner, 2005: 220).

Rather than being fearful of business links, the post-war Japanese bureaucracy created institutionalized channels for the negotiation and renegotiation of policies in cooperation with the private sector. The fact that relations in some areas of activity became too cosy and less than transparent over time cannot entirely erase their effectiveness in the catch-up period. We cannot ignore the social and political setting in which institutions are embodied. In Japan, institutionalized relationships based on trust were unlike the more conventional legalistic enforcement of contracts, but they reflected a particular set of social values that were not necessarily less 'efficient' (Beeson, 2002: 11).

4.4 The distinctiveness of post-war institutionalism

Japan's high-growth record stands alongside the 'consensual techno-cracy', 'bargained compromise' and those other facets of relational contracting that neoclassical economists berate as inimical to allocative efficiency (Dore, 1987). But what needs to be emphasized is that as a latecomer to industrialization, Japan had a compelling desire to catch up with the West and it was this that drove the post-war trajectory. With such a national rallying call, it was inevitable that the Japanese system would take on different characteristics to those found in earlier pioneering countries. The adoption and adaptation of new technologies required dedicated forms of capital finance, new corporate structures, and a stable and educated labour force, together with institutions for regulating product and labour markets and nurturing cooperation and competition.

At its heart, the endeavour was informed not so much by the search for allocative efficiency as an economist might define it as by a set of social arrangements. This embraced, in Dore's words, 'the compromises made in favour of people who would lose out from the free working of market forces, the mobilizing of a sense of obligation and personal commitment in employment relations' together with 'customer market relations' generating 'a sense of fairness which enables people to work cooperatively, conscientiously, and with a will'. It is arguable from this perspective that Japan gained a form of 'x-efficiency' or 'production efficiency' just as important for explaining differences in national economic performance as is 'allocative efficiency'. And if the incentive was to compromise and restrain the use of market power out of consideration for the bargaining partners engaged in the search for national competitiveness, that in turn required the incentive-providing, coordinating, conciliating and adjudicating role of government (Dore, 1987: 18).

If we are to understand properly the institutional foundations of Japan's high-growth period, and in turn be able to delineate which features became sclerotic and the precursors of future economic malaise, it is necessary to see post-1945 developments as rather more than an evolutionary progression of inter-war and wartime trends or even the culmination of the state's long-standing pursuit of modernization dating back to the Meiji period. As Teranishi has argued, Japan's strategic post-war economic endeavour was a more complex and interrelated affair than this monotonic evolutionary approach might suggest. Much of the institutional and relational developments of the high-growth period

Table 4.4 Characteristics of Japan's economic systems

Sub-system	**Meiji-Taishô economic system**	**High-growth-period economic system**
(Peak time period)	**Mid-1900s to early 1920**	**Mid-1950s to 1980s**
Government–Market division of labour	Market mechanism	Government intervention
Government–Private sector interface	Inter-regional	Inter-industrial
Private sector	Large shareholders	'Japanese-style' firms
	Banks finance indigenous industries	Bank-centered financial system

Source: Teranishi, 2005: 29.

were the result of a reaction against the vicissitudes and failures of the pre-1945 period rather than a natural outcome of its central premises (Teranishi, 2005).

Although Japan had pursued a modernization and developmental strategy from the mid-nineteenth century, the roles of the principal economic agents and the institutional settings in which they operated were anything but monolithic. As Table 4.4 indicates, Japan's economic system to the early 1920s was market-based with limited government intervention. Workers were highly mobile between firms, income distribution was unequal, corporate governance was dominated not by banks but by large shareholders, including regional merchants and large landlords, and the focus of economic activity and lobbying was not between the state and the private sector but rather within the regional economy through which capital, resources, information and guidance were disseminated (Hashino and Saito, 2004: 254).

Direct intervention within the economy for development, redistributive and planning purposes grew steadily between the wars and during the Second World War. It was during the 1920s and 1930s, moreover, that direct efforts were made to alter the relationship between the government and the private sector and to promote particular industries. Industrial associations were developed to encourage greater representation of distributive interests between the state and the private sector, while embryonic forms of the much-lauded 'Japanese employment system', incorporating seniority wage systems and long-term employment, were developed within large zaibatsu firms. Nothing could be more distinct from Japan's post-1945 developmental state, its bank-centred finance, its managerial rather than shareholder-based employment system and its orchestrated government–business interface (Teranishi, 2005: 28–30, 296–7).

The pre-1945 system stumbled badly between the wars as Japan faced severe international competition in key industrial sectors, especially heavy and chemical industries. The foundations of the system were also weakening. The agricultural sector slowed, the banking system grew increasingly unstable, and the impulse to preserve vibrant regional economies faded midst disputes between tenants and landlords and a broader desire by particular social classes and industrial interests to seek their own betterment rather than that of a regional community (Teranishi, 2005). During the war, direct government intervention, economic planning, the control of employment and wage systems, and the use of industrial associations to assist the flow of information and directives all intensified (Okazaki and Okuno-Fujiwara, 1999). War-related financial lendings were organized via financial syndicates with bank lending under the direct control of the state. In short, politicians, bureaucrats and entrepreneurs had been challenged for decades before 1945 to establish an economic system compatible with both intensified government intervention and an active and potentially rent-seeking private sector.

None of this meant that Japan had necessarily to compromise the private sector to gain success. Authors like Calder (1988), Friedman (1988), Okimoto (1989) and Samuels (1987) see the relationship of the government and the private sector as zero-sum whereas it was always a more complex affair. During the period 1931–40 the Japanese state on the whole delegated control to private industrial cartels (the zaibatsu) run in response to state incentives. State control existed during the period 1940–52 in the sense that state institutions were imposed onto the private economy which displaced many private cartels. But there was never complete self-control in the former period with steel, rail and communications run by the state, nor was there complete state control thereafter. Moreover, neither state control nor self-control worked well (Johnson, 1999: 57–9). Faced with the shortcomings of earlier decades, the compelling imperative from post-war reform and reconstruction onwards was to build an economic system fashioned for national growth and security. If there was little faith that the free market would deliver this with certainty, efficiency or fairness, there was little evidence either that impulses from the past, be they cultural or modernizing, would in themselves be sufficient. The differing systems which emerged after 1945 were those consciously chosen for declared ends.[1]

Economic warfare in peacetime was to embrace strategy, persuasion, compliance and direction. What is significant is that the Japanese state effected new relations with labour and capital and succeeded, whereas it had faltered in earlier periods. These relations were not fashioned according to Western profit-maximizing instincts; they were designed to encourage cooperation in pursuit of nationally sanctioned objectives. The links between public and private, between the formal and the informal, and between government and market-driven activity were always blurred in Japan. As Johnson notes, state and civil society needed one another such that:

> The concept 'developmental state' means that each side *uses* the other in a mutually beneficial relationship to achieve developmental goals and enterprise viability. When the developmental state is working well, neither the state officials nor the enterprise managers prevail over the other. The state is a 'catalytic' agency ... and the managers are responding to incentives and disincentives that the state establishes. (Johnson, 1999: 60)

Such a strategy was to prove risky and uncertain and demanded regular review and assessment if its ultimate objectives were to be met. And it had to draw upon the political, economic, social and cultural fibres of the nation to sustain commitment and momentum. Nonetheless, these post-war impulses add a rather more subtle interpretation of Japan's economic development down to the 1990s than would be gleaned from a 'catch-up' based merely upon an opportunistic exploitation of cheap labour and capital in a benign national and international environment. They focus on a developmental state in which the government worked through various institutions to lower transaction costs as a way of encouraging an export-oriented growth process, spurred by both internal and external competition (Crafts, 2003).

Japan's experience, therefore, was more the result of a pragmatic and urgent need to learn and borrow from the past, to adapt to circumstance and opportunity, and to fashion and refashion relations amongst the principal economic agents in a manner and to an extent that was far from predetermined (Abe and Gourvish, 1997). The plan-rational developmental state and the distinctive Japanese employment system clearly remain features of the high-growth period. But as Teranishi argues, the amalgam of post-war policies, interventions, administrative interference and relational arrangements, which in their entirety offend many of the basic principles of neoclassical economics, emerged less as a natural post-war manifestation of Japan's economic building blocks dating from the Meiji period than as the means whereby earlier but unfulfilled attempts to establish working relations between government and business and to promote the private sector without aggravating distributive conflict could be enjoined for the urgent purpose of national economic reconstruction and security.

4.5 Conclusion

The themes of this chapter are not new: economists, historians and political scientists have been arguing the relative merits of states and markets for generations past. But by emphasizing an arbitrary dichotomy between the state and the private sector, and by inference between politics and economics, we compound our misunderstanding of how economies fare (Coates, 2005). State socialism, social democracy and state-business models of national economic management have in recent years lost something of their previous appeal. In consequence, the major industrial nations are now seeking that alchemy mix of state intervention and the free play of market forces knowing that neither route has historically proved sufficient in itself to meet the twin demands of economic efficiency and social stability.

Japan had grasped that point in its search for a role in the post-war economic order. But therein lay the 'paradox of catch-up'. During the high-growth period the Japanese government had become a powerful instrument in promoting economic development, largely as a coordinator of capital allocations across domestic industries and production activities, using economic information and technology from advanced nations at low transaction cost to reap gains that were particularly beneficial to Japan at its stage of economic maturity. But once the path of state-led development had been embarked upon, it proved difficult to alter institutional developments and practices, least of all abruptly (Gao, 2001). As Japan journeyed on that path down to the 1990s, it developed a set of institutional attributes that were well fitted for the purpose of catch-up but were potentially, without adequate or timely adaptation, likely to compromise its ability to sustain economic leadership. Although Japan displayed a degree of flexibility in its responses to the oil crises of the 1970s, it had at the same time fostered a restricted domestic market and an underdeveloped transaction service sector.

It found it especially hard, moreover, to quicken the pace of radical technical innovation (as distinct from the incremental use of borrowed technology) after 1990. State-led development gradually compromised the government's ability to retain neutrality in the enforcement of property rights so critical to innovation, to deepen capital markets, to connect consumer wants to effective demand, or to link them to domestic production (Grimes, 2001; Tan, 2005). Japan paid a heavy price from the 1990s for its failure to adapt its institutions, its relational contracts, and its belief in the efficacy, politically and economically, of an elite bureaucracy.

That said, it is worth remembering that those countries which capitalized on their post-war opportunities to gain and retain comparative advantage did so by examining how they could mould and alter inherited structures, markets and technology to medium- and long-term advantage. For the greater part of the post-1945 period Japan realized that the state could undertake selective intervention in growing, tertiary and declining industries, could shape tax and research and development expenditures, especially in high-technology sectors, and could invest in human capital accumulation. The cumulative effect of doing so was that firms could maintain their competitive advantage in international markets to such a degree that over time they were able to reshape the comparative advantage of the nation as a whole.

This is not to imply that countries are forever wedded to their past; the rapid economic convergence of the post-war period demonstrates otherwise. The critical point is that in Japan the industrial, political and financial will was there to be exploited for the purpose of national growth and success. Japan was very willing to adapt, borrow and refashion against past practice. It was this capacity of the Japanese state both to set the goals of a state–business relationship and to preserve the autonomy of each that can readily be overlooked in criticism of developmental policies during the high-growth period and immediately beyond (Woo-Cumings, 1999). The semi-coercive manner in which MITI and the Ministry of Finance in post-war Japan exercised authoritative intervention was soon replaced by processes of regular consultation with business leaders and representatives of trade associations and academia. It was a process of consensual adjustment rather than diktat. The ability of MITI and the Economic Planning Association, for example, to broker the interests of various interest groups who might otherwise engage in rent-seeking and thereby distort resource allocation for the greater part of the high-growth period was conspicuous in its absence in other industrialized nations. It is the market-conforming rather than market-supplanting feature of Japanese experience that is worth recalling.

The Japanese government was not always in the driving seat of economic progress and at times certainly failed to prevent excesses, corruption and over-dependence. Nonetheless, the Japanese state proved relatively successful during the critical period of post-war reorientation in brokering disparate political interests. As such, direct government intervention was less critical than was the authorities' capacity to enable market forces to work through the bureaucracy rather than in spite of it. It was a matter of balance and always risky. Indeed, Stiglitz has argued that the post-1997 financial crisis in Japan was caused in part by too little government regulation (or perverse or ineffective government regulation) in some areas, and too many misguided government controls in others (Stiglitz, 1998: 1).

The institutional setting within which Japan forged its 'economic miracle' remains significant, as even its harshest critics have come to realize. 'If Japanese policymakers', writes Porter, 'hope to restore the nation's long term health, they must address the underlying causes of its decline. That means beginning with an accurate reading of what drove Japan's success in the first place' (Porter, 2000: 2). In that regard, the Japanese government's role in enhancing the market without itself always being the dominant or proactive force could give rise to a more nuanced interpretation of the 'developmental state' than the hubris of the recent past might suggest.

Note

The themes developed here are explored in greater detail in the author's forthcoming study of the political economy of Japan's growth and decline, 1945–2000.

1. Debate continues as to whether the post-1945 reforms introduced in Japan were as significant as customarily believed. Okazaki and Okuno-Fujiwara(1999) have argued strongly that the principal features of the post-war Japanese economic system which many believe underpinned the country's high-growth experience – including management practices, the 'main bank system', active industrial policy and the raft of administrative guidance and intervention – were actually established during the early 1940s as Japan sought to impose control over the wartime economy. According to this thesis, the significant structural break for Japan occurred at the time the country was developing a command economy rather than during the post-war reform period.

References

Abe, E. and Gourvish, T. (eds), *Japanese Success? British Failure? Comparisons in Business Performance Since 1945* (Oxford: Oxford University Press, 1997).

Abramovitz, M. 'Catch Up and Convergence in the Post-War Boom and After', in W. Baumol, R. R. Nelson and E. Wolff (eds), *Convergence of Productivity* (Oxford: Oxford University Press, 1994): 86–125.

Beason, D. and Patterson, D. *The Japan That Never Was* (Albany: State University of New York Press, 2004).

Beason, R. and Weinstein, D. 'Growth, Economies of Scale, and Targeting in Japan (1955–1990)', *Review of Economics and Statistics*, 78 (2) (1996): 286–95.

Beeson, M. (ed.), *Reconfiguring East Asia. Regional Institutions and Organisations After the Crisis* (London: Routledge Curzon, 2002).

Block, F. 'Disorderly Coordination: The Limited Capacities of States', in L. Burlamaqui, A. C. Castro and H.-J. Chang (eds), *Institutions and the Role of the State* (Elgar: Cheltenham, 2000): 53–71.

Boyd, R. and Ngo, T. W. *Asian States: Beyond the Developmental Perspective* (London: Routledge, 2005).

Brenner, R. 'The Capitalist Economy, 1945–2000', in D. Coates (ed.), *Varieties of Capitalism, Varieties of Approaches* (New York: Palgrave Macmillan, 2005).

Burlamaqui, L., Castro, A. C. and Chang, H.-J. (eds), *Institutions and the Role of the State* (Elgar: Cheltenham, 2000).

Burlamaqui, L. 'Evolutionary Economics and the Economic Role of the State', in L. Burlamaqui, A. C. Castro and H.-J. Chang (eds), *Institutions and the Role of the State* (Elgar: Cheltenham, 2000): 27–52.

Calder, K. E. *Crisis and Compensation: Public Policy and Political Stability in Japan* (Princeton: Princeton University Press, 1988).

Callon, S. *Divided Sun: MITI and the Breakdown of Japanese High-tech Industrial Policy, 1975–1993* (Stanford: Stanford University Press, 1995).

Chang, H.-J. 'An Institutional Perspective on the Role of the State: Towards an Institutional Political Economy', in L. Burlamaqui, A. C. Castro and H-J. Chang (eds), *Institutions and the Role of the State* (Elgar: Cheltenham, 2000): 3–26.

Chang, H.-J. 'Breaking the Mould: An Institutionalist Political Economy Alternative to the Neo-liberal Theory of the Market and the State', *Cambridge Journal of Economics*, 26 (2002): 539–59.

Coates, D. *Models of Capitalism. Growth and Stagnation in the Modern Era* (Oxford: Blackwell, 2000).

Coates, D. (ed.), *Varieties of Capitalism, Varieties of Approaches* (New York: Palgrave Macmillan, 2005).

Crafts, N. R. 'The East Asian Escape from Economic Backwardness', in P. A. David and M. P. Thomas (eds), *The Economic Future in Historical Perspective* (Oxford: Oxford University Press, 2003): 209–30.

Dore, R. *Taking Japan Seriously. A Confucian Perspective on Leading Economic Issues* (London: Athlone Press, 1987).

Eichengreen, B. 'Capitalizing on Globalization', *Asian Development Review*, 19 (1) (2002): 14–61.

Evans, P. *Embedded Autonomy – States and Industrial Transformation* (Princeton: Princeton University Press, 1995).

Friedman, D. *The Misunderstood Miracle: Industrial Development and Political Change in Japan* (Ithaca: Cornell University Press, 1988).

Gao, B. *Japan's Economic Dilemma: The Institutional Origins of Prosperity and Stagnation* (Cambridge: Cambridge University Press, 2001).
Garside, W. R. 'A Very British Phenomenon? Industrial Policy and the Decline of the Japanese Coal Mining Industry Since the 1950s', *Australian Economic History Review*, 45 (2) (2005): 186–203.
Gordon, A. *The Wages of Affluence: Labor and Management in Postwar Japan* (Cambridge, MA: Harvard University Press, 1998).
Grimes, W. *Unmaking the Japanese Miracle: Macroeconomic Politics, 1985–2000* (Ithaca: Cornell University press, 2001).
Hashino, T. and Saito, O. 'Tradition and Interaction: Research Trends in Modern Japanese Industrial History', *Australian Economic History Review*, 44 (3) (2004): 241–58.
Hodgson, G. M. 'From Micro to Macro: The Concept of Emergence and Role of Institutions', in L. Burlamaqui, A. C. Castro and H-J. Chang (eds), *Institutions and the Role of the State* (Elgar: Cheltenham, 2000): 103–26.
Huang, X. *The Rise and Fall of the East Asian Growth System, 1951–2000. Institutional Competitiveness and Rapid Economic Growth* (London: Routledge, 2005).
Johnson, C. *MITI and the Japanese Miracle: The Growth of Industrial Policy 1925–1975* (Stanford: Stanford University Press, 1982).
Johnson, C. 'The Developmental State: Odyssey of a Concept', in M. Woo-Cumings (ed.), *The Developmental State* (Ithaca: Cornell University Press, 1999): 32–60.
Kim, J. and Lau, L. J. 'The Sources of Economic Growth of East Asian Newly Industrialized Countries', *Journal of the Japanese and International Economies*, 8 (1994): 235–71.
Kim, S. and Lee, Y. H. 'The Productivity Debate of East Asia Revisited: A Stochastic Frontier Approach', *Applied Economics*, 38 (14) (2006): 1697–1706.
Kitson, M. 'Measuring Capitalism: Output, Growth and Economic Policy', in D. Coates (ed.), *Varieties of Capitalism, Varieties of Approaches* (New York: Palgrave Macmillan, 2005): 29–46.
Krauss, E. S. 'Political Economy: Policy-making and Industrial Policy in Japan', *Political Science and Politics*, XXV (1) (1992): 44–57.
Krugman, P. 'The Myth of Asia's Miracle', *Foreign Affairs*, 73 November–December (1994): 62–78.
Lin, C. 'The Transition of the Japanese Keiretsu in the Changing Economy', *Journal of the Japanese and International Economies*, 19 (1) (2005): 96–109.
Maddison, A. *Explaining the Economic Performance of Nations: Essays in Time and Space* (Cheltenham: Edward Elgar, 1995).
Masina, P. *Rethinking Development in East Asia. From Illusionary Miracle to Economic Crisis* (London: Curzon, 2002).
Miwa, Y. *State Competence and Economic Growth in Japan* (London: Routledge, 2004).
Miwa, Y. and Ramseyer, J. M. 'The Fable of the Keiretsu', *Journal of Economics and Management Strategy*, 11 (2) (2002): 169–224.
North, D. C. *Institutions, Institutional Change and Economic Performance* (Cambridge: Cambridge University Press, 1990).
North, D. C. 'The Institutional Foundations of East Asian Development: A Summary Evaluation', in Y. Hayami and M. Aoki (eds), *The Institutional Foundations of East Asian Economic Development* (Basingstoke: Macmillan, 1998): 552–60.

Okazaki, T. and Okuno-Fujiwara, M. (eds), *The Japanese Economic System and Its Historical Origins* (Oxford: Oxford University Press, 1999).
Okimoto, D. *Between MITI and the Market: Japanese Industrial Policy for High Technology* (Stanford: Stanford University Press, 1989).
Porter, M., Takeuchi, H. and Sakakibara, M. *Can Japan Compete?* (Basingstoke: Macmillan Press, 2000).
Samuels, R. J. *The Business of the Japanese State* (Ithaca: Cornell University Press, 1987).
Stiglitz, J. *The Role of International Financial Institutions in the Current Global Economy* (Chicago: Council on Foreign Relations, 1998).
Tabb, W. K. *The Postwar Japanese System: Cultural Economy and Economic Transformation* (Oxford: Oxford University Press, 1995).
Tan, L. *The Paradox of Catching Up. Rethinking State-led Economic Development* (Basingstoke: Palgrave Macmillan, 2005).
Teranishi, J. *Evolution of the Economic System of Japan* (Cheltenham: Edward Elgar, 2005).
Tolliday, S. (ed.), *The Economic Development of Modern Japan, 1945–1995: From Occupation to the Bubble Economy* (Cheltenham: Elgar, 2001).
Woo-Cumings, M. (ed.), *The Developmental State* (Ithaca: Cornell University Press, 1999).

5 The Developmental Logic of Financial Liberalization in Taiwan

Elizabeth Thurbon

The Asian crisis of 1997–98 for many pundits appeared to 'discredit' the region's developmental states, projecting them as a symbol of the incompatibility of financial openness with efforts to govern the market. In the standard accounts, something has got to give, and invariably it is the developmental state that must lose out (Pang, 1998; Moon and Rhyu, 2000; Jayasuriya, 2001; Pirie, 2005). However, this widely held view misleads, not only because it sets up a false dichotomy between governing the market and financial openness, but also because it overstates the uniformity of developmental states in their liberalizing objectives and approach.

In developing this proposition, we shall argue that financial liberalization in pre-crisis Taiwan was driven primarily by a 'developmental logic', indeed, that it constituted a key part of the state's evolving developmental strategy.[1] We shall therefore seek to show how the *ideas* behind Taiwan's liberalizing shift over the 1980s and early 1990s strongly reflected the state's traditional priorities of industrial development and upgrading in the name of national security – priorities definitive of a developmental state – and how these ideas were institutionalized in a key agent of liberalization: Taiwan's Central Bank. Through a variety of case studies, we argue that the primary goals of liberalization in Taiwan have been twofold. First, liberalization has been aimed at meeting evolving economic challenges wrought by years of rapid growth, particularly the need to upgrade financial sector arrangements to meet the changing needs of Taiwanese firms and individual investors, and the desire to reorient the economy towards more service-oriented sectors in line with Taiwan's changing competitive advantage. Meeting these challenges is seen by the policy-making elite as critical to sustained economic prosperity, a prosperity which continues to form the basis of Taiwan's claims to an independent status in the international arena. Secondly, liberalization in Taiwan reflects a relatively new strategy on behalf of the ruling elite to come to terms with an old problem: diplomatic isolation arising from the China situation. This strategy involves seeking entry into such economic institutions as the World Trade Organization (WTO), trading the requisite liberalizing concessions for enhanced recognition as an international player in its own right, and diversifying the basis of Taiwan's international economic enmeshment so as to increase the stake of its foreign trade and investment partners in the country's future security and prosperity.

However, while policy-makers have strategically adopted liberalization as a tool to meet evolving developmental challenges, we also argue that Taiwan's distinctive brand of developmentalism, which places dual emphasis on growth *and* stability, has ensured that policy-makers have balanced liberalizing measures with the extension of regulatory controls in critical areas to ensure that liberalization does not threaten financial stability. The result has been the very gradual and cautious approach to liberalization that is so characteristic of Taiwan.

The key conclusion of this chapter is that in order to explain adequately Taiwan's approach to financial liberalization, it is necessary to take into account the *ideational* and *organizational* environment – or the *institutional* framework – in which liberalization has been planned and implemented. This chapter thus draws inspiration from, and owes a theoretical debt to, the growing body of institutional analyses of liberalization and globalization, particularly Vogel's (1996) examination of the ways in which domestic institutions have shaped distinctive national approaches to liberalization in advanced industrial countries, and Weiss's (2003) comprehensive exposition of the mediating role played by domestic institutions in producing distinctive national responses to external economic and political pressures.

In developing our own institutionalist interpretation of liberalization in Taiwan, we begin with an examination of the somewhat neglected face of Taiwanese developmentalism: finance. Our aim is to demonstrate the ways in which financial sector arrangements over the post-war period became the organizational embodiment of Taiwan's distinctive brand of developmentalism, characterized by the commitment of the policy-making elite to 'growth with stability' (GWS). We then turn to examine the *continuity* in Taiwan's financial policy orientation over the 1980s and 1990s, highlighting the impact of Taiwan's developmental ideas and institutions on the liberalization process through a number of case studies, including the liberalization of the banking sector and the stock exchange, Taiwan's Asia-Pacific Regional Operations Centre (APROC) initiative and its bid to join the WTO, and the somewhat paradoxical combination of liberalization and the creation of new sources of development financing. The aim of these case studies is to demonstrate how liberalization in Taiwan prior to the crisis was shaped primarily by the traditional developmental concerns of GWS. In highlighting the developmental logic of liberalization in Taiwan, we conclude that developmentalism may ironically live *because of* – not simply *in spite of* – financial liberalization.

5.1 Taiwan's distinctive brand of developmentalism and its financial policy implications

As noted above, throughout the post–Second World War period, Taiwan adhered largely to the developmental state model of national governance. The term 'developmental state' was coined by Chalmers Johnson (1982) to describe the institutional foundations, both ideational and organizational, that underpinned the rapid industrial development of post-war Japan: an elite consensus surrounding the primary goal of industrial development and transformation; an autonomous and highly skilled economic bureaucracy able to devise coherent national development strategies; and institutionalized cooperative relations between government and business designed to facilitate the effective formulation and implementation of developmental plans. The state's position of 'senior partner' in this relationship was guaranteed by stringent control over key resources, particularly finance, which provided both carrots (for example, preferential credit treatment) and sticks (for example, credit denial) to secure business compliance with developmental objectives (Amsden, 1989). Inspired by Japan's success and influenced by long periods of Japanese colonialism, Taiwan and Korea proved successful emulators of the Japanese developmental state model over the post-war period, and together with Japan now constitute perhaps the most successful examples of late industrialization in history.

In all three countries, the prioritization of industrial development above all other goals – their *developmental orientation* – was born out of the perceived need to defend the nation-state against geopolitical threats via rapid industrialization. In the case of Taiwan's ruling Kuomintang (KMT) party, military threat from the mainland provided the developmental impetus. Following defeat by the Chinese communists in 1949, the KMT retreated to Taiwan with the intention of using the island as a temporary base from which to launch a renewed offensive. The communists, however, soon proved a more resilient force than expected, and it became clear that economic development was essential to secure both the legitimacy of KMT rule on the island and the resources needed to survive in isolation and defend against invasion.

For Taiwan then, as for all developmental states, the economy became imbued with a geo-political purpose: that of nation-building. This emphasis on the goal of nation-building via industrialization informs a developmental state's *strategic* view of the economy; as economic outcomes have a long-term, political purpose, the state necessarily plays an active role in ensuring that economic actors direct their energies towards the promotion of broader nationalistic goals. For the new KMT leaders on Taiwan, such ideas about the state's role in the pursuit of industrialization had a long history, being a key focus of the teachings of Sun Yat-sen, the founder of the KMT on the mainland. Sun had advocated the rapid industrialization of China under the auspices of an extremely powerful state in order to address the threat of foreign imperialism which he believed threatened the Chinese nation and civilization with certain extinction (Sun, 1924). To this end, Sun promoted a combination of the private ownership of capital and state control in critical areas (including finance and key industries) to ensure that industrialization went hand in hand with the principle of the 'people's livelihood'.[2]

The influence of Sun's ideas on the state-guided industrialization strategy adopted by the KMT on Taiwan in such areas as land reform, the establishment of state monopolies in key industries and the encouragement of privately owned small and medium sized enterprises (SMEs) in consumer production has since been well documented in the literature (Gregor, 1981; Lee, 1988: 78–94).[3] However, it is the impact of developmental ideas on *financial policy* in Taiwan that is central to my argument, and this has received much less attention in the literature. This is perhaps because, unlike the developmental states of Japan and South Korea, Taiwan's financial policies have *not* resulted in the rise of massive private conglomerate capital, the chaebol in Korea and the keiretsu in Japan, which so distinguish these countries' political economies. However this is certainly not to say that financial policy was of less developmental significance in Taiwan. Indeed, the way in which Taiwan's *growth* priorities became institutionalized in financial sector arrangements geared towards industrial promotion over the post-war period has been well documented in the literature, and does not require full elaboration here.[4] However, while the manipulation of the financial sector for industrial development ends was a key characteristic of Taiwan's post-war development strategy, there were important tactical differences in the way in which financial policy was managed in Taiwan: differences which reflect Taiwan's distinctive brand of developmentalism or, more specifically, its prioritization of 'growth with stability'.[5]

Taiwan's reluctance to use financial policy to create massive, privately owned national champions (as in Korea and Japan) reflected a combination of Sun's aforementioned ideas about the importance of 'growth with equity' (read: social and political stability) and the KMT's desire to check the growth of large, private corporations which might challenge its political stronghold on the island. However, it was the KMT's obsession with *financial* stability that exerted perhaps the strongest influence on Taiwan's financial policy approach, and on the institutional set-up of its financial system throughout the post-war period. This obsession was a legacy of the rampant inflation suffered under the KMT on the mainland prior to the Party's retreat to Taiwan. Inflation had undermined the popular support base of the KMT, particularly amongst the urban, middle-class constituency, leading to a crisis of legitimacy (Li, 1995: 43). This was understood by KMT leaders to be the key reason for the party's eventual defeat on the mainland. As such, following the KMT's retreat to Taiwan, one of the most significant institutional innovations was the establishment of a powerful and independent central bank, which has remained the most influential financial policy institution in Taiwan ever since. Immediately upon its establishment in 1961,[6] the Central Bank of China (CBC) had its independence guaranteed and price stability enshrined as its primary goal. The CBC was also granted extensive powers to enforce the rule that growth must not come at the expense of stability.[7]

For example, in addition to controlling monetary policy, the CBC was also granted extensive regulatory authority over the banking system and the capital market. This has guaranteed a structural position of power for the CBC in the nation's financial policy-making apparatus. So, while the Taiwanese state is not necessarily a unitary actor, and while Taiwan's financial policy-makers have not always agreed about financial policy decisions, the CBC has maintained ultimate discretion over the liberalization process, even more so than the Ministry of Finance (MOF), which deals more directly with the constituencies of the financial sector.[8] This has meant that any plans to liberalize financial markets have been balanced carefully against the priority of financial stability institutionalized in the CBC.

So, while not an exhaustive review of the evolution of Taiwan's distinctive brand of developmentalism and its financial policy implications (such a review is impossible given the scope of this chapter), these select examples demonstrate how developmentalism Taiwan-style, which combined the prioritization of industrial development in the name of national security with the KMT's obsession with financial stability, became institutionalized in financial sector arrangements over the post-war period. In the following section we demonstrate how the shift towards liberalization over the 1980s and up until the onset of the Asian crisis was largely informed by the distinctive developmental ideas that had shaped Taiwan's financial policies since the 1950s.

5.2 The developmental logic of financial liberalization in Taiwan

By the time of the 1997–98 Asian crisis, Taiwan had adopted an extensive array of liberalizing measures in a range of important areas, including interest rate, foreign exchange rate and capital account liberalization, and the opening up of the banking sector to foreign participation (Thurbon, 2001). However, far from signifying the demise of developmentalism, it is our contention that liberalization in Taiwan prior to the crisis formed a key part of the state's evolving developmental strategy. This is evidenced in a range of areas, including the liberalization of the banking sector and the stock exchange, as well as the liberalizing measures surrounding Taiwan's APROC initiative and its WTO accession bid. In the following sections we seek to highlight the *developmental* logic of liberalization in Taiwan through an examination of both the *origins* and the *execution* of financial liberalization. In terms of the *origins* of liberalization, we seek to demonstrate how liberalization measures prior to the crisis were motivated primarily by the traditional developmental concerns of industrial development and national security. More specifically, we argue that liberalization formed a key part of the state's industrial upgrading strategy, as well as a part of its new approach to securing international legitimacy in the light of the lingering China threat. In terms of *execution,* we argue that the developmental logic of liberalization in Taiwan is further evidenced by the state's cautious and guarded liberalizing approach, which combined liberalization with re-regulation aimed at ensuring that increased financial freedom did not undermine the ultimate goal of 'growth with stability'.

5.3 Liberalization of the domestic banking sector

The liberalization of Taiwan's domestic banking sector involved the easing of entry barriers to private domestic and foreign players, the liberalization of interest rates on bank loans and deposits, as well as the encouragement of the internationalization of Taiwanese banks. We suggest that the motivations behind these liberalizing measures were both economic and political, and embodied the traditional developmental concerns of industrial competitiveness and national security.

Economically, a key motivation was to address the inadequacies of the nationalized system in meeting new economic challenges, which by the late 1980s were threatening to undermine both industrial competitiveness and financial stability. Up until that point, Taiwan had enjoyed four decades of rapid economic growth, driven largely by the success of its export-oriented industrialization strategy. This success, however, brought with it new challenges, including sharp increases in labour and land prices. These challenges threatened to undermine the competitiveness of Taiwan's labour-intensive manufacturing industries and discourage new industrial investments. Furthermore, the accumulation of a massive current account surplus since 1981, also a legacy of Taiwan's export success, had led to the build-up of excessive domestic liquidity, forcing a 60 per cent appreciation of the New Taiwan dollar between 1985 and 1992, further harming exporters.

These economic challenges demanded a change in industrial strategy. Increasing offshore investment, particularly in Southeast Asia, which boasted much lower production costs, became imperative to maintain the competitiveness of Taiwanese firms. Increasing overseas Foreign Direct Investment (FDI) would also provide an effective solution to the problem of excess liquidity. This new industrial strategy, however, also had a strong political motivation. Increasingly unfavourable economic conditions at home had begun to see domestic firms shift production to the mainland. By the early 1990s, Taiwan's leaders were increasingly fearful that this would lead to de facto reunification via Taiwan's economic absorption into China (Munro, 1994). Encouraging the diversification of Taiwanese firms into Southeast Asia, it was hoped, would stem this dangerous tide, while helping to develop the region's economies in order to counterbalance China's rapidly growing market. These economic and political motivations were the rationale behind the government's 1994 'Go South' policy, which provided numerous incentives for Taiwanese firms to invest in Southeast Asian countries.

Significantly for our purposes, Taiwan's new industrial strategy transformed the financial requirements of Taiwanese firms. Faced with increasing pressures to expand and diversify their investments abroad, Taiwanese firms needed to rely on banks not only for financial assistance, but also for better counsel on cash management, fund-raising and investment making, and even on hedging (Lee and Wang, 1995: 10). Furthermore, Taiwanese firms investing overseas would require on-the-ground financial support and advice in target countries, which in turn necessitated the establishment of overseas branches of Taiwanese banks. However while Taiwan had achieved a remarkable level of industrial transformation, Taiwan's banking sector had changed very little since the early 1960s. These new requirements fell well outside the capacities of Taiwan's state-owned banking sector. The rapid upgrading of the skills and services of the banking sector and the promotion of the internationalization of Taiwanese banks was a must to guarantee a future for Taiwan's export-oriented firms.[9]

Even in the absence of such external pressures, however, the limitations of the state-owned banking sector in meeting the more general financing needs of Taiwan's privately owned SMEs, the engines of Taiwan's growth, would alone have necessitated banking reform. Taiwan's SMEs had long suffered under the lending bias of state-owned banks towards large state-owned enterprises (SOEs), which forced SMEs to rely on the underground banking industry for much of their financing. By 1990, loans from the underground banking industry accounted for one-third of all working capital of Taiwan's SMEs (*Free China Journal*, 16 April 1990). Such transactions fell outside the scope of regulatory and supervisory controls, posing risks to financial stability. The establishment of commercial banks catering to the needs of SMEs would not only make their financial transactions easier to regulate, but also increase the quality of financial services to SMEs, further facilitating their development.

Of course it was not only Taiwanese *firms* that were suffering under outdated banking sector arrangements. Years of rapid economic growth had also transformed the financial requirements of Taiwan's *individual* investors, with increasing income levels and expanding political freedoms leading to demands for more attractive investment options. In the absence of competitive commercial banks in which to deposit their savings, consumers turned to the speculative and unpredictable Taiwan Stock Exchange (TSE) to try to increase their returns, or to real-estate investment, or simply declined to invest at all, leaving a lot of idle money washing around the economy (*Free China Journal*, 16 April 1990).

By the early 1990s, the inability of the domestic banking sector to transfer effectively the country's high levels of savings into productive investment was becoming increasingly apparent, with speculation in the TSE and real-estate rife, threatening to destabilize the domestic economy. Without banking reforms that would attract funds back into formal financial institutions, the industrial sector would continue to be milked of funds for productive investment while the 'casino' economy continued to balloon and to undermine financial stability (*Free China Journal*, 27 September 1990).

Evidently then, banking sector reform was critical to promote both skill and service upgrading to meet the changing needs of Taiwanese firms and individual investors and to divert funds out of speculative and into productive investments. For Taiwan's financial policy-makers, liberalization of market access, combined with interest rate liberalization, was seen as an effective means by which to meet these new developmental challenges. The understanding was that the increased competition wrought by liberalization would force banks to compete for deposits by enhancing their skills and services, thus leading to the modernization and upgrading of the banking sector. This was clearly the thinking of the then CBC Governor Shieh, who outlined the intention of entry-barrier liberalization thus:

> [I]n an effort to promote financial efficiency through market competition, the (CBC) and (MOF) have worked together to lower entry barriers to the financial industry... This move will induce greater competition to the banking industry and help promote its modernization.
>
> (Shieh, 1992: 4)

The then director of the MOF's Department of Monetary Affairs revealed a similar understanding of the goals of entry-barrier liberalization: 'Since the new entrants would in effect push all banks to improve their quality of services and to promote financial innovation, enterprises and individuals would be provided with better services' (Chen, 1990). Actions do speak louder than words, however, and the way in which the opening of the domestic market to foreign intermediaries was executed is perhaps the most telling of the developmental logic that lay behind liberalization in this area. For example, while foreign banks were allowed greater freedom to set up shop in Taiwan from 1994, access continued to be highly regulated in order to maximize possibilities for technology transfer and 'learning by viewing'. To begin, only banks ranking amongst the world's top 500 in terms of capitalization or with a business turnover of more than $US1 billion were allowed to set up branches. Failing these requirements, banks could qualify on the condition that they had conducted at least $US300 million worth of business in Taiwan in the past, indicating that they had a long-term commitment to the domestic market. All foreign branches were also required to have a minimum paid-in capital of US$5.7 million, an increase from the previous US$3 million requirement.[10] Such restrictions meant that only large and successful banks would be permitted to operate in the domestic market. The developmental logic that lay behind such measures is further indicated by the admission of an anonymous source close to the then Finance Minister Wang that 'the door will be open but only ajar. That is typical of Taiwan. They really want technology transfer to teach the locals how to do it, then in the future they can do it on their own' (cited in Sargent, 1992: 14).

Further evidence of the developmental logic shaping liberalization is that the state has retained extensive regulatory controls over the operations of foreign financial intermediaries, regulations which are aimed at ensuring that their activities do not contradict the broader goal of national industrial development. To this end, foreign banks operating in Taiwan are subject to the same administrative guidance as domestic banks to ensure that their operations ultimately benefit the domestic industrial economy. For example, in November 1998, after a few high-profile Taiwanese firms defaulted on their loans, CBC Governor Fai-nan Perng and Finance Minister Paul Chiu summoned representatives from 23 foreign banks operating in Taiwan to their offices and requested that they keep their credit lines open to local firms at the current level so as not to destabilize further the corporate sector. Although the regulators stopped short of threatening to deny favours to bankers who ignored the government's appeal (as they did in two previous meetings with domestic banks), most foreign bank representatives said after the meeting that they would heed the government's advice (CNA 1998).

Evidently then, liberalization of the banking sector in Taiwan reflects a *developmental logic*. Liberalization has served the developmental objectives of the Taiwanese state, being aimed at upgrading Taiwan's financial institutions to meet the changing needs of Taiwanese firms and individuals, drawing speculative and idle funds into the formal financial market to be used for productive purposes while at the same time ensuring that financial operators, both domestic and foreign, continue to work in line with the state's overall objectives of GWS. A similar logic can be traced behind the liberalization of the TSE, to which we now turn.

5.4 Liberalization of the stock exchange

Far from indicating the state's surrender to global market pressures, the liberalization of the TSE provides another clear example of the developmental logic shaping Taiwan's liberalizing path. Based upon evidence presented herein, we argue that liberalization prior to the crisis was aimed primarily at introducing a degree of stability to the TSE so that it could become a more reliable source of development financing for Taiwanese firms.

Due to the dominance of individual investors in the TSE (individual investors account for about 90 per cent of trading on the local bourse) Taiwan's stock market has tended to be extremely unstable and speculative, with negative economic and social implications. The emergence of the stock-market bubble in 1987 and the eventual crash of 1989 were a clear indication of this tendency, the bursting of the bubble providing the government with real impetus to reform the financial sector. Liberalization of the TSE in 1990 to allow the purchase of Taiwanese stocks by Qualified Foreign Institutional Investors (QFIIs) was seen by the government as one effective means by which to stabilize the exchange. The logic was that the introduction of large, experienced institutional investors would reduce the room for speculative activity and encourage a longer-term approach amongst Taiwanese investors. According to the then Finance Minister Wang Chien-shien, taming the TSE was the main reason behind opening the market to QFIIs in 1991 (*Free China Journal*, 17 September 1990).

The government's intention to foster a more stable stock exchange via liberalization is clearly evidenced by the way in which liberalization was executed. When the market was opened to QFIIs in December 1990, only a very select group were allowed to apply for permission to invest: banks, insurance companies and fund management companies. In order to gain investment approval, QFIIs had to meet strict size and experience standards set out by Taiwan's Securities and Exchange Commission (SEC).[11] Even then, stringent conditions were placed on both their inward and outward remittances to guarantee a focus on long-term productive, as opposed to short-term speculative, investments. For example, the principal amount invested by QFIIs could not be remitted abroad for three months after the original remittance, and where inward remittances were made in instalments, the three-month period applied to each instalment separately (Liu, 1991). If a QFII remitted all of its funds and then wished to reinvest, it had to go through the whole application process again, which discouraged outward remittances once the original investment had been made.

The waiting period for outward remittances also took a very long time. An outward remittance application had to be filed with the SEC, then another with the CBC, which imposed a one-month waiting period on all applications. If the QFII wished to remit returns on the investment, it had to supply numerous documents, including financial statements certified by a certified public accountant in Taiwan, as well as tax clearance certificates, which often took a very long time to obtain. In the light of all of these regulations, Liu concluded in 1991 that 'the new program will attract only longer-term investors [but] [t]his is exactly what the regulators intend; there are already too many short-term investors, mostly individuals, in Taiwan' (Liu, 1991: 6). While foreigners found this restrictive approach 'intensely annoying', the then Finance Minister Wang Chien-shien defended the government's position arguing that limiting access to institutional investors and regulating remittances 'makes a significant contribution to strengthening and stabilising the market' (cited in Sargent, 1992: 14).

Of course, drawing attention to the developmental motivations behind banking sector and stock exchange liberalization is not to deny the existence of external pressures for liberalization in these areas, which certainly existed over the period in question, particularly from the United States. However, in weighing the relative importance of these pressures upon Taiwan's liberalizing decisions, we suggest that Taiwan's very cautious and gradual approach to liberalization indicates the great importance of developmental concerns in shaping liberalization outcomes.[12] Of course, the developmental attitude of the government and the CBC towards liberalization is not so surprising, given the continuing practice of appointing developmentally oriented bureaucrats to the position of CBC governor. We have shown elsewhere that throughout the 1990s, the upper echelons of the CBC have been staffed by sceptics of the benefits of liberalization for purposes other than developmental (GWS) goals (Thurbon, 2001). However, the view that the proper role for the financial system is one of supporting the government's overriding goal of GWS is not confined to the CBC. In fact, throughout his reign over the 1990s, President Lee Teng-hui provided a strong link with the developmental philosophies of Sun Yat-sen. Lee was the successor of President Chiang Ching-kuo (1978–88), who was the son of Taiwan's first President Chiang Kai-shek (1949–78), Sun's most devoted disciple. Within hours of President Chiang Ching-kuo's death in 1988, Lee, describing himself as 'a decade-long pupil of President Chiang Ching-kuo in the art of nation building' (*Free China Journal*, 18 January 1988), publicly vowed to carry out Chiang's last will: the maintenance of national security and prosperity by virtue of adherence to the principles outlined by Sun Yat-sen.

Since that time, at nearly every major public occasion over the course of his presidency, Lee confirmed his commitment to working towards the goal of industrial development based on Sun's 'growth with equity' (read: economic and political stability) principles. In 1997, President Lee invoked the spirit of Sun Yat-sen in his call for the upgrading of the Taiwanese economy, including the establishment of Taiwan as an Asia Pacific Regional Operations Centre (APROC):

> Nearly a century ago, Dr. Sun Yat-sen drew up blueprints for the development of a democratic, free, and equitably prosperous Republic of China ... Today, we can proudly say that ... the ideals of Dr. Sun Yat-sen have already been realised ... And now, having pushed our nation to new heights of development, we must continue our efforts ... we must coalesce the energy of our people towards promoting a national re-engineering that continues to spur national development ... We will spare no effort in our drive to transform Taiwan into an Asia Pacific Regional Operations Center.
>
> (Lee, 1997: 1)

It is to a closer examination of the liberalizing commitments surrounding Taiwan's APROC initiative, and the developmental logic driving this scheme, to which we now turn.

5.5 Liberalization and the APROC initiative

Most of Taiwan's major liberalizing initiatives in the area of finance prior to the crisis, including the liberalization of the foreign exchange market (both inward and outward remittances) and the liberalization of the offshore activities of domestic banks, surrounded the plan to establish Taiwan as an APROC. The APROC initiative and the attendant plan to establish Taiwan as a regional financial hub formed a key element of the 1991 Six Year National Development Plan, although the idea of establishing Taiwan as a regional financial centre was first mooted as early as 1972.

The APROC initiative was born out of the aforementioned decline in Taiwan's competitive advantage as a labour-intensive exporter, and its obvious suitability as an operational headquarters for multinational activities, including its geographic location, its highly developed economy and educated workforce, its established global trade network and close ties with Southeast Asia, and its political and social stability. Reorienting Taiwan's development strategy towards the provision of value-added services was seen as critical to Taiwan's future economic competitiveness. The then Central Bank Governor Sheu outlined the developmental rationale behind the APROC initiative thus:

> Currently our country, in terms of its economic development, is at a critical stage. The need to upgrade both industry and the economy to respond to increased international competition requires that we adopt a new and effective development strategy. Faced with the challenges of rapid economic development in Asia-Pacific countries and spurred by the rapid development of economic relations across the Taiwan Strait, the [APROC] plan has been conceived. The [APROC] plan is concerned with developing Taiwan into a center for six regional economic activities, namely manufacturing, sea transportation, air transportation, finance, telecommunications and the mass media. The purpose of the [APROC] plan is to promote economic liberalization and internationalization in Taiwan, and attract multinational enterprises to set up their headquarters for the East Asian market in Taiwan.
>
> (Sheu, 1995: 1)

For Sheu, the creation of a financial centre formed a key part of this 'new and effective development strategy', both as part of the regional 'hub' concept and also because it would hasten the upgrading and internationalization of Taiwan's own financial service industry, and help elevate Taiwan's position in international financial markets (see, for example, Sheu, 1995: 2). To this end, in 1991 the Executive Yuan formally included the *Plan to Develop Taipei into a Regional Financial Center* as one of the major objectives of the Six Year National Development Plan. In July 1994 a more detailed plan was formulated, placing emphasis on promoting Taiwan as a regional *funding* centre. The key strategy of this plan was to develop Taiwan's financial markets along the lines of the Singapore model, in which domestic and offshore financial operations are treated separately. In line with the philosophy of 'internal control, external freedom', the plan was to liberalize the *offshore* operations of Taiwan's financial institutions, promoting Taiwan as a regional funding centre, while taking a much more cautious and gradual approach to liberalizing *domestic* financial activities so as to protect financial stability whilst promoting financial sector upgrading (see, for example, Sheu, 1995: 4). As such, while liberalization was advocated to the extent that it would facilitate the establishment of Taiwan as a regional financial centre in line with the APROC initiative, ultimate emphasis clearly remained on maintaining stable foundations for national *industrial* development and financial stability – or GWS.

Our examples thus far have concentrated on the government's developmental strategy of employing liberalization to facilitate financial sector upgrading in pursuit of industrial development and financial stability. As noted earlier, these goals were not seen as ends in themselves by the ruling elite, but rather formed the foundation of Taiwan's national security, KMT legitimacy and the basis of the country's claims to an independent status in the international arena. We now turn to a closer analysis of the role of liberalization in the state's new strategy to manage its diplomatic isolation. Taiwan's bid to join the WTO is a useful lens through which to view this aspect of the developmental logic shaping liberalization in Taiwan.

5.6 Liberalization and the WTO

Taiwan's WTO accession bid reflected a strong developmental logic, constituting a central pillar of the state's new strategy to come to terms with the increasing costs of diplomatic isolation. Taiwan's desire to join such international institutions as the WTO was largely born out of a crisis of international political legitimacy dating back to the 1970s. While Taiwan enjoyed widespread recognition as the sole legal government of China up until 1970, in 1971 countries began to switch their diplomatic recognition from Taiwan to the mainland government. By 1978 the number of countries maintaining official ties with Taiwan had fallen to only 21, and in 1979 the United States severed its diplomatic relations. By 1980, Taiwan had been forced out of all influential international organizations including the United Nations (UN), the International Monetary Fund (IMF) and the World Bank, leaving Taiwan with a link to only one international governmental organization (IGO) of any significance: the Asian Development Bank (ADB) (Kau, 1992: 237–8).[13]

Taiwan's initial strategy of dealing with this situation was to refuse diplomatic ties with any country that formally recognized the People's

Republic of China (PRC), for fear of undermining its own claim as the legitimate government of China. As a countermeasure to its (partially self-imposed) isolation, over the 1970s and 1980s the KMT sought to extend 'substantive' but 'unofficial' international ties via the promotion of private sector relations, while avoiding direct government-to-government contact with foreign countries. However, by the mid-1980s, the diplomatic costs associated with the absence of official foreign relations were becoming increasingly apparent.[14] Furthermore, Taiwan's diplomatic isolation was having major political ramifications on the domestic front. Kau points to an increasing sense of frustration amongst the Taiwanese people over the government's inability to translate the country's growing economic strength into political stature abroad. This impacted negatively upon public perceptions of the political integrity of the KMT, raising fears among the Taiwanese people about the long-term viability of the Republic of China (Taiwan) (ROC) as a nation in its own right and increasing support for non-KMT parties. Eventually, Taiwan's Democratic Progressive Party picked up on the public's discontent with the nation's diplomatic isolation and put the pursuit of UN membership on the table, leading to a massive increase in the opposition party's popularity and forcing the KMT to reconsider its foreign policy stance (Munro, 1994).

In the light of growing challenges from without and within, upon coming to power in 1988, President Lee Teng-hui sought to redress the terms of Taiwan's diplomatic isolation, softening the government's attitude towards establishing diplomatic ties with countries recognizing the PRC, and aggressively pursuing inclusion in IGOs and non-governmental organizations (NGOs) with semi-governmental character. This reflected a new commitment on behalf of the ROC government to exercise its rights as an independent entity and sovereign state in the international arena (Kau, 1992: 246). In response to Taiwan's shift in strategy, China reaffirmed its commitment to 'coercive diplomacy', terminating its formal ties with Grenada, Liberia and Belize upon their establishment of diplomatic ties with Taiwan in 1989. This only strengthened Taiwan's resolve to defend its independent status via the establishment of official relations with as many countries as possible. Reaffirming this stance in 1997, President Lee committed the country to 'actively take part in international organizations and activities, so that nations around the world must acknowledge the reality of the ROC's existence and development. This will enhance our international status, and uphold our dignity in the world' (Lee, 1997: 2).

As Taiwan's economic strength was perhaps its greatest claim to recognition as an independent nation, entry into major international economic organizations was of utmost importance. When viewed in this light, the political motivations behind Taiwan's WTO bid become apparent: membership in such organizations formed a key part of the strategy to establish Taiwan in the international arena as a sovereign entity in its own right. Furthermore, by becoming more closely enmeshed in economic relationships with developed countries via increasing trade and FDI (which WTO membership would facilitate), Taiwan's safety would be ensured 'because so many other powerful nations – in addition to increasingly powerful transnational actors – have a genuine and growing stake in Taiwan's well-being' (Klein, 1992: 272).

Munro (1994) points out that diversifying the basis of Taiwan's foreign trade and investment relations would also serve to counter 'reunification by stealth': the situation of China gaining increasing influence over Taiwan via increased economic relations. As noted earlier, this was perceived as a real threat in the early 1990s, with approximately 45 per cent of Taiwan's capital outflow being pumped into the mainland in 1993 alone. In the face of this threat, Taiwan's leaders sought to diversify their international economic connections to stem the outflow and to thereby 'offset the risk of being absorbed economically and politically by the mainland' (Munro, 1994: 115). In addition to the 'Go South' policy outlined above, which saw a substantial decline in investment in the mainland from 1994 onwards, WTO entry would deepen Taiwan's economic relationships with a variety of powerful countries outside the region, which in the long term would perhaps be more critical for security purposes.

From this perspective, the liberalizing commitments that come as part and parcel of membership in such organizations as the WTO are a small price to pay for securing Taiwan's national security and independence. However, the competitive challenges that WTO membership will bring have not been met lying down. In anticipation of the heightened competition that will accompany its accession obligations, the Taiwanese state has been engaging in regulatory reforms aimed at enhancing the competitiveness of Taiwan's financial institutions, thus enabling them to capitalize on the expanding opportunities associated with increasing economic openness. Prior to Taiwan's WTO accession in 2002, the government set about encouraging mergers and acquisitions (M&As) to strengthen the domestic banking sector. This has been crucial to boosting the competitiveness of Taiwanese banks, particularly as over-banking has been a major problem in Taiwan.[15] Fierce competition for deposits has long kept banking institutions small, the combined assets of Taiwan's top three banks totalling only 26 per cent of domestic bank assets. The ability of such small institutions to compete with much larger foreign players in an open environment is indeed limited.

Up until 2000, the government encouraged mergers mainly amongst state-owned banks, but on 24 November 2000 the Merger Law of Financial Institutions was enacted, providing tax and non-tax incentives to all financial institutions willing to merge, and allowing domestic banks to merge with foreign banks. Under the new law, new financial institutions formed through mergers are allowed to deduct past losses from institutions involved in the merger from their profits (*Taiwan Headlines*, 2000). In the light of the government's strategy, there were 15 bank mergers between 1997 and 2001 in Taiwan.

As such, while membership of the WTO entails substantial liberalizing commitments, Taiwan has been introducing new regulations to upgrade and enhance the competitiveness of Taiwan's financial institutions so that they may compete more effectively in the new internationalized environment. Clearly then, insofar as Taiwan's WTO accession bid was inextricably tied up with the promotion of Taiwan's status as an independent entity in the international arena, liberalization has been carried out in such a way as to enhance the strength of Taiwan's domestic economy, upon the strength of which Taiwan's claims to political independence are based.

5.7 The expansion of development financing

A final piece of evidence pointing to the endurance of developmentalism in Taiwan is the fact that financial liberalization prior to the crisis was accompanied by the *expansion* of the sources of development financing, not a reduction in the state's developmental capacities. The expansion of development financing came in numerous guises, including the recycling of foreign exchange reserves for developmental purposes and the creation of new forms of joint public–private development financing schemes in line with growing constraints on deficit financing. This latter strategy we have detailed elsewhere (Thurbon, 2001). As such, this section will briefly detail the former strategy of foreign reserve recycling.

Taiwan's infamous hoard of foreign exchange reserves is largely the result of years of maintaining a current account surplus.[16] However, given Taiwan's exclusion from such international institutions as the IMF, there is also a strong political rationale behind maintaining huge reserves, as Taiwan may be forced to rely on its own resources in the event of a speculative attack or a financial meltdown. Up until the late 1980s, Taiwan invested the majority of its reserves (about 90 per cent) in US deposits. However, since that time, evolving economic challenges have led Taiwan to redeploy these reserves for more productive purposes, particularly to facilitate the internationalization of Taiwanese banks and firms. In 1989 the CBC began to deposit foreign exchange reserves in the overseas branches of Taiwanese banks, and on 15 April 1990 the CBC promulgated its guidelines for the utilization of the country's massive foreign exchange reserves to finance local firms' overseas investments. CBC Governor Shieh explained the developmental logic behind this strategy thus:

> In terms of what we do with our reserves, the theory is to use them to the best advantage of the domestic economy. Taiwan is a small island with no resources, only manpower. Part of achieving our goal of 7% GNP growth is financing our industry and export sector for global expansion. This is done by channelling money through commercial banks to enterprises going overseas for resource development, or acquisition of high-technology entities.
>
> (Shieh, cited in *Global Custodian*, 1991)

Such assistance was made available to assist internationalizing firms in a variety of ways, including the purchasing of foreign firms, exploiting overseas resources, advancing technology and management know-how through transfers, and building production and marketing networks (*Free China Journal*, 25 October 1990). However, funds were offered on the proviso that the firms invest in strategically designated industries and remain domestically based or, as the then Governor Shieh put it, 'keep their roots in Taiwan' (cited in *Free China Journal*, 25 October 1990). On 23 November 1991, Shieh announced that forex reserves would also be made available to help purchase the imported capital goods needed for investment in *domestic* projects under the Six Year National Development Plan (*Free China Journal*, 3 December 1991). These examples clearly demonstrate the CBC's strong emphasis on *national industrial development*, despite liberalization.

Since the early 1990s, reserves have been extended to local businesses willing to 'Go South.' There was also a clear political rationale behind this move: increasing Taiwan's role as net creditor to Southeast Asia would provide Taiwan with greater diplomatic leverage in the region. As Kuo-shu Liang, the then Board Director of the Bank of

Communications, noted in 1992: 'The Republic of China is well aware that expanding the flow of outward direct foreign investment (DFI) is one of the most effective ways of combating isolation in the global arena' (Liang, 1992: 12). To this end, Taiwan has also used its reserves for the purposes of foreign aid in the form of soft loans and technical assistance. In 1988, Taiwan established the International Economic Cooperation and Development Fund (IECDF)[17] to provide low-interest loans and technical assistance to countries in Asia and Latin America. Taiwan has also made financial commitments to multilateral development organizations such as the Inter-American Development Bank and the European Bank for Reconstruction and Development, and was a founding member of the ADB, to which it makes major contributions. In fact, Taiwan is the first country to make a transition from ADB borrower to ADB lender.

Evidently then, far from undermining state capacity for industrial governance, liberalization in Taiwan has gone hand in hand with the expansion of the state's industrial financing role, indicating the endurance of developmentalism in Taiwan despite increased economic openness.

5.8 Conclusion

An institutionalist analysis of Taiwan's pre-crisis liberalizing efforts reveals that liberalization has been driven primarily by a developmental logic, and shaped by Taiwan's distinctive brand of developmentalism. More specifically, liberalization in Taiwan has been strategically employed to promote economic upgrading and national security, but balanced with re-regulation to ensure that liberalization does not undermine financial stability.

This conclusion should be qualified with two important points. First, in highlighting the role of domestic institutions in shaping liberalizing decisions and outcomes in Taiwan, we are not suggesting that external market pressures for liberalization did not exist. Rather, we are suggesting that the globalist interpretation, with its exclusive focus on external market pressures, does not tell the full story of liberalization in Taiwan. In this chapter we have sought to highlight the *developmental* motivations for liberalization (that is, economic upgrading and national security) as they tend to be overlooked in the mainstream literature. But regardless of the *origins* of liberalizing pressures, the cautious and gradual way in which liberalization was actually *executed* in Taiwan indicates that liberalization was shaped by something more than 'global pressures'. The combination of liberalization with re-regulation to enhance the capacities of the state to promote GWS is evidence itself of the developmental logic of financial liberalization in Taiwan.

Second, the argument that liberalization in Taiwan was shaped by a developmental logic does not mean that liberalization in Taiwan has been, or will be, problem-free. In the wake of the crisis, a number of high-profile scandals in the banking and stock markets have revealed some weaknesses in Taiwan's evolving financial sector arrangements. As such, the existence of a developmental motivation driving liberalization does not necessarily mean that liberalizing outcomes will always be entirely as the state hopes or expects. However, compared with its neighbours, it is clear that Taiwan's pre-crisis liberalizing measures were indeed relatively successful in advancing the state's goals of 'GWS'. This is a far cry from the outcomes of liberalization in countries like Korea, where the increasing influence of neoliberal economic doctrine saw liberalization carried out rapidly and recklessly, resulting in near financial meltdown.[18]

As such, while certainly not perfect, Taiwan's experience indicates that developmentalism and liberalization are not mutually exclusive. Indeed, an institutional analysis of liberalization in Taiwan suggests that developmentalism and increasing economic openness may go hand in hand.

Notes

1. We focus specifically on liberalization in the *pre-crisis* period as it was Taiwan's unique liberalizing approach during this period that so distinguished it from other states in the region, particularly South Korea (see Thurbon, 2001). For an examination of the enduring impact of developmentalism on industrial and financial governance in Taiwan in the post-crisis period, see Weiss and Thurbon (2004) and Thurbon and Weiss (2006).
2. Along with 'nationalism' and 'democracy', 'the people's livelihood' was identified by Sun as one of the three 'Principles of the People', upon which China's progress was ultimately dependent. For Sun, the people's livelihood, or *min sheng*, was the fundamental law of social progress: '... if livelihood does not go right, social culture cannot advance, economic organization cannot improve, morals will decline, and many injustices such as class war, cruelty to workers, and other forms of oppression will spring up... All social changes are effects; the search for livelihood is the cause' (Sun, 1924: 176). The fulfilment of the people's livelihood involved at the most basic level a minimum standard of living for all in which everyone was adequately housed, fed and clothed. Essentially, *min sheng* meant 'growth with equity'.

3. Indeed, Sun's influence is enshrined in Article 142 of the Constitution of the ROC, which states that the 'national economy shall be based on the Principle of People's Livelihood'.
4. Such measures included, for example: nationalization of the banking sector (1949); the establishment of specialized financial institutions for the promotion of industrial development (1960s onwards) (such as the Postal Savings System to encourage savings, the Bank of Communications to supply medium-to-long term loans to existing industries, and the China Development Corporation to channel funds into new industrial developments); the highly regulated entry of foreign banks to promote access to the international capital market and much needed technical know-how (1960s); the establishment of the Development Fund to extend policy loans to 'strategic' enterprises at below market rates to promote industrial deepening (1973); and the re-organization of the Postal Savings System to redirect deposits into development banks for distribution as industrial policy loans (1982). See for example Wade (1985), Wade (1990) and Cheng (1993).
5. The term 'growth with stability' was actually popularized by the KMT itself during the 1950s in Taiwan and has remained a famous catch-cry of politicians and bureaucrats ever since.
6. The year in which restructuring of the financial system to facilitate industrial development began in earnest in Taiwan.
7. It should be noted here that industrial development and financial stability were not seen as incongruous goals; rather, financial stability was seen as a precondition for sustained growth. For example, speculative investments in areas such as real estate not only artificially inflate prices, but also have a negative developmental effect by drawing funds away from productive investments.
8. For example, throughout the 1990s the MOF advocated a much speedier approach to foreign exchange liberalization than the CBC, which was more concerned about the inherent risks of economic destabilization. See, for example, Thurbon (2001) and Chu (1999: 198).
9. In the words of then CBC Governor Shieh, 'In order to respond to the changing needs of industrialists to develop overseas, it is becoming increasingly important to speed up the promotion of financial internationalization in order to allow the ROC's financial markets to gradually become integrated with international financial markets, so that the scope of services and products can be expanded and funds be more effectively utilised' (Shieh, 1993: 9); see also Chen (1990).
10. Furthermore, foreign banks had to report all capital remittances to their home country to the Ministry of Finance, which meant that the Ministry could freeze the local assets of foreign banks if parent banks ran into trouble, thus protecting Taiwanese depositors (*Free China Journal*, 17 March 1994).
11. For example, foreign banks wishing to invest in the TSE had to rank amongst the 500 largest banking institutions in the free (that is, non-communist) world, as measured by total assets. Foreign insurance companies had to have been in the business for at least 10 years and have securities holdings of at least US$500 million, while fund management companies had to have been operating for at least 5 years and have securities holdings of $US500 million or more. See Liu (1991).

12. The government's very gradual approach to lifting the strict foreign ownership caps on foreign investment in the TSE, coupled with the CBC's extensive powers to intervene in – or even close down – the stock market if it looks to be undermining the financial stability or domestic economic competitiveness, is also a strong indication of the developmental logic informing liberalization in Taiwan, which we have detailed elsewhere (Thurbon, 2001: 252–4). The same might be argued in relation to the role of domestic interest-group pressures, particularly business, in promoting liberalization, especially following democratization. Given Taiwan's SME-dominated industrial structure, business groups obviously had a relatively lower capacity than their Japanese and Korean counterparts to influence government decisions. However, even if business pressures were important in promoting liberalization, the very strategic way in which liberalization was carried out is indicative of something *more* than a purely interest-group explanation of liberalization. For example, most measures that could be explained in terms of business interests, such as the liberalization of the issuance of overseas bonds, have been coupled with the introduction of new measures to ensure that liberalization promotes the state's goals of 'growth with stability', such as legislating that the proceeds of overseas bond issuances must be invested in industrial expansion or upgrading at home.
13. Unless otherwise stated, information in the following two paragraphs is based on Kau (1992).
14. Kau (1992: 243) notes five main limitations of non-official relations for Taiwan: (1) they are open to pressure and influence by the PRC; (2) they are overlooked by international law which makes them difficult to rely on to facilitate intergovernmental negotiation; (3) they do not facilitate access to high-level government offices for policy negotiation/administrative coordination; (4) they are generally barred from access to arms sales and military technology transfer (except in the US case); and (5) they fail to give respect and dignity to ROC citizens as people with a first-class developing economy.
15. Prior to the M&A wave, Taiwan's 21 million people were serviced by no less than 50 domestic and 46 foreign banks, 60 credit cooperatives, 314 farmers' and fishermens' credit unions, and the postal savings system, all competing for deposits.
16. Taiwan's reserves have fluctuated between US$85 billion and US$100 billion over the past decade.
17. The International Cooperation and Development Fund (ICDF) since July 1996.
18. For an institutional examination of the waning influence of developmental ideas, the rise of neoliberalism and the implications for financial liberalization prior to the crisis, see Thurbon (2003).

References

Amsden, A. *Asia's Next Giant* (Oxford: Oxford University Press, 1989).

Central News Agency (CNA). 'Finance Officials Urge Foreign Banker's Not To Crunch Credit', 20 November (1998), online edition.

Chen, M.-T. 'The Financial System and Financial Policy in the Republic of China', *Economic Record*, July–August (1990): 1–15.

Cheng, T.-J. 'Guarding the Commanding Heights: The State as Banker in Taiwan', in S. Haggard, C. H. Lee and S. Maxfield (eds), *The Politics of Finance in Developing Countries* (Ithaca: Cornell University Press, 1993): 55–92.

Chu, Y.-H. 'Surviving the East Asian Financial Storm: The Political Foundation of Taiwan's Economic Resilience', in T.-J. Pempel (ed.), *The Politics of the Asian Economic Crisis* (Ithaca: Cornell University Press, 1999).

Free China Journal, 'New Leader Taught by Chiang', 18 January (1988), (online edition).

Free China Journal. 'ROC Takes Giant Step in Privatizing Banks', 16 April (1990), online edition.

Free China Journal. 'Taiwan Looking for 'Practical' Investors', 17 September (1990), online edition.

Free China Journal. 'Time to Fix Financial Market', 27 September (1990), online edition.

Free China Journal. 'Forex Strength Props Up Overseas Ventures', 25 October (1990), online edition.

Free China Journal. 'Forex to Purchase Six Year Plan Capital Goods', 3 December (1991), online edition.

Free China Journal, 'Financial Focus', 17 March (1994), online edition.

Gregor, A. *Ideology and Development. Sun Yat-Sen and the Economic History of Taiwan* (Berkeley: University of California, 1981).

Johnson, C. *MITI and the Japanese Miracle* (Stanford: Stanford University Press, 1982).

Jayasuriya, K. 'Globalization and the Changing Architecture of the State: The Regulatory State and the Politics of Negative Coordination', *Journal of European Public Policy*, 8 (1) (2001): 101–23.

Kau, M. Y. 'The ROC's New Foreign Policy Strategy', in D. F. Simon and M. Y. Kau (eds), *Taiwan: Beyond the Economic Miracle* (Armonk: M. E. Sharpe, 1992): 237–56.

Klein, D. W. 'The Political Economy of Taiwan's International and Commercial Links', in D. F. Simon and M. Y. Kau (eds), *Taiwan: Beyond the Economic Miracle* (Armonk: M. E. Sharpe, 1992): 257–74.

Lee, K.-T. *Economic Transformation of Taiwan* (London: Shepherd Walwyn Ltd, 1988).

Lee, T.-H. 'President Lee Teng-hui's National Day Message', *Central News Agency*, 9 October (1997).

Lee, Y.-S. and Wang, H.-S. 'The Recent Development in the Banking Industry in Taiwan', *Economic Review*, September–October (1995) 9–15.

Li, K.-T. *The Evolution of Policy Behind Taiwan's Development Success* (Singapore: World Scientific, 1995).

Liang, K.-S. 'Background and Lessons of Financial Reform in the Republic of China', *Economic Review*, March–April (1992): 10–14.

Liu, L. S. 'Taiwan-Securities Market-Opening Measures: An Analysis', *East Asian Executive Reports*, 13 (1) (1991): 9–13.

Moon, C.-I and Rhyu, S.-Y. 'The State, Structural Rigidity, and the End of Asian Capitalism: A Comparative Study of Japan and South Korea', in R. Robison, M. Beeson, K. Jayasuriya and H-R Kim (eds), *Politics and Markets in the Wake of the Asian Crisis* (London: Routledge, 2000): 77–98.

Munro, R. H. 'Giving Taipei a Place at the Table', *Foreign Affairs*, 73 (6) (1994): 109–22.
Pang, E.-S. 'The Financial Crisis of 1997–98 and the End of the Asian Developmental State', *Contemporary Southeast Asia*, 22 (3) (1998): 570–93.
Pirie, I. 'The New Korean State', *New Political Economy*, 10 (1) (2005): 25–42.
Sargent, S. 'Will the Tiger Be Released From Its Cage?', *Asia Money and Finance*, March (1992): 14.
Sheu, Y. D. 'Developing Taipei into a Regional Financial Center', *Economic Review*, November–December (1995): 1–9.
Shieh, S. C. 'Shieh's Gotta Have It: Taiwan's Power Behind The Thrown', *Global Custodian*, September (1991), online edition.
Shieh, S. C. 'The Outlook for Taipei as a Regional Financial Centre in Asia', *Economic Review*, March–April (1992): 6–15.
Shieh, S. C. 'Balance of Payments Adjustment, Financial Liberalization, and Financial Surplus Recycling in the R.O.C', *Economic Review*, January–February (1993): 9–15.
Sun, Y.-S. *San Min Chu I (The Three Principles of the People)* (Taiwan: Taiwan Publishing Co., 1924).
Taiwan Headlines. 'Incentives Offered For Bank Mergers', 11 October (2000), online edition.
Thurbon, E. 'Two Paths to Financial Liberalization: South Korea and Taiwan', *The Pacific Review*, 14 (2) (2001): 241–67.
Thurbon, E. 'Ideational Inconsistency and Institutional Incapacity: Why Financial Liberalization in South Korea Went Horribly Wrong', *New Political Economy*, 9 (3) (2003): 341–61.
Thurbon, E. and Weiss, L. 'Investing in Openness: The Evolution of FDI Strategy in Korea and Taiwan', *New Political Economy*, 11 (1) (2006): 1–24.
Vogel, S. *Freer Markets, More Rules* (Ithaca: Cornell University Press, 1996).
Wade, R. 'East Asian Financial Systems as a Challenge to Economics: Lessons From Taiwan', *California Management Review*, 27 (4) (1985): 106–27.
Wade, R. *Governing the Market* (Princeton: Princeton University Press, 1990).
Weiss, L. (ed.) 'Bringing Domestic Institutions Back In', *States in the Global Economy* (Cambridge: Cambridge University Press, 2003): 1–16.
Weiss, L. and Thurbon, E. 'Where There's a Will There's a Way: Governing the Market in Times of Uncertainty', *Issues and Studies*, 40 (1) (2004): 61–72.

6
The Institutional Legacy and the Development of an Australian National Innovation System

Simon Ville

6.1 Introduction

Institutions are the rules of the game that help to shape the long-term historical development of societies. They mediate human interaction and can be more or less formal (or tangible) in nature ranging from systems of government to common modes of behaviour. Most formal institutions can be distinguished as economic, social, political or cultural in nature although such distinctions are more difficult to make for informal institutions. What is certain is the pervasive impact of all types of institutions on a country's multifaceted development. Thus, economic performance may be shaped as much by a nation's legal system as by its trade policy.

In this chapter we sketch the origins and development of institutions that have had a significant bearing upon innovation as one of the mainstays of the economic growth of Australia since White Settlement two centuries ago. Most existing studies of relevant Australian institutions have focused on the period since Federation, and little attempt has been made to analyse the institutions–economic development relationship.[1] Our description of institutions and analysis of their bearing upon economic progress is underpinned by the new institutionalism, particularly that of Douglass North. North's contribution is most striking in his rejection of rational choice models and the so-called 'efficiency theory': for him, a society's set of institutions evolve through a wide range of influences or ideologies, which rarely provide for an optimal economic outcome.[2]

6.2 Institutions and economic change

North developed a dynamic theory of institutional change composed of three elements: informal 'constraints', formal 'constraints' and enforcement mechanisms. Both formal and informal institutions play a 'constraining' role in the sense that they bring some order to the chaos of human interactions. Informal constraints include norms of behaviour, conventions and codes of conduct. They are embodied in the belief systems, cultures and ideologies of a society that evolve gradually over long periods of time and have the ability to endure through major historical events. A continuum exists from informal to formal constraints, with the latter including the law, systems of government, public policy and economic markets. These can alter markedly over shorter time periods in response to major events and changes in the dominant actors.

More specifically, in the economic sphere, institutions bring order to production and exchange, and it is their effect on the cost of exchange and production that largely explains their influence on economic performance. Thus, for example, a well-defined and respected system of property rights will encourage cost-reducing innovation by protecting the value of the rents associated with new ideas. Particular codes of conduct will be conducive to low transaction costs, thereby making exchange more efficient.

While the effect of institutions generally is to reduce uncertainty in human interaction, this does not inevitably provide the most efficient economic outcomes. North noted three reasons why suboptimality often results: our limited understanding of our own reality and how it changes over time; our imperfect belief systems; and our blunt tools for implementing change and development. As a result, North rather depressingly concluded: 'Economic history is an endless depressing tale of miscalculation leading to famine, starvation, deceit and warfare, death, economic stagnation and decline, and indeed the disappearance of whole civilizations' (North, 1999: 18). In this light, the economic enrichment of 'Western' nations over the last two centuries can be viewed as the exception rather than the rule, since most societies have failed to establish the institutional structure necessary for sustainable economic modernization.

Western exceptionalism is explained by North through *adaptive efficiency*: 'the ability of some societies to adjust flexibly in the face of shock and evolve institutions that effectively deal with altered reality' (North, 1999: 18). Stable but unchanging institutions do not provide the impetus for economic growth.[3] Rosenberg and Birdzell emphasize the role of institutional change in their explanation of 'How the West Grew Rich' (Rosenberg and Birdzell, 1986). They cite nine institutional innovations favourable to economic development in Western Europe by the eighteenth century, which cover a range of broad or specific legal, financial, religious and political contexts. They are the legal enforcement of contracts and property claims; the evolution of bills of exchange and modern banking systems; insurance; the replacement of arbitrary confiscation with regular taxation and recognized property rights; economic association without kinship; double-entry bookkeeping; religious and moral systems conducive to commercial activity; the mercantilist partnership; and political fragmentation in Europe.

Rosenberg and Birdzell's institutional innovations coalesce with North's thinking on adaptive institutions. A key aspect of modern economic development is the shift from personal to impersonal systems of exchange. Personal trade occurs on a small local scale with few players where monitoring is easy. A wider market may be possible where behaviour is constrained by social network membership, but this is limited to the size of the network. Impersonal exchange permits transactions to occur at a distance between parties unknown to each other. This provides a wider market for the seller and consequent cost economies from larger-scale production and increased specialization. However, impersonal exchange is founded on what North calls a *credible commitment* by both parties to cooperate rather than defect. Creating or adapting institutions that can foster credible commitment is thus a key aspect of modern economic development. Formal institutions associated with commercial law clearly play a role, but they would be limited in their effectiveness without the reinforcement of informal norms of behaviour that legitimize impersonal exchange. This is, perhaps, where North's third element, the enforcement mechanism, plays a key role, especially in terms of third-party enforcement by an impartial and legitimate state. North concludes that the critical watershed distinguishing Western Europe's economic ascendancy from the rest of the world was the shackling of arbitrary government in Britain in 1689. This process was repeated among neighbouring nations as monarchs were forced to bargain rights in return for revenue in order to survive (North, 1981). The result was the evolution of a legitimate legal structure (including mercantile law), the growth of science and technology, and the development of military technology that facilitated European hegemony (North, 1993: 17).

In practice, this was merely the occasion of major institutional change, which was brought to a head by a much longer period of incremental adjustment in informal institutions or value systems conducive to modern systems of exchange and production. North accounts for institutional change by a process of interaction between organizations (the players) and institutions (rules and conduct). In particular, competition among organizations is important to encourage their investment in new skills and knowledge, which in turn will shape future perceptions and belief systems.

Previous historical experience therefore plays a major role in subsequent institutional change. While North emphasizes this process as change, not necessarily progress, not all would agree entirely with his explanation of what drives institutional change. Value systems are shaped by many aspects of historical experience, both economic and non-economic in nature. Not only can institutions be socially inefficient, as North would acknowledge, neither need they be privately efficient.

6.3 Phases of institutional development in Australia

One can identify three broad phases of institutional development and change in Australia since British settlement. For much of the nineteenth century, Australian institutions were those of the British Empire, imported into Australia but insufficiently adapted to local conditions. Emerging self-determination, economic crisis in the 1890s and the move to federated nationhood in 1901 invoked the development of distinctive national institutions, though barricaded within a siege-like mentality from international influences. The final two decades of the twentieth century witnessed a more outward-looking institutional structure, embracing multilateral relationships from a multicultural society in an era of globalization. Each of these institutional structures constituted a punctuation or marked shift from the previous one: colonial to national to global. This punctuation or transition from one stage to the next has been driven, to a large degree, by the tension between the existing domestic institutional structure and a changing international environment, and between changing informal belief systems and more entrenched formal institutional structures.

6.3.1 Colonial institutions: Beneficent servants of empire

6.3.1.1 Establishment

Australia was the fortuitous importer of the institutional structure most conducive to rapid economic development. The economic hegemony achieved by Britain at the end of the eighteenth century drew heavily upon the type of institutional innovations identified by North and by Rosenberg and Birdzell. In Britain, these included a system of government that emphasized the rule of law and legitimate authority ahead of arbitrariness in behaviour and in the exercise of power. In the economic sphere, institutional innovativeness included sophisticated financial, commodity and insurance markets, accounting systems and mercantile law. An array of legal forms of business enterprise served as the vehicles for expanded production and exchange; these included the chartered and joint stock companies, the partnership, and ownership by tenants in common. The family firm was the dominant and largely successful form of ownership and management, reinforced by powerful social and economic networks of entrepreneurs. Together the family and the network reduced transaction costs and enhanced flows of information, commodities and credit.[4]

While benefiting from this legacy, there were few formal institutions in Australia during the earliest years of British settlement, and those in existence served the specific needs of a British penal colony rather than a market economy. Where formal institutions were called upon, such as legal or political representation, they were more likely to be located in London than Sydney, resulting in delays, misunderstandings and asymmetries of information. Thus, for example, when the Bank of New South Wales sought the legal status of a joint stock company, it received Governor Macquarie's agreement locally, but permission from the British government was refused, leaving the Bank in the invidious position of trading as a joint stock company in organization but an unlimited liability partnership in law.

With a paucity of formal institutions, of particular interest for the early years of settlement are the informal institutions represented in belief systems and codes of conduct brought to Australia by British migrants. On the one hand, the fact that many were convicted criminals suggests that the levels of trust and credible commitment required in economic transactions may have been in short supply. Against this, it must be borne in mind that many were convicted of petty offences, often the result of desperation from abject poverty. It is doubtful that most of these convicts were part of a hardened criminal class (Nicholas, 1990; Shlomovitz, 1990). Moreover, some brought with them business experience, entrepreneurial values and trade skills (Oxley, 1996). Many came from close-knit working-class and ethnic communities, particularly in East London, where a strong emphasis was placed upon trustworthy behaviour within their group.[5] Significantly, early forms of enterprise in Australia largely took the form of personal exchange, relying upon repeated dealing among small local firms as a basis for honest behaviour. Kinship and social networks added to the sense of trust (Ville, 1998).[6]

It has been suggested by Greene that British migrants carried with them to the colonies large stocks of social capital, which helped to form a European-style civil society in these nations. Moreover, the partibility, adaptability and enhancibility of social capital made it especially transferable to very different economic and social contexts (Greene, 2001). 'Social capital' is a widely defined and used term but is best thought of as the development of shared social norms and values based on cooperation, trust, reciprocity and obligation.[7] Greene adopts a very broad definition which in effect covers most institutional forms. Others have focused more closely on trust and cooperation. McIntosh's study of English communities, 1300–1640, makes a case for the development of large stocks of social capital established through the actions of both local bodies such as the church, charities and the courts, and informal groups such as kinship, friendship, co-workers and neighbourliness. The role of organizations as lubricators of cooperation has been widely discussed in the social capital literature, particularly in the light of the central role attributed to them by Robert Putnam. Analyses of European medieval guilds, however, suggest they were also capable of generating divisiveness and exclusivity (Putnam, 2000; Ogilvie, 2003).

While social capital carries notions of a cooperative community spirit, other writers have identified individualism as the predominant British belief system, resonating strongly with an entrepreneurial and inventive ethos. It has been widely argued that Britain made a transition from a peasant society to an individualistic and commercial one in the sixteenth and seventeenth centuries, although Macfarlane controversially argued for a much earlier genesis of English individualism.[8]

After about 1800, the arrival of more 'free' immigrants to Australia, many of whom were merchants from British and Indian houses, the increasing numbers of emancipated convicts ('emancipists'), a change in official attitudes towards them from Macquarie's governship onwards, and pressure from London for financial self-sufficiency in the colonies provided new opportunities for economic activity beyond the jail and out of the control of the New South Wales Corps. By the time of Commissioner Bigge's 1821 reports into the colonies, many of his recommendations were already under way including the preferred assignment of convicts to private employers and the encouragement of private investors. As Butlin has noted, a mixed economy began to take shape after 1810, comprising a conventional public sector alongside a rapidly growing private sector (Butlin, 1994: 3).

Nonetheless, for most of the nineteenth century, economic expansion remained largely under the custodianship of British institutions: Australian wool and other commodities were largely sold in London; 'colonial capital' was raised on the London Stock Exchange and managed by British boards of directors; economic policies, such as the Navigation Laws, were British; and technological innovation focused upon the needs of the industrializing British economy with a very different climate and set-of-factor costs from primary-producing Australia. The dominant groups ('elites') driving institutional change were British or 'Anglo-Australian', that is settlers in Australia who still considered Britain their home.

6.3.1.2 Local adaption of colonial institutions

British institutions, nonetheless, were tempered by an environment for which they were not designed. As a result, institutions evolved as they adapted to local Australian conditions, while still remaining fundamentally British and colonial. Environmental differences centred around location, climate and factor costs. Australia's location in the south Pacific made it the antipode of Britain and remote from the regions of major human settlement and modern economic progress, the so-called 'tyranny of distance' thesis (Blainey, 2001). Its hot, dry climate contrasted with Britain's mild and wet one. Australia's land abundancy but labour deficiency was similarly the converse of the small but populous British Isles.

These environmental differences helped to shape the evolution of Australian belief systems in the nineteenth century, or what North calls 'mental models'. The issue of distance was not just that with the rest of the world: communications among a colony's rural settlements and, intercolonially, between the major centres of Sydney and Melbourne, were slow and unreliable. The sense of isolation of small communities added to the great uncertainty of small-scale farming in a hot, dry climate and helped to develop a strongly supportive frame of mind. With few alternative distractions and the need to share knowledge, assets, skills and experiences, communities were thrown together in a plethora of local organizations of a strongly inclusive and socially interactive nature: social and sporting clubs, charity groups, religious gatherings, agricultural and horticultural societies and farmers clubs were all to be found in most pastoral and farming districts of Southeastern Australia by the late 1850s. While this sense of community was akin to the experiences of British rural life, the additional factors of extreme isolation, limited social hierarchies and class symbols, and convictism, and a predominantly male population at first, generated a greater sense of equality and mutual help as reflected in high levels of social capital and the idea of mateship.

While the church was an important institution of colonial Australian communities, the accompanying religion was more rational and secularist than in Britain, sometimes referred to as civil religion. This has been attributed to the use of religion as an ethics system in the early penal colony and the adoption of a practical and 'here-and-now' approach to life in the face of great hardships on the frontier and a strong sense of uncertainty. This took precedence over esoteric ideology and personal sacrifice for a hereafter life that could not easily be verified (Gillman, 1999: 239–42). Religious interdenominationalism was rarely a source of conflict in contrast to European experience. Relations between Catholics and Protestants in rural Australia, for example, were generally 'harmonious and cooperative', helped by non-extreme forms of doctrinal interpretation if not a degree of irreligiosity (Swan, 1970; Jackson, 1987; Campbell, 1997; Logan, 2000: 121).

By mid-century, cooperative behaviour was furthered by a relatively homogeneous group of settlers, educated and of medium-to-high social rank. They frequently came from the same region of Britain, shared similar cultural values and religious beliefs, and included large extended-family groupings.[9] Scots, with their strong emphasis upon family and clan, were numerous. Former military officers and employees of the East India Company were also common (Roberts, 1935: 368–75; James, 1949: 63). The arrival of non-British migrants rarely engendered distrust and social dislocation. Outside the highly itinerant goldfields, European–Chinese relations were generally characterized by 'mutual cooperation and benefit'. Lancashire has noted the support of rural institutions such as the judiciary, local press and large landowners for their Chinese communities against prejudicial legislation emanating from urban central government, which may suggest some tension between local and British influences upon institutional development (Lancashire, 2000: 229, 237–8).

The adaptiveness of colonial Australia's institutions is perhaps best illustrated by the Victorian gold mining boom of the 1850s. The discovery of gold in July 1851 led to a rapid influx of diggers, with the population of the Victorian goldfields rising from 19,000 to 144,000 during 1851–60. Most of the prospecting occurred on public land and, with additional concerns over social stability, the Victorian government introduced a system of property rights to govern mining, which included a licence fee and a defined size of claim. These rules proved defective in terms of incentives and were difficult to enforce, which, when combined with rapid changes in the technology and geology of mining, contributed to the unrest that culminated in the Eureka Stockade rebellion of 1854. While suppressing the rebellion with armed force, the Victorian government took note of the complaints and introduced major institutional reforms in the mining communities. These reforms provided more effective allocation of property rights and political representation, which secured social stability and improved resource exploitation (La Croix, 1992).

Two environmental forces shaping the growth of formal as well as informal institutional structures before 1900 were distance and population size. Distance and poor communication between the colonies emphasized the sense of independence and with it the development of separate and distinctive institutional structures. The legacy of this has been fragmented and, arguably, inefficient institutions creating a framework of federated nationhood, sustained by the particularism of individual states. Distance, combined with small population bases, has necessitated governments to champion the construction of expensive infrastructure, using their resources and taxing capability to raise funds for the purpose on the London Stock Exchange. This 'colonial socialism' has also generated a legacy of interventionism for twentieth-century Australia (Butlin, 1959).

Both firms and markets were British-dominated in the nineteenth century. The Australian economy was heavily oriented towards the export of primary products, most notably wool, meat, dairy products, grain and gold. The main market for each of these products was in London, not Sydney or Melbourne. Wool was sold by auction at the London coffee houses before moving to a separate Wool Exchange in 1875 (Maughan, 1931: 73). In mid-century about 80 per cent of Australian wool was thus sold (Barnard, 1958: 47). Australian wool growers had to wait months to receive the proceeds of a sale in a distant market about which they understood little and from which price trend and other commercial information were slow to emerge. Sales were controlled by British consignors and brokers such as Dalgety and Australian Mercantile Land and Finance Company, and it was London firms in ancillary and related industries that benefited from the location of the market.

Financial markets were equally dependent upon London with the London Stock Exchange providing far greater levels of funding for the

Australian colonial economies than the embryonic local exchanges, which dealt in a small number of mostly thinly traded scripts (Hall, 1963, 1968; Salsbury and Sweeney, 1988). British banks were also major providers of firm finance as were a wide range of British firms across many industries through personal networks and ongoing trading relationships.[10] The 1830s witnessed the establishment of British banks in Australia, notably the Bank of Australasia, the Union Bank and the Bank of South Australia, which were larger branch institutions channelling British investment and providing related services such as foreign exchange. Adapting to the needs of the Australian economy, many banks broke with British orthodoxy by lending on the collateral of landed property, livestock and other relatively illiquid securities (Merrett, 1997: 184).

Banks and wool consignors are two important examples of a specific type of British multinational that was widely represented in nineteenth-century Australia: the free-standing company (Wilkins, 1988). Frequently, their domestic operations in Britain physically amounted to little more than a nameplate over a door in the City of London although, within the context of mid-nineteenth-century Australia, they were both very large and highly specialized. As late as 1910 six of the leading ten companies operating in Australia were of this type (Ville and Merrett, 2000: 34). The intention behind these companies was to secure natural resources and farming output needed by the industrializing British economy, although the benefits to the complementary Australian economy were also substantial, particularly in terms of inflows of entrepreneurship, knowledge, finance and technology and the outflow of pastoral and mining exports.

Firms domiciled in Australia drew mostly upon British laws dealing with economic association, notably incorporation as a joint stock company, partnership and tenancies in common. In the first half of the nineteenth century, incorporation was a special privilege achieved through a private Act of the British Parliament or the consent of its executive government, which was a lengthy and expensive process based upon unclear statutory and legal foundations. The problems experienced by the Bank of New South Wales were mentioned earlier. Incorporation provided a clearly defined legal status, the free transferability of shares and, frequently, limited liability. In the first half of the century the first two benefits were of little value to small private businesses while the third, limited liability, was regarded with suspicion, particularly in the eyes of creditors. There were only about 71 incorporations in New South Wales during 1835–51, and 14 in Melbourne by 1852.

Such companies were concentrated in a few capital-intensive industries such as transport and utilities, were floated in cyclical booms by a small number of promoters and had high failure rates (Hall, 1968: 3; Salsbury and Sweeney, 1988: 6–7).

Local incorporation laws were introduced in mid-century by the Australian colonies in largely identical form. It was the importance of free-standing multinationals that prompted this. Local laws facilitated joint flotation on the British and Australian colonial stock markets and the existence of Boards of Directors in both countries. However, it was the impact of the local mining boom of the 1850s that caused Victoria to be the first colony to introduce legislation, covering mining companies in 1860 and extending to all sectors four years later. New South Wales followed with legislation in 1861 and 1874 respectively. While the legislation drew closely upon the British in freely granting incorporation to businesses which provided the names of seven people, a memorandum of association, and were registered with the Registrar of Companies, there were some important differences. In 1853 Victoria and New South Wales broke with British tradition by introducing limited liability for partnerships, excluding banking and insurance. More significantly, in 1871 Victoria took the radical step of introducing no-liability for shareholders in mining ventures, which freed investors from the normal legal commitment to meet unpaid calls on their shares from the company or its creditors. Instead, forfeiture of the shares resulted from unpaid calls without further payment. Again New South Wales took a decade to replicate this law. This novel legislation helped to maintain the flow of investment into an industry with large capital needs but very high risks.

6.3.2 National institutions: Self-serving insularity

6.3.2.1 Crisis, opportunity and assertion

A major institutional shift took place around the end of the nineteenth century with the growth of local Australian institutions, which increasingly replaced those of the British Empire. No particular cause or event singularly defines this punctuated equilibrium. That informal institutions or belief systems, less susceptible to direct imperial control, had adapted and changed more than colonial formal institutions during the nineteenth century created a tension between these constraints on human interaction. As noted earlier, belief systems were heading in the direction of an Australian perspective on many matters, distinct from the British or even colonial perspective. It took a series of events to bring these frictions to a head.

The 1890s was a decade of crisis in Australia: a major economic downturn, the collapse of several leading financial institutions, prolonged drought conditions, and industrial relations conflict. These circumstances exerted enormous pressures on existing colonial institutions that ultimately weakened their role in Australia. British investors turned their back on many Australian companies following losses on speculative mining ventures, while the London boards of free-standing companies in Australia began to understand the growing ineffectiveness of management by remote control. Strikes by shearers and maritime workers asserted the egalitarian aspirations of the Australian workforce, while colonial institutions had no solution or effective response to the drought. Accompanying the crisis, but in some respects a response to it, were new economic opportunities associated with the diversification of production and exchange, a widening range of primary produce and mining, new manufacturing, and the expansion of non-British trading partners.

Crisis and opportunity therefore revealed shortcomings in the institutional legacy from Britain, and led to a reassessment of the latter's nature and place in Australia. This turn of events would reinforce evolving Australian perspectives and attitudes to engender nationhood and foment a shift to local institutions reflecting national aspirations.

Much is often made of the impact of the First World War, especially the Gallipoli campaign, on Anglo-Australian relations and, later, that of the surrender in Singapore during the Second World War. While there remained strong cultural, economic and political ties that made the two countries firm allies in wars throughout the twentieth century, Australia had already begun to develop multilateral political and economic relationships before 1914, including a growing trade balance with wartime foes Japan and Germany.[11] These new trading relationships occurred within an environment of growing Australian self-determination in the face of the United Kingdom's traditional role as the imperial power and intermediary in Australia's economic and political relations with the rest of the world. War, however, served as a catalyst in the growth of domestic economic institutions including local markets and government policies.

6.3.2.2 Institutional shifts

One of the key institutional shifts in the economic sphere was the repatriation of commodity and capital markets from Britain back to Australia.

Wool and other commodities had largely been sold in London in the mid-nineteenth century, as noted above. By the final two decades of the century, local sales were increasing in size and share of total disposals. This reflected the growing multilateralism of Australia's international economic relations. More wool, for example, was being sold to Continental European than British buyers by the 1890s, while shipping routes had similarly diversified. Less than 30 per cent of total wool exports had been sold in Australia at the beginning of the 1880s, but this grew to an average of 53 per cent in the following decade, and continued to rise sharply to 76 per cent in the first decade of the twentieth century and 93 per cent in the second (Ville, 2005: 76). During the First World War, Britain was able to acquire the whole of the Australian wool clip for its wartime needs under the Imperial Wool Purchase Scheme, but this was under circumstances of tough Australian negotiations that resulted in highly beneficial terms for the Australian grower, as Tsokhas has shown (Tsokhas, 1990).

While repatriation of the wool market was largely the product of economic imperatives and the actions of wool brokers, changes in other primary produce markets were more closely associated with government action in response to economic uncertainty in evolving produce markets, resulting from war and depression. These included marketing boards, price support, and international commodity agreements. Kenwood has noted, 'The involvement of some ten federal and more than fifty state statutory marketing authorities... has thus been the most prominent feature of Australian agricultural marketing since the 1920s' (Kenwood, 1995: 51). Operating over a wide range of commodities, the Boards had broad responsibilities, particularly price support, product promotion, and capital and technical assistance. As single desk authorities, they played a key part in the price stabilization ('home consumption pricing') policies of successive governments, which fixed home prices artificially high and stable on the justification of a wage-cost disadvantage. A logical third string to agricultural support was the negotiation of international commodity agreements to mitigate price fluctuations in overseas markets. Most agreements, however, were relatively short-lived with only marginal effects on prices (Kenwood, 1995: 53).

The local capital market matured rapidly in the first half of the twentieth century. The disapprobation of the London capital market in the 1890s, together with the growth opportunities provided by trade barriers, population expansion, and a diversifying economic structure were the triggers. The resulting domestic capital market was increasingly focused on the private sector and provided for most of Australia's capital formation needs through the twentieth century. Major improvements in the efficiency of its operations and the range of its services took place. It broadened its scope from its high-risk mining origins in the nineteenth century to a wide range of more stable but expanding industrials and quasi-government stocks by the interwar period. Government's role included the assumption of note issue in 1910, the establishment of the Commonwealth Bank as a quasi central banker in 1912, and the statutory powers conferred on the Loans Council in 1929 to fix the volume of public sector borrowing (Merrett, 1997).

More broadly, markets began to move from personal to impersonal. The personal business networks of the British Empire began to yield to impersonal trade and finance flows that traversed cultural and linguistic boundaries, for example with Japan and Germany mentioned above, and which required a credible commitment to function effectively.

Labour markets took a highly regulated character for at least the first half of the twentieth century, particularly in the form of centralized wage-fixing polices. The egalitarian ethos associated with the labour unrest of the 1890s and the associated breakdown of effective collective bargaining lay at the foundation of quasi-judicial compulsory arbitration, implemented by a Commonwealth Court and State Tribunals. The 1907 Harvester Judgement introduced the idea of the 'basic wage' or 'living wage' necessary to maintain a breadwinner, his wife and three children. Social policy and material need, therefore, determined wages rather than the nature of employment, although a 'secondary margin' took some account of training, skills, experience and the needs of particular industries. Between 1922 and 1953 quarterly cost-of-living adjustments were made to the basic wage. The link to economic policy, instead, was through the tariff and price maintenance, which, it was claimed, gave employers the resources to pay living wages.

Support was provided to manufacturing beginning effectively with the 1908 Lyne Tariff. Infant industry arguments were proffered in the face of foreign competition in traded goods. The need for a more balanced and diverse economy and greater stability of employment and earnings were additionally invoked as justifications. Duties were raised in 1911 and 1914 before the Greene Tariff of 1921 used national defence reasons to justify further increases, taking the range of dutiable imports to 71 per cent (Kenwood, 1995: 69–70). Import quotas were also periodically introduced. Variations in protection levels were used to prosecute development policies; for example, preferential rates were used to foster a local automobile industry at the end of the Second World War (Conlon and Perkins, 2001: 115–16).

While multinationals continued to play an important role in twentieth-century Australia, the dominance of British-registered free-standing companies diminished. Of the top 25 non-financial firms domiciled in Australia in 1910, 12 were foreign-registered (all British). By 1930 this figure had declined to eight and then to three by 1952. Firms registered in New South Wales or Victoria began to take their place (Ville and Merrett, 2000). Where British multinationals remained in Australia, they faced tensions between the rights of local management and their London boards. Helped by improved communications, those firms willing to delegate substantial responsibilities to local management often gained a consequential competitive advantage. Among the major wool brokers, the slowness of the London boards of the New Zealand Loan and Mercantile Agency (NZLMA) and the Australian Mercantile Loan and Finance Company (AMLF) to relinquish tight control was reflected in their loss of market share in the first half of the twentieth century (Ville, 2000). Benefiting from early incumbency and tariff protection, many leading Australian firms began to expand nationally in the first half of the twentieth century.

British free-standing companies were largely superseded by American multinationals that located manufacturing subsidiaries in Australia. They provided much of the technological and organizational know-how underpinning the industrial diversification of Australia, which provided a *quid pro quo* for the tariff protection sought by such firms.

6.3.3 Globalizing institutions: Convergent efficiency

6.3.3.1 Declining competitiveness and fragmented federalism

The substitution of local institutions more akin to, and providing greater control over, Australia's twentieth-century development was a major step forward. It helped to provide the foundations for rapid economic growth and modernization, and appeared to be based upon a high degree of consensus and egalitarian behaviour led by actors who viewed themselves increasingly as Australian rather than Anglo-Australian or British. Nonetheless, it was a 'White' Australian consciousness in which other racial groups were disadvantageously treated. Economically, it was limited in its ability to promote sustainable competitive advantages. Two factors largely explain its economic shortcomings: the creation of a high-cost, high-price economy and the failure to complete the national integration of political and economic institutions.

Protectionism and labour market regulation, while designed to diversify the economy and foster industrial harmony through justice, were primarily responsible for a cost-price structure that was not internationally competitive and reduced domestic consumer demand. Tariffs raised domestic production costs and, by mitigating foreign competition, sustained small firms and industries that were probably not competitive beyond an infant industry period, thus limiting resource reallocation to more promising long-term growth sectors and firms. Moreover, they encouraged competition-shy firms, including powerful multinationals attracted by the external tariff, to invest in rent-seeking political lobbying activity to maintain or even raise protection, rather than focus upon increased operational efficiencies particularly through innovation.[12] Centralized wage determination, by largely ignoring economic imperatives such as skill and product differences, fostered labour markets relatively unresponsive to the needs of structural change. Finally, 'human protectionism', in other words the 'White Australia' immigration policy, shut out sources of productive low-wage workers (Brennan and Pincus, 2002: 64). In 1972 the OECD drew attention to Australia's declining competitiveness, which it particularly attributed to tariffs as high as 36 per cent. Domestically, a 1977 government White Paper and the Crawford Report in 1979 advocated a change in direction for trade and industry policies.

Australia's constitutional structure developed in a genuinely federal manner with final decisions on some policies lying at the state level. The structure provides some benefits in terms of checks and balances. On the other hand, it creates ambiguities regarding lines of responsibility and chains of accountability, and encourages power games amongst state and federal regulatory bodies with overlapping jurisdictions in areas such as industrial relations and agricultural support. However, Australia's is a fragmented federalism, where differences exist between the individual state constitutions, thus adding considerably to the complexity of federal–state government relations and, indeed, state–state government relations (Costar, 1999). The incomplete constitutional transformation is also seen by Olson as allowing institutional sclerosis to take hold in Australia and with it the capture of government policy by interest groups (Olson, 1984; Marks and Sadeghi, 1998). Incomplete integration can also be seen in economic institutions. Stock exchanges operated from the capital cities of each state, each with their own rules and *modus operandi*, the Australian Stock Exchange only coming into being in 1987. A uniform Companies Act for each state only came into existence in 1961–62.[13]

6.3.3.2 Deregulation and engagement

A decisive change of direction occurred from the 1970s and 1980s and, as at the beginning of the century, it was driven by changing belief systems at home and a shifting external environment. Australia's nationalist economic policies had achieved rapid economic growth but with the slowdown of global growth in the 1970s, more attention was focused on boosting efficiency and competitiveness. As we saw above, Australia's high-cost structure, rent-seeking political economy and fragmented federalism had contributed to declining international competitiveness. Much blame was attached to the cosy consensus that provided powerful rent-seeking corporations protection from competition by trade barriers and price regulation in return for high wages for labour unrelated to levels of productivity.

The break with that conventional wisdom was as decisive and as widely accepted as its original introduction nearly a century beforehand. Changing belief systems evolved from a concern over Australia's declining relative position in the world economy and from an awareness of similar institutional re-evaluations occurring overseas. It was the Hawke and Keating Labour governments of the 1980s and early 1990s that made the decisive policy changes, but these largely had the bipartisan support of the coalition parties whose traditional philosophies they most closely reflected, and who continued the policies under the Howard governments from 1996. What ensued may be summarized as the replacement of inward-looking, nationalist protection and regulation with outward deregulation and competition drawing upon multicultural values. While particularly applied to economic institutions in this chapter, these terms range broadly over social and political change, which in turn impinged upon economic performance. The ending of a 'White Australia' immigration policy, for example, was as important to more efficient labour markets as the dismantling of centralized wage fixing.

Key areas of change centred upon the institutions of labour and capital markets, trade policy and competition policy. Tariffs were progressively reduced with the effective rate of assistance declining from 35 to 5 per cent during 1972/73–2000/01 (Meredith and Dyster, 1999: 328). Various industrial incentives were offered, partly as a *quid pro quo*, to ease the transition to free trade, and as part of a change of focus towards the pursuit of efficiency and environmental responsibility. The stated intentions were the promotion of investment, exports, innovation, competitiveness and resource sustainability (Brennan and Pincus,

2002: 75). In financial markets, foreign exchange controls were ended, the dollar was allowed to 'float', foreign banks were permitted to apply for licences to operate in Australia, and most remaining barriers between domestic and international financial markets were removed (Merrett, 1998). Labour market decentralization reduced the powers of federal arbitration tribunals and encouraged a focus upon enterprise-level negotiations and awards. This had the effect of reducing the role of central awards to a safety net for the low paid (Castles, 2002: 48–9). Labour skills were enhanced by the substantial expansion of participation in tertiary education as a result of elevating many educational institutions (Colleges of Advanced Education) into universities and introducing a partial user-pay funding system (Higher Education Contribution Scheme) that could handle the vast increase in expenditure. In addition, greater attention was given to the fostering of skills that addressed employment needs (Cowie, 1999).

While shifts in the institutional structure governing labour, capital and trade largely involved loosening the reins of government control, competition policy headed in the opposite direction. The absence of effective competition policy until the final third of the twentieth century contributed to the uncompetitive business environment, allowing interfirm collusion to flourish. Butlin, Barnard and Pincus aptly summarized the situation: 'all the restrictive practices known to man were exploited in the Australian economy' (Butlin *et al.*, 1982: 125).[14] A change of emphasis began with the Trade Practices Act (1967), which created the Trade Practices Court to investigate anti-competitive behaviour. Various enhancements to the policy have followed, including the introduction of a dominance test in 1977 and closer attention to merger activity as well as interfirm collusion. Since 1993 the *structuralist* approach of dominance has been largely replaced by a *behavioural* or *conduct* test of competition. The Australian Competition and Consumer Commission was created in 1995 with wide-ranging powers and coverage, and employs economic ideas and concepts to evaluate levels of competition (King, 2003). Competition has additionally been enhanced by removing the industry monopolies of government enterprises at both federal and state levels, privatization, the admission of competing firms, or contracting out the right to provide particular services (*Reserve Bank of Australia Bulletin*, December 1997).

Associated with these shifting institutional patterns, particularly enhanced competition and domestic market maturity, has been the demise of the distinctive proprietary capitalism of early-twentieth-century Australia and its replacement with more modern corporate forms, based on stronger organizational structures and more effective corporate strategies, which converge to a large degree with advanced forms of capitalism in other developed nations and have led large numbers of firms to reverse the institutional legacy by expanding overseas (Fleming *et al.*, 2004: 203).

6.4 Institutional change and innovation

One of the key drivers of a nation's nature and pace of economic development is innovation, particularly through the development of cost-reducing processes and the introduction of new products and services. Thus, a consequential issue arising from our broad survey of institutions and economic development in Australia is the impact the changing institutional structure has had upon the nature and rate of innovation. Secondly, generalizing about the institutional legacy from historical experience, we investigate the extent to which a distinctive national innovation system has evolved.

Imported British colonial institutions of the nineteenth century provided strong social, knowledge, financial and legal foundations for innovation. Thus, for example, the system of patents together with secure property rights helped to protect the value of rents associated with innovation. Well-founded networks provided the trust, cooperation and information exchanges that facilitate research and development activity. Imports of human and financial capital and modern forms of business organization further contributed to the munificent environment for innovative behaviour and provided access to wider international sources of information and expertise. Innovation opportunities in turn impact upon a nation's institutional structure, much of the microeconomic reform of recent decades being designed to increase Australia's exposure and receptiveness to overseas technology in high-growth industries.

The informal institutions associated especially with mental models or belief systems supported an innovative culture. These included a mixture of social capital-style cooperation, sharing the diagnosis of problems and their solution, while at the same time a strong dose of individualism that drove many inventors to look at problems and their solution from a unique perspective. Indeed, the setting for much nineteenth-century inventive activity was the individual rather than the organization. The secularist, 'here and now' approach that developed in the nineteenth century suggests on the one hand a practical frame of mind associated with problem-solving, while on the other hand a limited interest in the long-term investments and improvements associated with experimental research and development.

However, the *forms* of innovation undertaken in Britain were rarely suited to the very different structure and composition of the Australian economy and natural environment. British free-standing companies in Australia, for example, provided financial support and sources of general management experience but only limited useful industry-specific know-how. While Britain provided access to international sources of information, it was carefully brokered, limiting multilateral communications with other nations.

The development of local institutions by the early twentieth century promised to align the innovation effort more closely with national interests and economic development. Government support became more important, either directly or through public research bodies such as the Commonwealth Scientific and Industrial Research Organization (CSIRO) (1949) and its predecessor, the Council for Scientific and Industrial Research (CSIR) (1926) (Schedvin, 1987). The widening range of industries, particularly in manufacturing, fostered by the changed environment enhanced the opportunity for applying new technologies, particularly those adapted from overseas. Australia's escape from British international intermediation provided more direct access to overseas sources of innovation. The arrival of many American manufacturing multinationals in the 1920s and 1930s provided important new sources of international technology transfer. The repatriation of decision-making in some companies and markets provided a stronger feedback mechanism and a greater focus on local needs and domestic research and development. Regulation and protection provided insulation against some forms of uncertainty for a small developing economy and thus a more conducive environment for research and development.

Against these positive aspects, however, the insularity, lack of competition and insufficient alignment of regulatory policy with economic incentives erected many barriers to innovation. For example, the disassociation of wages with labour productivity reduced the incentives for the workforce to support productivity-enhancing innovations. Internal and external price support encouraged firms to focus on maintaining or advancing these policies rather than concentrate upon raising their internal efficiency. The survival of inefficient small firms and some industries denied resources to large firms in successful industries able to undertake extensive in-house research. In addition, fragmented federalism, particularly in the multiplicity of federal and state economic authorities, distorted and confused the market signals and policy rules upon which effective innovation relies.

There are grounds for greater optimism about the third stage of institutional evolution over the final two or three decades of the twentieth century. The emphasis upon competition and efficiency, through deregulation and microeconomic reform, provides a much closer alignment of government, entrepreneurial and worker incentives with innovation. The returns to corporate rent-seeking, either through collusion with other producers or by lobbying government, have diminished, while the returns to labour, primed with higher skills and a broader ethnic mix, are much more closely aligned with the economic incentives of the industry. Not only have the returns to Olsonian distributional coalitions diminished, but the fundamental changes in mental modes and formal institutions have, perhaps, overturned the encroaching institutional sclerosis. In addition, mature and internationally integrated capital markets are better able to distinguish dynamic and innovative organizations within Australia and provide them with access to more extensive resources and support overseas. The belated emergence of modern, large-scale industrial enterprise in Australia has provided greater opportunities to absorb and adapt effectively foreign sources of technology to suit the local environment, as well as enhanced domestic research and development capabilities (Fleming *et al.*, 2004: 227–9).

6.5 Conclusion: Towards a national innovation system

The adaptiveness of Australian institutions to profound environmental change over two centuries and the rapid establishment of impersonal markets suggest, overall, an institutional structure receptive to the opportunities presented by innovation. While much of this chapter has emphasized historical change in Australia's institutional structure, elements of continuity also exist – key patterns, moderated by historical experience. Such patterns or layers, by setting some distinctive ground rules, have helped to give shape and coherence to a multilayered national framework for innovation at the beginning of the twenty-first century. These continuing facets include surmounting the problems of geographical distance, small population size, and fragmented institutions, while harnessing the benefits of social cohesion, networking skills, a secularist state of mind, the influence of foreign direct investment, a richness of natural resources, the rule of law and a mixed economy. These continuities, combined with the periodic shifts discussed here, provide the distinctive institutional legacy for the generation and reception of knowledge flows in Australia and thus the shaping of a contemporary national innovation system that is currently a subject of much discussion and analysis (*Mapping Australian Science and Innovation*, 2003).

Notes

1. Exceptionally, see White (1992). Post federation, see Henningham (1999) and Brennan and Castles (2002). Kenwood (1995) provides some good evidence, though focuses rather narrowly on economic policy and formal economic institutions.
2. Of particular importance are North (1990), North and Weingast (1989), North (1993), Hirsch and Lounsbury (1996) and North (1999).
3. He gives the examples of the 'suq' and the caravan trade (North, 1990: 125–6).
4. There is a wide literature dealing with these ideas including Jones and Rose (1993), Muldrew (1998) and Boyce and Ville (2002: chapter 9).
5. For later in the nineteenth century, see Godley (1986).
6. New South Wales shipowning was said to be 'entwined in a complex set of relationships' (Hainsworth, 1971: 23).
7. See Ville (2004) for a recent survey of the subject.
8. For a recent assessment of the debate, see French and Hoyle (2003).
9. Knack and Keefer (1997: 11) concluded that levels of trust tend to be higher in ethnically homogeneous communities following non-hierarchical religions, particularly Protestantism.
10. For example, see the substantial trade finance and industrial investment provided by British trader Robert Brooks in Broeze (1993: 81–90).
11. For example, see Meredith and Dyster (1999: 101), Tweedie (1994), Purcell (1981) and Perkins (1989).
12. For example, see Bell (1993: 20, 32–1, 103).
13. A national listing of all securities commenced in 1972.
14. The Australian Industries Preservation Act of 1906 is generally viewed as having only a limited and temporary impact. For example, see Fleming and Terwiel (1997).

References

Barnard, A. *Australian Wool Market, 1840–1900* (Melbourne: Melbourne University Press, 1958).

Bell, S. *Australian Manufacturing and the State. The Politics of Industry Policy in the Postwar Period* (Cambridge: Cambridge University Press, 1993).

Blainey, G. *The Tyranny of Distance: How Distance Shaped Australia's History* (Sydney: Macmillan, 2001).

Boyce, G. and Ville, S. *The Development of Modern Business* (Basingstoke: Palgrave, 2002).

Brennan, G. and Castles, F. G. (eds), *Australia Reshaped. 200 Years of Institutional Transformation* (Cambridge: Cambridge University Press, 2002).

Brennan, G. and Pincus, J. 'Australia's Economic Institutions', in G. Brennan and F. G. Castles (eds), *Australia Reshaped. 200 Years of Institutional Transformation* (Cambridge: Cambridge University Press, 2002): 53–85.
Broeze, F. *Robert Brooks and the Australian Trade. Imperial Business in the Nineteenth Century* (Melbourne: Melbourne University Press, 1993).
Butlin, N. G. 'Colonial Socialism in Australia', in H. G. J. Aitken (ed.), *The State and Economic Growth* (New York: Social Science Research Council, 1959): 26–78.
Butlin, N. G., Barnard, A. and Pincus, J. J. *Government and Capitalism: Public and Private Choice in Twentieth Century Australia* (St Leonards, NSW: Allen & Unwin, 1982).
Butlin, N. G. *Forming a Colonial Economy, Australia 1810–1850* (Melbourne: Cambridge University Press, 1994).
Campbell, M. *The Kingdom of the Ryans: The Irish in South West New South Wales, 1816–1890* (Sydney: University of New South Wales Press, 1997).
Castles, F. G. 'Australia's Institutions and Australia's Welfare' in G. Brennan and F. G. Castles (eds), *Australia Reshaped. 200 Years of Institutional Transformation* (Cambridge: Cambridge University Press, 2002): 25–52.
Conlon, R. and Perkins, J. *Wheels and Deals. The Automobile Industry in Twentieth-Century Australia* (Aldershot: Ashgate, 2001).
Costar, B. 'State Government', in J. Henningham (ed.), *Institutions in Australian Society*, second edition (Melbourne: Oxford University Press, 1999): 34–52.
Cowie, R. 'Education', in J. Henningham (ed.), *Institutions in Australian Society*, second edition (Melbourne: Oxford University Press, 1999): 159–83.
Fleming, G. and Terwiel, D. 'What Effect Did Early Australian Antitrust Legislation Have on Firm Behaviour? Lessons from Business History', *Australian Business Law Review*, 27 (1) (1999): 47–56.
Fleming, G., Merrett, D. and Ville, S. *The Big End of Town. Big Business and Corporate Leadership in Twentieth-Century Australia* (Melbourne: Cambridge University Press, 2004).
French, H. R. and Hoyle, R. W. 'English Individualism Refuted and Reasserted: The Land Market of Earls Colne (Essex), 1550–1750', *Economic History Review*, 56 (4) (2003): 595–622.
Gillman, I. 'Religion', in J. Henningham (ed.), *Institutions in Australian Society*, second edition (Melbourne: Oxford University Press, 1999): 234–50.
Godley, A. 'Jewish Soft-loan Societies in New York and London and Immigrant Entrepreneurship, 1880–1914', *Business History*, 38 (3) (1996): 101–16.
Greene, J. P. 'Social and Cultural Capital in Colonial British America: A Case Study', in R. I. Rotberg (ed.), *Patterns of Social Capital: Stability and Change in Historical Perspective* (New York: Cambridge University Press, 2001): 491–509.
Hainsworth, D. R. *The Sydney Traders. Simeon Lord and his Contemporaries, 1788–1821* (Melbourne: Cassell Australia, 1971).
Hall, A. R. *The London Capital Market and Australia, 1870–1914* (Canberra: Australian National University Press, 1963).
Hall, A. R. *The Stock Exchange of Melbourne and the Victorian Economy, 1852–1900* (Canberra: Australian National University Press, 1968).
Henningham, J. (ed.), *Institutions in Australian Society* (Melbourne: Oxford University Press, 1999).
Hirsch, P. M. and Lounsbury, M. D. 'Rediscovering Volition: The Institutional Economics of Douglass C. North', *Academy of Management Review*, 21 (3) (1996): 872–73.

Jackson, H. R. *Churches and People in Australia and New Zealand, 1860–1930* (Wellington: Port Nicholson Press, 1987).

James, G. F. (ed.), *A Homestead History: The Reminiscences and Letters of Alfred Joyce of Plaistow and Norwood, Port Phillip, 1843–64* (Melbourne: Melbourne University Press 1949).

Jones, G. and Rose, M. B. *Family Capitalism* (London: F. Cass, 1993).

Kenwood, A. G. *Australian Economic Institutions Since Federation* (Melbourne: Oxford University Press, 1995).

King, S. P. 'Competition Policy and Regulation', in I. McAllister, S. Dowrick and R. Hassan (eds), *The Cambridge Handbook of Social Sciences in Australia* (Cambridge: Cambridge University Press, 2003): 31–44.

Knack, S. and Keefer, P. 'Does Social Capital Have an Economic Payoff? A Cross-Country Investigation', *Quarterly Journal of Economics*, 112 (4) (1997): 1251–88.

La Croix, S. J. 'Property Rights and Institutional Change During Australia's Gold Rush', *Explorations in Economic History*, 29 (2) (1992): 204–27.

Lancashire, R. 'European-Chinese Economic Interaction in a Pre-Federation Rural Australian Setting', *Rural Society*, 10 (2) (2000): 229–41.

Logan, J. 'Sectarianism in Ganmain: A Local Study, 1912–21', *Rural Society*, 10 (2) (2000): 121–38.

Macfarlane, A. *The Origins of English Individualism: The Family, Property and Social Transition* (Oxford: Blackwell, 1978).

Mapping Australian Science and Innovation (Canberra: Department of Education Science and Training, 2003).

Marks, A. and Sadeghi, M. 'Testing the Olson Hypothesis Within the Australian Context', *Australian Economic Review*, 31 (2) (1998): 130–44.

Maughan, C. *Markets of London* (London: Pitman, 1931).

McIntosh, M. K. 'The Diversity of Social Capital in English Communities, 1300–1640 (With a Glance at Modern Nigeria)', *Journal of Interdisciplinary History*, 29 (3) (1999): 459–90.

Meredith D. and Dyster, B. *Australia in the Global Economy* (New York: Cambridge University Press, 1999).

Merrett, D. T. 'Capital Markets and Capital Formation in Australia, 1890–1945', *Australian Economic History Review*, 37 (3) (1997): 181–201.

Merrett, D. T. 'Capital Markets and Capital Formation in Australia, 1945-90', *Australian Economic History Review*, 38 (2) (1998): 135–54.

Muldrew, C. *The Economy of Obligation: The Culture of Credit and Social Relations in Early Modern England* (Basingstoke: Macmillan, 1998).

Nicholas, S. 'Reinterpreting the Convict Labour Market', *Australian Economic History Review*, 30 (2) (1990): 50–66.

North, D. C. and Thomas, R. P. *Rise of the Western World: A New Economic History* (Cambridge: Cambridge University Press, 1973).

North, D. C. *Structure and Change in Economic History* (New York: Norton, 1981).

North, D. C. and Weingast, B. R. 'Constitutions and Commitment: The Evolution of Institutions Governing Public Choice in Seventeenth-Century England', *Journal of Economic History*, 49 (4) (1989): 803–32.

North, D. C. *Institutions, Institutional Change and Economic Performance* (Cambridge: Cambridge University Press, 1990).

North, D. C. 'Institutions and Credible Commitment', *Journal of Institutional and Theoretical Economics*, 149 (1) (1993): 11–23.

North, D. C. *Understanding the Process of Economic Change*, London, Institute of Economic Affairs for the Wincott Foundation, Occasional Paper No. 106 (1999).

Ogilvie, S. *A Bitter Living: Women, Markets, and Social Capital in Early Modern Germany* (New York: Oxford University Press, 2003).

Olson, M. *Australia in the Perspective of the Rise and Decline of Nations*. Canberra, Centre for Economic Policy Research, Australian National University, Discussion Paper No. 109 (1984).

Oxley, D. *Convict Maids: The Forced Migration of Women to Australia* (Melbourne: Cambridge University Press, 1996).

Perkins, J. 'German Shipping and Australia Before the First World War', *Australian Economic History Review*, 29 (1) (1989): 42–59.

Purcell, W. R. 'The Development of Japan's Trading Company Network in Australia, 1890–1941', *Australian Economic History Review* 21 (2) (1981): 114–32.

Putnam, R. D. *Bowling Alone: The Collapse and Revival of American Community* (New York: Simon & Schuster, 2000).

Reserve Bank of Australia. 'Privatisation in Australia', *Reserve Bank of Australia* Bulletin, December (1997) http://www.rba.gov.au/PublicationsAndResearch/Bulletin/bu_dec97/bu_1297_2.pdf.

Roberts, S. H. *The Squatting Age in Australia, 1835–47* (Melbourne: Melbourne University Press, 1935).

Rosenberg, N. and Birdzell, L. E. *How the West Grew Rich. The Economic Transformation of the Industrial World* (New York: Basic Books, 1986).

Salsbury, S. and Sweeney, K. *The Bull, the Bear and the Kangaroo: The History of the Sydney Stock Exchange* (Sydney: Allen & Unwin, 1988).

Schedvin, C. B. *Shaping Science and Industry: A History of Australia's Council for Scientific and Industrial Research* (Sydney: Allen & Unwin, 1987).

Shlomovitz, R. 'Convict Workers: A Review Article', *Australian Economic History Review*, 30 (2) (1990): 67–88.

Swan, K. *A History of Wagga Wagga* (Wagga: City Council, 1970).

Tsokhas, K. *Markets, Money & Empire. The Political Economy of the Australian Wool Industry* (Melbourne: Melbourne University Press, 1990).

Tweedie, S. *Trading Partners. Australia and Asia, 1790-1993* (Sydney: University of New South Wales Press, 1994).

Ville, S. 'The Relocation of the International Market for Australian Wool', *Australian Economic History Review*, 45 (1) (2005): 73–95.

Ville, S. 'Social Capital: An Insight Revealed or a Concept Too Many?', *Working Papers in Economics*, (University of Wollongong, 2004).

Ville, S. *The Rural Entrepreneurs. A History of the Stock and Station Agent Industry in Australia and New Zealand* (Melbourne: Cambridge University Press, 2000).

Ville, S. 'Business Development in Colonial Australia', *Australian Economic History Review*, 38 (1) (1998): 16–41.

Ville, S. and Merrett, D. T. 'The Development of Large Scale Enterprise in Australia, 1910–64', *Business History*, 42 (3) (2000): 13–46.

White, C. *Mastering Risk. Environment, Markets and Politics in Australian Economic History* (Melbourne: Oxford University Press, 1992).

Wilkins, M. 'The Free-Standing Company 1870–1914: An Important Type of British Foreign Direct Investment', *Economic History Review*, 2nd ser., 41 (2) (1988): 259–82.

7
The Deep Determinants of Long-run Growth and Economic Development

P. Dorian Owen and Clayton R. Weatherston

7.1 Introduction

As conventionally measured by per capita GDP (gross domestic product), average living standards in the richest countries in the world are estimated to be more than one hundred times greater than those in the poorest countries.[1] Why are some countries so much poorer than others and what can be done to reduce such differences? A definitive explanation of this staggering variation is the 'holy grail' of modern macroeconomics, not least because important insights could potentially lead to drastic improvements in the welfare of a large proportion of the world's population.

A recent wave of influential empirical studies in the economics literature has attempted to identify the fundamental factors that underpin long-term economic growth and development and that account for such large differences in average living standards across countries. The key contenders are a country's geographical characteristics, the quality of its institutions, the extent of its integration with world markets, and differences in culture. Existing empirical studies have attempted to evaluate how much of the overall variation in per capita real income levels across countries can be explained by representative proxies for some or all of these factors and, because each has different implications for policy, to assess their relative importance. Most of the recent debate has centred on the roles of institutions versus geography, an emphasis that is reflected in our discussion.

The aim of this chapter is to provide an accessible critical overview of this literature, emphasizing the basic arguments that lie behind the statistical exercises and the various attempts to make statements about the relative strength of causal relationships. In Section 7.2, we consider the nature of 'proximate' versus 'fundamental' or 'deep' determinants of development, briefly summarize the various mechanisms by which the candidate deep determinants affect development, and outline the main proxy measures used in the empirical studies. In Section 7.3, we discuss the methods used to distinguish empirically between the effects on per capita real income of the different hypothesized deep determinants. We also examine the extent to which useful conclusions can be obtained in practice, given the nature of the data used and the endogeneity of, for example, institutions and openness. In Section 7.4 we critically review some of the key contributions in this literature. The different studies produce conflicting results, which we attribute, at least partly, to a failure in modelling methodology. Section 7.5 contains concluding comments.

7.2 'Proximate' versus fundamental determinants

Much of the research on economic growth in the last 25 years has adopted a 'production function' approach to try to explain variations in rates of economic growth and levels of development across different countries and across time. Following Solow (1956, 1957), this relates a country's aggregate output (typically measured by real GDP) to the level of its inputs into the productive process, as illustrated in Figure 7.1. These inputs, or factors of production, include physical capital (machinery, factories, and infrastructure), labour (the number of workers or hours worked), human capital (reflecting the quality of the human inputs into production due to the level of education, on-the-job training and health status), and technology (the available knowledge about how to produce output). From this point of view, *growth* of output

Inputs	→	Aggregate Production Function	→	Output
Physical Capital (K)		$Y=f(K,L,H,A...)$		GDP (Y)
Labour (L)				
Human Capital (H)				
Technology (A)				

Figure 7.1 Determination of aggregate output – the production function approach

arises due to the *growth* of inputs into the production process, particularly technological change and the accumulation of physical and human capital.

This type of decomposition can allow us to determine empirically, for example, that the United States is richer than Chad because the United States has a higher rate of physical capital investment and a more highly educated labour force, and uses these inputs more efficiently. However, while such an analysis provides useful insights, it does not fully explain the underlying sources of the United States' advantages in producing output, and raises as many questions as it answers. For example, why has the United States saved and invested more than Chad and so accumulated higher levels of physical and human capital? Why does the United States use its inputs more efficiently than Chad?

Lower rates of accumulation of physical and human capital, technological backwardness and inefficiency in the use of the factors of production can themselves be viewed as *outcomes*, and thus are often labelled 'proximate determinants' of aggregate output.[2] There must be some more *fundamental* or *deeper* underlying factors that lead to these outcomes which, in turn, lead to the divergence in economic well-being across nations. To try to get to the root of this, a recent body of literature has evolved that distinguishes between the proximate determinants of differences in living standards across countries (such as physical and human capital accumulation and technology) and the deep, fundamental or ultimate factors that determine the proximate determinants and, consequently, income levels.

The search for deep determinants of investment, technology and efficiency has focused on relatively slowly changing, durable characteristics that have a pervasive effect on a country's economy over extended periods of time. These include a country's geography, the quality of its institutions, the extent to which it is integrated into the international trading system, and a society's culture, reflected in its attitudes, beliefs and values.

7.2.1 Geography and economic development

There is a long tradition of emphasizing the importance of geography for economic development; the French philosopher Montesquieu ([1748], 1977, Book XIV: 243), for example, noted that 'people are . . . more vigorous in cold climates'. However, despite a succession of authors examining the implications of factors such as temperature, humidity, rainfall, soil quality and the presence of rivers (Marshall, 1890; Gilfillan, 1920; Huntington, 1924; Wittfogel, 1957; Kamarck, 1976), geographical variables were, initially, largely ignored in most of the empirical work on economic growth in the 1990s (see the surveys by Barro and Sala-i-Martin (1995) and Durlauf and Quah (1999)).[3] More recently, the role of geography has been re-emphasized (Diamond, 1997; Landes, 1998; Parker, 2000). Among economists, 'geographical fundamentalism' is most strongly associated with Jeffrey Sachs and his colleagues (Bloom and Sachs, 1998; Gallup *et al.*, 1999; Gallup *et al.*, 2003; McArthur and Sachs, 2001; Masters and McMillan, 2001; Sachs, 2001, 2003a, b; Sachs and Malaney, 2002).

There are many dimensions of geography, and these can influence economic development through a range of different mechanisms.[4] Geography can affect a country's openness to international trade through its access to the coast, which determines its ability to ship goods by sea, and its proximity or remoteness with respect to major markets (Gallup *et al.*, 1999).

Climate directly affects work effort and hence agricultural productivity, while the incidence of diseases has an impact on the quality of labour inputs (Schultz and Tansel, 1997; Gallup *et al.*, 1999). Sachs and Malaney (2002) discuss the multiple channels through which malaria, in particular, has adverse effects on economic development. As well as medical costs and income forgone due to morbidity-induced reductions in worker productivity and premature mortality, malaria also has indirect effects through higher fertility rates and consequent reductions in investment in education (especially for girls), decreased household saving, reduced labour mobility, and reduced foreign investment and tourism.[5] Masters and McMillan (2001) emphasize the positive influence of climates that produce frost, which kills exposed organisms detrimental to human, animal and plant health, which, in turn, improves the productivity of investment in human capital and agriculture. Poor health directly reduces the acquisition of human capital, via reduced attendance at school (Bleakley, 2002; Miguel and Kremer, 2004) and impairment of cognitive development and learning ability (Sachs and Malaney, 2002), and as a direct result of the shorter horizons over which to reap the benefits from such investment because life expectancy is reduced (Becker, 1993).

Resource endowments (including water, soil fertility, minerals, and energy resources) can also affect the path of development, although there is much debate about why the abundance of natural resources spurs economic growth in some countries but appears to be a 'curse' in others (Sachs and Warner, 1995; Engerman and Sokoloff, 1997, 2002).

Diamond (1997) argues that the emergence of sedentary agriculture was first initiated in mid-latitude areas where the biogeographical potential in terms of suitable plants and animals for domestication was most favourable. This allowed societies to move out of a hunter-gatherer lifestyle, to acquire immunity to animal-borne diseases and to develop a non-food producing sector of the economy so that people could specialize, study to accumulate human capital, and advance their technology and their political and economic institutions. In addition, the East–West axis of Eurasia (as opposed to the North–South axis of the African and American continents) meant that animal and plant species and advances in agricultural technology were more easily diffused across areas with a similar climate. This, in turn, induced a sustained process of institutional development. According to Diamond, the key in explaining these outcomes was geography.

Overall, the *geography hypothesis* maintains that the climate, topography, landmass orientation, rivers, access to the sea, location, geology, ecology and prevalence of diseases of a nation profoundly influence the incentives, technologies and outcomes in a society. On this view, natural geographical factors are the primary fundamental determinants of the wealth of nations. This does not necessarily imply that 'geography is destiny', as Bonaparte is reputed to have observed, but it does mean that environment-specific types of investment may be required to overcome, for example, malaria in tropical areas or inaccessibility and high transport costs in landlocked countries (Sachs, 2003b).

Various measures of geography have been used in the deep-determinants empirical literature, both as possible deep determinants in their own right and as sources of exogenous variation in institutions. Given that many of the world's poorest countries are located in the tropics, as illustrated in Figure 7.2, a commonly used proxy for geography is distance from the equator (Acemoglu *et al.*, 2001; Easterly and Levine, 2003; Olsson and Hibbs, 2005). Other geography measures include the proportion of the population living with the risk of malaria transmission (Acemoglu *et al.*, 2001; Sachs, 2003a; Rodrik *et al.*, 2004; Batten and Martina, 2007), whether a country is landlocked (Easterly and Levine, 2003), the proportion of the land area (or population) within 100 km of the coast (Sachs, 2003a; Carstensen and Gundlach, 2006), mean temperature (Acemoglu *et al.*, 2001), frost prevalence (Masters and McMillan, 2001), whether the continent has an East–West (as opposed to North–South) axis (Olsson and Hibbs, 2005), the share of the population in temperate climate zones (Sachs, 2001, 2003a), continent size (Olsson and Hibbs, 2005), the number of plants and domesticable animals known to exist in prehistoric times (Olsson and Hibbs, 2005), and whether a country produces certain crops (Easterly and Levine, 2003).

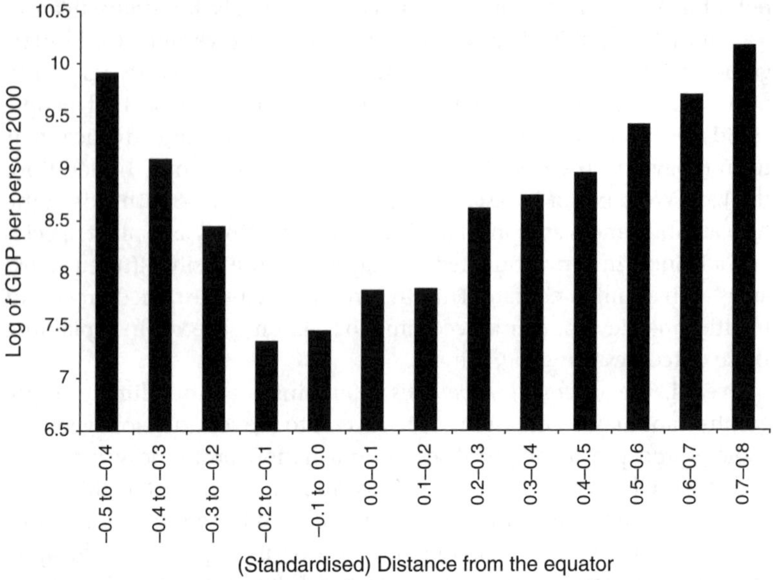

Figure 7.2 Countries further from the Equator have higher incomes
Data sources: Standardized distance from the Equator from La Porta *et al.* (1999); GDP per person from Olsson and Hibbs (2005).

While covering a range of dimensions of geography, this list is clearly not exhaustive.

7.2.2 Institutions and economic development

The *institutions hypothesis* maintains that institutions, interpreted as 'the rules of the game in a society … the humanly devised constraints that shape human interaction' (North, 1990: 3), 'are the underlying determinant of the long-run performance of economies' (North, 1990: 107). This view also has a long history (Smith [1776], 1976) and has experienced a recent major revival in the economics literature. The 'institutionalist' school in economics emphasizes the importance of property rights, legal systems and the rule of law, land tenure, political stability, and other formal and informal social institutions (Engerman and Sokoloff, 1997, 2002; Hall and Jones, 1999; Acemoglu *et al.*, 2001, 2005; Djankov *et al.*, 2003).

These factors had been neglected for some time because it was previously felt that such institutions developed *as a result of* economic development, but the institutions hypothesis argues that institutions are a *causal determinant* of growth and development. Institutions are seen as a deep determinant because they mainly change relatively slowly over time (Williamson, 2000) and because they affect the incentives to accumulate physical and human capital, and to innovate and adopt new technology, thus having an important effect on the proximate determinants of output. Consequently, 'Third World countries are poor because the institutional constraints define a set of payoffs to political and economic activity that do not encourage productive activity' (North, 1990: 110). 'Good institutions' are generally regarded as having three main characteristics: (1) security of property rights for a broad coverage of individuals in society; (2) effective constraints on the abilities of powerful subgroups or elites (including politicians) to expropriate the returns from production; and (3) some degree of equality of opportunity applying to a broad cross section of society (Acemoglu *et al.*, 2005).

There are different views on how institutions have developed to produce, for example, different degrees of protection of property rights. The *legal origin* viewpoint emphasizes historic differences in legal traditions as the main reason for cross-country differences in property rights (La Porta *et al.*, 1998, 1999). It highlights the difference between English common law and French civil law, which developed to reflect the historical contexts in their host countries and spread to become the most widely used legal systems worldwide. Common law places more emphasis on private property rights and, because of its greater reliance on jurisprudence, is also regarded as more flexible in responding to a changing economy; it is therefore argued to be more favourable for economic development (Levine, 2005).

An alternative view maintains that differences in *endowments*, such as climate, disease environment, crops, and natural resources, affected the type of institutions developed. For example, Acemoglu *et al.* (2001) emphasize the importance of disease environment for European colonization strategies. They argue that where settler mortality rates were high because of an unfavourable disease environment, as in many parts of Africa and Latin America, European colonists set up *extractive colonies*. Rather than settling in large numbers and establishing institutions that protected property rights for a broad coverage of the population, they concentrated on extracting the returns to be made from minerals, plantation crops and other natural resources for the benefit of the privileged colonizing minority elite, often using slave labour, as in the Caribbean, or forced indigenous labour, as in Central America. By contrast, where settler mortality rates were low, because of a more favourable disease environment, colonizers settled in larger numbers and brought with them or created institutions that enforced property rights for the bulk of the population, limited the power of the state, and avoided creating extreme inequality in wealth and income. Classic examples of such *settler colonies* are Australia, Canada, New Zealand and the United States. Whereas Acemoglu *et al.* (2001) focus on the disease environment, Engerman and Sokoloff (1997, 2002) emphasize mineral and crop endowments as the driving force behind the choice of extractive versus settler colonies. Abundance of minerals and crops such as sugarcane, tobacco and cotton, allied with dense indigenous population, encouraged plantation agriculture, slave labour, and inequality; by contrast, endowments suited to grain and livestock, combined with sparse population, promoted more egalitarian family farming.

A crucial part of the argument is that the early institutions persisted after the end of colonization and so continued to have long-lasting effects on current institutions and economic activity that endure to the present day. In short, favourable disease environments and/or grain and livestock endowments initially made for 'good' institutions, whereas unfavourable environments and/or minerals and plantation crops led to 'bad' institutions, and these largely endured to affect current living standards. Although this view of the development of institutions emphasizes the role of geographical endowments, it differs crucially from the geography view in arguing that any effect of geography is *indirect*; it is only to the extent that geography affects institutions that geography has any effect on development.

The concept of 'institutions' is multifaceted and includes the working of markets, contract enforceability, bureaucratic efficiency, risk of expropriation, infrastructure quality, and repudiation of contracts by government; not surprisingly, such a broad concept is hard to pin down empirically. The empirical literature has adopted a variety of different measures of institutions. The most common are survey-based assessments of institutional quality and/or government effectiveness. Such measures are typically derived from sources such as the Political Risk Services (PRS) Group's International Country Risk Guide (ICRG), Business Environment Risk Intelligence (BERI), or the Economist Intelligence Unit, and are based on assessments by experts of different aspects of the institutional environment, such as corruption, law and order, and the protection of property rights.

For example, in their proxy for social infrastructure, Hall and Jones (1999) include a measure of government anti-diversionary policies (which includes data from the ICRG on law and order, bureaucratic quality, corruption, the risk of expropriation and government repudiation of contracts). Acemoglu *et al.* (2001, 2002) adopt the extent of legal protection of private property and enforcement of such laws as a proxy for institutions. They use the ICRG measure of protection against expropriation risk of private foreign investment by government.

Another data set that has been widely used to measure institutional quality is that of Kaufmann *et al.* (2002, 2004, 2005) who construct composite indices of six different dimensions of institutional quality (voice and accountability, political stability and the absence of violence/corruption, government effectiveness, 'light' regulatory burden, rule of law, freedom from graft) from ratings by country experts (including the ICRG and BERI) and surveys. The Kaufmann *et al.* data on institutions are used, for example, by Rodrik *et al.* (2004) and Easterly and Levine (2003).

An alternative, and less commonly used, set of measures aims to capture the limits on executive power of political leaders. The primary data source for a measure of such constraints is the Polity IV data set compiled by Jaggers and Marshall (2000).[6] Some measures focus on constitutional or electoral rules, such as the 'plurality' and proportional representation variables constructed by Beck *et al.* (2001).

7.2.3 Other potential deep determinants of economic development

'Openness' (reflecting the degree of integration with world markets) is often argued to be a key force driving improvements in productivity and living standards (Frankel and Romer, 1999; Brunner, 2003). Standard economic theory suggests that the effects are ambiguous as efficiency gains from trade can be offset by the implications of reallocating resources in response to changing relative prices of tradable goods. More recent analysis identifies a wider set of mechanisms that can enhance the positive effects of openness on growth, such as market-size effects boosting R&D, the possibility of international R&D spillovers, and access to imported inputs embodying new technology (see Helpman (2004: chapter 5) and Brunner (2003) for a more detailed discussion of the theory and the conflicting views that emerge from the empirical growth literature). Measures of openness are included in some of the empirical deep-determinants studies, usually the ratio of trade (exports plus imports) to GDP, or Sachs and Warner's (1995) index of openness.[7]

Culture, despite its role in shaping beliefs, values, social norms, and preferences in a society, and its relatively slowly changing nature as it is transmitted across generations, has received less attention in the economics literature, perhaps because of its very broad nature and the difficulty of specifying and testing precise, refutable hypotheses (Guiso *et al.*, 2006). The main focus in the empirical growth literature is the role of religion in influencing growth, echoing the long-held view that certain religions, specifically Protestantism following Weber ([1904], 1930), are more conducive to growth. Reflecting this view, some of the empirical studies of deep determinants include religion variables, although primarily as controls rather than as a main focus of interest. Acemoglu *et al.* (2005) dismiss evidence of a causal effect of religion on economic growth on the grounds that 'religious beliefs are endogenous, both to economic outcomes and to other fundamental causes of income differences'. In itself, this is not entirely convincing given that exactly the same concern applies to economic institutions, their preferred deep determinant, as discussed below.

The importance of sound macroeconomic policy (including fiscal and monetary policy) for growth rates and current economic development has long been championed by multilateral development institutions such as the OECD, IMF, and World Bank. Reflecting this, some studies, for example Easterly and Levine (2003), include a range of macroeconomic policy variables (such as budget deficits and inflation rates) as determinants of income levels. However, Rodrik *et al.* (2004) argue that policy actions are better matched with macroeconomic aggregates measured over the short term; therefore, such policy variables are better included in regressions explaining cross-country *growth* rates, whereas institutions representing the cumulative impact of a series of policy actions are more appropriately included in models explaining income *levels*.

As most of the debate in the empirical literature on deep determinants has centred on the relative importance of geography and institutions, we focus on these in the discussion that follows.

7.3 Geography versus institutions: An empirical contest

How can we empirically distinguish between the competing 'geography versus institutions' views? At face value, the distribution of (the natural logarithm of) levels of GDP per capita by latitude appears to lend strong support to the geography view. Tropical regions, on average, have low levels of GDP per capita, whereas countries in higher latitudes have higher income levels, giving rise to what Theil and Chen (1996) termed the 'Equatorial Grand Canyon' representation of cross-country variation in GDP per capita (see Figure 7.2). However, while there is a strong correlation between latitude and average income levels, this does not, in itself, prove causation. There are many different explanations about why different aspects of geography affect development (the endowments variant of the institutions hypothesis provides one such alternative to the direct effect of geography), and there are usually exceptions (for example, Singapore and Hong Kong).

Geography is arguably 'as exogenous a determinant as an economist can ever hope to get' (Rodrik *et al.*, 2004: 133) in the taxonomy of deep determinants. However, this is not even necessarily true for all aspects of geography. The ability of humans to suppress diseases, such as malaria, increases with development. Similarly, the harvesting and exhaustion of natural resources will be partly determined by need, availability of technology and/or substitutes, and environmental policies. This endogeneity can give rise to an econometric problem when, for example, using malaria burden as a measure of the exogenous effect of geography in cross-country empirical studies.

'Institutionalists' point to the *reversal of fortune* as an important argument against the geography hypothesis (Acemoglu *et al.*, 2002). Former European colonies that were relatively wealthy in 1500, before colonization (for example, Bolivia), are among the less well off today, and former colonies that are relatively wealthy today (for example, New Zealand) were poor in 1500.[8] At face value, this constitutes a natural experiment because geography is held constant. The changes in economic fortunes are argued to stem from systematic changes in institutions brought about during colonization. However, critics of this view argue that the only spectacular reversal of fortune involved the four 'neo-European' British colonies (Australia, Canada, New Zealand, and the United States) and question whether initial institutions are always reliable predictors of current institutions, especially for constraint measures such as the limits on executive powers of political leaders (Przeworski, 2004a, b).

Plots of GDP per capita against measures of the quality of institutions (Figure 7.3) also reveal a strong association. As well as the same sorts of concerns raised about the latitude–GDP correlations, there is a further problem with institutions. Institutions, being 'humanly devised', are at least partly endogenously determined by a variety of factors, including the level of income of the country.[9] Richer countries can afford higher-quality institutions; poorer countries have fewer resources available for building institutions. This suggests that institutions co-evolve with a country's wealth. The possibility of reverse causality makes it difficult to look at the association in Figure 7.3 and separate out the effects of institutions on GDP per capita from the effects of GDP per capita on institutions.

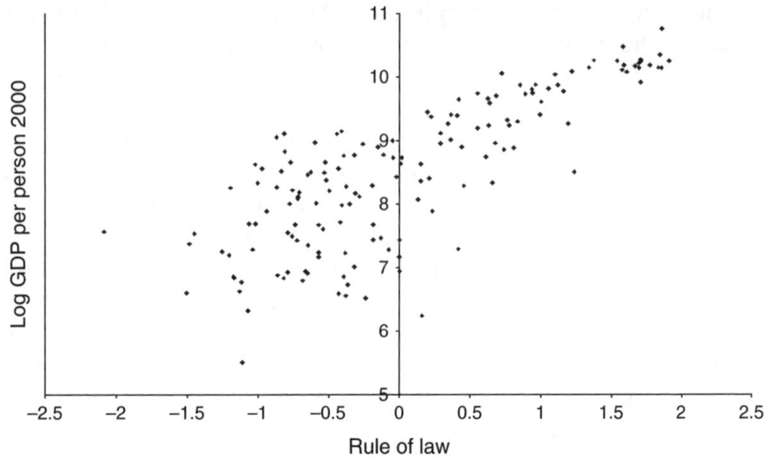

Figure 7.3 Countries with better institutions have higher incomes
Data sources: Rule of Law index from Kaufmann *et al.* (2002); GDP per person from Olsson and Hibbs (2005).

In the deep determinants literature, exogeneity is therefore not considered a necessary requirement for a deep determinant, otherwise geography would presumably dominate by default. To some critics, the endogeneity of institutions is a critical weakness of the whole exercise, arguing that '[i]nstitutions are not a deeper cause than the supply of factors or technology' (Przeworski, 2004a: 184). A less extreme interpretation of this would be that the decision to focus on institutions (which can be interpreted as an aspect of technology, *A*, in Figure 7.1) but exclude other endogenous inputs into the production function (such as human capital) is based on other perceptions, such as relative stability over time.

However, concerns about endogeneity are exacerbated by the choice of the hierarchical level of institutions examined and the nature of the proxy variables chosen. In terms of Williamson's (2000) classification scheme for institutions, these studies focus on 'Level 2' institutions, formal rules defining property rights and the legal system, rather than deeper 'Level 1' institutions, primarily informal institutions, such as traditions, norms, and customs. The former are interpreted as changing over a relatively long horizon (10–100 years) but are at least partly endogenous. The latter are perceived as normally changing over very long horizons (hundreds or even thousands of years) and are more plausibly interpreted as exogenous; they are therefore more reasonable choices for deep determinants, given the emphasis on persistence as a characteristic of deep determinants, but they overlap with aspects of culture and are difficult to measure.

The problem of lack of exogeneity is made worse by the widespread use in this literature of what are essentially *outcome* measures of the Level 2 institutional set-up rather than descriptive or classificatory variables that reflect the *constraints* imposed by the institutions (Glaeser *et al.*, 2004). Glaeser *et al.* (2004) argue that institutions should reflect constraints on government and be permanent, or at least durable, features of the economic environment (that is, better fit the criteria for a deep determinant). Indeed, Glaeser *et al.* (2004) and *The Economist* (2004) question the validity of the measures used in the literature to quantify 'institutional quality'. Subjective investor survey-based indicators and even the measures of constraints on the executive from Polity IV, discussed in Section 7.2.2, not only tend to improve with increases in real per capita GDP, that is are endogenous, but may reflect the results of governments' behaviour and not permanent and durable features of the economic environment.[10] Indeed, in Argentina the standard indices of 'institutions' fluctuate wildly with the electoral cycle, which is clearly not a desirable feature for a variable purporting to measure a deep determinant (*The Economist*, 2004). Also, lower levels of bureaucratic constraints on government are not necessarily disadvantageous (as is the presumption) for institutional quality because dictators can choose to secure property rights without enshrining this in rules. Indeed, Glaeser *et al.* (2004: 285) conclude that 'objective measures of institutions, those that actually describe the constitutional rules that limit the power of the sovereign, have no predictive power for the growth of per capita income'.

Although it is recognized that economic development is a complex phenomenon, recent empirical studies have estimated simple models using data for a broad cross section of countries to attempt to evaluate the overall and relative importance of geography versus institutions in explaining cross-country variations in income levels. These studies aim to give a 'big picture' generalization on the importance of the various factors based on the large variation observable in samples that include countries covering widely differing levels of development. Compared to detailed case studies of experience in individual countries or comparative historical analyses, cross-country econometric analyses consign potentially important individual-country effects into the implied error terms in the models, but, unlike many case studies, they are based on an (admittedly simple) explicit analytical framework, allow researchers to control for other relevant factors, and provide a way of quantifying the average effect of the deep determinants on income levels.

However, there are clearly limitations inherent in such cross-country analyses (Bardhan, 2005; Pande and Udry, 2005), including concerns over the lack of consistency in the quality of the data and the coverage of variables of interest across countries at different levels of development; lack of coverage can lead to overly parsimonious models and omitted variables bias. Also, cross-country analyses do not allow for heterogeneity in the implementation of institutions at a local level within a country, for example across regions or individuals.

To attempt to deal with reverse causality, it is necessary to find something that provides an exogenous explanation of the variation in institutions across countries that is unaffected by a country's level of development. In econometric terms, instrumental variables (IV) estimation provides a method for consistently estimating the effect of institutions on GDP per capita in situations such as this where ordinary least squares (OLS) regressions yield biased and inconsistent estimates. In order to provide desirable statistical properties, IV estimation requires variables to act as instruments that are relevant (that is, are highly correlated with the endogenous deep determinant, such as institutions) and exogenous (in the sense that they are uncorrelated with the model's error term).

Hall and Jones (1999), in one of the earliest cross-country studies to hypothesize that the fundamental determinant of a country's long-run economic performance is the quality of its institutions, provide an illustration of how this works in the context of an extremely parsimonious (and surely oversimplified) model:

$$\log(Y/L) = \alpha + \beta S + \varepsilon \tag{7.1}$$

$$S = \gamma + \delta \log(Y/L) + \theta X + \eta \tag{7.2}$$

where S is a measure of social infrastructure, Y/L is output per worker and X is a vector of exogenous variables that affect S but do not *directly* affect Y/L (an exclusion restriction with respect to Equation (7.1)). If these X variables are relevant, that is have a non-trivial role in explaining cross-country variation in S ($\theta \neq 0$), and exogenous, that is are uncorrelated with ε in Equation (7.1), then they would make ideal instruments as they can be used to isolate the exogenous variation in S, uncorrelated with ε, and use this variation to estimate β, the effect of S on Y/L. Hall and Jones, in their choice of instrumental variables, rely on various measures of the extent of Western European influence including distance from the equator, the fraction of a country's population speaking one of the five major Western European languages (English, French, German, Portuguese or Spanish), and the fraction of the population speaking English as their first language.[11] A concern, noted by Acemoglu *et al.* (2001), McArthur and Sachs (2001), and Olsson and Hibbs (2005), with, for example, using distance from the equator as an instrument is that a country's latitude will affect its agricultural productivity, and thus does not satisfy the exclusion restriction (that is, it has a direct effect on income levels over and above its effect on institutions); this compromises the consistency of the estimate of β in Equation (7.1). The search for appropriate instruments for endogenous deep determinants of income levels is, therefore, a major challenge.

The endowments variant of the institutions hypothesis provides a clever way of approaching the instrumentation problem. Acemoglu *et al.* (2001) use data on the mortality of settlers in the colonies, which should be exogenous with respect to current institutions, as predictors of the institutions established during colonization, which, they argue, persist. So, settler mortality should provide an exogenous source of variation that can explain current institutions. Although very innovative and widely used, there are some potential problems with this approach. Settler mortality is correlated with the present-day disease environment, which is likely to have a direct effect on current GDP per capita that has nothing to do with institutions. Also, settlers took with them human capital, which in itself would have fostered economic development and institution building, so the linkages involved are far from unambiguous (Glaeser *et al.*, 2004). Olsson (2004) argues that the colonial story behind the settler mortality instrument, while plausible for Asian and neo-European colonies, is not relevant for the heterogeneous process of settling in mainly Latin American colonies (in the period 1500–1830) and primarily African colonies set up after 1885. Also, in the 1500s, well-developed property rights institutions barely existed in Europe, so that the 'assignment' of extractive versus productive institutions was not a feasible option, regardless of the disease environment encountered.[12]

7.4 Empirical studies on the deep determinants of income levels

Table 7.1 provides a summary of the specifications and key findings of some of the main empirical studies in this literature. Notwithstanding concerns about whether the instruments used are adequate, the results

Table 7.1 Primary empirical studies on the deep determinants of income per capita

Study	Institutions variable (Instrument)	Trade variable (Instrument)	Geography variable (Instrument)	Other controls	Base sample	Key findings
Hall and Jones (1999)	*SOCINF* (***ENGFRAC***, ***EURFRAC***, ***LATITUDE***)	*YRSOPEN*, component of *SOCINF* (**ln*FR***)	*LATITUDE* (in robustness check only)	No	127 countries	'Differences in social infrastructure across countries cause … large differences in income across countries.' (p. 114)
Acemoglu *et al.* (2001)	*EXPROP* (**ln*SETTMORT***)	–	*LATITUDE*, *TEMPERATURE*, *SOILQUAL*, *NATRESC*, *LANDLOCK*, *HUMIDITY*, *MALFAL94* (*Not instrumented*)	Yes	64 ex-colonies	Settler mortality acts as an instrument for modern institutions. '[W]e estimate large effects of institutions on income per capita. Once the effect of institutions is controlled for, countries in Africa or those closer to the equator do not have lower incomes.' (p. 1369)
Easterly and Levine (2003)	*INSTINDEX* (**ln*SETTMORT***, ***LATITUDE***, ***LANDLOCK***, ***CROPS/ MINERALS***)	*YRSOPEN* (*Generic instrument set*)	Omitted from second-stage regressions	Yes	72 ex-colonies	'[T]ropics, germs, and crops do not explain economic development beyond their impact on institutions.' (p. 35)

Sachs (2003)	*EXPROP*, *INSTINDEX*, *RULELAW* (in turn) (**ln*SETTMORT***, ***KGPTEMP***)	–	*POP100KM*, *MALFAL94* or *MAL94P* (***ME***)	No	*EXPROP*: 59 ex-colonies, *INSTINDEX*: 62 ex-colonies, *RULELAW*: 69 ex-colonies	'[M]alaria transmission, which is strongly affected by ecological conditions, directly affects the level of per capita income after controlling for the quality of institutions.' (p. 1)
Rodrik *et al.* (2004)	*RULELAW* (**ln*SETTMORT***)	ln(*TRADE/GDP*) (**ln*FR***)	*LATITUDE*	Yes	79 ex-colonies	'The quality of institutions "trumps" everything else.' (p. 131)
Olsson and Hibbs (2005)	*POLENV* or *SOCINF* (*not instrumented*)	*YRSOPEN*, component of *SOCINF* (*not instrumented*)	*BIOCON* or *GEOCON*	No	102 countries (excl. Neo-Europes and extractive)	'[A]s much as half of the ... international variation in log output per person can be explained by ... exogenous geography and prehistoric biology ... robust to controls for political and institutional variables.' (p. 936)

Notes: The dependent variable is commonly log of GDP per capita (or a variant such as log of GDP per worker) in a single year (most commonly 1995, but varying from 1988 to 1997). 'Instrument' (in bold) denotes a variable in the first-stage regression that is excluded from the second-stage regression in IV estimation; it is included in the instrument set for its particular relevance for the endogenous regressor to which it is attached in parentheses. Variables are defined in the Appendix to Table 7.1.

from the earliest influential studies (Acemoglu *et al.*, 2001; Easterly and Levine, 2003; Rodrik *et al.*, 2004) reached a strong consensus indicating that, although geographic conditions affect development, they have done so only through their impact on the development of different types of institutions; after controlling for institutional quality, geography appears to have little direct effect on income. This early evidence, therefore, strongly supports the institutions hypothesis.

As a counter example, however, Sachs (2003a) demonstrates that a measure of malaria transmission is statistically significant when added to representative specifications from these three studies, implying that geographical variables do have a direct effect on GDP per capita as well as an indirect effect via institutions. In a similar vein, Carstensen and Gundlach (2006) and Presbitero (2006) report results that support this view of the broader influence of geography. Also, Olsson and Hibbs (2005) formalize and empirically test Diamond's (1997) hypotheses on the biogeographic determinants of relative levels of development; their results provide strong support for the importance of geographic and prehistoric biogeography in explaining cross-country variation in levels of income per capita, even after controlling for the effect of institutions. From a different perspective, Glaeser *et al.* (2004) criticize the view that institutions cause growth by arguing that the indicators of institutional quality used in the empirical studies are inappropriate, as noted in Section 7.2, and that human capital is more important and less volatile than conventional measures of institutions. Overall, the initial apparent consensus on the primacy of institutions has therefore been undone by more recent empirical work.

At least part of the explanation for this diversity of conclusions stems from the differences in coverage, in terms of explanatory variables, of the different model specifications. This literature considers only relatively few categories of deep determinants; despite this, the various studies do not all include representative proxies from each of these broad categories. Some earlier studies (for example, Ram, 1997) examine the relationship between income levels and distance from the equator, but do not control for other deep determinants. Acemoglu *et al.* (2001) focus on the role of institutions and, in some regressions, control for geographical determinants, but not for the effects of integration. Measures of integration are also given little or no attention in the studies by Easterly and Levine (2003), Carstensen and Gundlach (2006) and Presbitero (2006). In contrast, Frankel and Romer (1999), Irwin and Terviö (2002), and Brunner (2003) focus on the effects of trade and integration on cross-country income levels; they control for some aspects of geography, such as area and latitude, but not for institutions. Both the studies by Alcalá and Ciccone (2004) and Dollar and Kraay (2003) focus on the partial effects of institutions and trade.[13]

Rodrik *et al.* (2004) criticize Acemoglu *et al.* (2001) and Frankel and Romer (1999) for not embedding their specifications in a broader framework. Rodrik *et al.* (2004) run a 'horse race' between institutions, trade and geography; they examine the relative significance of each in the determination of income, using the Frankel and Romer (1999) instrument for trade and the Acemoglu *et al.* (2001) settler mortality instrument.[14] Although this framework is broader than many of the other studies in including three potential deep determinants, it still reduces the multifaceted aspects of geography and institutions to a single measure of each.

Studies that include a richer menu of geographical or institutional variables tend to be less well developed in other dimensions. Acemoglu and Johnson (2005) 'unbundle' institutions and include proxies for both 'property rights institutions' and 'contracting institutions' but additional control variables in their empirical specifications are limited to including, in separate regressions, latitude, religion variables, or macroeconomic policy variables. Bardhan (2005) extends the notion of institutional quality relevant for development from a focus on property rights to include the strength of democratic participation rights and institutions of coordination, but in his empirical work focuses solely on the effects of institutions on income levels. Olsson and Hibbs (2005) incorporate different facets of biogeography but, although they include a proxy for institutions, they ignore its potential endogeneity and do not include openness.

The highly parsimonious approach to model specification and the selective coverage of the many different aspects of institutions and geography are likely to have serious effects. Including just one broad representative proxy for institutions in the estimated models means that it is not possible to identify the relative importance of specific institutional features, which limits the usefulness of the results for policy purposes. Indeed, given that the broad proxies are weighted aggregates of the various specific institutional components, the arbitrary weights will affect the estimated effect of a broad cluster of institutions on income (Pande and Udry, 2005). Acemoglu (2005) emphasizes that identifying the role of specific institutions is a more challenging task and will require a richer range of instruments or new methods.

In addition, the results summarized above demonstrate that the conclusions obtained in existing studies are sensitive to the combination of variables included in the chosen model. This suggests that model uncertainty, the unavoidable uncertainty about the relevance of *any* theoretical model, which has been identified as a major problem in the empirical growth literature (Temple, 2000; Brock and Durlauf, 2001; Durlauf *et al.*, 2005), is also a problem in the related literature on deep determinants. Brock and Durlauf (2001) emphasize that growth theories are 'open-ended', in that the relevance of one growth determinant does not normally preclude the relevance of other potential determinants. As the different growth determinants are not usually orthogonal, omitted variables bias is a potentially serious problem, and parameter estimates and standard errors can be sensitive to the model specification.[15]

Most studies of deep determinants estimate extremely parsimonious models; their assessment of the robustness of their results relies on examining the sensitivity of the size and significance of the parameter on, say, institutions to piecemeal variation in a limited number of additional regressors. Such a methodology, termed the 'average economic regression' approach by Gilbert (1986), risks imposing several untested exclusion restrictions and consequently does not adequately address the issue of model selection. Our contention is therefore that the conflicting conclusions obtained partly stem from a failure in the dominant methodology used in the current empirical literature on deep determinants of cross-country income levels; as Gilbert (1986) emphasizes, the approach used in these studies 'illustrates' rather than rigorously tests different competing models.

There are different ways of attempting to deal with model uncertainty, including extreme bounds analysis (Levine and Renelt, 1992), Bayesian model averaging (Brock and Durlauf, 2001), and general-to-specific modelling (Hendry and Krolzig, 2005), and such methods are beginning to be applied in the deep determinants literature (for example, Owen and Weatherston, 2007).

7.5 Conclusions

Although the effects of institutions and geography on economic development have received considerable attention from social scientists and economic historians, empirical studies assessing the impact of institutions and other 'deep' or fundamental determinants are relatively recent.

This chapter critically reviews the key empirical contributions in the economics literature on the deep determinants of income levels. We identify three main themes. The first is the existence of conflicting conclusions between 'institutionalists' (for example, Acemoglu *et al.*,

2001; Easterly and Levine, 2003; Rodrik *et al.*, 2004), who argue that geography matters only insofar as it impacts on the formation of institutions, and 'geographists' (for example, Sachs, 2003; Olsson and Hibbs, 2005), who, while not denying the relevance of institutions, maintain that geography also has a direct impact on levels of GDP per capita.

The conflicting results in the empirical literature may be inherently related to the second theme, which is the non-overlapping nature of the models used in different studies. The results are sensitive to the proxies adopted for institutions and geography, the instruments adopted for the endogenous regressors, and the choice of other exogenous controls. Moreover, the empirical methodology adopted in most of the existing studies is not well suited to deal with concerns about model uncertainty. Further analysis that directly confronts the issue of model uncertainty and parameter heterogeneity across groups of countries is needed.

Following the decision that endogenous (albeit slow-moving) variables are admissible as deep determinants, a third recurrent theme in this literature is the empirical challenge involved in attempting to identify exogenous sources that can explain a significant portion of the variation in the key endogenous factors – including the quality of institutions, some aspects of geography (such as disease burden), and integration with world markets – in order to assess the causal impacts of these factors on the level of GDP per capita using IV estimation techniques. The search for appropriate instruments for endogenous deep determinants of income levels is problematical; in particular, the difficulty in obtaining more than a handful of more-or-less plausible instruments for the quality of a country's institutions is a major limitation of cross-country analysis. The most commonly used instruments restrict analysis to the domain of countries that were allocated a cluster of institutions as a result of European colonization, but there are legitimate concerns about the ability of any single instrument to explain the development of institutions in all ex-colonies. There may be a need for a wider set of instruments to capture adequately the heterogeneous experiences of colonization as the effects on institutional development of climate, relative land abundance, slavery, and plantation agriculture are not mutually exclusive. In addition, there is a need for more rigorous testing for weak instruments.

With the caveat that the commonly used measures of institutions are less than ideal and the application in this literature of more rigorous approaches to deal with model uncertainty and identification of weak instrument problems is still in its early stages, the current consensus appears to have shifted from being strongly supportive of the view that institutions are all that matter for economic development to a broader view that identifies a direct role for geography.[16]

Policy implications of this literature are relatively sparse because of the highly aggregated nature of the measures used. Even if a broad institutions measure is found to be statistically and numerically significant in explaining cross-country variation in income levels, this provides relatively little guidance to policy makers in terms of a blueprint for institutional reform, as the authors of these studies (for example, Rodrik *et al.*, 2004: 157–8) clearly recognize. Progress is likely to proceed along several fronts, including more detailed micro-level analysis, complementary historical case studies, and a more rigorous approach to cross-country analysis that addresses the issues of model uncertainty, parameter heterogeneity, and the quality of instruments used.

Appendix to Table 7.1 Variable definitions

Variable code	**Variable definitions**
SOCINF	Average of an index of the quality of government (*GADP*) and the degree of trade openness (*YRSOPEN*)
GADP	Index of the quality of government ('government antidiversion policies') averaging five categories from the ICRG: law and order, bureaucratic quality, corruption, risk of expropriation, and government repudiation of contracts
YRSOPEN	Index of trade openness constructed by Sachs and Warner (1995), identifying the fraction of years from 1950 to 1994 that an economy is 'open', as defined in Note 7
ENGFRAC	Fraction of the population speaking English as a first language
EURFRAC	Fraction of the population speaking one of the major European languages (including English) as a first language
LATITUDE	Distance from the equator (degrees of absolute latitude divided by 90)
ln*FR*	Natural logarithm of trade shares predicted by Frankel and Romer's (1999) gravity model
EXPROP	Average protection against expropriation risk, average for 1985–1995, based on survey indicators of the risk of expropriation of private foreign investment by government from ICRG
ln*SETTMORT*	Natural logarithm of estimated mortality rate for European settlers, constructed by Acemoglu *et al.* (2001)

TEMPERATURE	Various temperature variables, including mean annual temperature, minimum monthly high, maximum monthly high, minimum monthly low, and maximum monthly low, all in degrees Celsius
SOILQUAL	Dummy variables for low-latitude steppe, low-latitude desert, mid-latitude steppe, mid-latitude desert, dry steppe wasteland, desert dry winter, and highland
NATRESC	Percentage of world gold reserves, per cent of world iron reserves, per cent of world zinc reserves, number of minerals present, oil resources (thousands of barrels per capita)
LANDLOCK	Dummy variable equal to 1 if country is landlocked
HUMIDITY	Morning minimum, morning maximum, afternoon minimum, afternoon maximum, all in per cent
MALFAL94	Proportion of a country's population that lives with the risk of malaria transmission multiplied by an estimate of the proportion of national malaria cases that involve the fatal species *Plasmodium falciparum* in 1994
INSTINDEX	Average of six indicators of institutional quality: (i) voice and accountability, (ii) political instability and violence, (iii) government effectiveness, (iv) regulatory burden, (v) rule of law, and (vi) corruption
CROPS/MINERALS	Series of 11 crop and mineral 0/1 dummy variables indicating whether a country produced any of the following crops and minerals in 1998–1999: bananas, coffee, copper, maize, millet, oil, rice, rubber, silver, sugarcane, and wheat
RULELAW	Kaufmann *et al.*'s (2002) composite indicator of a number of elements that capture the protection afforded to property rights as well as the rule of law
KGPTEMP	Share of a country's population in temperate eco-zones in 1995 based on the Koeppen–Geiger eco-zone classification system
POP100KM	Percentage of the population living within 100km of the coast
MAL94P	Proportion of each country's population that lives with the risk of malaria transmission in 1994
ME	Combined measure of malaria ecology, including temperature, species abundance, and vector type, which is predictive of malaria risk but exogenous to economic conditions and public health interventions constructed by Kiszewski *et al.* (2004)
RULELAW	Kaufmann *et al.*'s (2002) composite indicator capturing 'the protection afforded to property rights as well as the rule of law' (Rodrik *et al.*, 2004, p. 138)

Appendix to Table 7.1 (Continued)

Variable code	**Variable definitions**
ln(*TRADE/GDP*)	Natural logarithm of the ratio of nominal trade (exports + imports) relative to nominal GDP (averaged over the period 1950–1998)
POLENV	Index of the political-institutional environment (equivalent to Hall and Jones' (1999) *GADP*) averaging five categories from the ICRG: law and order, bureaucratic quality, corruption, risk of expropriation, and government repudiation of contracts
BIOCON	A proxy of initial biogeography based on the first principal component of the number of annual or perennial wild grasses (with mean kernel weight greater than 10 mg) and the number of mammals (greater than 45 g in weight) capable of being domesticated in prehistory
GEOCON	A proxy for geographical conditions based on the first principal component of four geographical variables: size of continent, major axis of continent, latitude, and climate

Note: More detailed discussion of the variables and the original sources of the data are available in the studies cited in Table 7.1.

Notes

Earlier versions of this chapter have been presented at the Institutions and Economic Development Symposium, University of Otago (March 2005), in the New Zealand Treasury's Economic Growth Seminar series (May 2005), and in a University of Otago Competitiveness Research Network seminar (June 2005). We are grateful to participants and to Stephen Knowles for helpful comments and suggestions. Financial support from a University of Otago Research Grant is also gratefully acknowledged.

1. Using GDP per capita in current 'international' dollars, derived using purchasing power parity (PPP) exchange rates, in 2003 the per capita GDP of Luxembourg was $62,298 compared to $548 in Sierra Leone (Source: World Bank, 2005).
2. North and Thomas (1973: 2) eloquently emphasize this point by noting that 'the factors we have listed (innovation, economies of scale, education, capital accumulation and so on) are not causes of growth; they *are* growth' (emphasis in original).
3. Olsson (2005) provides a critical summary of both the earlier and the more recent theoretical arguments on the influence of physical geography on economic development.

4. Olsson (2005) classifies geographical characteristics into four subgroups: (1) climate, relating to the average and variability in conditions above the ground surface; (2) topography, relating to the conditions of the ground surface, including shape, elevation, cartography and orientation; (3) geology, describing the character of the soil and the quality and quantity of existing minerals; and (4) biogeography, referring to the spatial distribution of plants and animals, and the geographical distribution of virus and disease vectors. Different aspects of each of these subgroups have been argued to be relevant factors in economic development.
5. Sachs and Malaney (2002: 681) argue that 'where malaria prospers most, human societies have prospered least'. Bloom and Sachs (1998) claim that the prevalence of malaria reduces the annual growth rate of sub-Saharan African economies by more than 1.3 percentage points a year.
6. Acemoglu and Johnson (2005) 'unbundle' formal institutions into 'property rights' institutions and 'contracting' institutions. The former are proxied by the risk of expropriation (from the ICRG) and by constraints on the executive from the Polity IV data set. Contracting institutions are proxied by a measure of the number of formal legal procedures necessary to evict non-paying tenants or collect an unpaid cheque.
7. The Sachs and Warner (1995) index assigns each country a score between zero and one depending on the fraction of years in the period 1950–94 that a country has been open. To be classified as 'open' a country must simultaneously satisfy five criteria relating to the extent of non-tariff barriers, average tariff rates, the black market premium on foreign exchange, whether the country is socialist, and the extent of state monopoly of exports.
8. Usually, prosperity in 1500 is measured by population density or urbanization rates on the grounds that only relatively developed societies could sustain bigger cities.
9. In contrast, geography is not endogenous in this sense; a country's latitude, for example, will not change as a result of an increase in its GDP per capita.
10. Pande and Udry (2005: 7) note that Political Risk Services informed them that to construct the 'protection against expropriation risk' measure they ' "infer" the risk involved from the degree of accountability of the government, the freedom of the judiciary, the level of application of the rule of law, and the level of apparent corruption', but the details are not transparent.
11. *S* is measured as an equally weighted average of a measure of 'government anti-diversion policy' (*GADP*), discussed in Section 7.2.2, and Sachs and Warner's (1995) index of openness, discussed in Section 7.2.3.
12. Despite concerns about the validity of instruments such as settler mortality and latitude, relatively few alternative instruments for institutions have been proposed, including legal origin (as discussed in Section 7.2.2), pre-colonial population density (Acemoglu *et al.*, 2002), state antiquity (Chanda and Putterman, 2004), and tradable pastoral production per capita (Fielding and Torres, 2005).
13. Alcalá and Ciccone's (2004) results suggest that trade and institutions are *both* relevant in explaining income levels, whereas Dollar and Kraay (2003) argue that it is difficult to disentangle the relative contributions of these two factors on income *levels*, but that trade has a significant partial effect on *growth*, and that institutions are less important.

14. Frankel and Romer (1999) instrument actual trade-to-GDP ratios using predicted trade-to-GDP shares constructed on the basis of a gravity equation for bilateral trade flows with geographical characteristics (country area, distance between the trade partners, whether countries share a common border, and whether they are landlocked) as regressors. Although initially constructed as an instrument for actual trade shares, this variable has also been widely used for other proxies for openness. For example, Hall and Jones (1999) use the Frankel and Romer instrument for the Sachs–Warner openness variable. This alternative proxy for openness is only weakly correlated with the Frankel and Romer instrument, which may yield a weak instrument problem.
15. Open-endedness of theory also has implications for evaluating the validity of instruments used in IV estimation (Brock and Durlauf, 2001). Exogeneity of chosen instruments cannot be justified purely on the basis of whether the 'instruments' are predetermined. Variables that may sensibly be regarded as 'predetermined' in an economic sense, including geographical or historical variables such as latitude or settler mortality, may not be exogenous in the statistical sense (that is, uncorrelated with the error term in the estimated model) because such variables can plausibly affect income through a variety of different mechanisms. If, say, settler mortality is used as an instrument for institutions, but it is correlated with the modern disease environment, which also has a direct effect on income that is not explicitly included in the structural model, then its direct influence will end up in the error term and therefore correlated with the selected instrument, even though settler mortality is 'predetermined'. However, because of the open-endedness of the theories and the consequent model uncertainty, it is difficult to ensure that all relevant variables are included in the model.
16. Interestingly, the final title of the review paper by Acemoglu *et al.* (2005), which is clearly institutionalist in stance, refers to 'institutions as *a* fundamental cause of long-run growth' (emphasis added), a subtle change from earlier drafts that referred to 'institutions as *the* fundamental cause'.

References

Acemoglu, D. 'Constitutions, Politics, and Economics: A Review Essay on Persson and Tabellini's *The Economic Effects of Constitutions*', *Journal of Economic Literature*, 43 (2005): 1025–48.

Acemoglu, D. and Johnson, S. 'Unbundling Institutions', *Journal of Political Economy*, 113 (2005): 949–95.

Acemoglu, D., Johnson, S. and Robinson, J. A. 'The Colonial Origins of Comparative Development: An Empirical Investigation', *American Economic Review*, 91 (2001): 1369–401.

Acemoglu, D., Johnson, S. and Robinson, J. A. 'Reversal of Fortune: Geography and Institutions in the Making of the Modern World Income Distribution', *Quarterly Journal of Economics*, 117 (2002): 1231–94.

Acemoglu, D., Johnson, S. and Robinson, J. A. 'Institutions as a Fundamental Cause of Long-Run Growth', in P. Aghion and S. N. Durlauf (eds), *Handbook*

of Economic Growth, Volume 1A (Amsterdam: Elsevier North-Holland, 2005): 385–472.
Alcalá, F. and Ciccone, A. 'Trade and Productivity', *Quarterly Journal of Economics*, 119 (2004): 613–46.
Bardhan, P. 'Institutions Matter, But Which Ones?', *Economics of Transition*, 13 (2005): 499–532.
Barro, R. J. and Sala-i-Martin, X. *Economic Growth* (New York: McGraw-Hill, 1995).
Batten, A. and Martina, A. 'Diseases Dominate', in W. R. Garside (ed.), *Institutions and Market Economies: The Political Economy of Growth and Development* (Basingstoke: Palgrave Macmillan, 2007).
Beck, T. G., Clarke, G., Groff, A., Keefer, P. and Walsh, P. 'New Tools in Comparative Political Economy: The Database of Political Institutions', *World Bank Economic Review*, 15 (2001): 165–76.
Becker, G. S. *Human Capital: A Theoretical and Empirical Analysis with Special Reference to Education*, third edition (Chicago: University of Chicago Press, 1993).
Bleakley, H. 'Disease and Development: Evidence from the American South', *Journal of the European Economic Association*, 1 (2002): 376–86.
Bloom, D. E. and Sachs, J. D. 'Geography, Demography, and Economic Growth in Africa', *Brookings Papers on Economic Activity*, 2 (1998): 207–73.
Brock, W. A. and Durlauf, S. N. 'Growth Empirics and Reality', *World Bank Economic Review*, 15 (2001): 229–72.
Brunner, A. D. 'The Long-Run Effects of Trade on Income and Income Growth'. International Monetary Fund, IMF Working Paper No. WP/03/37 (2003).
Carstensen, K. and Gundlach, E. 'The Primacy of Institutions Reconsidered: Direct Income Effects of Malaria Prevalence', *World Bank Economic Review*, 20 (2006): 309–39.
Chanda, A. and Putterman, L. 'Early Starts, Reversals and Catchup in the Process of Economic Development', Brown University Economics, Working Paper No. 2004-04 (2004).
Diamond, J. *Guns, Germs and Steel: The Fates of Human Societies* (New York: W. W. Norton, 1997).
Djankov, S., Glaeser, E., La Porta, R., Lopez-de-Silanes, F. and Schleifer, A. 'The New Comparative Economics', *Journal of Comparative Economics*, 31 (2003): 595–619.
Dollar, D. and Kraay, A. 'Institutions, Trade, and Growth', *Journal of Monetary Economics*, 50 (2003): 133–62.
Durlauf, S. N. and Quah, D. T. 'The New Empirics of Economic Growth', in J. B. Taylor and M. Woodford (eds), *Handbook of Macroeconomics, Volume 1A* (Amsterdam: North-Holland Elsevier Science, 1999): 235–308.
Durlauf, S. N., Johnson, P. A. and Temple, J. R. W. 'Growth Econometrics', In P. Aghion and S. Durlauf (eds), *Handbook of Economic Growth* (Amsterdam: North-Holland Elsevier Science, 2005): 555–677.
Easterly, W. and Levine, R. 'Tropics, Germs, and Crops: How Endowments Influence Economic Development', *Journal of Monetary Economics*, 50 (2003): 3–39.
Engerman, S. L. and Sokoloff, K. L. 'Factor Endowments, Institutions, and Differential Paths of Growth Among New World Economies', in S. Haber (ed.), *How Latin America Fell Behind: Essays on the Economic Histories of Brazil and Mexico, 1800–1914* (Stanford: Stanford University Press, 1997): 260–304.
Engerman, S. L. and Sokoloff, K. L. 'Factor Endowments, Inequality, and Paths of Development among New World Economies', *Economica*, 3 (2002): 41–109.

Fielding, D. and Torres, S. 'Cows and Conquistadors: A Comment on the Colonial Origins of Comparative Development', University of Otago, Economics Discussion Paper No. 0504 (2005).

Frankel, J. A. and Romer, D. 'Does Trade Cause Growth?', *American Economic Review*, 89 (1999): 379–99.

Gallup, J. L., Gaviria, A. and Lora, E. *Is Geography Destiny? Lessons from Latin America* (Palo Alto, CA. and Washington, DC: Stanford University Press and World Bank, 2003).

Gallup, J. L., Sachs, J. D. and Mellinger, A. D. 'Geography and Economic Development', *International Regional Science Review*, 22 (1999): 179–232.

Gilbert, C. L. 'Professor Hendry's Methodology', *Oxford Bulletin of Economics and Statistics*, 48 (1986): 283–307.

Gilfillan, S. C. 'The Coldward Course of Progress', *Political Science Quarterly*, 35 (1920): 393–410.

Glaeser, E. L., La Porta, R., Lopez-de-Silanes, F. and Shleifer, A. 'Do Institutions Cause Growth?', *Journal of Economic Growth*, 9 (2004): 271–303.

Guiso, L., Sapienza, P. and Zingales, L. 'Does Culture Affect Economic Outcomes?', *Journal of Economic Perspectives*, 20 (2006): 23–48.

Hall, R. E. and Jones, C. I. 'Why Do Some Countries Produce So Much More Output Per Worker Than Others?', *Quarterly Journal of Economics*, 114 (1999): 83–116.

Hendry, D. F. and Krolzig, H.-M. 'The Properties of Automatic *Gets* Modelling', *Economic Journal*, 115 (2005): C32–C61.

Helpman, E. *The Mystery of Economic Growth* (Cambridge, MA: Belknap Press of Harvard University Press, 2004).

Huntington, E. *Civilization and Climate*, third edition (New Haven: Yale University Press, 1924).

Irwin, D. A. and Terviö, M. 'Does Trade Raise Income? Evidence from the Twentieth Century', *Journal of International Economics*, 58 (2002): 1–18.

Jaggers, K. and Marshall, M. G. *Polity IV Project*, University of Maryland, Center for International Development and Conflict Management (2000).

Kamarck, A. M. *The Tropics and Economic Development: A Provocative Inquiry into the Poverty of Nations* (Baltimore: Johns Hopkins University Press, 1976).

Kaufmann, D., Kraay, A. and Zoido-Lobatón, P. 'Governance Matters II – Updated Indicators for 2000/01'. World Bank Policy Research Department, Working Paper No. 2772 (2002).

Kaufmann, D., Kraay, A. and Mastruzzi, M. 'Governance Matters III: Governance Indicators for 1996, 1998, 2000, and 2002', *World Bank Economic Review*, 18 (2004): 253–87.

Kaufmann, D., Kraay, A. and Mastruzzi, M. 'Governance Matters IV: Governance Indicators for 1996–2004', World Bank, Policy Research Working Paper No. 3630 (2005).

Kiszewski, A., Mellinger, A., Spielman, A., Malaney, P., Ehrlich Sachs, S. and Sachs, J. 'A Global Index Representing the Stability of Malaria Transmission', *American Journal of Tropical Medicine and Hygiene*, 70 (2004): 486–98.

Landes, D. *The Wealth and Poverty of Nations: Why Some Are So Rich and Some So Poor* (New York: W. W. Norton, 1998).

La Porta, R., Lopez-de-Silanes, F., Shleifer, A. and Vishny, R. 'Law and Finance', *Journal of Political Economy*, 106 (1998): 1113–55.

La Porta, R., Lopez-de-Silanes, F., Shleifer, A. and Vishny, R. 'The Quality of Government', *Journal of Law, Economics, and Organization*, 15 (1999): 222–82.

Levine, R. 'Law, Endowments and Property Rights', *Journal of Economic Perspectives*, 19 (2005): 61–88.

Levine, R. and Renelt, D. 'A Sensitivity Analysis of Cross-Country Growth Regressions', *American Economic Review*, 82 (1992): 942–63.

McArthur, J. W. and Sachs, J. D. 'Institutions and Geography: Comment on Acemoglu, Johnson and Robinson (2000)'. Cambridge, MA, National Bureau of Economic Research, Working Paper No. 8114 (2001).

Marshall, A. *Principles of Economics* (London: Macmillan, 1890).

Masters, W. A. and McMillan, M. S. 'Climate and Scale in Economic Growth', *Journal of Economic Growth*, 6 (2001): 167–86.

Miguel, E. and Kremer, M. 'Worms: Identifying Impacts on Education and Health in the Presence of Treatment Externalities', *Econometrica*, 72 (2004): 159–217.

Baron de Montesquieu, C.-L. de Secondat. *The Spirit of Laws: A Compendium of the First English Edition*, translated by T. Nugent and edited by D. W. Carrithers (Berkeley: University of California Press, [1748], 1977).

North, D. C. *Institutions, Institutional Change and Economic Performance* (Cambridge: Cambridge University Press, 1990).

North, D. C. and Thomas, R. P. *The Rise of the Western World: A New Economic History* (Cambridge: Cambridge University Press, 1973).

Olsson, O. 'Unbundling Ex-Colonies: A Comment on Acemoglu, Johnson and Robinson 2001'. Göteborg University, Working Papers in Economics No. 146 (2004).

Olsson, O. 'Geography and Institutions: Plausible and Implausible Linkages', *Journal of Economics*, Suppl. 10 (2005): 167–94.

Olsson, O. and Hibbs Jr, D. A. 'Biogeography and Long-run Economic Development', *European Economic Review*, 49 (2005): 909–38.

Owen, P. D. and Weatherston, C. R. 'What Really Matters for Long-term Growth and Development? A Re-examination of the Deep Determinants of Per Capita Income', University of Otago, Department of Economics, mimeograph (2007).

Pande, R. and Udry, C. 'Institutions and Development: A View from Below'. Yale University, Economic Growth Center Discussion Paper No. 928 (2005).

Parker, P. M. *Physioeconomics: The Basis for Long-Run Economic Growth* (Cambridge, MA: MIT Press, 2000).

Presbitero, A. F. 'Institutions and Geography as Sources of Economic Development', *Journal of International Development*, 18 (2006): 351–78.

Przeworski, A. 'The Last Instance: Are Institutions the Primary Cause of Economic Development?', *European Journal of Sociology*, 45 (2004a): 165–88.

Przeworski, A. 'Geography vs. Institutions Revisited: Were Fortunes Reversed?', Department of Politics, New York University, mimeograph (2004b).

Ram, R. 'Tropics and Economic Development: An Empirical Investigation', *World Development*, 25 (1997): 1443–52.

Rodrik, D., Subramanian, A. and Trebbi, F. 'Institutions Rule: The Primacy of Institutions Over Geography and Integration in Economic Development', *Journal of Economic Growth*, 9 (2004): 131–65.

Sachs, J. D. 'Tropical Underdevelopment'. Cambridge, MA, National Bureau of Economic Research, Working Paper No. 8119 (2001).

Sachs, J. D. 'Institutions Don't Rule: Direct Effects of Geography on Per Capita Income', Cambridge, MA, National Bureau of Economic Research, Working Paper No. 9490 (2003a).
Sachs, J. D. 'Institutions Matter but Not for Everything: The Role of Geography and Resource Endowments in Development Shouldn't Be Underestimated, *Finance & Development*, June (2003b): 38–41.
Sachs, J. and Malaney, P. 'The Economic and Social Burden of Malaria', *Nature*, 415 (2002): 680–5.
Sachs, J. and Warner, A. M. 'Economic Reform and the Process of Global Integration', *Brookings Papers on Economic Activity*, 1 (1995): 1–95.
Schultz, T. P. and Tansel, A. 'Wage and Labor Supply Effects of Illness in Côte d'Ivoire and Ghana: Instrumental Variable Estimates for Days Disabled', *Journal of Development Economics*, 53 (1997): 251–86.
Smith, A. *An Inquiry into the Nature and Causes of the Wealth of Nations.* (Chicago: University of Chicago Press, [1776] 1976).
Solow, R. M. 'A Contribution to the Theory of Economic Growth', *Quarterly Journal of Economics*, 70 (1956): 65–94.
Solow, R. M. 'Technical Change and the Aggregate Production Function', *Review of Economics and Statistics*, 39 (1957): 312–20.
Temple, J. 'Growth Regressions and What the Textbooks Don't Tell You', *Bulletin of Economic Research*, 52 (2000): 181–205.
The Economist, 'Development Piecemeal: Small Policy Changes, Not Upheaval, May Be the Trigger of Growth', *The Economist*, 5 August (2004).
Theil, H. and Chen, D. 'The Geographic Distribution of Gross World Product, 1950–1990', in H. Theil with D. Chen, K. Clements and C. Moss (eds), *Studies in Global Econometrics* (Dordrecht: Kluwer, 1996): 7–46.
Weber, M. *The Protestant Ethic and the Spirit of Capitalism* (London: Unwin University Books, [1904], 1930).
Williamson, O. E. 'The New Institutional Economics: Taking Stock, Looking Ahead', *Journal of Economic Literature*, 38 (2000): 595–613.
Wittfogel, K. *Oriental Despotism: A Comparative Study of Total Power* (New Haven: Yale University Press, 1957).
World Bank, World Development Indicators CD-ROM 05 (Washington, DC: World Bank, 2005).

8

The Deep Determinants of Health and Education: Institutions versus Geography

Michael Jones, Stephen Knowles, and P. Dorian Owen

8.1 Introduction

Why are some countries so underdeveloped in economic terms relative to others? This is the central question of a widely cited literature within economics, which has become known as the deep-determinants literature. Within this literature, proximate determinants of development are defined as those that appear in the aggregate production function, such as physical and human capital per worker. Deep determinants, by contrast, are the variables that explain differences in the proximate determinants; hence they are the underlying, or deep, determinants of development. Frequently cited papers in this literature include Hall and Jones (1999), Acemoglu *et al.* (2001, 2002, 2003), Easterly and Levine (2003), Rodrik *et al.* (2004), Sachs (2003), and Olsson and Hibbs (2005).[1] Many of these papers have attempted to answer the question as to whether geography or institutions is the key deep determinant of economic development. The earlier contributions to the debate tended to conclude that institutions 'trump' geography as the key deep determinant of economic development, but the papers by Sachs (2003) and Olsson and Hibbs (2005) suggest there is an important role for geography. This literature is reviewed in more detail by Owen and Weatherston (2007) in this book.

All of the papers cited in the previous paragraph use data on income per capita to proxy for the level of development. We argue that this is not necessarily the best measure of economic development available. Admittedly, some studies have been careful to note that their focus is on the level of income per capita only. For example, the papers by Hall and Jones (1999) and Sachs (2003) have 'income' or 'output' in their titles, not 'economic development'. On the other hand, Acemoglu *et al.* (2001, 2003), Easterly and Levine (2003), Rodrik *et al.* (2004), and Olsson and Hibbs (2005) all mention 'development' or 'economic development', rather than 'income' in their titles. In addition, this literature is sometimes referred to as the 'levels of development' literature (Bhattacharyya *et al.*, 2005).

Although it is not unusual within the general field of economics to use income per capita as a proxy for the level of economic development, it has been widely recognized, for some time, in the *development* economics literature that income per capita is only one dimension of economic development. Within development economics, rather than just focusing narrowly on the level of income per capita, other measures of the level of economic development are widely used, including the structural composition of the economy, and levels of education and health. The Human Development Index (HDI), a composite index which includes income per capita, education and health, has become a popular alternative measure of the level of economic development.

It would appear, therefore, that there is a gap in the existing literature on the effect of institutions on economic development, in that almost all of the existing research focuses on only one facet (income per capita) of economic development.[2] A rare exception is the chapter in this book by Batten and Martina (2007), which analyses the effect of institutions, geography, and the risk of malaria on the HDI. Our approach differs from that of Batten and Martina in that we focus on the effect of institutions and geography on measures of education and health separately, rather than the HDI. We also argue that the risk of malaria, as an important aspect of the disease environment, is too closely associated with any proxy for health, such as life expectancy, to be considered one of its deep determinants; hence, we do not include malaria risk in attempting to model empirically the deep determinants of life expectancy. This chapter seeks to fill a gap in the literature by providing a preliminary analysis of the effect of institutions, and geography, on education and health outcomes, within a deep-determinants framework.

Section 8.2 discusses the measurement of economic development in more detail. Section 8.3 briefly reviews the literature on the effect of institutions and geography on income per capita, emphasizing the distinction between proximate and deep determinants of development. Section 8.4 presents some theoretical arguments as to why institutions and geography can be thought of as deep determinants of health and education. Section 8.5 analyses the relationship between institutions and geography, and education and health outcomes in an informal manner, using simple scatter plots. These relationships are analysed more formally, using multiple regression analysis and instrumental variables estimation methods, in Section 8.6. Section 8.7 concludes.

8.2 Measuring economic development

Very few economists, if any, would argue that economic development (or 'welfare' as it is defined in many first-year textbooks) can be *defined* as narrowly as the level of income per capita. However, there is a debate over whether economic development can be adequately *measured* using the level of income per capita, or whether this needs to be supplemented with other data.

The view that economic development can be measured by income per capita, even though by definition it is a broader concept, is a view that permeates most *macroeconomics* textbooks. In such texts it is standard to argue that, although income per capita is not the same thing as economic welfare, using GDP per capita as a *measure* of welfare is justified. A typical defence of this practice can be found in Frank and Bernanke (2004: 460), who state that 'real GDP is *not* [emphasis in original] the same as economic well being'. The reasons they give for this include the fact that GDP does not include non-market activities, that it does not include leisure time, that it ignores the environment, poverty, inequality, crime, traffic congestion, and so on. However, Frank and Bernanke (2004: 461) then go on to argue that 'real GDP per person *does* [emphasis in original] tend to be positively associated with many things people value, including a high material standard of living, better health and life expectancies and better education'.

Most *development* economists, however, are less willing to accept that income per capita is an ideal *measure* of economic development. Development economics textbooks typically begin with a lengthy discussion of the different variables that should be considered when measuring the level of economic development, including, in addition to income per capita, variables measuring education, health, the distribution of income, access to safe water and sanitation facilities, the structural composition of the economy, population growth, and so on (see, for example, Ray, 1998; Perkins *et al.*, 2001; Todaro and Smith, 2006).

In the development economics literature, the HDI is the measure of economic development most commonly used, since the early 1990s, as an alternative to income per capita. The HDI is a composite index measuring three different aspects of development: income per capita, education (as proxied by a weighted average of the adult literacy rate and the combined primary, secondary and tertiary enrolment rate) and health (as proxied by life expectancy at birth). The construction of the index is such that each country receives an HDI score between zero (the lowest possible score) and one (the highest possible score). For details on how the HDI is constructed, see Todaro and Smith (2006: 59–61) or United Nations Development Programme (UNDP) (2003: 340–1).

Critics of the HDI, however, have raised a number of technical objections to the way that the separate components are aggregated into an index, including whether the weights attached to each component are appropriate (see, for example, Kelley, 1991; Trabold-Nubler, 1991; Noorbakhsh, 1998). A detailed discussion of these issues is beyond the scope of this chapter, but one example may prove helpful. Ravallion (1997) points out that the HDI is computed in such a way that an extra year of life is implicitly valued much more highly in a high-income country than a low-income country, which seems questionable from a philosophical point of view. Given the potential difficulties with the HDI, we choose to focus on measures of education and health separately, rather than the HDI, as indicators of different aspects of economic development.

In terms of whether it is reasonable to use income per capita as a proxy for economic development, the key question is *not* whether income per capita is the same thing as economic development, but whether income per capita can be used to *measure* economic development adequately. The answer to this question hinges on how highly correlated income per capita is with other dimensions of economic development. Not only do the correlations between income per capita and other measures of development need to be statistically significant, they need to be high enough that income per capita can be used to predict other development outcomes reasonably accurately for all countries. The more countries there are that have high incomes but low measures of other dimensions of development, or vice versa, the less satisfactory is income per capita as a proxy for economic development. It also needs to be considered whether income per capita is measured with sufficient accuracy; if not, it may not be a good measure of average incomes, let alone welfare or development. Each of these questions will now be addressed in turn.

8.2.1 The correlation between income per capita and other measures of development

In order to assess whether economic development can simply be proxied by income per capita, we analyse the extent to which income per capita is correlated with education and health. The data used for these calculations are for the years 2000–01 and are taken from UNDP (2003). The correlation between income per capita and life expectancy, 0.610, is far from perfect. The correlation between income per capita and the combined school enrolment rate is slightly higher, at 0.637. These correlations are both statistically significant, but hardly high enough to suggest that income per capita can be used as a reliable proxy for the level of economic development more generally.

The fact that the correlations between income per capita and other dimensions of development are less than perfect implies that there will be countries with high incomes but low levels of education and health, and vice versa. Examination of the data reveals that, for example, Cuba, Panama, Jamaica and Sri Lanka all enjoy reasonably high levels of education and health, without having high levels of income per capita. High incomes per capita, but low levels of education and health, are found in many of the oil-exporting countries, and in countries such as Botswana and South Africa. Given the existence of such exceptions, which is reflected in the fact that the correlations between income per capita and education and health are less than perfect, income per capita cannot be considered a perfect proxy for the level of economic development. Data on income per capita should be supplemented with data on other variables such as education and health.

8.2.2 Measuring income per capita

A problem with measuring income per capita, acknowledged in most economics texts, is that only *market* transactions are included in the official measure of income. In other words, only the monetized economy is counted. Hence, if a family buys their vegetables, this is included in the official measure of income; if they grow their own, it is not (although any money spent on seeds or other gardening inputs is included). Comparing values for a particular country's income per capita over time does not present any serious problems, assuming that the size of the non-monetized economy is a reasonably constant proportion of income per capita. However, there is more of a problem when comparing the incomes per capita of different countries, particularly if making comparisons between countries at different stages of economic development. In a developed country, most families will buy most of their food, clothing and so on; in a less developed country, many people will produce their own. Hence, in less developed countries a much higher proportion of production is non-monetized, over-stating the gap between rich and poor countries.

This section of the chapter has considered whether income per capita is a good proxy for the level of economic development. Two arguments have been presented to suggest that it is not. Because the size of the non-monetized economy differs across countries at different levels of development, income per capita, as it is measured, will overstate the gap between rich and poor countries. Hence, income per capita is measured with error. It has also been shown that, although there are positive correlations between income per capita and other dimensions of economic development, these correlations are far from perfect. Hence, although income per capita conveys useful information on the level of economic development, it is advisable to supplement this with other information.

8.3 Institutions and geography as deep determinants of income per capita

As noted in the introduction, there is a growing literature on the role played by institutions in determining why some countries are rich and others poor. North (1990: 3) defines institutions as 'the rules of the game in a society or, more formally, [they] are the humanly devised constraints that shape human interaction. In consequence, they structure incentives in human exchange, whether political, social or economic.' Good institutions are typically thought of as those that encourage investment and exchange by protecting property rights, ensure the enforceability of contracts, minimize corruption, discourage rent-seeking, promote law and order, and remove obstacles to setting up businesses. North (1990: 9) suggests that poor institutions can help explain the economic backwardness of many parts of the world, arguing that many Third World countries are characterized by institutional arrangements that favour redistribution and rent-seeking over productive activity, create monopolies rather than competition, and do not create incentives for investing in human capital.

Acemoglu *et al.* (2002: 1262–3) also outline arguments as to why institutions will influence productivity. They define good organization of society as a cluster of political, economic and social institutions that ensure that a broad cross section of society has effective property rights. They define such institutions as *institutions of private property*. By contrast, other societies will have *extractive institutions*, where the majority of the population faces a high risk of expropriation and hold-up by the government, the ruling elite or other agents. Institutions of private property are thought to create the incentives required for investment, whereas extractive institutions are not. If the majority have no property rights, then potential entrepreneurs will not invest. Hence, investment will be lower in countries that do not have good institutions.

There are also arguments in the literature to suggest that geography is the underlying reason why many parts of the world remain undeveloped. For example, some geographic areas are more suitable than others for agricultural production. Sachs (2001) notes that for rice, maize and wheat, agricultural productivity is lower in tropical regions than in temperate regions, arguing that this is the result of lower soil fertility (due to heavy rainfall and high temperatures), a higher prevalence of pests and parasites (due to high temperatures and an absence of frost), lower net plant photosynthesis and low rates of water availability (due to high rates of evaporation and transpiration of water through plant surfaces).

Diamond (1997) argues that bio-geographic conditions in prehistoric times can explain much of the current world distribution of income. For example, Africa is not as economically advanced as Eurasia because Africa had fewer animals that could be domesticated and fewer plants suitable for farming, so it was in Eurasia that a hunter-gatherer culture gave way to sedentary farming. This in turn enabled Eurasians to live in villages and produce a food surplus which could feed specialists such as inventors and soldiers. Hence Eurasia was able to develop technologies and institutions that were then used to dominate the rest of the world.

8.4 Why institutions may affect health and education

The key focus of this chapter is not the effect of institutions on income per capita, but their effect on health and education. There are a variety of reasons as to why institutions may lead to favourable health and educational outcomes. As noted above, Acemoglu *et al.* (2002) argue that institutions can be separated into two groups: extractive institutions and institutions that protect property rights. They suggest that the type of institutions a country has today can be traced back to colonial times. In areas where the incidence of settler mortality was low, and which were not heavily populated already, the colonial powers tended to favour large-scale European settlement and, hence, transplanted European-style institutions. These institutions protected property rights and encouraged economic development. On the other hand, in areas where settler mortality was high and/or population density was high, the colonial powers were interested only in extracting raw materials from the colony and set up institutions with that in mind. Granting property rights to the majority of the population was not important; ensuring a supply of cheap native labour was. Such institutions would not be likely to promote economic development for the majority of the population. Acemoglu *et al.* (2002) argue that these institutional arrangements have persisted in the post-colonial era.

The question that needs to be addressed in this chapter is what effect these different institutional arrangements would be likely to have on health and education. In countries where European institutions were transplanted, it is likely that facilities will have been set up that promoted access to health and education facilities for the majority of the population, at least for the European settlers, mirroring those in Europe. However, in cases where extractive institutions were set up, the colonial powers will have had little interest in promoting the health and education of the native population. As long as native labour was abundant in the colonies, unhealthy workers could easily be replaced, and workers did not require an education in order to perform the manual labour demanded by the colonial powers. If these institutions have persisted to this day, we would expect that, in countries with institutions of private property, education and health outcomes will be better than in countries with extractive institutions.

A good institutional environment will not only protect property rights, but will be one characterized by a lack of corruption. Corruption within the education and health sectors could lead to the misappropriation of funds and/or medical equipment, hence reducing the effectiveness of the health and/or education sectors, leading to suboptimal health and/or educational outcomes. Good institutions will also ensure that teachers and doctors carry out the work that is expected of them. Woolcock (1998) suggests that, in many developing countries, hospitals and schools may exist, but the doctors and teachers who are meant to staff them are often not at work. This problem is, in part, due to the fact that the institutions normally used to monitor the performance of government employees are lacking.

A poor institutional environment, where one group within society is favoured at the expense of another, could also lead to violent conflict, which has obvious implications for health and, to some extent, education. Many countries in post-colonial Africa, for example, have had rulers who favour their own particular ethnic group, which leads to political instability and violent conflict (for specific examples, see Meredith, 2005). Not only will people be killed in such conflict, reducing life expectancy, but conflict may also lead to the destruction of hospitals and schools, affecting both health and educational outcomes.

We now turn our attention to the question of why geography may affect health outcomes. Put simply, many diseases are more prevalent in certain geographic areas. As argued by Landes (1998: 7), '[h]eat, especially year round heat,... encourages the proliferation of life forms hostile to man'. Sachs (2001: 17) argues that 'malaria transmission generally requires an ambient temperature of 18 degrees centigrade or higher for the anopholene mosquitoes to be infective'. The absence of frost in tropical countries, except those at high altitudes, also contributes to the spread of disease. As discussed in Section 8.3, the extreme heat and humidity in tropical countries also contributes to low soil fertility, reducing food production, which has consequences for health. Sachs (2001) empirically tests this relationship and finds that life expectancy is lower, and infant mortality higher, in the tropics, after controlling for the level of income per capita.

The effects of climate and other aspects of geography on health also feed through to investment in human capital. Sachs and Malaney (2002) summarize some of the mechanisms by which malaria, for example, affects human capital acquisition, including school absenteeism and impairment of cognitive development (see Chapter 7 in this book for further discussion).

8.5 An informal examination of the relationship between institutions, geography and development

Section 8.4 outlined arguments as to why institutions and geography may be expected to affect health and educational outcomes. This section of the chapter informally analyses, using simple scatter plots of cross-country data, whether these variables are in fact correlated. A more formal analysis of the data is undertaken in Section 8.6.

We proxy for institutions using the Kaufmann *et al.* (2002) data on institutional quality. Kaufmann *et al.* construct an index of property rights that includes measures of voice and accountability, political stability and the absence of violence, government effectiveness, light regulatory burden, rule of law and freedom from corruption. The data underlying this index are from a variety of sources, with most being from surveys or evaluations by experts. The maximum possible value of this variable is 2.5, with a minimum possible value of −2.5. These data have been widely used to proxy for institutions in the deep-determinants literature, for example by Easterly and Levine (2003) and Rodrik *et al.* (2004); however, such measures have drawbacks, as discussed by Owen

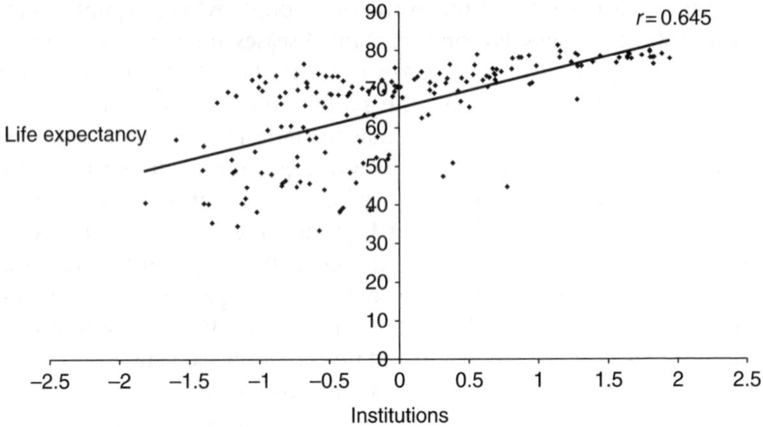

Figure 8.1 Relationship between institutions and life expectancy
Notes: Data for life expectancy are from UNDP (2003) and for institutions from Kaufmann *et al.* (2002).

and Weatherston (2007). The relationship between this measure of institutions and life expectancy is depicted in Figure 8.1.

Figure 8.1 shows that, generally speaking, countries with better quality institutions tend to have higher life expectancies. The correlation coefficient between these two variables, 0.645, is statistically significant and reasonably high. There are no obvious outliers in this relationship. Although institutional differences across countries do not explain all of the variation in life expectancy, they do explain some of the variation.[3] The relationship between institutions and the combined enrolment rate is depicted in Figure 8.2. This correlation is also positive (0.664) and statistically significant.

We now turn our attention to the relationship between geography and our two measures of economic development. Our chosen proxy for geography is mean temperature, measured in degrees Celsius. It was noted earlier that some papers in the deep-determinants literature (such as Sachs, 2003) have found a positive correlation between geography and income per capita. Sachs' key result is that income per capita is correlated with the risk of fatal malaria, even after controlling for institutions. However, given that one of our dependent variables, life expectancy, is a proxy for health, we can hardly argue that the risk of fatal malaria, an important aspect of the disease environment, is a deep determinant of health. That a higher proportion of the population at risk of a fatal disease reduces life expectancy, other things equal, is not particularly

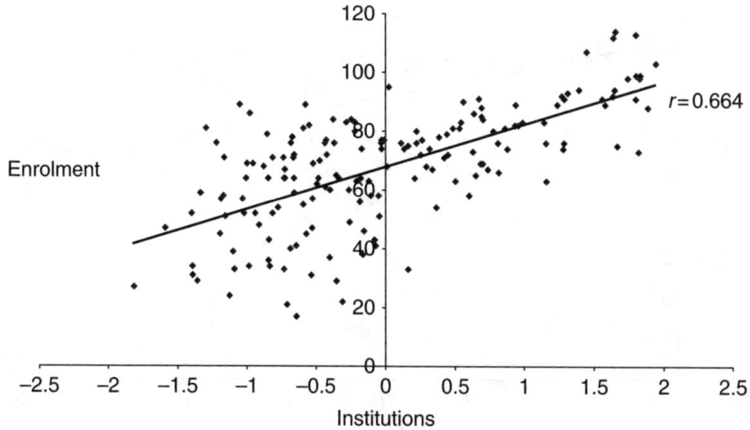

Figure 8.2 Relationship between institutions and combined enrolment
Notes: Data for combined school enrolment are from UNDP (2003) and for institutions from Kaufmann *et al.* (2002).

surprising. For this reason, we choose not to proxy for geography using the risk of fatal malaria, nor any other health-related geography measure, in models attempting to explain life expectancy.[4]

The arguments presented in Section 8.4 suggest that high temperatures have an adverse effect on health; hence, we would expect to find a negative correlation between mean temperature and life expectancy. Also, if mean temperature adversely affects health, and if less healthy people are less likely to attend school, then a negative correlation between mean temperature and the combined enrolment rate would follow.

The relationship between mean temperature, our geography proxy, and life expectancy is presented in Figure 8.3. As expected, for the reasons outlined in the previous section, in countries where mean temperature is higher, life expectancy is lower ($r = -0.494$). A statistically significant negative relationship ($r = -0.658$) is also found between mean temperature and the combined enrolment rate, which is shown in Figure 8.4.

The data analysis in this section provides some evidence consistent with the hypothesis that institutions and geography are deep determinants of other dimensions of economic development, not just income per capita. More specifically, the data suggest that institutional and geographic factors are associated with educational and health outcomes. It should be acknowledged, however, that although examining the simple

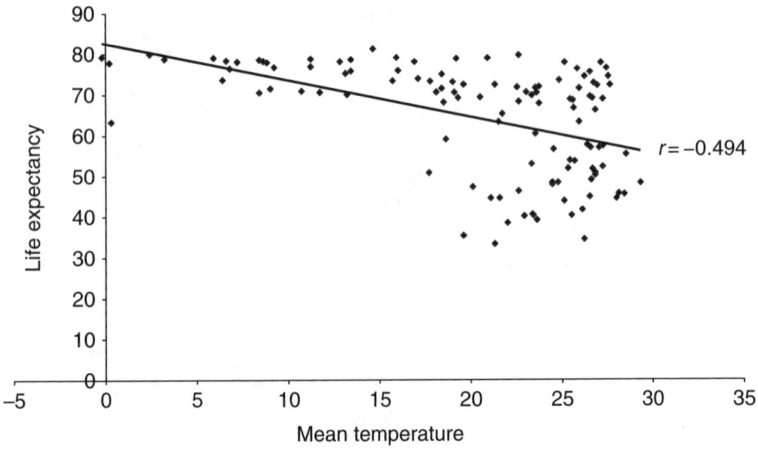

Figure 8.3 Relationship between mean temperature and life expectancy
Notes: Data for life expectancy are from UNDP (2003) and for mean temperature from McArthur and Sachs (2001).

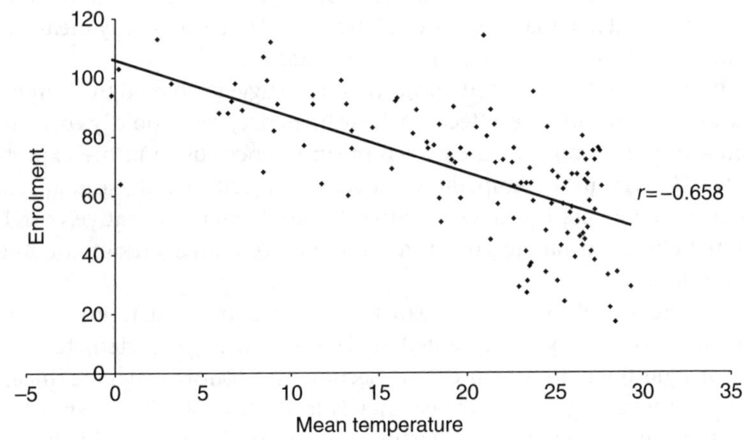

Figure 8.4 Relationship between mean temperature and combined enrolment
Notes: Data for combined school enrolment are from UNDP (2003) and for mean temperature from McArthur and Sachs (2001).

correlation between two variables has the advantage of ease of interpretation, this overlooks the possibility of omitted variables bias and endogeneity. Section 8.6 will examine whether the results presented in this section still hold when analysed in a more formal manner.

8.6 Formal empirical analysis

The scatter plots presented above, although easy to interpret, fail to take into account that more than one variable may affect development outcomes. We have argued that both institutions and geography are likely to affect development outcomes; hence we need to control for the level of institutions when examining the effect of geography on development outcomes, and control for the level of geography when examining the effect of institutions on economic development. This can be achieved using multiple regression analysis applied to data for a cross section of countries. It is also likely that institutions are affected by the level of economic development; if institutions are endogenous, this potentially biases the estimated coefficient on the institutions variable. The problem of endogeneity, and how it is typically addressed in the deep-determinants literature, through the use of instrumental variables estimation methods, is discussed in more detail in Owen and Weatherston (2007).

In order to test more formally for the effect of institutions and geography on our measures of economic development we obtain two-stage-least-squares (2SLS) estimates of the following equation:

$$DEV = \alpha + \beta_1 GEOG + \beta_2 INSTIT + \varepsilon \tag{8.1}$$

where *DEV* is the development indicator of interest (life expectancy or the combined enrolment rate), *GEOG* is a proxy variable for geography, such as mean temperature (*MeanTemp*), *INSTIT* is a measure of the quality of institutions, α a constant term, β_1 and β_2 the coefficients to be estimated, representing the partial effect of each explanatory variable on *DEV*, and ε a country-specific error term. As *INSTIT* is potentially endogenous, we instrument for this variable using the settler mortality variable proposed by Acemoglu *et al.* (2001); see the discussion in Chapter 7 for more details.

The empirical results obtained from 2SLS estimation of Equation (8.1) are presented in Table 8.1. Columns (1)–(3) give results for the combined school enrolment rate and columns (4) and (5) for life expectancy. The results from estimating the model in Equation (8.1), including *MeanTemp* as a proxy for geography and the Kaufmann *et al.* (2002) measure of institutional quality for *INSTIT*, suggest that an increase in institutional quality leads to improvements in both the combined school enrolment rate (column (1)) and life expectancy (column (4)). This is consistent with the plots presented in Figures 8.1 and 8.2. However, the

Table 8.1 2SLS results

	Dependent variable				
	School enrolment			Life expectancy	
	(1)	(2)	(3)	(4)	(5)
Constant	72.312**	72.074**	79.049**	53.810**	53.624**
	(5.44)	(4.72)	(16.28)	(6.26)	(5.42)
INSTIT	24.863**	25.224**	4.283	18.804**	19.086**
	(4.42)	(2.61)	(0.87)	(5.18)	(3.05)
MeanTemp	−0.220	−0.187		0.544	0.570
	(0.35)	(0.20)		(1.35)	(0.93)
Pop100km		−0.869	−0.896		−0.678
		(0.07)	(0.15)		(0.09)
Malfal			−36.418**		
			(4.70)		
R^2	0.395	0.386	0.598	0.278	0.262
N	74	74	77	74	74
CD-F	22.50	9.47	11.28	22.50	9.47
Partial R^2	0.241	0.119	0.377, 0.561	0.241	0.119
Shea Partial R^2	0.241	0.119	0.240, 0.357	0.241	0.119

Notes: Absolute values of asymptotic *t*-statistics are given in parentheses. ** indicates statistical significance at the one per cent level, on the basis of a two-tailed test. *CD-F* is the *F*-stat form of the Cragg-Donald statistic for weak instruments. With more than one endogenous explanatory variable, the first value for the Partial R^2 statistics relates to *INSTIT* and the second value to *Malfal*.

estimated coefficients on mean temperature are not statistically significant at conventional significance levels, suggesting that this particular geography proxy has no effect on the combined school enrolment rate or life expectancy, once the quality of institutions has been controlled for. The R^2 measures of the goodness of fit of the models in columns (1) and (4) are relatively modest, but the Stock and Yogo (2005) implementation of the Cragg-Donald *F*-statistic does not indicate that there is a problem with weak instruments.[5]

The proportion of the population living more than 100 kilometres from the coast (*Pop100km*) is another geography proxy found to be a statistically significant deep determinant of income per capita in some of the models estimated by Sachs (2003). We re-estimated the model including this variable as an additional geography proxy; the results, reported in columns (2) and (5), suggest that this geography proxy also does not have a statistically significant effect on either the combined school enrolment rate or life expectancy.[6] Taken at face value, these results suggest that institutions trump geography in explaining cross-country variation in education and life expectancy, mirroring the early consensus in the studies on the deep determinants of income levels (Acemoglu *et al.*, 2001; Easterly and Levine, 2003; Rodrik *et al.*, 2004).

We noted earlier, however, that in some of the more recent deep-determinants studies, other geographic variables, in particular the risk of fatal malaria, have been found to be statistically significant in explaining income per capita. While we have argued that including a measure of the population at risk of fatal malaria does not provide a particularly profound explanation of life expectancy, it is more informative to consider its relevance as a determinant of the school enrolment rate. The results in column (3) are for a model including a measure of malaria risk (*Malfal*) in addition to *INSTIT* and *Pop100km*.[7] The instrument set includes the settler mortality variable and a measure of malaria ecology, due to Kiszewski *et al.* (2004), which Sachs (2003) argues is both exogenous and a good predictor of *Malfal*. This model provides the best overall fit of the models estimated but, with two endogenous explanatory variables and two excluded instruments, the Cragg-Donald test statistic suggests that this model is more prone to the weak instruments problem, which could affect the reliability of the tests of significance of the partial effects of the explanatory variables.[8] However, with this caveat, *Malfal* has a statistically significant negative effect on the school enrolment rate, but the coefficient on the institutions measure is no longer statistically significant. Thus, these preliminary estimates for the deep determinants of school enrolment rates and life expectancy appear to exhibit the same type of sensitivity to model specification, choice of proxies and instrument choice observed across the studies examining deep determinants of income per capita, as discussed in Chapter 7. Not surprisingly, given the use of the same explanatory variables in a cross-country context, the issues of model uncertainty and weak instruments identified in the literature on the deep determinants of levels of income per capita are also relevant in the analyses of the determinants of other measures of development.

8.7 Conclusions

The deep-determinants literature analyses the effect of institutions and geography on cross-country differences in economic development, using income per capita as a proxy for economic development. This chapter has argued that income per capita is too narrow a proxy for economic development, meaning there is a gap in the literature with respect to examining the effects of institutions and geography on other facets of economic development.

This chapter shows that life expectancy and the combined school enrolment rate are not perfectly correlated with the level of income per capita, suggesting that income per capita is not an ideal proxy for economic development more generally. The chapter then examines the correlations between two other measures of economic development, life expectancy and the combined school enrolment rate, and both institutions and geography (as proxied by mean temperature). The simple correlations reported in Section 8.5 suggest that institutions and mean temperature are, respectively, positively and negatively correlated with our two measures of economic development. However, in the more formal statistical analysis carried out in Section 8.6, the (partial) correlations between mean temperature and the measures of economic development are not statistically significant. Further testing suggests that the proportion of the population living more than 100 kilometres from the coast also does not have a statistically significant effect on the two measures of development. However, a measure of the population at risk of fatal malaria has a statistically significant effect on the school enrolment rate and, when this variable is included, the effect of institutions on the enrolment rate is no longer statistically significant.

It is a common finding in the deep-determinants literature that better quality institutions lead to higher levels of economic development, when economic development is interpreted narrowly as the level of income per capita. Our results suggest that better quality institutions also lead to higher levels of economic development, when economic development is interpreted more broadly, except in the case where the population at risk of fatal malaria is a control variable. Such variation in conclusions depending on model specification mirrors similar results obtained in the literature on the deep determinants of levels of income per capita, suggesting that concerns about model uncertainty and weak instruments, discussed in Chapter 7, need to be given more serious consideration in future work.

Notes

1. To give an example of how widely cited this literature is, a search on Google Scholar in February 2007 revealed that Acemoglu *et al.* (2001) has been cited in over 1200 scholarly works.

2. Sachs (2001) analyses the effect of geographic, but not institutional, variables on health.
3. In Section 8.2 we argued that for income per capita to be considered a good proxy for broader dimensions of economic development, for example life expectancy, the correlation between the two had to be relatively high. When examining the correlation between life expectancy (or the combined enrolment rate) and institutions we are concerned with whether variation across countries in institutions can explain *any* of the cross-country variation in life expectancy.
4. This does not imply that there are not potentially important channels of causation from malaria risk to levels of income per capita through to general health status, over and above the very direct effects of mortality due to malaria on life expectancy.
5. If instruments are 'weak', that is they do not have high (partial) correlations with the endogenous explanatory variables, 2SLS estimates can be badly biased and hypothesis tests based on these estimates can be prone to size distortion, making tests of statistical significance unreliable. Stock and Yogo (2005) derive critical values for the Cragg-Donald *F*-statistic, as a test of weak instruments, for different values of the number of included endogenous regressors (n), the number of excluded instrumental variables (K_2) and the desired maximal size of a 5 per cent Wald test if using 2SLS. For the models in columns (1) and (4), as $n = 1$, the Cragg-Donald statistic is equivalent to the first-stage *F*-statistic and the critical values are 16.38, 8.96 and 6.66 for, respectively, the 10 per cent, 15 per cent and 20 per cent sizes; hence, with a calculated Cragg-Donald value of 22.50, the null of weak instruments is rejected in the most stringent case where the maximum 2SLS size is no more than 10 per cent, corresponding to a maximum size distortion of 5 per cent. Also reported in Table 8.1 is the conventional partial R^2, which measures the squared partial correlation between the endogenous regressor and the excluded instrument(s), and the Shea (1997) partial R^2 measure; if $n = 1$ the latter equals the conventional partial R^2, but for $n > 1$ it takes into account intercorrelations between the instruments. For *INSTIT* and settler mortality, the partial R^2 of 0.241 is relatively modest.
6. The lack of statistical significance of *Pop100km* is not affected by removing *MeanTemp* from the model. The main difference is that omitting *MeanTemp* leads to a Cragg-Donald statistic of 38.99 compared to 9.47 for the model in column (2), for which the weak instrument null is rejected only for a 15 per cent maximum size.
7. *Malfal* measures the proportion of each country's population that lives with the risk of malaria multiplied by an estimate of the proportion of national malaria cases involving the fatal species *Plasmodium falciparum* (Sachs, 2003).
8. The value of the Cragg-Donald statistic for this model (11.28) implies rejection of the null of weak instruments only for a maximum size of 20 per cent (with a critical value of 8.75), implying a maximum size distortion of 15 per cent. In addition, the Shea partial R^2 values are noticeably lower than the conventional partial R^2 values, which may also indicate a weak instrument problem.

References

Acemoglu, D., Johnson, S. and Robinson, J. A. 'The Colonial Origins of Comparative Development: An Empirical Investigation', *American Economic Review*, 91 (2001): 1369–401.

Acemoglu, D., Johnson, S. and Robinson, J. A. 'Reversal of Fortune: Geography and Institutions in the Making of the Modern World Income Distribution', *Quarterly Journal of Economics*, 117 (2002): 1231–94.

Acemoglu, D., Johnson, S. and Robinson, J. A. 'Disease and Development in Historical Perspective', *Journal of the European Economic Association*, 1 (2003): 397–405.

Batten, A. and Martina, A. 'Diseases Dominate', in W. R. Garside (ed.), *Institutions and Market Economies: The Political Economy of Growth and Development* (Basingstoke: Palgrave Macmillan, 2007).

Bhattacharyya, S., Dowrick, S. and Golley, J. 'Institutions and Trade: Competitors or Complements in Economic Development?', Paper presented at the EDGES Road to Riches Workshop, Australian National University, November 2005.

Diamond, J. *Guns, Germs and Steel: A Short History of Everybody for the Last 13,000 Years* (New York: W. W. Norton, 1997).

Easterly, W. and Levine, R. 'Tropics, Germs, and Crops: How Endowments Influence Economic Development', *Journal of Monetary Economics*, 50 (2003): 3–39.

Frank R. H. and Bernanke, B. S. *Principles of Economics*, second edition (Boston: McGraw-Hill Irwin, 2004).

Hall R. E. and Jones, C. I. 'Why Do Some Countries Produce So Much More Output Per Worker Than Others?', *Quarterly Journal of Economics*, 114 (1999): 83–116.

Kaufmann, D., Kraay, A. and Zoido-Lobatón, P. 'Governance Matters II – Updated Indicators for 2000/01'. World Bank Policy Research Department, Working Paper No. 2772 (2002).

Kelley, A. C. 'The Human Development Index: Handle With Care', *Population and Development Review*, 17 (1991): 315–24.

Kiszewski, A., Mellinger, A., Spielman, A., Malaney, P., Ehrlich Sachs, S. and Sachs, J. 'A Global Index Representing the Stability of Malaria Transmission', *American Journal of Tropical Medicine and Hygiene*, 70 (2004): 486–98.

Landes, D. S. *The Wealth and Poverty of Nations: Why Some Are So Rich and Some So Poor* (New York: W. W. Norton, 1998).

McArthur, J. W. and Sachs, J. D. 'Institutions and Geography: Comment on Acemoglu, Johnson and Robinson (2000)'. Cambridge, MA, National Bureau of Economic Research, Working Paper No. 8114 (2001).

Meredith, M. *The State of Africa: A History of Fifty Years of Independence* (London: Simon and Schuster, 2005).

Noorbakhsh, F. 'The Human Development Index: Some Technical Issues and Alternative Indices', *Journal of International Development*, 10 (1998): 589–605.

North, D. C. *Institutions, Institutional Change and Economic Performance* (Cambridge: Cambridge University Press, 1990).

Olsson, O. and Hibbs Jr., D. A. 'Biogeography and Long-run Economic Development', *European Economic Review*, 49 (2005): 909–38.

Owen P. D. and Weatherston, C. R. 'The Deep Determinants of Long-run Growth and Economic Development', in W. R. Garside (ed.), *Institutions and Market Economies: The Political Economy of Growth and Development* (Basingstoke: Palgrave Macmillan, 2007).

Perkins, D. H., Radelet, S., Snodgrass, D. R., Gillis, M. and Roemer, M. *Economics of Development*, fifth edition (New York: W. W. Norton, 2001).
Ravallion, M. 'Good and Bad Growth: The Human Development Reports', *World Development*, 25 (1997): 631–8.
Ray, D. *Development Economics* (Princeton: Princeton University Press, 1998).
Rodrik, D., Subramanian, A. and Trebbi, F. 'Institutions Rule: The Primacy of Institutions Over Geography and Integration in Economic Development', *Journal of Economic Growth*, 9 (2004): 131–65.
Sachs, J. D. 'Tropical Underdevelopment'. Cambridge, MA., National Bureau of Economic Research, Working Paper No. 8119 (2001).
Sachs, J. D. 'Institutions Don't Rule: Direct Effects of Geography on Per Capita Income'. Cambridge, MA, National Bureau of Economic Research, Working Paper No. 9490 (2003).
Sachs, J. and Malaney, P. 'The Economic and Social Burden of Malaria', *Nature*, 415 (2002): 680–5.
Shea, J. 'Instrument Relevance in Multivariate Linear Models: A Simple Measure', *Review of Economics and Statistics*, 79 (1997) 348–52.
Stock, J. H. and Yogo, M. 'Testing for Weak Instruments in Linear IV Regression', in D. W. K. Andrews and J. H. Stock (eds), *Identification and Inference for Econometric Models: Essays in Honor of Thomas Rothenberg* (Cambridge: Cambridge University Press, 2005).
Todaro M. P. and Smith, S. C. *Economic Development*, ninth edition (Harlow: Pearson Addison-Wesley Longman, 2006).
Trabold-Nubler, H. 'The Human Development Index – A New Development Indicator', *Intereconomics*, 26 (1991): 236–43.
United Nations Development Programme. *Human Development Report 2003: Millennium Development Goals: A Compact Among Nations To End Human Poverty* (New York: Oxford University Press, 2003).
Woolcock, M. 'Social Capital and Economic Development: Toward a Theoretical Synthesis and Policy Framework', *Theory and Society*, 27 (1998): 151–208.

9
Diseases Dominate

Aaron Batten and Alan Martina

9.1 Introduction

What underlying or deep factors determine the distribution of social well-being across the nations of the world?

Variations of this question have received the attention of many over the centuries. Clearly Adam Smith, in *An Inquiry into the Nature of the Causes of the Wealth of Nations* (1776), addressed this question. In far more recent times, economic historians and others have attempted to provide, implicitly at least, cogent answers – authors such as Rostow (1960), Reynolds (1983), North and Thomas (1973), North (1990, 1994, 1995), Diamond (1997) and Bernstein (2004). The most recent group of contributors to the debate have been economists: in particular, Hall and Jones (1999), Acemoglu *et al.* (2001, 2002, 2005), Easterly and Levine (2003), Sachs (2003) and Rodrik *et al.* (2004).

The amount of attention given recently to attempting to answer versions of this generic question is not surprising given the contemporary world as it is. For instance, if a broad measure of social welfare is adopted, such as the Human Development Index (HDI), then in 1994 the measure for the country with the highest level was some 5.6 times greater than that for the country with the smallest measure. (Canada had the highest level of 0.9801 and Sierra Leone the smallest with a measure of 0.176).

In our attempt to answer the question posed we re-examine the empirical results, based on cross-country data sets, presented in Rodrik *et al.* (2004) and Acemoglu *et al.* (2001) respectively. Both sets of authors conclude that the variation across countries of a proxy variable that measures the quality of relevant economic institutions – that are solely concerned with ensuring the rule of law and the protection of individual property rights – is the dominant deep determinant that explains the variation in per capita GDP across countries in the mid-1990s. (The other deep determinants of economic development taken into account in Rodrik *et al.* (2004) were a measure of the level of integration of a country into international trade and a measure of the geography for this country).

We depart from their general approach in two ways. First, we, like others (for instance, Sen (1985, 1999), Dasgupta (1993) and Ranis (2004)), believe that a measure of per capita GDP for any community inadequately captures the range of relevant considerations that may influence the level of social well-being in this community, and presumably it is the variation in the level of social well-being across countries that most needs to be explained. For this reason we concentrate our attention on attempting to explain the variation across countries of a measure of the HDI in 1994.[1] While this measure of social well-being has been criticized on a number of grounds,[2] in our view it still is to be preferred to the use of per capita GDP. The second way that we depart from previous approaches is that we include one additional possible deep determinant of economic development besides the three considered by Rodrik *et al.* (2004), that is the percentage of the population at risk of contracting malaria (hereon called 'malaria risk'). This measure should be thought of as a proxy measure for the level of virulent diseases associated with malaria that are present in a community. (As pointed out in Section 9.3.2.2, the reduction in the prevalence of malaria in a community results in a fall in the child mortality rate from all causes of death).

We find that malaria risk is the dominant deep determinant (of the four determinants considered) that explains most of the variation of the HDI across countries in the mid-1990s. In particular, we find that on applying the standard tests of statistical significance the regressor representing economic institutions (namely the rule of law) is sometimes not statistically significant, whereas malaria risk is always statistically significant in all the estimated regression equations presented later in which both malaria risk and the rule of law (along with other relevant variables) are included as regressors. We also find that the coefficient estimates for relevant regression equations imply that a reduction in the level of malaria risk by one standard deviation (SD) always has a greater influence on increasing the level of the HDI than does a one-SD improvement in the measure of the rule of law. Exactly how much greater falls somewhere within the range of 1.25–5.68. Moreover, within this range the most reliable values probably are towards the lower bound. This is indicated by an argument developed in Section 9.4.4.1 that sets out a number of reasons why ordinary-least-squares (OLS) estimates of relevant regression equations may be more reliable than those generated by using two-stage-least–squares (2SLS) estimation procedures. These empirical results only apply to the average country in the late twentieth century. When the full data set is split into two sub-sets – one made up of countries in which malaria risk is present and the other made up of countries in which this risk is absent – we find that the regressor 'economic institutions' is not statistically significant for countries in which malaria risk is present. Naturally, malaria risk is a highly statistically significant regressor for these countries. In contrast, in those countries in which there is no malaria risk the regressor 'economic institutions' is highly statistically significant.

While these empirical results emphasize the importance of malaria and related diseases for explaining the variation in the level of well-being across countries, Rodrik *et al.* (2004: 151), in contrast, assert that because malaria is a debilitating rather than a fatal disease it is unlikely to have a marked influence on the level of per capita GDP. The relevant medical literature suggests otherwise. For instance, in 1994 some 46 per cent of the world's population was exposed to the risk of contracting malaria (Hay *et al.*, 2004: 328). In addition, in 2001 near to three million people died from malaria in Africa alone and, in that year, this disease was responsible possibly for two-thirds of the mortality rate from all causes for children under five years of age living in mildly to heavily malaria-infected regions on that continent.[3] Should a person survive a severe attack of this disease, what, as emphasized by Bremen (2001: 1), is '[p]articularly devastating to development are the long-duration effects of malaria, manifest in learning and behavioral disorders and decreased capacity to work'. For a country in which these long-term consequences are prevalent amongst the population, they are likely to have profound detrimental economic consequences.[4] (These matters will be explored a little further in Section 9.3.2.2).

For these reasons, we take seriously a result presented by Sachs (2003), namely that the risk of contracting malaria is a statistically significant regressor in explaining the variation in the level of per capita GDP across countries. Indeed, motivated by this result, we reconsider this matter here in some detail by taking into account a range of issues not considered by Sachs (2003).[5] To begin with, we allow for a wider range of regressors in the estimation of relevant regression equations. Whereas in Sachs (2003) the dependent variable was per capita GDP, we replace this dependent variable by considering a measure of social well-being (the HDI). We further question the use by Sachs (and others such as Acemoglu *et al.* (2001) and Rodrik *et al.* (2004)) of instrumental variables (IVs) within a 2SLS estimation procedure to estimate relevant coefficients and suggest, instead, that coefficient estimates derived from the application of OLS may be more reliable. For the sake of completeness, however, we do generate some empirical results by applying IVs within a 2SLS estimation procedure while also indicating how certain useful IVs can be exploited by drawing upon the theory, developed by Stock and Yogo (2005), for identifying weak IVs. Making use of the full data set only provides empirical results for the average country in the mid-1990s. To determine the influence of malaria risk and economic institutions on sub-groups of countries we split the full data set into two groups: countries that are faced with malaria risk and countries that are not.

Some readers may not be convinced by the econometric evidence to be presented later. We point out, however, that a brief perusal of the history of epidemics or pandemics of virulent infectious diseases (VIDs) suggests that these diseases have had a profound influence on how various societies have evolved over time.[6] One only needs to think of the Black Death pandemic that spread through Europe from 1347 to 1350 and the waves of pandemics of various VIDs that struck the civilizations of the Americas through the sixteenth century. The Black Death caused mortality rates of 30–40 per cent (Hays, 2003: 37) while the total population of the Americas was reduced from 50–100 million to below 10 million by the middle of the seventeenth century. Much of this reduction was due to pandemics of VIDs (Hays, 2003: 72–77) accidentally introduced from Europe. The long-term consequences of these dramatic demographic changes for the societies concerned were profound.

This theme is taken up in the next section, where we consider a case history from the late nineteenth century. During this episode History conspired, accidentally, with Nature to create a near-perfect controlled experiment to demonstrate the influence that an epidemic of VIDs alone can have on the economy of the community concerned. During this quasi-controlled experiment the level of economic institutions (from hereon, institutions) were of a comparatively high order.

An inference that can be drawn from this quasi-controlled experiment is that if, in the mid-1990s, some VIDs were widespread and their virulence varied markedly in intensity across the regions of the globe, then the presence of these VIDs must explain some proportion of the variation in the level of social well-being across countries. As indicated above (and as explained in more detail in Section 9.3.2.2), malaria and its associated diseases in the mid-1990s were just such a set of diseases. Naturally, this particular line of argument does not allow us to quantify how important malaria and associated diseases were relative to other factors (such as institutions) in the late twentieth century. To do so requires the application of econometric analysis.

The argument developed here is not meant to imply that we regard institutions as being of no importance. If possible, fatal contagious diseases need to be brought under control through the provision of the institution of public health. Once this has been done, then, and most likely only then, do the provision of a reasonable level of the rule of law and the protection of individual property rights come into their own in facilitating further economic development. What is more, just containing VIDs without subsequently providing a reasonable level of the rule of law and the protection of individual property rights probably will do relatively little to facilitate further expansion of the level of the HDI for the country concerned. As indicated by the analysis developed below, and culminating in Section 9.4, there seems to be a particular sequence of steps that need to be taken by a community before it can experience a sustained rise in the level of its HDI. VIDs have to be contained first before making provision for the rule of law and the protection of individual property rights.[7]

While we recognize the particular role that economic institutions have to play in the attempt to expand the level of social well-being for a poor community, we cannot agree with the following bold statement made by Bernstein (2004: 293):

> Institutions, not the bounty of nature or freedom from imperialist domination, separate the winners from the losers in the global economy. First and foremost, it is the degree of respect and reverence for the Rules of the Game – rule of law, equality under the law, and respect for the civil liberties of all – that dominates the wealth of nations.

This emphasis on the overarching importance of the institution of the Rules of the Game is not supported by the evidence presented here. The relevant issues are rather more complicated than Bernstein suggests. The presence or absence of widespread virulent contagious disease in the various communities of the world has to be part of any cogent story that attempts to explain the separation of 'the winners from the losers in the global economy'.[8]

The plan of this chapter is as follows. In Section 9.2 the History-Plus-Nature case study is considered. The basic regression model and data used to estimate this model are both discussed in Section 9.3. The core of the regression analysis is presented in Section 9.4. In Section 9.5 the data set used to estimate the regression model is extended to determine how robust the initial regression results are. In Section 9.6 we split the data set into those countries that, in the mid-1990s, were faced with malaria risk and those that were not. Concluding comments are made in Section 9.7.

9.2 Quasi-controlled experiment generated by History-Plus-Nature

9.2.1 The Panama Canal case

The controlled experiment takes the following form: in the initial situation in the community concerned there is a comparatively high level of the rule of law, and the protection of individual property rights (Rule) is in place. A VID is present in the environment of this community, however. Those who invest in the economy for this community are not aware of this fact, or disregard it. The question is, will this investment prove to be privately profitable? Or more generally, will it be possible, at reasonable cost, to develop the economy for this community? To answer this question we consider the attempt to build the Panama Canal between 1881 and 1914.

After Ferdinand de Lesseps created his company to raise financial capital to fund the building of the Panama Canal, construction began in 1881.[9] Clearly investors in this project perceived that the quality of the rule of law and the protection of individual property rights were adequate; otherwise, presumably, they would not have invested in this project. Within a short time, however, deaths caused by either yellow fever or malaria began to occur amongst the workforce. By the end of 1888 the level of mortality had risen to an estimated 30,000. (At some locations along the building corridor for the canal it is likely that two out of every three workers died from these diseases). At this point, this civil engineering project was abandoned by the French entrepreneurs.

While there were engineering and geological difficulties that also needed to be overcome for this project to be completed, it seems reasonable to infer from these facts regarding mortality that the main constraint on this investment project becoming privately profitable was that created by the prevalent fatal contagious diseases. That the institutions of the rule of law and individual property rights were in place did not alter this situation. This argument was understood by senior members of the United States Federal government when it took over the task of building the canal in 1904.

In response to an outbreak of yellow fever that had occurred along the canal corridor in the first part of 1905, John Stevens, on being appointed the chief engineer for the canal project in that year, immediately called for building work on the canal to cease. Stevens then allocated all available resources to William Crawford Gorgas – who had gained considerable experience in controlling the breeding of mosquitoes (in particular *Aëdes aegypti*) in Cuba between 1900 and 1904 in the attempt to contain yellow fever[10] – to allow him to mount a vigorous campaign aimed at drastically reducing the mosquito population along the canal corridor. Above all, Stevens and Gorgas realized that until this task had been performed successfully it would not be economically efficient to attempt to construct the canal. This decision received the support of President Theodore Roosevelt on the advice, in particular, of his friend Dr William David Lambert, who stated the following: '...If you [President Roosevelt] fall back upon the old methods...you will fail, just as the French failed. If you back up Gorgas and his ideas and let him pursue his campaign against the mosquito, you will get your canal' (McCullough, 1977: 77, 467–8). Roosevelt heeded this advice and gave his support to Stevens and Gorgas. One consequence was that only two per cent of the workforce used in the building of the canal was hospitalized in the period 1904–14 compared to about a 33 per cent mortality rate during the period 1881–88.

9.2.2 Inference and interpretation

This well-documented case history, and other case histories not discussed here,[11] indicate that controlling VIDs is a necessary condition that has to be satisfied before sustained economic development is possible in any community. In particular, this case history indicates that an adequate level of the rule of law is not the only institution that a society needs to have in place to ensure that its economy functions reasonably effectively. It also is crucially important to have in place institutions that facilitate the provision of an adequate level of public health. In the present study, however, the reason for not allowing for public health in the econometric analysis is that the variable we attempted to use to represent public health – namely the level of the effectiveness of government to provide public services – is so highly correlated with the rule of law. It is not possible to distinguish easily between these two measures of the quality of quite different types of institutions. (The simple correlation coefficient between the rule of law and government effectiveness is 0.9098).[12]

9.3 Model to be estimated and its variables

In the previous section advantage was taken of quasi-controlled experimental evidence to draw the inference (bearing in mind relevant information presented later in Section 9.3.2.2) that malaria and associated diseases must be of significant importance in explaining the variation in the level of social well-being across countries in the mid-1990s. Attention now turns to attempting to confirm this inference and to quantifying the relative importance of malaria and associated diseases in explaining the variation in the level of social well-being across countries.

9.3.1 The basic model

To guide the selection of the data, we draw on and extend the model sketched out by Rodrik *et al.* (2004). This model is indicated in Figure 9.1, which indicates that a range of variables are assumed to interact with each other and with the level of social well-being for the representative country. The variables Rodrik *et al.* (2004) employed were GDP per capita, geography, institutions and the level of integration of the economy into international trade for the country concerned. We have added to this list the disease burden that the representative country faces. We also have replaced GDP per capita with the HDI, a variable that is used to represent the level of social well-being.

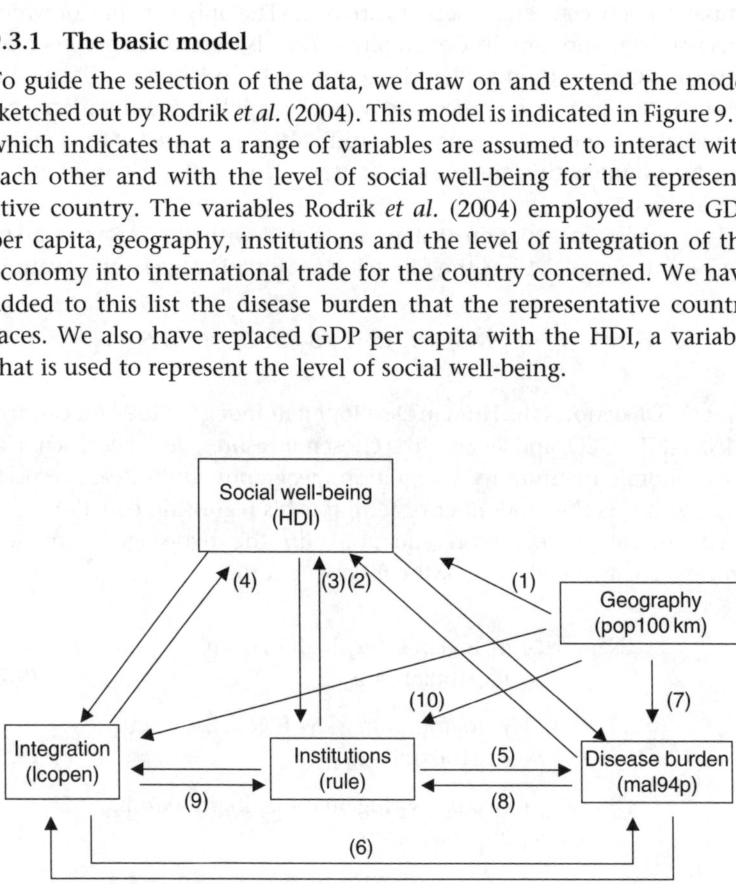

Figure 9.1 Channels of inter-causality between the deep determinants: Extended model separating geography into disease burden and ease of access to water transport

It can be seen in Figure 9.1 that some of the arrows have been numbered, indicating the lines of causation. In this section and the next, we are particularly interested in the arrows marked (1), (2), (3) and (4). In Section 9.3.3 we also will consider the line causation associated with the arrows marked (8) (the influence of the disease burden on the level of institutions) and (5) (the influence of the level of institutions on the disease burden) while also allowing for other considerations (such as the influence of Geography on Institutions).

The main technical difficulty associated with estimating at least part of the system represented in Figure 9.1 is the endogeneity or reverse causation between certain sets of variables. (The only variable for which this issue does not arise is Geography, which is treated as an exogenous variable). One method for handling this problem is the use of suitable IVs in a 2SLS estimation procedure. While we apply this estimation technique later, there are some practical difficulties associated with applying this technique within the present context. This matter is considered in Section 9.4.4.1.

The regression equation system associated with the arrows marked (1) – (4) in Figure 9.1 has the following as its basic regression equation:

$$\mathrm{HDI}_i = \beta_o + \beta_1\ \mathrm{INS}_i + \beta_2\ \mathrm{INT}_i + \beta_3\ \mathrm{GEO}_i + \beta_4\ \mathrm{DIS}_i + \varepsilon_i, \qquad (9.1)$$

where HDI_i denotes the Human Development Index for 1994 for country i, INS_i, INT_i, GEO_i and DIS_i are the chosen measures, yet to be discussed, for economic institutions, integration, geography and disease respectively, and ε_i is the random error term for this regression equation.

The first-stage regression equations (in the two-stage estimation process) are assumed to be of the following form:

$$\mathrm{INS}_i = \alpha_o + \alpha_1\ \mathrm{logem4}_i + \alpha_2\ \mathrm{logfrankrom}_i + \alpha_3\ \mathrm{me}_i + \alpha_4\ \mathrm{Pop100km}_i + \varepsilon_{i\mathrm{INS}}; \qquad (9.2)$$

$$\mathrm{INT}_i = \gamma_0 + \gamma_1\ \mathrm{logfrankrom}_i + \gamma_2\ \mathrm{logem4}_i + \gamma_3\ \mathrm{me}_i + \gamma_4\ \mathrm{Pop100km}_i + \varepsilon_{i\mathrm{INT}}; \qquad (9.3)$$

$$\mathrm{DIS}_i = \kappa_o + \kappa_1\ \mathrm{me}_i + \kappa_2\ \mathrm{logem4}_i + \kappa_3\ \mathrm{logfrankrom}_i + \kappa_4\ \mathrm{Pop100km}_i + \varepsilon_{i\mathrm{DIS}}. \qquad (9.4)$$

The regressors in these three regression equations are IVs that are listed and specified in Table 9.1. These IVs are discussed later. The terms $\varepsilon_{\mathrm{INS}}$ and so on refer to error terms in first-stage regression equations.

Table 9.1 Descriptive statistics of key variables

	(1) Mean	(2) Standard deviation	(3) Max Observations	(4) Min	(5) Max
Human development index 1994 (HDI94)	0.6643	0.23	169	0.176	0.98
OLS estimators					
Rule of law (Rule)	0.003	0.95	168	−2.16	1.91
Log nominal openness (Lcopen)	4.12	0.59	170	2.55	5.78
Population within 100 km of navigable waterways 1995 (Pop100 km)	432	0.37	150	0	1.00
Percentage of population at risk of contracting malaria (Mal94p)	0.36	0.44	165	0	1.00
Instrumental variables					
Log European settler mortality during 17th, 18th and 19th centuries (logem4)	4.66	1.21	81	2.14	7.99
Percentage population speaking English (engfrac)	0.07	0.24	182	0	1.00
Percentage population speaking European languages (eurfrac)	0.22	0.38	185	0	1.00
Log constructed trade share (logfrankrom)	3.01	0.80	163	0.83	5.64
Malaria ecology (me)	3.66	6.42	173	0	31.55

Note: Sources for all data provided in Appendix A.

The estimates of these first-stage regression equations provide the basis for generating the predicted values of INS, INT and DIS that are used as instruments to estimate regression equations (Equation 9.1).

9.3.2 The regressors

An interpretation of one aspect of what is attempted in this section is that we decompose the measure of geography (Geo) used in Rodrik *et al.* (2004: 162). There, this measure was defined as the distance of the capital of the country concerned from the equator (measured as the absolute latitude divided by 90). In our view, this measure is too all-encompassing. There are many dimensions of the geography of a country which capture quite different aspects of the given economic and climatic environment in which the country operates.[13] For this reason we essentially consider two variables that measure two quite different aspects of the geography of a country.

9.3.2.1 Distance from water transport

This variable draws on the observation that a nation's degree of access to navigable waterways has been shown to play an important role in its development since it will influence the extent to which a region can specialize in the production of goods in which it has a comparative advantage (Gallup *et al.*, 1998, 1999; Radelet and Sachs, 1998). For this reason we use the proportion of a nation's population within 100 km of the coast or navigable waterways (Pop100 km).

The other variable is the risk of contracting malaria, the level of which is determined to some extent by the country's location relative to the equator. (The risk of contracting malaria in a region also is influenced by the altitude of the region, the amount of rainfall and types of mosquitoes and malaria parasites to be found in this region). Both these variables were employed in Sachs (2003). He applied these variables separately, however, in different regression equations. Later we employ both variables in a single regression equation to estimate regression equation (Equation 9.1).

9.3.2.2 Malaria

On consulting estimates for the 1990s and beyond of the mortality rate and disease burden (measured by disability-adjusted life years) imposed by malaria, relative to that for a range of other contagious diseases (Murray and Lopez, 1997a, Table 3; Murray and Lopez, 1997b, Table 3; WHO, 2002), the impression may be gained that malaria imposes a relatively small disease burden. In 1990, malaria ranked only sixth of all contagious diseases, with lower respiratory infections and diarrhoeal diseases appearing to have imposed far greater burdens on the world community. However, as Snow *et al.* (2004) point out, these estimates are based on the incorrect assumption that an individual death or morbidity event is caused by a single disease. In contrast, empirical evidence they present indicates that in sub-Saharan Africa, malaria contributes in indirect ways towards the death of children under the age of five from a range of diseases. The upper limit of their estimates, based on statistical inference, suggests that when allowing for these indirect mechanisms, about two-thirds of all deaths for this age group are caused by malaria.[14]

Snow *et al.* (2004) qualify their estimates since they emphasize they have not been confirmed by satisfactory controlled experimental evidence that would allow for all confounding factors or where, during the experiment, malaria is eliminated completely from the relevant population. Nevertheless, their estimates are suggestive.[15,16]

Two inferences follow from these observations. One is that, clearly, actual mortality and morbidity rates for malaria (where malaria is treated as the single cause of death or morbidity) would understate (possibly by a large amount) the true burden imposed by this disease. For this reason the indicator used here for the disease burden imposed by malaria in a given country is the risk of contracting malaria in that country. The other inference is that since malaria interacts with various other diseases, the risk of contracting malaria could be viewed as a proxy variable for the risk of contracting a range of infectious diseases.

A further reason for treating this variable as a proxy variable is that a range of less virulent tropical diseases, such as sleeping sickness (trypanosomiasis), hookworm (ancylostomiasis), bilharzia (shistosomiasis) and yellow fever, are to be found in geographic regions of the world in which the risk of contracting malaria is also comparatively high. (This point can be established by consulting the world map of the distribution of incidence of malaria (Hay *et al.*, 2004) and comparing it with the various relevant world maps of the geographic distribution of the incidence of various relevant tropical diseases (Kiple, 1993)).

Figure 9.2 indicates the various channels along which malaria (and its associated diseases) are thought to influence the level of the HDI. In this regard it is noteworthy that Sachs and others have argued that the prevalence of malaria in a country can have a significant *direct* impact on the level of development of this country. (See the references cited in Endnote 5). For example, even when workers who are ill do attend their place of employment they are likely to function well below their normal levels of productivity due to reduced energy levels and an impaired ability to concentrate. In addition, a life plagued with sickness almost certainly will reduce an individual's life expectancy, which, in turn, is likely to reduce the value of the human capital invested in this person. Consequently this will tend to reduce the incentive for employers to invest in the education of the workforce.

For younger individuals who are sick regularly, it will be difficult to find the energy needed to attend school. In a study by Foster and Leighton (1993: 11) of the economic impacts of malaria in Kenya and

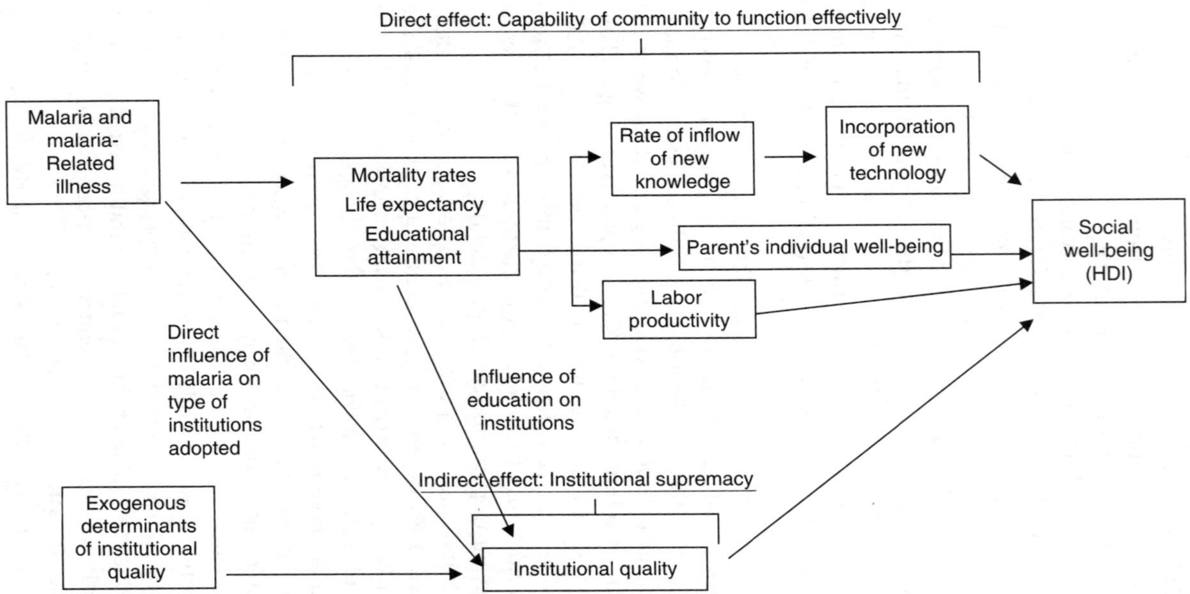

Figure 9.2 Flow chart of hypothesized channels of influence of disease burden on levels of social well-being

Nigeria it was estimated that school children in Kenya miss, on average, 11 per cent of their schooling due to malaria and malaria-related illness. (In this study malaria is also estimated to deprive the economy of anywhere up to 14 per cent of its workforce due to worker absenteeism and reduced productivity per year). In addition, the comparatively high child mortality rate caused by malaria is likely to reduce the incentive for parents to invest in their children's education.

The risk of contracting malaria will also tend to reduce the flow of information from low-malarious to the higher-malarious regions of the world (Malaney and Sachs, 2002: 684; Malaney *et al.*, 2004: 143–4). For instance, since foreign direct investment is one of the most important channels along which new knowledge and technologies flow into a developing country, the increased level of risk associated with foreign investment in comparatively highly malarious areas will retard the flow of useful information into these areas. In addition, the relatively high risk of foreigners contracting malaria, as a result of visiting malarious countries, also has the potential to impede the flow of relevant knowledge to these countries.

Figure 9.2 also indicates that the risk of contracting malaria will influence directly the well-being of parents who see their children dying in relatively large numbers. This in turn influences the level of social well-being in the community concerned. The matter of immunity from malaria, and specifically the immunity that children inherit in the form of the sickle cell trait from one parent, is relevant here. Those children that inherit this immunity receive a haemoglobin mutation which effectively renders the carrier comparatively immune to the transmission of malaria. However, if this sickle cell trait is inherited from both parents then the carrier often contracts Sickle Cell Anaemia, a condition that cannot be cured. This illness in effect incapacitates the infected individual for extended periods over a life which usually ends prematurely.[17]

Finally, Figure 9.2 also suggests that malaria has an indirect influence on social well-being. In this instance malaria operates along two channels to influence the level of institutions, which, in turn, influences the level of social well-being. Along one channel an increase in the level of malaria risk directly reduces the level of institutions. (This line of causation was indicated by Acemoglu *et al.*, 2001). Along the other channel, an increased level of malaria risk reduces the level of education, which, in turn, reduces the level of institutions. This line of causation is suggested by a point made by Glaeser *et al.*, 2004; that is, the higher the level of education in a community, the higher the level of institutions. Glaeser *et al.* did not mention, however, the influence of malaria, or other diseases, on the level of education. The possible influence of malaria risk on the level of institutions is discussed further in Section 9.3.3.

9.3.2.3 *Rest of the regressors*

The other two regressors in the basic model are the institution of the rule of law and the protection of individual property rights (Rule) and the integration of a country into the world economy as measured by the logarithm of the openness of the economy to international trade (Lcopen). The preferred measure of integration is an index adopted from Rodrik *et al.* (2004), which is the natural logarithm of a ratio of nominal imports plus nominal exports compared to nominal GDP, measured in nominal US dollars averaged over all available data for the period 1950–98. It might be argued that this last variable, Lcopen, overlaps with Pop100 km since the ease of access to water transport would facilitate international trade. This does not seem to be the case, however, as the simple correlation coefficient between these two variables for the cross-county data sets we use for these two variables is just 0.1193.

9.3.3 Instrumental variables

As indicated in Figure 9.1, endogeneity and reverse causality are assumed to exist between all the variables (except Geography) referred to in that figure. It could be argued that to allow for this endogeneity relevant IVs should be applied within a 2SLS estimation procedure. While this point of view will be questioned in Section 9.4.4.1, for the present the IVs that are applied later are considered, briefly, here. The IV for Rule is that provided by Acemoglu *et al.* (2001: 1370): the mortality rates for colonists from the seventeenth, eighteenth and nineteenth centuries (henceforth logem4). The hypothesis is that a high level of these mortality rates within a given region would have reduced the rate of adoption of desirable economic institutions in that region. In addition, since these colonial mortality rates are unlikely to be correlated with the current levels of economic activity, it might be thought that this variable serves as an appropriate instrument for contemporary measures of institutional quality. This belief is questioned in Section 9.4.4.1.

Frankel and Romer (1999) constructed an instrument for international trade by estimating a bilateral trade equation, and then aggregated the fitted values for this equation in order to estimate the geographic component of a nation's overall trade relations. The constructed trade share variable (logfrankrom) is used as the IV for international integration. The IV chosen to control for the potential endogeneity of malaria risk is an index (me) devised from Kiszewski *et al.* (2004) that estimates a nation's malaria burden based upon its comparative ecologically based transmission vectors. This index has been criticized by Rodrick *et al.* (2004: 151) amongst others as not being truly exogenous and, therefore, not a satisfactory IV for malaria risk. This view could be challenged since this index measures mosquito species, parasite type, regional ambient temperatures and rainfall conditions – factors that tend to be exogenous to any reasonable intervention by human action. Hence, this IV appears to possess the required desired properties. (Gundlach (2004: 10) makes a similar point). Nevertheless, the use of this IV can be questioned for reasons other than those mentioned by Rodrick *et al.* (2004). The relevant argument is sketched out in Section 9.4.4.1.

9.4 Estimated regression results

9.4.1 Ordinary-least-squares estimations

As a point of reference the influence of diseases, institutions, geography and integration on HDI is estimated using OLS.[18] In the regression results presented in Table 9.2 allowance has been made for heteroscedasticity within the context that the data set is of a limited or finite size.[19] (This implies that robust *t*-statistics are estimated).

In this table a variation of the core OLS estimate of Equation 9.1 is set out in column 1. The estimated coefficients for Geography and Institutions are highly statistically significant and with their expected signs. The Integration coefficient is neither statistically significant nor correctly signed. This result is consistent with the findings reported in Rodrik *et al.* (2004).

Next, Disease (malaria risk) is added to the regression equation to be estimated. The estimated coefficients are set out in column 2 in Table 9.2. Again, all estimated coefficients, except that for integration, have the desired properties. Hence malaria risk appears to matter in determining the level of HDI.

If these coefficient estimates are interpreted as accurately representing the causal links amongst each of these variables then, as a general rule, those nations with a low exposure to malaria risk, high-quality institutions and a large proportion of their population residing near water transport could be expected to have substantially higher levels of social well-being (as defined) in the mid-1990s compared to those

Table 9.2 Determinants of development: The Human Development Index for 1994 is the dependent variable using ordinary-least-squares estimations

Regressors	(1)	(2)	(3)
Integration	0.0165	−0.0108	−0.0035
(Lcopen)	(0.64)	(−0.61)	(−0.20)
Geography	0.0985***	0.0953***	0.0649**
(Pop100 km)	(2.70)	(3.35)	(2.42)
Institutions	0.1606***	0.0766***	0.0811***
(Rule)	(12.96)	(6.95)	(7.25)
Disease	–	−0.328***	−0.2197***
(Mal94p)		(−12.19)	(−6.51)
Sub-Saharan Africa dummy variable			−0.1465***
			(−4.51)
Adj. R^2	0.5066	0.7685	0.8060
No. Obs.	138	138	128
F-Statistic	83.46	184.03	145.09

Note: Robust *t*-statistics in parenthesis (according to the two-tailed test significant at the five per cent level (*), two per cent level(**), and one per cent level (***)).

nations that were exposed to high levels of malaria risk, had low-quality institutions and were landlocked without easy access to navigable rivers.

Next, to assess the importance of malaria risk in influencing the level of the HDI, the coefficient estimate for malaria risk (Mal94p) in Table 9.2, column 2, is multiplied by an improvement in the level of this variable (that is, the level of malaria risk is reduced in size) by one SD. (The value of the SD for this regressor is found in Table 9.1 and in column 1 in Appendix C). The resulting adjusted value (0.328×0.44) is 0.144. The same adjustment, *mutatis mutandis*, is made to the coefficient estimate for each of the other regressors listed in Table 9.2, column 2. These adjusted coefficient estimates are set out in Appendix C, column 2.[20] These calculations indicate that malaria risk has the greatest impact on the level of the HDI, having nearly twice as much impact than do Institutions (Rule), and over four times more impact than does Geography (*Pop100 km*). These calculations based on OLS estimates of relevant coefficients suggest, therefore, that diseases dominate in explaining the distribution of the HDI across all countries.

9.4.2 Allowing for the sub-Saharan African dummy

Approximately 90 per cent of the morbidity due to malaria takes place in the tropical and sub-tropical regions of Africa (Hay *et al.*, 2004: 333). This fact raises the following question: Is the disease burden created by malaria significant in its own right in explaining the cross-country variation in the level of the HDI, or is malaria risk simply acting as an alternative indicator for some other unidentified variable(s) closely related to sub-Saharan Africa?

In the attempt to answer this question a dummy variable for sub-Saharan Africa – a variable that represents a range of factors unique to this area of the world – is included in the basic regression equation. The resulting coefficient estimates are set out in Table 9.2, column 3. The coefficient estimate for Disease remains statistically significant, as do the coefficient estimates for all the other regressors (except that for Integration). The size of the coefficient estimate for Disease, however, is now smaller than previously.

Next, these coefficient estimates are adjusted as before to determine the influence of a particular variable on the level of the HDI. The results are set out in Appendix C, column 3. Now Disease has 26 per cent more impact on the level of the HDI than do Institutions, and still over four times more impact than does Geography.

9.4.3 Allowing for the indirect influence of Disease on Institutions

It is indicated in Figures 9.1 and 9.2 that Disease also may influence the level of Institutions, which in turn will influence the level of the HDI. It also is indicated in Figure 9.1 that Institutions may influence the level of Disease. These matters are considered here. The OLS regression results presented in Table 9.3, column 1 tend to support the conjecture that Disease influences the level of Institutions.

In that regression the level of Disease (for 1994) and the average years of schooling (over the period 1970–1985) have a lagged influence on the average level of the rule of law (for 2000 and 2002). All the coefficients have the expected sign and are highly statistically significant.[21]

It follows that a one-SD reduction in the level of Disease increases the level of the Institutions by ($0.44 \times 0.6862 =$) 0.3019 units, which in turn would raise the level of the HDI. This calculation is taken into account in column 2 in Appendix C. Now Disease has 2.29 times more impact than do Institutions on the level of the HDI. A similar re-calculation is done for column 3 in Appendix C (where the sub-Saharan African dummy variable is included in the relevant regression equation in Table 9.2) so that now Disease has 58 per cent more impact on the

Table 9.3 Factors determining the level of the rule of law 2000–02 and the level of malaria risk (1994)

Regressors	**(1)** **Rule of law 2000 – 02** **OLS estimate**	**(2)** **Disease (mal94p)** **2SLS estimate**
Disease	−0.6862***	
(mal94p)	(−3.48)	
Geography	0.6204***	
(Pop100 km)	(3.60)	
Average years of schooling	0.1835***	0.0711
1970–1985	(6.41)	(0.63)
Institutions		0.5538
(Rule 1990s)		(−1.35)
Latin American	−0.7422***	
dummy variable	(−4.63)	
Sub-Saharan		−0.3657***
dummy variable		(2.86)
Adj R^2	0.6785	0.1164
No. Obs.	103	59

Note: Robust *t*-statistics in parenthesis (according to the two-tailed test significant at the five per cent level(*), two per cent level(**), and one per cent level (***)).

level of the HDI than do Institutions. These re-calculations are shown in brackets in columns 2 and 3 respectively in Appendix C.

The lagged structure present in the regression equation represented in Table 9.3, column 1, implies that, in that equation, there should be no reverse causation going from the average level of the rule of law (for 2000 and 2002) through to the level of the malaria risk (in 1994) and the average level of schooling (from 1970 through to 1985). An alternative test of the possible presence of this reverse causality was devised by making use of a 2SLS estimation procedure. In this case an IV (the mortality rate for settlers) was used as the instrument for the rule of law (for the 1990s). In this test it was found that the rule of law had no statistically significant influence on malaria risk. The relevant coefficient estimates are set out in Table 9.3, column 2.

9.4.4 Two-stage-least-squares estimations

9.4.4.1 Should instrumental variables be applied?

As indicated in Figure 9.1 and within the context of the basic regression model set out in Equations 9.1–9.4, it is assumed that there is reverse causality running from the level of the HDI through to the level of each of the regressors on the right-hand side of Equation (9.1), except for Geography. Does it follow, however, that an attempt should be made to correct for this assumed endogeneity by making use of IVs within a 2SLS estimation procedure when estimating relevant regression equations? There are grounds for arguing that no such correction should be made.[22]

First, while the presence of endogeneity will bias the relevant coefficient estimate away from zero, there are other factors at work that may bias these estimates in the opposite direction. One such factor is measurement errors that are present in the estimation of the coefficients presented in Table 9.2. This is so since most of the regressors in Equation (9.1) are only proxy variables for the true values of the variables we wish to measure. For instance, the variable used to measure the influence of malaria risk does not measure directly the level of mortality and morbidity caused by this disease in the country concerned. Similarly, the regressor Rule is only a proxy variable for the quality of economic institutions. That being the case, the coefficient estimates for regression equations (9.3) and (9.4) in Table 9.2 will suffer from attenuation bias. It is not possible to determine the direction of this bias, however, given that a number of the regressors in those regression equations suffer from measurement errors (Green, 2003: 83–6).

Another bias is probably caused by the presence of omitted variables, because there is a wide range of regressors that possibly should have been included in the regression equation estimates set out in Table 9.2. Because of the presence of multi-collinearity, however, these variables could not be identified. Consequently they were omitted from those regression equations, which will also tend to result in relevant coefficient estimates being biased.

It follows that the influence of the simultaneous presence of endogeneity, measurement errors and omitted variables within a relevant regression equation, estimated by using OLS, implies that it is not at all clear in which direction the coefficient estimates, set out in Table 9.2, are biased. The overall consequence possibly is that these estimates are not unduly biased. If that is the case then IVs should not be used (along with 2SLS) to re-calculate the regression equation estimates set out in Table 9.2. This is especially so if the IVs that are available do not possess satisfactory properties.

A satisfactory IV must possess the following two properties: (a) it is adequately correlated with the regressor for which it is the instrument; and (b) it is uncorrelated with the error term in the regression equation being estimated. While the IVs listed in Table 9.1 may satisfy property (a), some do not satisfy (b). For instance, the IV for the rule of law – settler mortality rates for the seventeenth to nineteenth centuries – will be correlated with contemporary variables such as tropical climate, regional dummies and malaria risk in a given country. In addition, these latter variables probably suffer from measurement errors (since they do not measure what is actually required). Consequently, settler mortality rates, if used as an IV in a 2SLS estimation of a relevant regression equation, will tend to be correlated with the error term in this equation. (Similar remarks apply to the IV (malaria ecology) for malaria risk). The resulting coefficient estimates consequently will tend to be biased.

If one combines these two lines of argument, it follows that the use of the IVs listed in Table 9.1 in a 2SLS estimation of relevant regression equations may result in coefficient estimates that are less satisfactory (that is, more biased) than those derived by just using OLS to estimate these equations. For the sake of completeness, however, some 2SLS estimates of relevant regression equations will be provided here by making use of the IVs listed in Table 9.1.

9.4.4.2 Applying the instrumental variables

In estimating regression equation (9.1), based on 2SLS procedures that make use of regression equations (9.2)–(9.4), it needs to be established whether the proposed instruments are sufficiently strongly identified with each of the endogenous regressors in Equation (9.1). To do so, the test proposed by Stock and Yogo (2005) is used.[23] This test requires that if a particular instrument is sufficiently strongly identified with its endogenous regressor then the estimated F-statistic, for the first-stage estimation of the 2SLS estimation procedure, will exceed a certain critical value. (A table of critical values is found in Stock and Yogo (2005, Table 2). The sizes of these critical values of the F-statistic are conditional on the number of endogenous regressors within the regression equation and on the number of IVs that are being applied. (In the present case there are three endogenous explanatory variables and three instruments).

A difficulty with applying this test in practice is that the critical values of the F-statistic are only provided in Stock and Yogo (2005: 59) up to a maximum of two endogenous regressors. Fortunately, however, it has been possible to extend this table up to three endogenous explanatory variables.[24] That being the case, the critical value in the present case – three endogenous regressors and three instruments – is 4.23.[25] This value is well below the smallest F-statistic (12.94) for the first-stage regression equations. The F-statistic for these equations is reported at the bottom

Table 9.4 Deep determinants of development: The Human Development Index for 1994 is the dependent variable in two-stage-least-squares estimations

Regressors	**(1)**	**(2)**
Integration	−0.1184	−0.0435
(Lcopen)	(−1.65)	(−0.94)
Geography	0.2086**	0.0983
(Pop100 km)	(2.06)	(2.50)
Institutions	0.0485	0.2530
(Rule)	(0.69)	(0.48)
Disease	−0.3572**	−0.4495***
(Mal94p)	(−2.60)	(−4.23)
Instruments	(logfrankrom, logem4, me)	(logfrankrom, engfrac, me)
Adj.R^2	0.6308	0.7283
No. Obs.	71	120
F-Statistic	30.49	53.92
F-Statistic for each of	20.71	25.57
the first-stage	12.94	10.92
regression equations	22.91	25.14

Note: Robust *t*-statistics in parenthesis (according to the two-tailed test significant at the five per cent level (*), two per cent level(**), and one per cent level (***)).

of column 1 in Table 9.4. Hence the IVs are non-weak for each of the endogenous variables.

Also set out in Table 9.4, column 1 are the 2SLS coefficient estimates and the descriptive statistics for the core regression equation. As can be seen there, Institutions are no longer statistically significant whereas Disease is. (While the relevant regression results are not shown, the inclusion of the sub-Saharan Africa dummy variable does not improve the situation since the coefficient estimate for this regressor is not statistically significant).

The regression estimates presented in Table 9.4, column 1, when multiplied by the SD for the relevant regressor, imply that Disease has a greater impact on the level of the HDI than any of the other regressors. As reported in Appendix C, Disease has some 3.41 times greater impact on the level of the HDI than do Institutions. But clearly this calculation is biased strongly in favour of Institutions since this regressor is not nearly statistically significantly different from zero according to the standard two-tailed test of significance. Disease also has 2.20 times more impact on the level of the HDI than does Geography.

9.5 Expanding the limited sample size

A reasonable criticism that can be levelled at the coefficient estimates presented in Table 9.4, column 1, is that they are based upon a comparatively small data set. This is the consequence of the use of the mortality rates for colonial settlers from the seventeenth through to the nineteenth centuries (logem4) as an IV for the rule of law. The question is, however, what IV or IVs can be used in place of logem4. Here we turn to Hall and Jones (1999: 100), where they argue that the influence that Western culture has had on the institutions that have evolved throughout the world can be measured by the percentage of a nation's current population that speak either English (engfrac) or a Western European (eurfrac) language as their first language.[26] The use of both or one of these alternative IVs will allow the data set to be expanded from 71 to around 120 sets of observations: about a 70 per cent increase in the sample size. This increase should assist in increasing the accuracy of the regression coefficient estimates by reducing the variance of these estimates. That said, these alternative IVs may be weak (according to the Stock–Yogo test) and, if so, should not be used.

To test if this is the case, we experimented with combinations of the alternative IVs (engfrac and eurfrac). The most satisfactory results were derived by applying enfrac as the IV for the rule of law. The *F*-statistics for each of the first-stage regression equations on applying this IV are set out at the bottom of column 2 in Table 9.4. Each is greater than the critical value of 4.23 and hence engfrac can be regarded as a non-weak instrument, along with the other IVs listed in Table 9.4, column 2.

The coefficient estimates that are derived by applying this alternative set of IVs are set out in Table 9.4, column 2. On comparing these results with those in column 1 in that table it is clear that Disease and Geography now are more statistically significant than when the settler mortality rate (logem4) is used as the IV for the rule of law. Also Institutions and Integration are now even more statistically insignificant than before. (While not shown, introducing the dummy variable for sub-Saharan Africa into the regression equation does not alter these results since the coefficient for this regressor is not statistically significantly different from zero on applying to the standard two-tailed test of significance).

The coefficient estimates in Table 9.4, column 2, also are adjusted by multiplying them with the SD for the relevant regressor to determine the influence that a particular regressor has on the level of the HDI. The consequent results set out in column 5 in Appendix C indicate that in this instance Disease has 5.68 times more impact on the level of the HDI than do Institutions. This is so even though this calculation is biased strongly in favour of Institutions since (as just noted) the coefficient estimate for this regressor is not statistically significantly different from zero. Disease also has 5.43 times more impact than does Geography on the level of the HDI.

9.6 The influence of Disease and Institutions on different groups of countries

9.6.1 Econometric results

The econometric results reported in Tables 9.2 and 9.4 and in Appendix C indicate that Disease dominates in explaining the level of the HDI for the average country in the late twentieth century. Is this still the case for subgroups of countries? Clearly, for one subgroup of countries this cannot be so because the citizens of these countries, in the mid-1990s, faced no risk of contracting malaria. Indeed, for the average country in this group, Institutions now completely dominate in determining the level of the HDI for this country. This is indicated by the relevant coefficient estimates for this group of countries reported in Table 9.5, column 3.

As for the group of countries that faced a non-zero malaria risk in the mid-1990s, Disease dominates again in determining the level of the HDI for the average country in this group. If the dummy variable for sub-Saharan Africa is taken into consideration then Disease is the only other regressor (besides the sub-Saharan Africa dummy) that is statistically significant. The relevant coefficient estimates are reported in Table 9.5, columns 1 and 2.[27]

9.6.2 Conjecture regarding development policy

The results presented in Table 9.5 along with those in Tables 9.2 and 9.4 suggest a conjecture regarding the path that a country, with a low level of the HDI and facing malaria risk, should adopt in an attempt to achieve for its citizens a sustained increase in the level of social well-being. First, malaria and associated infectious diseases have to be contained. Once this has been accomplished, then it becomes essential to provide the rule of law and the protection of individual property rights. The first part of this line of argument is suggested by the coefficient estimates in Tables 9.2 and 9.4 (when taken in conjunction with the results reported in Appendix C), and those in Table 9.5, columns 1 and 2 – results

Table 9.5 The influence of the deep determinants of development on the HDI when the risk of contracting malaria and associated diseases in a group of countries is non-zero or zero

Regressors	**Dependent variable**		
	HDI for countries for which the risk of contracting malaria is non-zero		**HDI for countries for which the risk of contracting malaria is zero**
	OLS Regression 1	**OLS Regression 2**	**OLS Regression 3**
Integration	0.0283	0.0599	−0.0258
(Lcopen)	(0.85)	(1.80)	(−1.95)
Geography	0.1830***	0.0872	−.0150
(Pop100 km)	(3.69)	(1.52)	(0.64)
Institutions	0.0488	0.0482	0.1034***
(Rule)	(1.65)	(1.82)	(12.05)
Disease	−0.4105***	−0.3177***	
(Mal94p)	(−9.05)	(−7.08)	
Sub-Saharan Africa		−0.1393***	
dummy variable		(−3.61)	
Adj. R^2	0.6145	0.6761	0.6398
No. of observations	71	71	67

Note: Robust *t*-statistics in parenthesis (according to the two-tailed test significant at the five per cent level (*), two per cent level(**), and one per cent level (***)).

that indicate that while malaria and associated diseases are virulent within the community, the level of well-being for this country is severely constrained by these diseases. Once these diseases have been contained, the coefficient estimates in Table 9.5, column 3, suggest that economic institutions come into their own and make a fundamental contribution towards increasing the level of social well-being for the average country in that group of countries that is free of the scourge of malaria and related diseases.

9.7 Conclusions

The quasi-controlled experimental evidence derived from History-Plus-Nature cited in Section 9.2 indicates that even with the institution of the rule of law and the protection of property rights of a comparatively high quality in place in a community, the presence of an epidemic of a virulent infectious disease will severely adversely affect the level of economic activity and well-being in this community. This quasi-controlled experimental evidence is then combined with the fact (noted in Section 9.3.2.2) that in the mid-1990s the risk of contracting malaria (where malaria risk is a proxy variable for the morbidity and mortality caused by malaria and a number of associated diseases) was widespread but varied in intensity across the regions of the globe. These two broad sets of observations allow the conjecture that the risk of contracting malaria must explain a significant amount of the variation in the level of the HDI across countries in the mid-1990s. This conjecture is not contradicted by the empirical results presented in Tables 9.2, 9.4 and 9.5 and the summary of the appropriate adjustments of these results in Appendix C. These results, especially those in Appendix C, indicate that Disease (as measured by the risk of contracting malaria) dominates over all other possible deep determinants that might contribute to the level of the HDI for the average country in the late twentieth century.

It is open to doubt, however, whether Disease is as dominant as is indicated by the summary results set out in columns 4 and 5 in Appendix C because these results are based upon coefficient estimates (reported in Table 9.4) that were derived by applying 2SLS estimation techniques along with certain IVs. As was pointed out in Section 9.4.4.1, the use of these techniques, along with applying questionable IVs, may not produce results that are to be preferred to those derived by applying OLS to generate relevant results (that are reported in Tables 9.2 and 9.5).

Nevertheless, whichever results are regarded as being the more reliable, the results reported in Appendix C indicate that Disease dominates in the sense that the coefficient estimates for this variable are always statistically significant (when malaria risk is included in the relevant regression equation to be estimated), and this variable (when appropriately adjusted) always has the greatest impact on the level of the HDI for the average country in the late twentieth century. Economic institutions, however, appear to have a role to play in the development process once malaria risk has been brought under control.

These conclusions have a number of implications. First, since 58 per cent of all malaria cases occur in the poorest 28 per cent of the world's population (Barat, 2004), it follows that the countries that could be expected to contribute most to any increased effort aimed at containing this disease would be those wealthier countries of the world that are not faced with the risk of contracting malaria. (This additional effort also would need to be combined with an increased effort to contain the other diseases associated with malaria). The theory of the supply of global public goods suggests, however, that comparatively little would be contributed by these countries as they would gain comparatively little economically from any contribution they may make.[28] Yet improvements have been made in the containment and treatment of malaria since the mid-1990s. For instance, Bremen *et al.* (2004: 1) note:

> There has been rapidly increasing optimism for greatly improved malaria control, particularly in Africa where the vast majority of people affected by the disease reside ... The new positive attitude is based on major advances in malaria research and public health practices, and careful epidemiological and economic analyses of malaria's burden and cost-effective ways to lessen it.

If malaria and related diseases are contained throughout the world in the next few decades, naturally this should result in a narrowing of the variation in the HDI across countries. This narrowing would be even greater, as emphasized in the previous section, if the reduction in the level of diseases in the countries concerned was also accompanied by an improvement in the level of economic institutions such as the rule of law and the protection of individual property rights.

Appendix A Data and sources

(asiae) = Dummy variable taking value of one if a country belongs in Southeast and East Asia, and zero if otherwise. *Source*: Own determination.

(engfrac) = Fraction of the population speaking English. *Source*: Hall and Jones (1999).

(eurfrac) = Fraction of the population speaking a major Western European language, including English, French, German, Portuguese and Spanish. *Source*: Hall and Jones (1999).

(hdi94) = United Nations Human Development Index for 1994. *Source*: United Nations Human Development Report (1997).

(laam) = Dummy variable taking value of one if a country belongs to Latin America or the Caribbean, and zero if otherwise. *Source*: Own determination.

(lcopen) = Natural logarithm of nominal openness averaged between 1950 and 1996. *Source*: Heston; Summers and Aten, (2001).

(logem4) = Natural logarithm of estimated European settlers' mortality rates. *Source*: Acemoglu *et al.* (2001).

(logfrankrom) = Natural logarithm of predicted trade shares based on a bilateral trade equation. *Source*: Jeffrey A. Frankel and David Romer (1999).

(mal94p) = Proportion of a population at risk of contracting malaria in 1994. *Source*: Gallup and Sachs (2003).

(me) = Estimate of a nation's malaria burden based upon its comparative ecologically based transmission vectors in 1995. *Source*: Kiszewski *et al.* (2004).

(pop100 km) = Proportion of the population within 100 km of a sea navigable waterway in 1995. *Source*: Gallup *et al.* (1999).

(rule) = Composite index for rule of law and the protection afforded to private property rights during the 1990s. *Source*: Kaufmann *et al.* (2002).

(rule of law for 2000–2002) = Composite index for rule of law and the protection afforded to private property rights during 2000–2002. *Source*: Kaufmann *et al.* (2005).

(safrica) = Dummy variable taking the value of one if a country belongs to Sub-Saharan Africa, and zero if otherwise. *Source*: RST (2004).

(schooling 1970–85) = Average years of schooling 1970–85. *Source*: Barro and Lee (2000). Data found at http://www.cid.harvard.edu/ciddata/ciddata.html.

(schooling 1970–85) = Average years of schooling 1990–2000. *Source*: Barro and Lee (2000). Data found at http://www.cid.harvard.edu/ciddata/ciddata.html.

Appendix B A truncated table of critical *F*-statistics to test for weak instruments in linear IV regression. Based on Stock and Yogo (2005).

The Stock and Yogo (2005) weak instruments test rejects an instrument for a 2SLS estimation, if its estimated first-stage *F*-Statistic is smaller than the critical value indicated in the table below. This critical value, g_{min}, is calculated as a function of the number of included endogenous regressors (n), the number of instrumental variables (K_2) and the desired maximal size (r) of a Wald test of $\beta = \beta_0$, when the significance level is 5 per cent. In each of the justifications made in this chapter, the minimum value of (r) is adopted to derive the critical rejection values to maximize the likelihood of the instruments passing the test for the maximal size $r = 0.10$. The table below, which in part is taken from Stock and Yogo (2005:59) and which is then extended to the $n = 3$ case (using the Gauss computer program provided by Motohiro Yogo and extended and run by Heather Anderson to generate the relevant critical values), reports these critical g_{min} values. (The full table, covering many more values of K_2 and two more values of r, is available upon request.)

Critical values for the 2SLS weak instruments test based on the size of first-stage F-statistic.

	$n = 1, r =$		$n = 2, r =$		n = 3, r =	
K_2	0.10	0.15	0.10	0.15	0.10	0.15
1	16.38	8.96				
2	19.93	11.59	7.03	4.58		
3	22.30	12.83	13.43	8.18	4.23	3.34
4	24.58	13.96	16.87	9.93	10.01	6.48
5	26.87	15.09	19.45	11.22	13.41	8.23
6	29.18	16.23	21.68	12.33	15.99	9.54
7	31.50	17.38	23.72	13.34	18.16	10.64
8	33.84	18.54	25.64	14.31	20.11	11.61

Appendix C Standard deviation adjustments to the size of the estimates of core coefficients

	Standard deviation	**Table 9.2 (Col. 2) Dep. variable HDI**	**Table 9.2 (Col. 3) Dep. Variable HDI**	**Table 9.4 (Col. 1) Dep. variable HDI**	**Table 9.4 (Col. 2) Dep. variable HDI**
	1	2	3	4	5
Integration (Lcopen) x SD	**0.59**	0.006*	0.002*	0.07*	0.0257*
Geography (Pop100 km) x SD	**0.37**	0.035	0.0.24	0.077	0.0364
Institutions (Rule) x SD	**0.95**	0.073	0.077	0.046*	0.0324*
Disease (Mal94p) x SD	**0.44**	0.144	0.097	0.157	0.1978
IV for (rule)				logem4	engfrac
Disease/ Institutions		**1.98 (2.29)****	**1.26 (1.58)****	**3.41**	**5.68**
Disease/ Geography		**4.11**	**4.04**	**2.02**	**5.43**

* Coefficient estimate for variable concerned not statistically significantly different from zero at the 5 per cent level according to the two-tailed test.
** Number in brackets is that calculated after allowing for the indirect influence of Disease on the level of Institutions.

Notes

We thank the following for comments made on earlier versions of this chapter: Steve Dowrick, and participants at seminars given in the Departments of Economics at The Australian National University and Oxford University, The London School of Hygiene and Tropical Medicine, and the symposium on Institutions and Economic Development, University of Otago. Considerable assistance was provided by James Stock, Motohiro Yogo and Heather Anderson with the provision of the empirical information set out in Appendix B. We remain, however, responsible for the contents of this chapter.

1. We adopt the year 1994 for consideration in order to avoid the influence that the pandemic of HIV/AIDS in sub-Saharan Africa is likely to have on the measure of the HDI after the mid-1990s.
2. See, for example, Dasgupta (1993), Ravallion (1997) and Noorbakhsh (1998).
3. See Breman *et al.* (2004: 3, 5) and Snow *et al.* (2004). These estimates are much larger than those provided by the World Health Organization (WHO) and others, because they fail to take into account that an increase in the prevalence of malaria also increases the severity of a range of other childhood diseases. This matter is discussed in more detail later in the Section 9.3.2.2.
4. See Breman (2001), Malaney and Sachs (2002), Breman *et al.* (2004) and Malaney *et al.* (2004) for surveys of the relevant medical and economic literature on this point.
5. Sachs, along with a number of co-authors, has published a range of stimulating papers that bear on the issue of the burden of disease on economic development (Bloom and Sachs (1998), Gallup *et al.* (1998), Gallup and Sachs (2001), McArthur and Sachs (2001), Malaney and Sachs (2002) and Malaney *et al.* (2004)).
6. See, for instance, Cartwright (1972), Kiple (1993), Porter (1997) and Hays (2003).
7. The conjecture in the main text is similar to an argument presented in Ranis *et al.* (2000). They, however, were concerned only with the matter of economic growth and not with the variance of well-being across countries. Also see Ranis (2004) and Ranis and Stewart (2001).
8. In the index for Bernstein's book *The Birth of Plenty* (2004), 'infectious disease', 'disease' and 'malaria' do not appear; nor is there mention of any of the other major fatal infectious diseases that afflict humankind.
9. The discussion in the main text draws on Hays (2003), McCullough (1997), Malaney and Sachs (2002), Porter (1997) and Spielman and D'Antonio (2001).
10. This mosquito-control programme arose out of the work by Carlos Juan Finlay, Jesse Lazaer, Aristedes Agramonte, James Carrol and Walter Reed. They all contributed in various ways to demonstrating in 1900 that *Aëdes aegypti* was the vector carrying yellow fever from person to person. Whereas Finlay in 1872 published his first paper on the possible link between the mosquito and yellow fever, others had hypothesized this link earlier; for instance, Dr Josiah Clark Nott in 1848 (McCullough, 1977: 142–3).
11. Some other case histories that demonstrate the importance of controlling malaria before sustained economic development can take place, in an

environment where an adequate level of economic institutions are in place, are Batavia in the mid-eighteenth century (van der Brug, 1997), Malaya from 1901 through to the mid-1920s (Watson, 1943) and Northern Rhodesia in the 1930s (Watson, 1953). Also see Keiser *et al.* (2005), Utzinger *et al.* (2001), Utzinger *et al.* (2002) and Gallup and Sachs (2001: 90–1).

12. The relevant data are taken from Kaufmann *et al.* (2002).
13. Sachs (2003) equally is critical of the use of distance from the equator as a measure of the geography of a country.
14. This predicted change is for a group of countries for which the average child mortality rate (CMR) in 1990 was 181 per 1000 live births. For the same year the CMR was 11 and below for the wealthy industrialized – and nearly all non-tropical – countries. See United Nations Children's Fund (2001: 3).
15. Also see Molineaux (1997), Bremen (2001: 7) and Bremen *et al.* (2004: 2–6) on this issue.
16. Kremer and Miguel (2004: 159) also illustrate the general point made in the main text; that is, that an externality is created by altering the prevalence of a particular parasite or vector in the environment. In their study they find that de-worming children in several villages across Kenya resulted in improved health outcomes more than twice as large as that estimated when considering only the direct health impacts of the de-worming programme.
17. Far more detailed medical information on Sickle Cell Anaemia is provided by the United States Department of Energy, Biological and Environmental Research, and Human Genome Project Information Program (online) http://www.ornl.gov/sci/techresources/HumanGenome/posters/chromosome/sca.shtml.
18. A list of data sources used to derive all the regression equations cited in the main text is given in Appendix A.
19. See MacKinnon and White (1985). Also see Durlauf *et al.* (2005) and the references cited there on the matter of allowing for heteroscedasticity when the data set is of a finite size.
20. The reason for collecting these results in the table in Appendix C and not in a table in the main text is that this appendix will be referred to on a number of occasions throughout the main text.
21. In estimating the regression results presented in Table 9.3 the variable logarithm GDP per capita (GDPPC) for 1995 was omitted from the regression equation. The reason is that there is a high level of multi-collinearity between GDPPC and malaria risk, and between GDPPC and the average years of schooling. (The simple correlation coefficient between GDPPC and malaria risk is 0.8205 and between GDPPC and schooling 0.8471.) In addition, it is known that the level of malaria influences the level of GDPPC and not the other way round (Gallup and Sachs, 2001: 88–90). Also, the comparatively long lag between the average years of schooling (for 1970–85) and GDPPC (for 1995) suggests that it is the level of schooling that influences the level of GDPPC and not the other way round. Therefore, it seems reasonable to omit GDPPC from the relevant regression equation rather than the malaria risk and the average years of schooling.
22. The discussion in the main text has been influenced by that found in Durlauf *et al.* (2005).

23. The fundamental reason for applying this test is that if the instrumental variables are comparatively weakly identified with the relevant endogenous regressor then the second-stage estimation may generate a bias in the estimated coefficients towards those estimated by using OLS (Stock, 2001: 7580; Stock and Watson, 2003: chapter 10).
24. These calculations were made possible through the generosity of two people: Motohiro Yogo, who provided the Gauss program used in the calculations reported in Table 2 in Stock and Yogo (2005: 59); and Heather Anderson, who extended this program and carried out the time-consuming calculations required for the three-endogenous-variable case. The relevant calculations are available upon request.
25. Appendix B sets out a truncated version of Table 2 in Stock and Yogo (2005) plus the additional critical values for the case where there are three endogenous variables.
26. These IVs have also been used by Dollar and Kraay (2003).
27. These various regression results were derived using OLS. Attempts made to use 2SLS to derive relevant regression results had to be abandoned. This was because the relatively low values for the *F*-statistics for the estimated first-stage regression equations indicated (on applying the Stock–Yogo test) that the IVs being applied were weak. To save on space these results are not presented here.
28. See Kaul *et al.* (1999) and Smith *et al.* (2003).

References

Acemoglu, D., Johnson, S. and Robinson, J. A. 'The Colonial Origins of Comparative Development: An Empirical Investigation', *The American Economic Review*, 91 (2001): 1369–401.

Acemoglu, D., Johnson, S. and Robinson, J. A. 'Reversal of Fortune: Geography and Institutions in the Making of the Modern World Income Distribution', *Quarterly Journal of Economics*, 117 (2002): 1231–94.

Acemoglu, D., Johnson, S. and Robinson, J. A. 'Institutions as the Fundamental Cause of Long-Run Growth', in P. Aghion and S. Durlauf (eds), *Handbook of Economic Growth* (Amsterdam: Elsevier, 2005): 385–472.

Aghion, P. and Durlauf, S. (eds), *Handbook of Economic Growth* (Amsterdam: Elsevier, 2005).

Barat, L. M. 'Do Malaria Control Interventions Reach the Poor? A View Through the Equity Lens', *American Journal of Tropical Medicine and Hygiene*, 71 (Suppl. 2) (2004): 174–8.

Barro, R. J. and Lee, J.-W. 'International data on Educational Attainment: Updates and Implications'. Center for International Development, Working Paper No. 42 (2000).

Bernstein, W. J. *The Birth of Plenty: How the Prosperity of the Modern World was Created* (New York: McGraw-Hill, 2004).

Bloom, D. E. and Sachs, J. 'Geography, Demography, and Economic Growth in Africa', *Brookings Papers on Economic Activity*, (2) 1998: 207–96.

Breman, J. 'The Ears of the Hippopotamus: Manifestations, Determinants, and Estimates of the Malaria Burden', *American Journal of Tropical Medicine and Hygiene*, 64 (2001): 1–11.

Breman, J., Alilio, G. J., Martin, S. and Mills, A. 'Conquering the Intolerable Burden of Malaria: What's New, What's Needed: A Summary', *American Journal of Tropical Medicine and Hygiene*, 71 (suppl. 2) (2004): 1–15.

Cartwright, F. F. *Disease and History* (London: Rupert-Davis, 1972).

Dasgupta, P. *An Inquiry into Well-Being and Destitution* (Oxford: Clarendon Press, 1993).

Diamond, J. *Guns, Germs and Steel: The Fates of Human Societies* (London: W. W. Norton, 1997).

Dollar, D. and Kraay, A. 'Institutions, Trade and Growth', *Journal of Monetary Economics*, 50 (2003): 133–62.

Durlauf, S. N., Johnson, P. A. and Temple, J. R. W. 'Growth Econometrics', in P. Aghion and S. N. Durlauf (eds), *Handbook of Economic Growth* (Amsterdam: Elsevier, 2005): 555–677.

Easterly, W. and Levine, R. 'Tropics, Germs, and Crops: How Endowments Influence Economic Development', *Journal of Monetary Economics*, 50 (2003): 3–39.

Foster, R. and Leighton, C. 'Economic Impacts of Malaria in Kenya and Nigeria', Research Paper 6, *Health Financing and Sustainability Project*, Agency for International Development, USA (1993).

Frankel, J. A. and Romer, D. 'Does Trade Cause Growth?', *The American Economic Review*, 89 (1999): 379–99.

Gallup, J. L., Mellinger, A. and Sachs, J. *Geography and Economic Development.* Cambridge, MA, National Bureau of Economic Research, Working Paper No. 6849 (1998).

Gallup, J. L., Mellinger, A. and Sachs, J. *Climate, Water Navigability and Development.* Harvard University, Centre for International Development, Working Paper No. 24 (1999).

Gallu, J. L. and Sachs, J. 'The Economic Burden of Malaria', *American Journal of Tropical Health and Hygiene*, 64 (2001): 85–96.

Glaeser, E. L., La Porta, R., Lopez-De-Sianes, F. and Schleifer, A. 'Do Institutions Cause Growth?', *Journal of Economic Growth*, 9 (2004): 271–303.

Greene, W. *Econometric Analysis*, fifth edition (Upper Saddle River, NJ: Prentice Hall, 2003).

Gundlach, E. 'The Primacy of Institutions Reconsidered: The Effects of Malaria Prevalence in the Empirics of Development'. Kiel Institute for World Economics, Working Paper No. 1210 (May 2004).

Hall, R. E. and Jones, C. I. 'Why Do Some Countries Produce So Much More Output per Worker than Others?', *The Quarterly Journal of Economics*, 114 (1999): 83–116.

Hay, S. I., Guerra, C. A., Tatem, A. J., Noor A. M. and Snow, R. W. 'The Global Distribution and Population at Risk of Malaria: Past, Present, and Future', *The Lancet: Infectious Diseases*, 4 (2004): 327–36.

Hays, J. N. *The Burdens of Disease* (New Brunswick, N.J.: Rutgers University Press, 2003).

Heston, A., Summers, R. and Aten, B. *Penn World Tables Version 6.0*, Centre for International Comparisons at the University of Pennsylvania (CICUP), December 2001 http://pwt.econ.upenn.edu/.

Kaufmann, D., Kraay, A. and Zoido-Lobatón, P. 'Governance Matters II—Updated Indicators for 2000/01'. World Bank Policy Research Department, Working Paper No. 2772 (2002).

Kaufmann, D., Kraay, A. and Zoido-Lobatón, P. 'Governance Matters IV—Governance Indicators for 1996–2004'. World Bank Policy Research Department, Working Paper No. 3630 (2005).

Kaul, I., Gruberg, I. and Stern, M. A. (eds), *Global Public Goods* (New York: Oxford University Press, 1999).

Keiser, J., Singer, B. and Utzinger, J. 'Reducing the Burden of Malaria in Different Eco-Epidemiological Settings with Environmental Management: A Systematic Review', *Lancet Infectious Diseases*, 5 (2005): 695–708.

Kiple, K. F. (ed.), *Cambridge World History of Human Diseases* (Cambridge: Cambridge University Press, 1993).

Kiszewski, A., Mellinger, A., Spielman, A., Malaney, P. Sachs, S. E., and Sachs, J. 'A Global Index Representing the Stability of Malaria Transmission', *American Journal of Tropical Medicine and Hygiene*, 70 (2004): 486–8.

Kremer, M. and Miguel, E. 'Worms: Identifying Impacts on Education and Health in the Presence of Treatment Externalities', *Econometrica*, 72 (2004): 159–217.

MacKinnon, J. and White, H. 'Some Heteroskedasticity-Consistent Covariance Matrix Estimators with Improved Finite Sample Properties', *Journal of Econometrics*, 29 (1985): 305–25.

McArthur, J. and Sachs, J. 'Institutions and Geography: Comment on Acemoglu, Johnson and Robinson 2000'. Cambridge, MA, National Bureau of Economic Research, Working Paper No. 8114 (2001).

McCullough, D. *The Path Between the Seas: The Creation of the Panama Canal 1870–1914* (New York: Simon and Schuster, 1977).

Malaney, P. and Sachs, J. D. 'The Economic and Social Burden of Malaria', *Nature*, 415 (6872) (2002): 680–85.

Malaney, P., Speilman, A. and Sachs, J. 'The Malaria Gap', *American Journal of Tropical Medicine and Hygiene*, 71 (Suppl 2) (2004): 141–46.

Molineaux, L. 'Malaria and Mortality: Some Epidemiological Considerations', *Annals of Tropical Medicine and Parasitology*, 91 (1997): 811–25.

Murray, C. J. L. and Lopez, A. D. 'Mortality by Cause for Eight Regions of the World: Global Burden of Disease Study', *The Lancet*, 349 (1997a): 1269–76.

Murray, C. J. L. and Lopez, A. D. 'Global Mortality, Disability, and the Contribution of Risk Factors: Global Burden of Disease Study', *The Lancet*, 349 (1997b): 1436–42.

Noorbakhsh, F. 'The Human Development Index: Some Technical Issues and Alternative Indices', *Journal of International Development*, 10 (1998): 589–605.

North, D. C. *Institutions, Institutional Change and Economic Performance* (Cambridge: Cambridge University Press, 1990).

North, D. C. 'Economic Performance Through Time', *The American Economic Review*, 84 (1994): 359–68.

North, D. C. 'The New Institutional Economics and Third World Development', in J. Harriss, J. Hunter and L. M. Lewis (eds), *The New Institutional Economics and Third World Development* (London: Routledge, 1995): 17–26.

North, D. C. and Thomas, R. P. *Rise of the Western World* (Cambridge: Cambridge University Press, 1973).

Porter, R. *The Greatest Benefit to Mankind: A Medical History of Humanity from Antiquity to the Present* (London: Harper Collins, 1997).

Radelet, S. and Sachs, J. 'Shipping Costs, Manufactured Exports, and Economic Growth', Paper presented at the annual meeting of the American Economics Association (January, 1998).

Ranis, G., Stewart, F. and Ramirez, A. 'Economic Growth and Human Development', *World Development*, 28 (2000): 197–219.

Ranis, G. and Stewart, F. 'Growth and Human Development: Comparative Latin American Experience'. Yale University, Economic Growth Centre, Discussion Paper No. 826 (2001).

Ranis, G. 'Human Development and Economic Growth'. Yale University, Economic Growth Centre, Discussion Paper No. 887 (2004).

Ravallion, M. 'Good and Bad Growth: The Human Development Reports', *World Development*, 25 (1997): 631–8.

Reynolds, L. G. 'The Spread of Economic Growth to the Third World: 1850–1980', *Journal of Economic Literature*, 21 (1983): 941–80.

Rodrik, R., Subramanian, A. and Trebbi, F. 'Institutions Rule: The Primacy of Institutions Over Geography and Integration in Economic Development', *Journal of Economic Growth*, 9 (2004): 131–65.

Rostow, W. W. *Stages of Economic Growth: A Non-Communist Manifesto* (Cambridge: Cambridge University Press, 1960).

Sachs, J. D. 'Institutions Don't Rule: Direct Effects of Geography on Per Capita Income'. Cambridge MA, National Bureau of Economic Research, Working Paper No. 9490 (2003).

Sen, A. K. *Commodities and Capabilities* (Oxford: Oxford University Press, 1985).

Sen, A. K. *Development as Freedom*, first edition (New York: Knopf Press, 1999).

Smith, A. *An Inquiry into the Nature of the Causes of the Wealth of Nations* (Oxford: Oxford University Press, 1976 (1776)).

Smith, R., Beaglehole, R., Woodward, D. and Drager, N. (eds), *Global Public Goods for Health* (Oxford: Oxford University Press, 2003).

Snow, R. W., Korenromp, E. L. and Gouws, E. 'Pediatric Mortality in Africa: *Plasmodium Falciparum* Malaria as a Cause or Risk?', *American Journal of Tropical Medicine and Hygiene*, 71 (Suppl 2) (2004): 16–24.

Spielman, A. and D'Antonio, M. *Mosquito: The Story of Man's Deadliest Foe* (London: Faber and Faber, 2001).

Stock, J. H. 'Instrumental Variables in Statistics and Econometrics', in N. J. Smelser and P. B. Baltes (eds), *International Encyclopaedia of Social and Behavioral Sciences* (Amsterdam: Elsevier Publishing, 2001): 7577–82.

Stock, J. H. and Watson, M. W. *Introduction to Econometrics* (Boston: Addison Wesley, 2003).

Stock, J. H. and Yogo, M. 'Testing for Weak Instruments in Linear IV Regression', in D. W. K. Andrews and J. H. Stock (eds), *Identification and Inference for Econometric Models: A Festschrift in Honour of Thomas Rothenberg* (Cambridge: Cambridge University Press, 2005): 80–108.

United Nations Children's Fund. *Progress Since the World Summit for Children: Statistical Review* (Paris: United Nations Children's Fund, 2001).

United Nations. *United Nations Human Development Report*, 1997 (New York: Oxford University Press, 1997).

Utzinger, J., Tozan, Y. and Singer, B. H. 'Efficacy and Cost-Effectiveness of Environmental Management for Malaria Control', *Tropical Medicine and International Health*, 6 (2001): 677–87.

Utzinger, J., Tozan, Y., Doumani, F. and Singer, B. H. 'The Economic Payoffs of Integrated Malaria Control in the Zambian Copperbelt Between 1930 and 1950', *Tropical Medicine and International Health*, 7 (2002): 657–77.

van der Brug, P. H. 'Malaria in Batavia in the 18th Century', *Tropical Medicine and International Health*, 2 (1997): 892–902.
Watson, M. *The Geographical Aspects of Malaria* (Washington, DC: United States Printing Office, 1943).
Watson, M. *African Highway: The Battle for Health in Central Africa* (London: John Murray, 1953).
World Health Organization. *World Health Report. Reducing Risks, Promoting Health Life* (Geneva: World Health Organization, 2002).

10
When Can the Rabble Redistribute? Democratization and Income Distribution in Low- and Middle-income Countries

Philip Nel

10.1 Introduction

The last decades of the twentieth century experienced an extensive introduction and/or deepening of electoral democracy in low- and middle-income countries (LMICs); a series of events that Diamond calls 'a democratic breakthrough without precedent in world history' (Diamond, 1999: 24).[1] However, contrary to the optimistic expectation of many analysts and decision-makers in Western democracies that all good things go together, the available evidence suggests that episodes of positive regime change in LMICs as a rule have seldom been followed by a reduction of wealth and income inequality in those countries. The purpose of this chapter is to propose an explanation for this anomaly.

Why should we be concerned at all about the relationship between economic (income and wealth) inequality and democracy in LMICs? Two sets of reasons have emerged in the recent literature. First, it is important to consider the effects that political institutions could have on reducing levels of economic inequality, given the emerging consensus that high levels of initial economic inequality have negative consequences for the overall development prospects of LMICs. In contrast to an earlier belief that there is an inescapable trade-off between growth and inequality in modernizing societies (Kuznets, 1955; 1963), a large number of studies in the 1990s and early 2000s postulated that economic growth and pro-poor development is retarded when income and asset inequality exceeds a certain threshold (Birdsall and Londono, 1997; Aghion and Garcia-Penalosa, 1999; Gugerty and Timmer, 1999;

Chen and Ravallion 2000; Birdsall, 2001; World Bank, 2001, 2005; Naschold, 2002; Nel, 2003; Cornia, 2004). Easterly (2002) shows that inequality, independently of other factors, is a large and statistically significant barrier to developing the institutional framework and human capital on which successful development depends. A recent study on inequality in Latin America concludes that inequality hinders the implementation of sensible macroeconomic strategies, retards demand, impedes the development of pro-poor trade policies, limits the growth of human capital stocks, raises social discontent, and limits the degree of political participation (Justino *et al.*, 2003: 64–5). There is also evidence that inequality can hamper poverty relief. The 2000/2001 World Development Report comments:

> while economic growth is systematically associated with poverty reduction, the rate at which growth translates into lower poverty depends on the initial level of inequality in the distribution of income and how that distribution changes over time.
>
> (World Bank, 2001: 35)

Dagdeviren *et al.* (2001) confirm this conclusion. They find that for a large sample of developing countries a strategy of marginal redistribution of wealth from the rich to the poor, or a strategy of equal distribution of growth benefits, is more effective in reducing poverty than increases in economic growth that are distributionally neutral.

Second, it has been suggested that the failure of emerging democratic regimes to spread wealth and income more equitably can undermine the trust of the populace in political institutions, can exacerbate civil strife and so at best can retard the consolidation of democratic advances, or at worst precipitate a slide back into authoritarianism.[2] Economic inequality and democracy are thus jointly determined, and much seems to be at stake in our attempt to find out why political institutions in recently democratized societies have such a poor track record when it comes to the mitigation of economic inequality.

The chapter proceeds by first defining the core concepts used and by reviewing the available evidence concerning the effect of democracy and democratization on inequality. An attempt is then made to develop an explanation for the empirical patterns reviewed. The final section draws some implications for our understanding of the determinants and effects of economic inequality, and for policy debates about the focus and nature of political reform in LMICs.

As is common in inequality studies, this chapter focuses on income inequality as an appropriate approximation of economic inequality in general (Champernowne and Cowell, 1998), based on the assumption that there is a significant correlation between income and wealth distribution, and between the distribution of both these social goods and the economic opportunity profile of the typical LMIC. This study forms part of the literature that explores how political factors shape income inequality, and we look in particular at the effect of democratization, which is defined as the process through which a political regime graduates to democracy (see below). Our time focus is prescribed by the availability of high-quality income inequality data, and we can therefore look only at the last four decades of the previous century. During this time, it was mostly LMICs that experienced democratic transitions, that is countries that by the end of the 1990s had a per capita income up to US$10,065.[3] They were joined by a small group of high-income countries, such as Taiwan and South Korea, who also made the successful transition from autocracy to democracy. LMICs consist of two distinct groups, namely ex-communist transition economies and what are generally referred to as developing countries. This chapter attempts in particular to explain why it is that the latter group has found it so difficult to translate political equality into a more equitable distribution of wealth and income, and most of the discussion therefore centres on developing LMICs. Part of the analysis is based on a cross-sectional time-series empirical analysis, and in order to ensure balance and the broadest possible spectrum of variation, a large sample of 108 countries, of which 26 are high-income and 82 LMICs, has been constructed from the income inequality dataset that is used as the primary data source (see Section 10.2).

10.2 Concepts and evidence

A political regime is the set of norms, rules and practices that determine the distribution of political rights between actors in a polity, how these rights can be exercised and what this means for the exercise of control over institutions of power such as the state (Sanders, 1981: 51–63; Przeworski *et al.*, 2000: 18). In a democracy the expectation is that those who find themselves in lower socio-economic positions will use the opportunities provided by political equality to reduce their disadvantage. In contrast, we have come to expect that in autocracies socio-economic inequalities will be mirrored in the concentration of political power in the hands of the few. Autocracies systematically exclude some sections of society from political rights in an attempt to prolong the exclusive control of one group or individual over the state. The crucial regime difference between autocracies and democracies is that the latter are characterized by popular sovereignty, while in the former, sovereignty resides in the hands of the few. In the useful terms suggested by Lane and Ersson (2003: 2), democracy is 'a political regime where the will of the people *ex ante* becomes the law of the country . . . *ex post*'. As Rueschemeyer *et al.* (1992: 41) comment, 'democracy, then, is a rather counterintuitive state of affairs, one in which the disadvantaged many have, as citizens, a real voice in the collective decision making of politics'.

There is, of course, more than one variant of democracy, and a number of distinguishing features have been emphasized in the literature. The crucial distinction, for our purposes, is between democracies that have institutionalized popular sovereignty and those in which regular competitive elections do take place, but where political veto power remains concentrated in the hands of a self-perpetuating elite within whose ranks leadership election is monopolized. Marshall and Jaggers (2002) conceive of democracy as consisting of three essential interrelated elements. The first is the presence of institutions of competitive elections in which the electorate can express effective preferences about competitively selected candidates and alternative policies. The second is the existence of effective institutionalized constraints on the exercise of power by the executive, and the third is the guaranteeing of civil liberties to all citizens. These three institutional characteristics combine to guarantee popular sovereignty, that is the legally entrenched right of the citizenry to exercise a veto over public officials and policies without fearing reprisal. This implies that privileged political positions for extra-parliamentary interest groups such the military, for example, are done away with and that constitutionalism and the rule of law have been institutionalized as means to secure horizontal constraints on the power of officials/leaders (Diamond, 1999: 10–11).

Keeping these requirements in mind, it is possible to distinguish between 'full', alternatively 'mature' or 'institutionalized' democracies on the one hand, and 'partial', 'incomplete', 'failing', 'pseudo' or 'defective' democracies on the other.[4] Among these terms, 'partial democracy' is perhaps the less pejorative, and in what follows we will distinguish between three regime types. First, *autocracies*, which refers to regimes in which elections are not based on universal franchise or, more commonly today, in which elections are not competitive in the sense that the electorate is not confronted with a real choice, or in which choices cannot be exercised in freedom. Secondly, *partial democracies*, in which there are competitive universal-franchise elections, but where popular sovereignty may be impeded by the undue influence of forces not under popular control (such as the military, for instance), where some restrictions on the rule of law and on civic and political freedoms may apply, and where the means for the electorate to exercise effective control over public officials may not be fully developed. Thirdly, *democracy*, in which civil and political liberties are respected, where there is effective control over the exercise of power by the executive, and where competitive elections are held regularly. Once these three requirements are met, we can speak of popular sovereignty having been institutionalized.[5]

The combined regime measure developed in the POLITY IV dataset (Marshall and Jaggers, 2000; 2002)[6] provides us with the means to operationalize the distinctions between these three regime types. *Autocracies* fall short on all three characteristics, but to varying degrees: they restrict or suppress civil liberties and political participation; executive selection usually takes place within a power elite; and there are few institutional constraints on the exercise of executive power. To capture the variety of autocracies, Marshall and Jaggers use an 11-point scale from −10 to 0. Similarly, they scale democratic regimes from +1 to +10, the latter score being an indicator of a full/institutionalized democracy. A regime that scores between +1 and +6 inclusive is here categorized as a *partial democracy*, because they fall significantly short on one of the three requirements. Those with a score of +7 to +10 are here regarded as *democracies*, because they meet well with all three requirements, but not necessarily comprehensively in respect of all three.[7] An episode of 'democratization' occurs whenever there is a *positive* regime transition from either autocracy or partial democracy to democracy.

The relationship between inequality and democracy in high-, middle- and low-income countries has received considerable attention,[8] with most studies concluding that democracy reduces inequality.[9] Muller (1988) finds that if analysts use a measure that combines depth and longevity of democracy, there is indeed a significant negative effect on inequality: durable democracies are less unequal. Burkhart (1997) uses only a depth measure of democracy but he also tests for the presence of a second-order polynomial relationship. He finds that (level of) democracy and inequality are indeed non-linearly related: partial democracies do not succeed in reducing inequality, but at about the midpoint of his scale measuring the depth of democracy, the effect is reversed. Earlier, Simpson (1990) also suggested an inverse, U-shaped relationship between the level to which political and civil rights are respected in a country and domestic inequality. Lee (2005) concludes that 'deeper' democracy is more inclined to reduce inequality, once we control for the size of the public sector, than do partial democracies.

There are a couple of problems with this literature, though. First, the quality of the income inequality data used in most of the extant studies can be questioned. It is notoriously difficult to get good-quality income data for a large cross section of developing LMICs, and none of the existing studies manages to solve the data quality problem in any consistent and persuasive manner. Second, as these studies use 'static' indicators of the independent variable (= the level of democracy), they do not explicitly ask how the time-variant dynamic of *democratization*, in contrast to the static of regime status, affects income distribution.[10]

The empirical strategy suggested here to overcome these two problems is, first, to use a high-quality cross-sectional time-series (panel) dataset, analysed by means of estimation models that can pick up not only the effect of the quality of democracy, but also how the dynamic of a transition to democracy affects subsequent income distribution relative to the dynamics in other countries. The income inequality panel data used here comes from the Estimated Household Income Inequality (EHII) dataset compiled by the University of Texas Inequality Project, under the leadership of James Galbraith. This is the most comprehensive within-country income inequality dataset available and is especially attractive because it is based on a quality source that remains consistent over time, namely the United Nations Industrial Development Organization (UNIDO) dataset on manufacturing pay or wage inequality. In contrast, alternative comprehensive inequality datasets, such as the widely used Deininger and Squire World Bank inequality dataset (Deininger and Squire, 1996, 1998) includes data that derive from different types of household survey sources and that have been collected using widely divergent methodologies across countries and across different time periods within countries. Clearly, this poses insurmountable problems for both cross-country and within-country time-series research, as Knowles (2005) points out. In addition, the coverage of the Deininger and Squire dataset of developing countries is fairly limited. The EHII dataset is produced by combining information from the UNIDO dataset with high-quality information from other household income inequality datasets, as well as other relevant information such as the ratio of manufacturing employment to total population, the degree to which a country's population has become urbanized, and population growth. This information is then combined in a regression that produces a pooled time-series of EHII (Galbraith and Kum, 2005).[11] We average the data over five-year periods, which produces a balanced pooled time-series of 551 observations covering 108 countries and spanning eight semi-decades, starting from 1960–64 and ending with the semi-decade 1995–99.

The second part of the empirical strategy used here is to employ a fixed-effects estimation model to test for the dynamic effect of democratization on subsequent income inequality. Fixed-effects models have the two advantages of controlling for omitted variables that differ between countries but are constant over time, and of allowing us to use changes over time in the included variables to estimate the effects of independents on the dependent. Our independent variable is a dummy (DEMDUM) which distinguishes between polities with a Polity2 score of more than 7 (dummy value = 1), and polities with a score of 6 and less (dummy value = 0) at any particular time. A lagged fixed-effects model picks up what the effect of changes in a country's DEMDUM status in one period is on the inequality level in that country in a subsequent period. As mentioned above, the literature suggests that there is an inverted U-curve relationship between level of democracy and inequality, and we are hence justified in expecting that the transition to deeper, more institutionalized democracy will be associated with the lowering of income inequality levels in subsequent periods, as poorer citizens use the vote to shift state spending in favour of their income opportunities (we will unpack this hypothesis in more detail in the next section).

Model 1 in Table 10.1 reveals that the effect of democratization in our full sample of 108 countries is to increase inequality, net of the effects of within-country variation in a vector of control variables captured by the lagged purchasing-power-parity value of Gross National Income per capita (GNIpc). Model 1 is the fixed-effects (within) estimation, and shows that a positive regime change in one time-period from autocracy to democracy, or from partial democracy to democracy, is systematically and significantly associated with higher levels of inequality in subsequent periods. This confirms the results of an earlier study that looked at the effects of democratization on the income shares of the poor, the middle class and the rich in 36 LMICs over an intense period of the spread of democracy, namely 1985–95 (Nel, 2005). This earlier study used comparable household survey data and found that the income share of the poor (lowest 40%) and the middle class (> 40 < 80%) as a rule declined subsequent to democratization, while the rich registered significant sharegains.

The fact that democratization tends to give rise to higher levels of inequality is at first glance counter-intuitive, especially in view of the well-established significant negative correlation between demo-

Table 10.1 Estimations of net effect of democratization on income inequality

	Model 1 (within: fixed effects)	**Model 2 (random effects)**
Dependent	*EHII Gini*	*EHII Gini*
DEMDUM	***1.950	.693
	(.487)	(.495)
GNI per capita	*.0001	*** –.000235
	(.00005)	(.000052)
Constant	41.381	44.349
	(.390)	(.554)
Observations	551	551
n	108	108
r^2	.314	.455

Coefficient values shown with standard errors in parentheses.
* = statistically significant at 0.1 level
** = statistically significant at 0.05 level
*** = statistically significant at 0.01 level
All explanatory variables lagged one time-period (semi-decade)

cracy/democratization and inequality: the cross-country Pearson correlation between level of democracy (Polity2) and the EHII Gini in our sample is –.340, and that between democratization (DEMDUM) and the EHII Gini –.364. In both cases the correlations are statistically significant at the 0.01 level, but they probably tell us no more than that countries with lower levels of inequality tend to be more democratic than those that are more unequal, and that positive regime transition is considerably less frequent in countries with high levels of inequality, as Boix (2003) and Acemoglu and Robinson (2006) have shown. What we are interested in, however, is the reverse causal arrow: not how inequality affects democracy, but how democratization affects inequality. By lagging the explanatory variables, and by using a fixed-effects model, we get a better handle on this reverse causal arrow than correlation analysis will allow us to do.

The results of the random-effects estimation in Model 2, however, place the finding of Model 1 in a better perspective. A random-effects model uses the available panel data more efficiently than the fixed-effects estimation, and allows us to draw conclusions also about variable variation *across* countries. The significant *negative* coefficient associated with GNIpc underlines that once we distinguish between levels of per capita income between countries, the inequality-increasing effect of democratization is no longer statistically significant. Considering that the events of positive regime change within countries during the period under consideration (1960–99) were restricted predominantly to LMICs, the findings suggest that there is a distinct dynamic at work in countries with lower per capita income levels which determines that democratization does not have the same equality-enhancing effect there as it has/had as a rule in higher-income countries. What is this dynamic?

10.3 Explaining the effects of democratization

The question to be answered in this section is, what are the conditions under which democratization in LMICs can (or cannot) mitigate income inequality? Empirically, this way of putting the question implies that clarity will have to be found on the vector of control variables that could affect the regularities identified in Table 10.1. A too-easy answer would be to argue that democracies in LMICs simply have not had enough time to consolidate the popular sovereignty that was postulated as such a central feature of democracy, compared to the long consolidation periods that most high-income democracies have gone through. While regime duration is indeed an important qualitative factor in predicting when democracies will manage to mitigate income inequality, and when not, as Muller (1988) has shown, this does not really answer the question about what exactly are the institutional and contextual features that allow durable democracies to achieve their salutary effects. We propose to answer this question by means of an extended *a priori* examination of the median voter hypothesis (MVH),[12] and then to test this explanation by means of an extension of the models used in Table 10.1.

At any point in time the gross income (income before tax and before redistributive transfers) of the typical individual is shaped by four factors: first, by the *factor endowment profile* of her society, that is the total amounts of the various factors of production available in the national unit to which she belongs; second, by the *share* that this individual's household has of the total amount of different factors of production; third, by the relative *returns* received by the different factors; and fourth, by the *size of her household*. The political process of democratization has the potential to affect the inter-household distribution of factors of production through fiscal means. It is likely that those who have been excluded from power before would use their new-found political clout to (a) enhance their family's share of the pool of human capital in a society by the extension of state-funded general education; and/or (b) change the ownership of fixed factors such as agricultural land and mineral resources by expropriation and redistribution. In an era of generalized economic openness and under conditions of the scarcity of foreign direct investment (FDI) capital, (b) becomes less attractive and less likely than (a).

The MVH asks us to imagine, not unrealistically, that a society is composed of members who are differentiated in terms of their individual share of total income. In high-inequality countries such as the LMICs, the citizenry is rather starkly divided into a rich, powerful elite and a poor mass public who compete with one another.[13] We assume further that median income level is less than the mean, which is the case in all 'real existing' societies. The regime is a democracy in which all adult citizens have the vote. The government sets the tax rate and can use the revenue earned to promote equality of opportunity through, amongst others, universal quality education. Two parties form and compete for the majority of the votes on the basis of a platform that consists of one item only, namely the desired tax rules that will tax all incomes at a common rate and deliver educational opportunities for everyone. A poorer citizen can be expected to vote for the party whose proposed tax rate will maximize her children's educational opportunities. In contrast, the elite power-holders would want to extend educational opportunities only marginally to favour economic growth, but not to the extent that it threatens their knowledge-based power. The MVH states that the tax rate chosen will coincide with the wishes of the voter whose income equals the median income. From a game-theoretic perspective the two competing political parties can reach a unique Nash equilibrium, that is an outcome where no player can benefit by changing his strategy while the other player keeps her strategies unchanged, if both parties propose the preferred tax rate of the median voter. The MVH entails two conclusions. First, assuming that all else remains equal, the introduction of the popular vote should enable the poor mass (those citizens whose income levels fall below the mean) to improve their income share anything up to the level of equality around the mean. Extending the vote to all adult citizens thus empowers the 'rabble to redistribute', implying that democracy may be more expropriative and therefore more equalizing than autocracy. Second, higher levels of inequality can be expected to lead to increased incentives on the median voter to favour deeper redistribution, seeing that the higher the level of income inequality, the bigger the gap between median and mean (Alesina and Rodrik, 1994; Persson and Tabellini, 1994).

Seen from this perspective, what autocracy with its restrictions on who may vote does is, in effect, to censor the distribution of voters on the income ladder, shifting the income position of the influential voter upwards (Rudra and Haggard, 2005: 1018). The likely result is that the decisive 'voter' in an autocracy – if voting takes place at all – is not the median-income earner whose income, as we said, falls below the mean, but someone with a higher income, and autocracies can be expected to be less committed systematically to redistribution.[14] One reason why episodes of democratization during the second half of the twentieth century have not been effective in terms of mitigating income inequality is that these episodes simulated the upward effect that autocracy has on the location of the influential voter. What are the conditions under which this may happen? Shapiro suggests that these conditions may have to do with both the *demand-* and the *supply-side* of redistribution (Shapiro, 2003).

10.4 Demand side

The demand for redistribution is a function of a number of factors. First and foremost, as our discussion of the MVH above illustrates, any censoring that takes place in the range of voters shifts the income level of the median voter upwards and could thus affect the preferences of the decisive voter. Such censoring is per definition part of autocracy, but it may also occur in a democracy when for whatever reason the median voter cannot effectively articulate her demand. Large differentials in income and wealth could be one of the reasons why some cannot 'afford' to vote, or cannot have their views adequately voiced. If we assume that political influence is a consumption good, then citizens with higher incomes should be able to secure more of it than those lower down the income and wealth ladder (Putterman, 1997; Bassett *et al.*, 1999). A high level of income inequality can thus mean that the median voter is too poor to have the political-demand effect that the MVH suggests. This does not imply that popular sovereignty is impossible in highly unequal societies, but the close positive correlation between income level and democracy, and the close negative correlation of both with inequality, suggests that highly unequal, relatively poor societies face exceptional challenges to institutionalize popular sovereignty. Widespread poverty (and geographic distance) may pose prohibitive costs for the median voter even to turn up at the ballot station. The median (influential) voter can only be found among the voters who turn up at the election booth (Downs, 1957; Lee and Roemer, 1998: 230, 238, footnote 8). If, for whatever reason, the median voter who votes occupies a position higher than the median on the income ladder, then the decisive income earner's effective demand for redistribution will accordingly diminish. As a rule, one would expect this to be less of a factor in a society where the fruits of education are widely spread, as there is a correlation between average levels of education achieved and participation in democratic practices.[15]

Second, the MVH's core assumption that the electorate faces only one issue at election time clearly is unrealistic and has to be relaxed (Roemer, 1998). Party platforms presented to voters usually contain a myriad of issues, and the median voter's eventual choice is determined by trade-offs amongst these and may depend on which party's package deal of issues is most attractive on balance, for her. This may affect her choice of what should be included in the favoured redistributive package, and how redistributive elements such as universal education, public health services, and old-age pensions (to name but a few) should be balanced. However, the degree of redistribution that she demands may also be affected by the public debates that surround the various party platforms between which she must choose. For instance, the preferences of the median voter concerning an ideal tax rate approaching unity may be offset by what she comes to believe about the likely effect of a particular redistributive strategy on future economic growth and political stability.[16] One important consideration in this regard is that the voter may have been persuaded that expropriation or the drastic increase of taxes on wealth in a relatively open global economy is a recipe to encourage capital flight, which could have dire consequences for future capital investment and growth prospects. Usually, there is no shortage of voices conveying this message during an era of globalization and although its proponents are clearly self-serving in how this is presented, it does indicate one of the strategic choices that the median voter has to consider and which may reduce her commitment to an expropriative tax rate. Work done by Boix (2003) and Acemoglu and Robinson (2006) shows that the mobility of capital is an important consideration for elites in highly unequal societies when they have to weigh up the relative costs of continued repression under autocracy versus the potential costs of redistribution. One explanation for the rush of democratization in many repressive autocracies in the latter decades of the twentieth century is that the liberal global regime of relaxing capital controls has made elites more inclined to accept democratization, as they can credibly threaten capital flight and hence restrict the redistributive costs under such a regime. As Boix puts it, 'The process of capital liberalization (in a politically fragmented world) fosters the exit option of asset holders that speeds up the introduction of democracy' (Boix, 2003: 240). The reverse also holds. The process of capital liberalization undermines the bargaining power of the median voter to effect significant redistribution, as the threat of capital flight holds the process of expropriation to ransom. Looked at from this perspective, the degree of capital controls applicable to a political jurisdiction may serve as an approximate indicator of the relative bargaining power of the median voter.[17]

Finally, the literature also suggests that demographic factors can affect the demand for redistribution. The higher the age of the median voter – which also makes them more likely to vote – and the more likely it is that they will reside in an urban area, the larger their demand for intergenerational redistribution will be (Perotti, 1996; Bassett, Burkett and Putterman, 1999; Boix, 2003; de Mello and Tiongson, 2003). In developing LMICs, where provision for the old is less well developed, the elderly are relatively better off in rural areas where they can continue to benefit from small agricultural production and extended families.

10.5 Supply side

Apart from conditions which could affect the demand for redistribution, the implementation of redistribution driven by popular sovereignty also depends on the ability and capability of public authorities to live up to the demands of the median voter. This means that we have to consider not only the demand-side but also the supply-side of the democracy-redistribution equation. Crucial in this regard is the capacity of the state to collect revenue and to manage effectively redistribution programmes such as a system of public education, basic health provision, social welfare, old-age pensions and anti-cyclical macroeconomic policy measures to offset the effects of economic contractions or external shocks.

Such external shocks were quite prominent during the latter part of the twentieth century, precipitated by generalized trade liberalization that increased income inequality in both high-income countries and LMICs. From the standard economic point of view, trade liberalization if followed by an increase in trade should contribute to equalizing incomes in developing societies with an abundance of unskilled labour. The Heckscher–Ohlin trade model concludes that under conditions of an open trading system countries will tend to export goods intensive in the factors that they have in abundance, while they will import goods that use factors that are relatively scarce. With the easing of trade that generalized openness brings, domestic prices of goods whose production uses scarce factors will tend to fall as imports drive down local prices, while local prices for goods that use abundant factors intensively will rise. Stolper and Samuelson (1941) extended this insight by adding that returns to the holders of factors of production that are intensively used will rise absolutely and disproportionately as prices for those goods rise, while the exact opposite will happen to the holders of scarce factors used in the production of goods whose prices fall. All else being equal, then, unskilled labour which is per definition relatively abundant in developing societies should benefit disproportionately from trade liberalization and the resulting specialization in competitive advantage (Ray, 1998: 648–52; Reuveny and Li 2003: 579). This should lead to an improvement in income inequality because the share of unskilled labour in national income increases and because we know that if the ownership of some factor *j* is more widely distributed than that of factor *k*, say, an increase in the national income share of *j* will reduce inequality (Anderson, 2005).

These expected inequality-reducing effects of greater openness could be neutralized, however, by a number of conditions. First, a preponderance of natural resources, such as oil, may alter the equation. The ownership of factors such as land, resources and capital has no 'natural' upper limit, in contrast to human skills, and their potential to increase inequality is therefore unbounded (Spilimbergo *et al.*, 1999: 81). Second, once we expand the basic trade model discussed above to include many countries with varying ratios of skilled to unskilled labour, the dynamics can also change. In general, openness in a large *n* system should raise the relative demand for skilled labour in middle-income developing countries, whose supply of skilled relative to unskilled labour is higher than the world average (Anderson, 2005: 1047). In addition, the presence in a relatively open world system of large producers and exporters of goods which use unskilled labour intensively may reduce the competitive advantage that smaller latecomers may have in unskilled labour, thus altering the demand-structure in favour of more skilled labour in these societies. If skilled labour is relatively scarce, though, this shifting demand will benefit only a few and thus increase overall inequality (Wood, 1997).

The available evidence suggests that low- and lower-middle-income developing countries are clearly much more vulnerable to the inequality-increasing effects of economic openness than their richer counterparts. Independent confirmation of this openness-vulnerability thesis is supplied by Milanovic (2002), who finds on the basis of solid evidence gleaned from household surveys that the inequality-increasing effects of openness and liberalization are much more pronounced in the case of low-income countries. Dependence on private capital inflows, including FDI, increased significantly since the 1970s, which increased access to technology and encouraged production away from low-tech goods which are relatively untradable due to the flooding of world markets by large low-skill producers. This led to an increase in demand for skilled labour, which is a factor endowment in relative short supply in these countries, due to the creation of long-term labour institutions that concentrated the ownership of human capital, and due to the relative failure of contemporary governments to disseminate skills more widely. In these countries, skills are disseminated only amongst a small segment of the labour force, which means that only a small group can benefit from the larger factor rewards brought about by technological innovation and trade specialization, with the result that the already high levels of wage differentials increase even further. Low-income countries are particularly vulnerable to these effects (Wood, 1995, 1997).

That factor underlines the important role that an efficient, honest and politically independent bureaucracy can play to cushion the potential disturbing effects of economic openness by raising revenue and spending it, amongst others, on disseminating appropriate skills in society through investment in education. The ability to deliver public goods such as universal education and health services is a matter of not only resource availability, but also the capacity and efficiency of the public institutions that are tasked to extract revenue and deliver public goods and services. In this context the relative political capacity of the state, approximated by the ratio between the amount of revenue raised and the potential revenue size, may be a good indicator of state efficiency. Lee finds that a one-point increase in government tax revenue as a percentage share of GDP decreases the Gini inequality score of an institutionalized democracy by up to eight percentage points. In partial democracies and autocracies, on the other hand, a larger public sector size is consistently associated with higher-income inequality (Lee, 2005: 174).

10.6 Test

In summary, then, there are a number of contextual and regime features that in combination with one another play an important part in determining whether democratization in LMICs will over time mitigate the high inequality levels that are common in these countries. We identified three important demand-side control variables that have to be added to our estimation of the effect of democratization on income inequality: (1) the average level of education achieved within a society; (2) the potential bargaining power of the median voter, approximated by the level of capital controls; and (3) the demographic structure of society. On the supply side, a relatively politically capable state, approximately indicated by its extractive capacity, seems to be an important redistributive factor under conditions of generalized economic openness. The next step is to see how these control variables fair in an extended version of the models used in Table 10.1, which is reflected in Models 3 and 4 in Table 10.2. Note that due to the co-linearity between GNIpc and some of the control variables introduced in these latter models, GNIpc is dropped as a control variable. In view of the common expectation, suggested first by Kuznets (1955, 1963) that economic growth may exacerbate inequality, especially in early phases of economic modernization, the lagged value of GDP growth is included instead.[18]

Table 10.2 Estimations of net effect of democratization on income inequality

	Model 3 (within: fixed effects)	**Model 4 (random effects)**
Dependent	*EHII Gini*	*EHII Gini*
DEMDUM	*.914	.733
	(.530)	(.544)
GDP growth	−.081	*** −.235
	(.056)	(.058)
Capital mobility	***.236	***.424
	(.0838)	(.081)
State's relative extractive capacity	* − 1.275	−.955
	(.659)	(.637)
OLD	.243	*** −.747
	(.191)	(.131)
Average years of schooling	*.329	−.220
	.175	(.159)
Constant	39.672	46.655
	(1.255)	(.986)
Observations	400	400
N	81	81
r^2	.392	.485

Coefficient values shown with standard errors in parentheses.
* = statistically significant at 0.1 level
** = statistically significant at 0.05 level
*** = statistically significant at 0.01 level

We estimate the effect of democratization (measured as before in Table 10.1) on the EHII Gini of 81 countries (58 LMICs), but now controlling for the following:

- *Capital mobility*, as measured by the Fraser Institute (Gwartney and Lawson, 2004), which uses an index that looks at the access that citizens have to foreign capital markets, and foreigners to domestic markets, plus the absence of restrictions on the freedom of citizens to engage in capital market exchange (higher value = less controls). Based on the preceding discussion, we expect the sign of this variable to be positive.
- *Relative extractive capacity* of a state, as calculated using the regression equation: Tax/GDP $= \beta0 + \beta1$ (time) $+ \beta2$(Mining/GDP) $+ \beta3$ (Agriculture/GDP) $+ \beta4$ (Exports/GDP) + error term (Feng *et al.*, 2000). The sign should be negative.
- *OLD*: The percentage of population who are 65 years and older (from the 2003 World Bank CD-Rom *World Development Indicators*). The hypothesis is that this variable's sign will be negative.
- *Average years of schooling* achieved by cohort 25 years and older (Barro and Lee, 2000). We expect the sign of this variable's coefficient to be negative.

As in Table 10.1, all independent variables lagged one time-period. Table 10.2 reports the results from the fixed-effects and the random-effects estimation using these variables.

The first notable point about Model 3, which is the fixed-effect model, is that the transition to democracy remains statistically significant but less so than in Model 1 (Table 10.1) now that we control for the effect of the demand- and supply-side factors listed above. In the random-effect model (Model 4), this significance – and with it the cross-country difference between democracies and non-democracies – disappears under the combined effects of these control variables. Five other findings also stand out: first, the reduction of capital controls within countries is highly significant and associated with rising subsequent inequality levels, and countries with less capital controls are more unequal than those with more. Models 3 and 4 thus strongly confirm the hypothesis that under the credible threat of capital flight it becomes less likely that the electorate will use the vote to institute measures that will drastically reshape patterns of income distribution in a country. Secondly, it is only in the within-country context that the growing capacity of the state is significant: as states democratize and the state grows stronger, the amelioration of inequality becomes more likely. However, the effect is not significant across countries. While the sign of the state capacity coefficient is still the expected negative, it does not seem to be such an important factor explaining variation between than within countries.

Third, countries with higher proportions of the elderly in their population clearly have a better track record in dealing with inequality under conditions of institutionalized democracy, as is the case in most high-income OECD countries, than do developing countries. As expected, the urban elderly in high-income countries are more politically active and capable than their relatively more numerous younger counterparts in LMICs, and articulate the demand for equality-increasing intergenerational transfers quite decisively. What little and insignificant impact the increase of the number of the elderly over time within countries has tends to worsen inequality.

Fourth, the results of Models 3 and 4 show that economic growth does have the potential to depress inequality, but this effect is not significant either within or between countries. The implications are, first, that there is no credible evidence of a growth-inequality trade-off within countries, contrary to the expectations generated by the Kuznets hypothesis[19] and, secondly, that democracy marginally helps to spread the fruits of faster economic growth somewhat more equitably than partial democracies or autocracies do.

Fifth, and surprisingly, the net effect of the average level of schooling is not significant in the random-effects, but is in the fixed-effects model. The latter shows that overall, when we account for all variation, higher levels of education seem to be associated only weakly with lower inequality. More significantly, rising levels of average schooling achieved within countries may worsen inequality, though. The sign of the coefficient in the fixed-effects model suggests that spreading education within a society does not *ipso facto* reduce inequality. Instead, before a critical level of the dissemination of skills is achieved, marginal educational advances can exacerbate income differentials between those that receive the higher level of education and those that do not, given the general income premium that there is on skilled labour. In this respect something of a Kuznets effect seems to be still relevant: as economies modernize and the premium on skilled labour increases, those who manage to improve their educational levels compared to the rest of society also draw more benefit in terms of higher relative income. Only when secondary and higher education becomes more universally available will the effect of the skill premium decline.

10.7 Conclusions

This study sets out to determine why it is that the spate of positive regime transitions to democracy in LMICs during the latter part of the twentieth century has not been accompanied by the reversal of patterns of income inequality. What sets this study apart from other investigations of the relationship between democracy and income distribution are the explicit focus on a dynamic factor, namely democratization, and the utilization of a consistent data source on gross income differentials in a large group of high-income countries and LMICs.

There are many factors that can account for the failure of regime transition from autocracy to give rise to greater economic equity in LMICs. As noted earlier, LMICs are composed of ex-communist transition economies on the one hand and the so-called 'developing countries' on the other. The literature has suggested specific reasons why inequality has risen during the latter decades of the twentieth century in the case of the ex-communist transition countries, including China. The primary explanations that have been offered for these trends in the transition economies are, in the case of China, the big divergence between rural and urban wages which resulted from the economic reforms since 1978 (Blecher, 2005), and the effect of the institution regulating population movement (the *hukou*) which severely inhibits mobility between the rural areas and the urban centres (Liu, 2005). In the case of the transition economies of Central and Eastern Europe and Central Asia, a number of factors contributed to the worsening of income inequality, among which were the rapid rise of unemployment as job security was removed in the wake of the capitalist reforms started in the late 1980s; the fall in minimum wage compared to the average wage as wage-setting norms changed in the wake of large-scale privatization; and the rise of the informal sector (Cornia, 2004: 7). To this list we can add the failure of the educational system to help the unemployed to re-school and re-tool; the effect of rapid inflation and macroeconomic instability; and the ability of the relatively well-off and politically powerful to capture rent-seeking opportunities at a direct cost to the less influential. Hellman *et al.* (2003) show how what they call a 'capture economy' has emerged in many transition countries, where the rapid and unregulated selling-off of state-owned enterprises in the absence of strong regulatory and democratic institutions provided opportunities for public officials and politicians to sell rent- and unequal wealth-generating advantages to private firms. There is good reason to believe that the latter factor of state capture by the elite, during and after the transition from autocracy, is also a major factor in accounting for the fact that partial democracies in the developing world are associated strongly with increasing inequality.

Moving beyond these more specific explanations of why partial democracies cannot redistribute, this chapter focused on the conditions under which poorer voters in institutionalized democracies (in contrast to partial democracies) can effect a mitigation of income inequality. MVH helps us to identify theoretically the conditions under which democratization could give rise to redistribution, but these conditions have become very circumscribed and scarce in an era of generalized economic openness. We noted that contrary to mainstream theory, economic openness in general tends to increase and not mitigate income inequality in countries where skilled labour is in short supply. Only in those countries with the requisite state capacity to disseminate skills amongst their populace on a broad scale can the electorate use the vote effectively to reduce the effects of this tendency. However, the demand for drastically enhanced state spending to spread educational opportunities more generally in poorer societies, which will depend on a form of expropriation through progressive taxation, can be suppressed if there is a credible threat of capital flight. Again, economic openness emerges as a threat and not a boon to attempts to lower inequality levels in developing LMICs in particular. As there are many reasons why we should be concerned about high levels of income inequality in the LMICs, as the 2006 World Bank *World Development Report* makes abundantly clear, these systemic obstacles to growth-enhancing and pro-poor redistribution have to receive more attention. At a minimum, the macroeconomic advisers of and in LMICs should reconsider the general assumption that economic openness, *tout court*, is desirable. While there is good reason to believe that trade openness can enhance growth and equity in societies which have achieved a certain level of human capital development, there are also reasons to be careful not to impose liberalization of the capital account on societies that have not yet achieved the required level of human capital development. The absence of capital controls makes it less likely that democratization would be followed by a broader dissemination of educational opportunities in these societies.

Finally, the evidence reviewed here also suggests that the promotion of democratization in LMICs, from within and from without, should be treated more circumspectly and discerningly. While positive regime transition to institutionalized democracy holds many potential benefits for societies with autocratic regimes or with partial democracies, it is clearly a mistake to assume that democratization in and of itself is a panacea for all the economic ills. Redistribution, in particular, is a policy outcome that has to be targeted separately and specifically under conditions of economic openness, and will not simply flow automatically from the extension of popular sovereignty.

Notes

1. See Doorenspleet (2000) for an analysis of this phase of global democratization.
2. In their comprehensive study of democracy and economic development, Przeworski *et al.* (2002: 122) find that 'democracies are less stable in societies that are more unequal to begin with, in societies in which household income inequality increases, and in societies in which labor receives a lower share of value added in manufacturing'.
3. Calculated by the World Bank using the exchange rate of the local currency against 1994 US Dollars (Atlas method).
4. See Epstein *et al.* (2003), Reich (2002) and Lee (2005).
5. This conception allows for a one-party-dominated regime to be recognized as an institutionalized democracy as long as the three Marshall and Jaggers criteria are met. This is a less stringent requirement than that proposed by Przeworski *et al.* (2000), who define democracies as regimes in which parties lose elections. This may set the bar unrealistically high for many LMICs, though; for example, the cases of Botswana and South Africa.
6. I use the Polity2 measure (revised combined polity score) which is geared towards the use of the POLITY regime measure in time-series analyses. It modifies the combined annual Polity score by applying a set of simple coding rules to deal with transitional periods and other exceptional circumstances (see Marshall and Jaggers, 2002: 8).
7. It is of course problematic to use what was intended as a continuous scale of democracy to arrive at a categorical distinction between types of democracy. Nevertheless, the POLITY IV dataset has so many advantages in terms of clarity of conceptualization and operationalization that researchers interested in the categorization of types of democracy prefer to use it instead of less transparent categorizations such as Reich (2002). The important question is where exactly to draw the line on this continuous scale between democracy and partial democracy, and the opinions differ on this (see Lee, 2005; and Epstein *et al.*, 2003). The cut-off used here, namely the score of seven, is deemed to be sufficiently stringent in terms of the three democracy criteria discussed above.
8. See Bollen and Jackman (1985) for a discussion of the early literature. See also Muller (1988), Simpson (1990), Burkhart (1997), Przeworski *et al.*, (2000), Gradstein, Milanovic and Ying (2001) and Lane and Ersson (2003).
9. One important exception is Bollen and Jackman (1985), who find no evidence of a direct relationship of depth of democracy on inequality, and argue that it is level of economic development that determines both. However, most recent work points out some problems with the Bollen and Jackman specification.

10. The one exception is the quasi-experimental study by Chan (1997), which looks at the effect of democratization in Taiwan, South Korea and Singapore on public policies that have redistributive effects. His results for Taiwan and South Korea indicate that public spending on education and social security did increase after the introduction of democracy. However, apart from being limited to three case studies, Chan's study also has two other shortcomings: first, it focuses on public expenditure *per se* and not on the distributive effects that public spending has on various income groups; second, his study is not based on an explicit theory that sets out the causal mechanism through which democratization can lead to redistribution.
11. Because it is based primarily on pay/wage data, this dataset is applicable only to analyses focusing on pre-tax and pre-transfer (= gross) income.
12. The MVH is an extremely parsimonious, some would say 'simplistic' model of voting outcomes and deliberately so. By keeping it parsimonious to the extreme, the MVH allows us to show in a controlled way what we have to add to the basic model to understand in a comparative manner what is actually taking place in 'real' democracies. Although there are clear limits to this way of approaching the study of comparative politics, it has obvious advantages as well, especially when we are confronted with such a complex and over-determined phenomenon such as democracy. It seems more constructive to start with a minimum model and then consider what to add to enable us to understand a phenomenon, rather than to try and grasp the complexity of the phenomenon in one comprehensive swoop. Although the ideas behind the MVH can be traced back to the liberal fears of the nineteenth century that democracies could be more expropriating than oligarchies (Lee, 2003), it was Downs (1957) and especially Meltzer and Richard (1981) that gave current currency to the MVH. For contemporary discussions, applications and tests of the MVH see Alesina and Rodrik (1994), Alesina and Perotti (1996), Persson and Tabellini (1994), Evans (2004), Mueller (2003), Congleton (2002), Borck (2003), Milanovic (2000) and de Mello and Tiongson (2003).
13. The discussion here is based on the very useful summary of the MVH that can be found in an unpublished paper by John Roemer (2001).
14. This does not mean that autocracies are never redistributive. Authoritarian redistributive populism of both leftist and rightist varieties has been a common occurrence in Southern Europe, Latin America, Southeast Asia and parts of Africa. As Wintrobe (1998) has argued, insecure authoritarian leaders also seek legitimacy through redistribution, while communist totalitarianism in East and Central Europe was associated with some of the lowest levels of income inequality that could be found anywhere in the twentieth century.
15. The relationship between level of education achieved and democracy is more complex than Lipset (1959) assumed. See Acemoglu *et al.* (2005) for a rebuttal of the view that higher average levels of education lead to democracy. However, within democracies, the more educated voters are, the more likely they are to become involved in electoral politics.
16. For extensive and very useful overviews of the reasons why the median voter may not necessarily prefer a tax rate of unity, or may not be able to secure it even if she prefers it, see Shapiro (2003: chapter 5), Putterman (1997), Borck (2003), Lee (2003) and Roemer (1998).

17. Structural features of the economy and specifically of the labour market may influence the median voter's bargaining power, thus affecting the demand for redistribution, if we entertain the plausible assumptions that the median-income earner is a relatively skilled labourer and that to voice effectively her demand for public redistribution she has to overcome typical collective action problems in developing LMICs. In a series of recent publications, Rudra has shown that the collective action resources of our median voter will be affected crucially by the presence of surplus labour and the ratio of skilled to unskilled labour in a society at any given time (Rudra, 2002; Rudra, 2005; Rudra and Haggard, 2005). She proposes the notion of 'potential labour power' (PLP) to capture the collective action potential of our median voter. PLP grows as the ratio of skilled to unskilled labour increases, but will decrease with the size of surplus labour, which is measured as the working-age population minus the economically active population and students in secondary and tertiary education. As we already have an alternative indicator of median voter bargaining power (see below), and since the PLP data is available only for a limited group of countries, we do not explore the effect of PLP any further here.
18. Figures for growth of GDP in purchasing-power-parity values are from the Penn World Tables, Heston, Summers and Aten (2003).
19. For a discussion, see Ray (1998).

References

Acemoglu, D. and Robinson, J. A. *Economic Origins of Dictatorship and Democracy* (Cambridge: Cambridge University Press, 2006).

Acemoglu, D., Johnson, S., Robinson, J. and Yared, P. 'From Education to Democracy?', *American Economic Association Papers and Proceedings*, 95 (2005): 44–9.

Aghion, P. E. C. and Garcia-Penalosa, C. 'Inequality and Economic Growth: The Perspective of the New Growth Theories', *Journal of Economic Literature*, 37 (4) (1999): 1615–60.

Alesina, A. and Rodrik, D. 'Distributive Politics and Economic Growth', *Quarterly Journal of Economics*, 109 (1994): 465-90.

Alesina, A. and Perotti, R. 'Income Distribution, Political Instability and Investment', *European Economic Review*, 81 (5) (1996): 1170–89.

Anderson, E. 'Openness and Inequality in Developing Countries: A Review of Theory and Recent Evidence', *World Development*, 33 (7) (2005): 1045–63.

Banerjee, A. and Duflo, E. 'Inequality and Growth: What Can the Data Say?'. Cambridge, MA., National Bureau of Economic Research, Working Paper No. 7793 (2000).

Barro, R. 'Democracy and Growth', *Journal of Economic Growth*, 1 (1) (1996): 1–27.

Barro, R. 'Inequality and Growth in a Panel of Countries', *Journal of Economic Growth*, 5 (1) (2000): 5–32.

Barro, R. J. and Lee, J. 'International Data on Educational Attainment: Updates and Implications'. Centre for International Development, Working Paper No. 42 (2000) http://www.cid.harvard.edu/ciddata/ciddata.html.

Bassett, W. F., Burkett, J. P. and Putterman, L. 'Income Distribution, Government Transfers, and the Problem of Unequal Influence', *European Journal of Political Economy*, 15 (1999): 207–28.

Bearse, P., Glomm, G. and Janeba, E. 'Why Poor Countries Rely Mostly on Redistribution In-kind', *Journal of Public Economics*, 75 (2000): 463–81.

Beer, L. and Boswell, T. 'The Resilience of Dependency Effects in Explaining Income Inequality in the Global Economy: A Cross-National Analysis, 1975-1995', *Journal of World Systems Research*, 8 (1) (2002): 30–59.

Benabou, R. 'Inequality and Growth'. London, Centre for Economic Policy Research, Discussion Paper No. 1450 (1996).

Birdsall, N. (2001) 'Why Inequality Matters: Some Economic Issues', *Ethics and International Affairs*, 15 (2): 3–28.

Birdsall, N. and Londono, J. 'Asset Inequality Matters: An Assessment of the World Bank's Approach to Poverty Reduction', *The American Economic Review*, 87 (2) (1997): 32–7.

Blecher, M. 'Inequality and Capitalism in China', unpublished report prepared for the American Political Science Association Task Force Conference on Inequality and Difference in Developing Societies (2005) http://www.apsanet.org/content_13916.cfm.

Boix, C. *Democracy and Redistribution* (Cambridge: Cambridge University Press, 2003).

Bollen, K. A. and Jackman, R. W. 'Political Democracy and the Size Distribution of Income', *American Sociological Review*, 50 (1985): 438–57.

Borck, R. 'Voting, Inequality, and Redistribution', DIW Working Paper, (July 2003) http://www.polecon.de/Redistribution.pdf.

Burkhart, R. E. 'Comparative Democracy and Income Distribution: Shape and Direction of the Causal Arrow', *Journal of Politics*, 59 (1) (1997): 149–64.

Castro-Leal, F., Dayton, J., Demery, L. and Mehra, K. 'Public Social Spending in Africa: Do the Poor Benefit?', *World Bank Research Observer*, 14 (1) (1999): 49–72.

Champernowne, D. and Cowell, F. *Economic Inequality and Income Distribution* (Cambridge: Cambridge University Press, 1998).

Chan, S. 'Democracy and Inequality: Tracking Welfare Spending in Singapore, Taiwan, and South Korea', in M. Midlarsky (ed.), *Inequality, Democracy, and Economic Development* (Cambridge: Cambridge University Press, 1997): 227–43.

Chen, S. and Ravallion, M. 'How Did the World's Poorest Fare in the 1990s?' World Bank Policy Research Working Paper No. 2409 (August 2000) http://www.worldbank.org/research/povmonitor/method.htm.

Congleton, R. 'The Median-Voter Model', contribution prepared for the *Encyclopedia of Public Choice* (2002) http://rdc1.net/forthcoming/medianvt.pdf.

Cornia, G. (ed.), *Inequality, Growth, and Poverty in an Era of Liberalization and Globalization* (Oxford: Oxford University Press, 2004).

Dagdeviren, H., van der Hoeven, R. and Weeks, J. 'Redistribution Matters: Growth for Poverty Reduction'. Geneva, Employment Sector, International Labour Office, ILO Employment Paper No. 2001/10 (2001).

de Ferranti, D. *et al. Inequality in Latin America and the Caribbean: Breaking with History?* World Bank Latin American and Caribbean Studies, Advanced Conference Edition (2003) http://www.cefe.net/forum/Inequality.pdf.

de Mello, L. and Tiongson, E. R. 'Income Inequality and Redistributive Government Spending', IMF Working Paper WP/03/14 (2003) http://www.imf.org/external/pubs/ft/wp/2003/wp0314.pdf.

Deininger, K. and Squire, L. 'Measuring Income Inequality: A New Data Base', *World Bank Economic Review*, 10 (3) (1996): 565–91.

Deininger, K. and Squire, L. 'New Ways of Looking at Old Issues: Inequality and Growth', *Journal of Development Economics*, 57 (1998): 259–87.

Diamond, L. *Developing Democracy: Towards Consolidation* (Baltimore: Johns Hopkins Press, 1999).

Doorenspleet, R. 'Reassessing the Three Waves of Democratization', *World Politics*, 52 (2000): 384–406.

Downs, A. *An Economic Theory of Democracy* (New York: Harper and Row, 1957).

Easterly, W. 'Inequality *Does* Cause Underdevelopment: New Evidence', Center for Global Development, Working Paper No. 1 (June 2002) http://www.cgdev.org/wp/cgd_wp001_rev.pdf.

Epstein, L., Bates, R., Goldstone, J., Kristensen, I. and O'Halloran, S. 'Democratic Transitions', unpublished paper (2003) http://www.cid.harvard.edu/cidpeople/bates/Transitions.pdf.

Evans, J. A. J. *Voters and Voting: An Introduction* (London: Sage, 2004).

Fan, S. and Rao, N. 'Public Spending in Developing Countries: Trends, Determination, and Impact'. Washington, D.C.: International Food Policy Research Institute, Environment and Production Technology Division, Discussion Paper No. 99, (2003) http://www.ifpri.org/divs/eptd/dp/papers/eptdp99.pdf.

Feng, Y., Kugler, Y. and Zak, P. J. 'The Politics of Fertility and Economic Development', *International Studies Quarterly*, 44 (1) (2000): 667–93.

Galbraith, J. K. and Kum, H. 'Estimating the Inequality of Household Income: A Statistical Approach to the Creation of a Dense and Consistent Data Set', *Review of Income and Wealth*, 51 (1) (2005): 115–43.

Gradstein, M., Milanovic, B. and Ying, Y. 'Democracy and Income Inequality: An Empirical Analysis', World Bank Research Department (2001) http://www.worldbank.org/research/inequality/inequalityandpolitics/dem,ineq.pdf.

Gugerty, M. K. and Timmer, C. P. 'Growth, Inequality, and Poverty Alleviation: Implications for Development Assistance'. Harvard Institute for International Development, Consulting Assistance on Economic Reform II, Discussion Paper No. 50, (December 1999) www.cid.harvard.edu/caer2/htm/content/papers/confpubs/paper50/paper50.pdf.

Gwartney, J. and Lawson, R. *Economic Freedom of the World: 2004 Annual Report* (Vancouver: The Fraser Institute, 2004) http://www.freetheworld.com.

Hellman, J., Jones, G. and Kaufmann, D. 'Seize the State, Seize the Day: State Capture and Influence in Transition Economies', *Journal of Comparative Economies*, 31 (2003): 751–73.

Heston, A., Summers, R. and Aten, B. 'Penn World Table Version 6.1', Center for International Comparisons at the University of Pennsylvania (CICUP) (2003) http://datacentre2.cass.utoronto.ca/pwt/docs/pwt61.html.

Justino, P., Litchfield, J. and Whitehead, L. 'The Impact of Inequality in Latin America', Poverty Research Unit at Sussex, Working Paper No. 21 (2003) http://www.sussex.ac.uk/Users/PRU.

Kanbur, R. 'Income Distribution and Development', in A. Atkinson and F. Bourguignon (eds), *Handbook on Income Distribution* (Amsterdam: North-Holland, 2000): 791-841.

Kentor, J. 'The Long-term Effects of Globalization on Income Inequality, Population Growth, and Economic Development', *Social Problems* 48 (4) (2001): 435–55.

Knowles, S. 'Inequality and Economic Growth: The Empirical Relationship Reconsidered in the Light of Comparable Data', *Journal of Development Studies*, 41 (2005): 135–59.

Kuznets, S. 'Economic Growth and Income Inequality', *American Economic Review*, 45 (1955): 1–48.

Kuznets, S. 'Quantitative Aspects of the Economic Growth of Nations: VIII. Distribution of Income by Size', *Economic Development and Cultural Change*, 11 (2: 2) (1963): 1–80.

Landa, D. and Kapstein, E. 'Inequality, Growth, and Democracy' (review article), *World Politics*, 53 (2001): 264–96.

Lane, J. and Ersson, S. *Democracy: A Comparative Approach* (London: Routledge, 2003).

Lee, C-S. 'Income Inequality, Democracy, and Public Sector Size', *American Sociological Review*, 70 (1) (2005): 158.

Lee, W. 'Is Democracy More Expropriative than Dictatorship? Tocquevillian Wisdom Revisited', *Journal of Development Economics*, 71 (2003): 155–98.

Lee, W. and Roemer, J. E. 'Income Distribution, Redistributive Politics, and Economic Growth', *Journal of Economic Growth*, 3 (1998): 217–40.

Lipset, S. M. 'Some Social Requisites of Democracy: Economic Development and Political Legitimacy', *American Political Science* Review, 53 (1959): 69–105.

Liu, Z. 'Institution and Inequality: The *Hukou* System in China', *Journal of Comparative Economics*, 33 (2005): 133–57.

Marshall, M. and Jaggers, K. 'Polity IV Project: Political Regime Characteristics and Transitions, 1800–1999', Center for International Development and Conflict Management, University of Maryland (2000) http:www.bsos.umd.edu/cidcm/inscr/polity.

Marshall, M. and Jaggers, K. POLITY IV PROJECT, Political Regime Characteristics and Transitions, 1980-2002, Dataset Users' manual (2002).

Meltzer, A. H. and Richard, S. F. 'A Rational Theory of the Size of Government', *The Journal of Political Economy*, 89 (5) (1981): 914–27.

Milanovic, B. 'The Median-voter Hypothesis, Income Inequality, and Income Redistribution: an Empirical Test with the Required Data', *European Journal of Political Economy*, 16 (2000): 367–410.

Milanovic, B. 'Can We Discern the Effect of Globalisation on Income Distribution? Evidence from Household Budget Surveys', World Bank Policy Research working paper 2876 (April 2002).

Muller, E. N. 'Democracy, Economic Development, and Income Inequality', *American Sociological Review*, 53 (1988): 50–68.

Mueller, D. C. *Public Choice III* (Cambridge: Cambridge University Press, 2003).

Naschold, F. 'Why Inequality Matters for Poverty'. UK Department for International Development Inequality, Briefing Paper No. 2 (March 2002).

Nel, P. 'Income Inequality, Economic Growth, and Political Instability in sub-Saharan Africa', *Journal of Modern African Studies*, 41 (4) (2003): 611–39.

Nel, P. 'Democratisation and the Dynamics of Income Distribution in Low and Middle-income Countries', *Politikon*, 32 (1) (2005): 17–43.

Nelson, P. 'Redistribution and the Income of the Median Voter', *Public Choice*, 98 (1999): 187–94.

Perotti, R. 'Growth, Income Distribution, and Democracy: What the Data Say', *Journal of Economic Growth*, 1 (2) (1996): 149–88.

Persson, T. and Tabellini, G. 'Is Inequality Harmful for Growth?' *American Economic Review*, 84 (3) (1994): 600–21.

Przeworski, A., Alvarez, M., Cheibub, J. and Limongi, F. *Democracy and Development: Political Institutions and Well-Being in the World, 1950–1990* (Cambridge: Cambridge University Press, 2000).

Putterman, L. 'Why Have the Rabble Not Redistributed the Wealth? On the Stability of Democracy and Unequal Property', in J. E. Roemer (ed.), *Property Relations, Incentives, and Welfare*, (London: Macmillan, 1997): 359–89.

Ray, D. *Development Economics* (Princeton: Princeton University Press, 1998).

Reich, G. 'Categorizing Political Regimes: New Data for Old Problems", *Democratization*, 19 (4) (2002): 1–24.

Reuveny, R. and Li, Q. 'Economic Openness, Democracy and Income Inequality: An Empirical Analysis', *Comparative Political Studies*, 36 (5) (2003): 575–601.

Robinson, W. *Promoting Polyarchy: Globalization, US Intervention ad Hegemony* (Cambridge: Cambridge University Press, 1996).

Rodrik, D. *The New Global Economy and Developing Countries: Making Openness Work* (Washington, D.C.: Overseas Development Council and the Johns Hopkins Press, 1999).

Roemer, J. 'Why the Poor do not Expropriate the Rich: An Old Argument in New Garb', *Journal of Public Economics*, 70 (1998): 399–424.

Roemer, J. 'Democracy, Educational Finance, and the Distribution of Human Capital: A Dynamic Analysis', unpublished paper (2001) http://mora.rente.nhh.no/projects/EqualityExchange/Portals/0/articles/roemer3.pdf.

Rudra, N. 'Globalization and the Decline of the Welfare State in Less-developed Countries', *International Organization*, 56 (2) (2002): 411–45.

Rudra, N. 'Globalization and the Strengthening of Democracy in the Developing World', *American Journal of Political Science*, 49 (4) (2005): 704–30.

Rudra, N. and Haggard, S. 'Globalization, Democracy, and Effective Welfare Spending in the Developing World', *Comparative Political Studies*, 38 (9) (2005): 1015–49.

Rueschemeyer, D., Stephens, E. H. and Stephens, J. D. *Capitalist Development and Democracy* (Chicago: University of Chicago Press, 1992).

Sanders, D. *Patterns of Political Instability* (New York: St Martin's Press, 1981).

Shapiro, I. *The State of Democratic Theory* (Princeton: Princeton University Press, 2003).

Simpson, M. 'Political Rights and Income Inequality: a Cross-national Test', *American Sociological Review*, 55 (1990): 682–93.

Spilimbergo, A., Londono, J. L. and Szekely, M. 'Income Distribution, Factor Endowments, and Trade Openness', *Journal of Development Economics*, 59 (1999): 77–101.

Stolper, W. and Samuelson, P. 'Protection and Real Wages', *Review of Economic Studies*, 9 (1941): 58–73.

Vanhanen T. *Democratizaion: A Comparative Analysis of 170 Countries* (London: Routledge, 2003).

Verdier, T, and Ades, A. 'The Rise and Fall of Elites: A Theory of Economic Development and Social Polarization in Rent-seeking Societies'. London Centre for Economic Policy Research, Discussion Paper No. 1495 (1996).

Wood, A. 'How Trade Hurts Unskilled Workers', *The Journal of Economic Perspectives*, 9 (3) (1995): 57–80.

Wood, A. 'Openness and Wage Inequality in Developing Countries: The Latin American Challenge to East Asian Conventional Wisdom', *The World Bank Economic Review*, 11 (1997): 33–57.

Wintrobe, D. *The Political Economy of Dictatorship* (Cambridge: Cambridge University Press, 1998).

World Bank. *Attacking Poverty – World Development Report 2000-2001* (Washington, D.C.: The World Bank, 2001).

World Bank. *World Development Indicators, CD-Rom* (Washington, D.C.: World Bank, 2003).

World Bank. Equity and Development: World Development Report 2005/2006 (Washington, D.C.: The World Bank, 2005).

11
Globalization as the Institutionalization of Neoliberalism: Commodification, Financialization, and the Anchorless Economy

Robert H. Wade

'Globalization' is normally taken to mean a high- or fast-rising level of economic interdependence across distances, and the informational connectivity that goes with it. But globalization in this sense is the surface manifestation of a more basic process in the political-economy world order, which could be described as the deepening institutionalization of a neoliberal mode of capitalism.

For the purposes of this chapter we take it as given that the world economy since the 1980s has become markedly more 'neoliberal' than in 1950–80, and that it has not been performing well. Median economic growth in OECD countries and developing countries is substantially lower than in 1960–80; the frequency and duration of growth stagnations in developing countries has increased; world income inequality has at best remained constant since 1980 and may have become more unequal (it has certainly become more unequal if one country, China, is excluded); the number of people living below an international extreme poverty line (PPP$1/day) increased in 1981–2001 when one country, China again, is excluded; the frequency of financial crises has been much higher in 1980–2000 than in the earlier decades; and developing countries outside East Asia have experienced no increase in share of global manufacturing value added (Wade, 2004a, 2008; Reddy and Minoiu, 2006). Deflationary tendencies have been evident in several OECD economies.

Here we shall discuss three mega-policies that help to explain the connection between the neoliberal mode and economic performance. The first is the far-reaching extension of private property rights (PPRs) to make the 'enclosed' assets commensurable through the price system and a large subset of them subject to sale on the same basic terms worldwide. We could call this 'expanding enclosure of private property', or the more familiar but uglier word, 'commodification'.

The second trend could be called 'financialization of the economy' (FOE). As PPRs advance, finance becomes more and more the universal unit of power. Financialization refers to the growing dominance of the financial economy over the real economy, as seen in the tightening institutional interlock and normative congruence around the interests of wealth holders; the rapid redistribution of national income towards capital-owners and away from labour (dependent on wages and salaries); and the rapid redistribution of national income towards the richest five per cent and one per cent of households in most of the OECD countries, notably the United States and the United Kingdom.

The third policy trend is the weakening of (non-market) institutions which in the post-war decades helped to stabilize and expand the world economy, with the unsurprising effect of increased instability and reduced expansion. We could call this 'the movement to an anchorless economy'.

These three forces move national political economies in a neoliberal direction, with the state functioning less as a coordinator of private economic actors and more as an umpire. They are very different to those given prominence in most of the burgeoning literature on 'institutions and economic growth'. This chapter illustrates how they affect economic performance of the world system and large sub-categories, and points to several more, or less, feasible policy measures to improve performance.

11.1 Enclosure, horizontal and vertical

To understand the force of enclosure, think of three sectors of a modern society: (1) the state and its organization for taking responsibility for the supply of collective goods and services, governed by a logic of the rights and duties of citizenship, supporting some degree of redistribution to those marginalized by market transactions; (2) the web of market exchange, governed by a logic of private property and individualism, where market exchange and individual liberty are treated as synonymous; and (3) the family, kin, neighbourhood, and associations based on intrinsic satisfactions, governed by affectivity and reciprocity (Lipschutz, 1997). The dominant trend in 'globalization' is the expansion of sector (2) into sectors (1) and (3), organizationally and normatively.

The expansion of market exchange is occurring through the radical extension of PPRs over assets. The 'enclosed' assets then become subject to price commensuration worldwide. The World Trade Organization (WTO) rules under the Trade-Related Investment Measures (TRIMS) and the General Agreement on Trade in Services (GATS) illustrate the principle of 'commensuration on the same basic terms worldwide'. They rule out a government giving domestic firms more favourable treatment than foreign firms.

The extension is happening 'horizontally' (raising the density of PPRs in peripheral regions from Mongolia to the Amazon) and also 'vertically' (raising the density of PPRs in types of assets formerly not governed by them). Natural resources are a particular target, including the seabed, naturally occurring genes, knowledge, even access to information collected at public expense. Even basic research, which used to be propelled by largely non-market calculations in sites insulated from market forces (such as university research laboratories), is being enfolded in corporations and privatized.

Private property rights enclosure is also happening in a range of formerly collectively provided goods and services, like education and health care. Drinking water is increasingly provided privately.[1] Civil services are being restructured away from Weberian-type bureaucracies towards task-related employment contracts and external recruitment, removing the segmentation between the civil service and the wider labour market.

The upshot is that an ever-larger part of people's lives is being subject to individualistic, market-based calculation, justified on the grounds that markets signal efficiency. The overarching unit of account in most of these transactions – if not directly then at one removed – is a hard currency: almost everywhere the US dollar, the centre currency of the world economy.

Hence the new world political order gives even more 'soft' power than before to the United States, as the source of the centre currency. If one of the basic political questions is 'Where does the king's writ end?', the answer today is that the United States is the modern king, and the king's writ now extends to the ends of the earth, to remote regions, and to previously non-market institutions like the family through the US-dominance of world finance (Wade, 2003a).

'Globalization', in short, is the reconstruction of power at the world level around finance, chiefly denominated in US dollars, by means of the extension of PPRs to all assets. This has deeply problematic impacts, such as the shift of what could be called 'infrastructural' power to those who control credit and the consequent increase of financialization. But in some domains it can also bring net social benefits, such as better environmental protection achieved through 'enclosing' air and water commons to the point where polluters have to pay.

All this is very abstract. Let us pin it down by illustrating the capillary processes by which private property rights and market relations are extended horizontally and vertically, and into the realm of cognitive and normative frameworks. The anecdotes can be read as bubbles on the stream of the big trends.

11.1.1 The neoclassical antibodies

The discipline of economics since the 1970s has become much more homogeneous than it was, in the sense that one paradigm, neoclassical economics, has marginalized other ways of seeing, including Keynesian, Kaldorian, and developmental state-ian perspectives. In the post–Bretton Woods era economics has lost much of its earlier 'biodiversity', even as it extended its scope of application far beyond the boundaries of orthodox economics. The reigning consensus over the 1980s and 1990s – not so much among the 'theorists' as among the policy community – has been a conservative combination of supply-side, free-market, and monetarist thoughts. It advocates a combination of fiscal conservatism, free financial markets as suppliers of capital, and monetary policy as the instrument of demand management (Baker, 2001). It is intolerant of ideas from the earlier 'Keynesian consensus' that market failure is endogenous, financial crises are normal in loosely regulated financial markets, governments should play a role in both macroeconomic demand management and microeconomic resource allocation, fiscal policy can be effective as a tool of demand management, and public investment can have high economic worth.

The extent to which non-neoclassical ideas have been extruded from the mainstream can be gauged from when George Bortz became editor of the *American Economic Review* (*AER*) in the early 1970s. Paul Davidson, a leader of the dwindling band of Keynesians, protested to Bortz that all his submissions under Bortz's editorship were being rejected, whereas under the previous editor most of his submissions had been accepted. Bortz informed him that the *AER* was not going to publish papers by Keynesians, and suggested that he and the Keynesians start their own journal. Davidson and colleagues went ahead with the *Journal of Keynesian Economics* – until someone noticed the acryonym and the title was quickly switched to the awkward *Journal of Post-Keynesian Economics*. The journal continues to publish, but is not rated as a 'top journal'.[2]

Through the 1970s Davidson was chair of the Rutgers University Economics Department. The department contained nearly 80 economists, of whom only five were clearly non-neoclassical. Davidson's friend, John Kenneth Galbraith, was a friend of the president of Rutgers. Galbraith urged the president to capitalize on the presence of a leading Keynesian and get some more Keynesians into the department. When the next vacancy occurred, in 1979, Davidson advertised for a Keynesian economist. The existing members were so dismayed that they appointed a delegation to protest to the president and provost. They suggested, in Davidson's words, that 'these types of non-mainstream economists would not be able to obtain lucrative government and foundation grants since the peer reviewers were much more mainstream'. They persuaded the president and provost to withdraw the Keynesian specification from the advertisement, and Davidson resigned the chairmanship. The irony is that the five non-neoclassical economists were publishing as much as the other 70+ economists combined (Paul Davidson, personal communication, 25 May 2005).[3] This is how the antibodies work to push non-neoclassical ideas to the margins.

11.1.2 How the US 'commentariate' sees 'nationalists' who stand in the way of worldwide free markets

Let us now consider how the American establishment has conceptualized the task of American foreign policy in the post–Cold War era. In this conceptualization, spreading free-market or neoliberal organizational arrangements and norms around the world, into every nook and cranny, is a central theme. In 1994 the US journal *Business Week* published an editorial (*Business Week*, 1994: 52), which asked, 'what should be the top foreign policy objective of the Clinton Administration, now that the Cold War is over?' It answered, 'the Cold-War strategy of containment must be replaced by the strategy of "enlargement" – unyielding promotion of an open global-market economy'. It went on to warn, 'to guarantee the spread of market economies overseas, the US must also contain the forces of reaction [reaction from those who "lose status and income" from the spread of market forces]'. The reaction of 'those dispossessed on the road to capitalism' often takes the form of nationalism or ultranationalism (and not class conflict, as Marx might have predicted). The United States must aim 'to preserve... nascent market economies and to contain the nationalists who threaten them', so as to 'further worldwide prosperity, spread democracy and ensure the peace', and so also extend the writ of the United States.

11.1.3 Mongolia

If we now ask how free-market ideas came to dominate the development agenda in developing countries, we can illustrate what happens at the coal-face end of the interaction between developing-country governments and the international financial institutions (IFIs). This interaction is one of the main channels through which neoliberal ideas and institutions are injected into developing countries. Creating the conditions in which assets can be bought or sold worldwide on the same terms, irrespective of the identity or nationality of the transactors, means removing the ability of a state to use policy instruments, such as trade protection, to put a wedge between the national economy and the international economy.

The story is about Mongolia. The government that took power in Mongolia after the end of communism in 1991 swung to the non-communist extreme and embarked on a programme of rapid economic liberalization, making it a star pupil of the Washington Consensus. The result was a collapse of the industrial sector, fast-rising urban unemployment, an influx into pastoralism, fall in pastoral yields, and a sharp deterioration in 'social indicators' (that had been relatively high in the era of protected industry, relative to Mongolia's per capita income).

However, the government did want to retain one 'industrial policy' instrument, namely an export tax on unprocessed wool. The Asian Development Bank offered the government a big loan, provided the government dropped the export tax. The government obliged, and now all Mongolia's wool is processed in China. Mongolia continues to struggle with high unemployment and a low-yield pastoral economy (Reinert, 2004). Mongolia's experience illustrates that the alternative to an 'inefficient' industrial sector (measured in world market prices) is often not an 'efficient' industrial sector, but none, which may be worse.

Fast forward to 2002, when a German Development Bank mission arrived in Ulan Bator to help with Mongolia's WTO accession. The mission discussed Mongolia's situation with the World Bank country director. It floated the idea of restoring an export tax on unprocessed wool. The World Bank country director objected strongly. As recalled by a participant, he said, 'That would be going backwards. We don't want the government to intervene in the economy. We want the government to stick to free trade.'[4] This flies in the face of the evidence of the non-growth effects of free trade.

11.1.4 Sri Lanka

The Sri Lankan government of 1989–93 had formulated and implemented a successful industrial policy aimed especially at promoting manufactured exports. The assassination of the prime minister in 1993 triggered the fall of the government, and the new government brought the pro-industrialization project to an end. The government at the start of the new century restarted work on an industrialization strategy, as an alternative to the World Bank-IMF-sponsored Poverty Reduction Strategy Paper (PRSP) that emphasized poverty alleviation, primary education, primary health care and the like.

The Bank and the International Monetary. Fund were unhappy; they wanted the government to abandon an industrialization strategy and stick strictly to the PRSP with its Washington-derived priorities (though presented as the result of Sri Lankan participation). They led a consortium of donors in holding out the carrot of a $2 billion grant for civil-war reconstruction after the peace deal of 2003. The Bank's country director informed the government – orally, not in writing – that it would have to stop work on its 'interventionist' industrial strategy as a condition of the grant.

The prime minister faced a choice: to continue with the industrial development push or win a sizeable grant. His ministers and coalition partners would have mutinied had he chosen the former, for the grant would provide kickbacks aplenty. The industry ministry reluctantly dismantled the cadre of experts who had been recruited to develop the industrialization strategy.[5] In the event the Bank/Fund/donor consortium did not even have to pay up since the government fell later that year on the issue of devolution of powers to the North and East.

11.1.5 Ethiopia

Before the Asian crisis broke, Ethiopia came under strong pressure from the Fund to open its capital account (to lift restrictions on money flows in or out and on foreign investment in the domestic economy), with the idea that Ethiopia would later also lift restrictions on the entry of foreign financial service firms to the domestic market. Yet Ethiopia, one of the poorest countries in the world, is of negligible interest to foreign speculators or investors; despite which, the Fund was determined to make the government open the financial system.

The Fund used the leverage of the Extended Structural Adjustment Program (ESAP), designed to give eligible poor countries cheaper access to Fund credits.[6] ESAP membership mattered not just because of cheap Fund credits, but also because lots of other cheap funds from other organizations rested on the Fund certifying a country as ESAP-eligible, including from the World Bank, the European Community and bilaterals. A country had to meet an array of conditions set by the Fund to be eligible, and was granted membership for a three-year period. But the Fund money was tranched. After an initial grant at the start of the programme, further tranches were conditional upon the country meeting a set of more specific time-bound benchmark conditions of the kind 'By date X you will have done Y.' The conditions related to the growth of money supply, the fiscal deficit, foreign exchange reserves, establishing a market in treasury bills, letting interest rates to be determined by supply and demand, and removing restrictions on flows of money in and out. Fund officials have much discretion in judging whether the government has met enough of the conditions to merit the next tranche, and therefore enough to merit all the other money cross-conditioned on ESAP.

The Board of the Fund approved an ESAP programme for Ethiopia in 1996. Then in 1997 the management of the Fund decided that the programme would stop; no more tranches would be given. Why?

A good part of the reason is that after the programme had been initiated in 1996 the Ethiopian government misbehaved in the eyes of the Fund, the US Treasury and a prominent American bank. Ethiopian Airlines, a state-owned enterprise, had earlier bought four Boeing aircraft with a loan from the American bank. The terms of the loan were onerous to the airline and lucrative to the American bank, because at the time Ethiopia had a very adverse risk rating. Not only was the interest rate high, the loan terms also contained the unusual provision that all four planes would be mortgaged to the American bank until the loan was paid in its entirety. By late 1996, Ethiopian Airlines wanted to renegotiate the loan. The American bank refused, so the government lent Ethiopian Airlines the money to pay off the loan in its entirety. The American bank was furious. It complained to the US Treasury that the Ethiopians had acted in bad faith.

Next, the US Executive Director at the Fund began to raise angry questions about Ethiopia's ESAP status. Negotiations were just beginning between the Fund and the government over the release of the 1997 tranche. The Fund officials negotiating with Ethiopia said the government had failed to meet some of the benchmarks, and the Fund toughened the requirements for financial liberalization and opening. For example, the government had to establish a treasury bill market (in a country whose whole financial system had assets equivalent to a small regional bank in the United States).

At this point the Ethiopian government said, 'Enough.' For all its need for the cheap financing, it was not prepared to open the capital account, which it considered too risky given that it would lose control of the interest rate and the exchange rate. Through a World Bank official it approached Joseph Stiglitz, the newly appointed chief economist and senior vice president at the World Bank, and persuaded him to visit Addis Ababa and advise it on how to negotiate with the Fund. Stiglitz arrived incognito in Addis Ababa in late 1997, and was deeply impressed by the development commitment and competence of the government. He devoted time to working through the government's negotiating strategy with the Fund. When the Fund found out that Stiglitz was in town it went apoplectic. The event became a milestone en route to Stiglitz's firing from the Bank in 2000 (Wade, 2002: 201–29).

By this time the Fund had succeeded in giving Ethiopia a bad name. Fund officials described Ethiopia as 'a reluctant reformer', a country 'off track'. In point of fact, Ethiopia had met the Fund's conditions to a degree that astonished Stiglitz and other World Bank officials, especially compared to the other African countries in ESAP programmes. But the Fund officials dealing with Ethiopia had by then decided that the country's ESAP status had to lapse until the government became more cooperative.

On his return from Addis Ababa, Stiglitz wrote a strong back-to-office report to World Bank President Wolfensohn, and repeated his points to several senior people in the Fund. In January 1998, Wolfensohn visited Ethiopia. Bank officials put the ESAP issue at the top of his briefing book, and he and the prime minister discussed it at length. Wolfensohn promised he would take it up. On his return he raised it with the Fund's Managing Director Camdessus at their regular breakfasts at least twice.

This pressure from the top of the World Bank to the top of the Fund worked. The Fund resumed negotiations for a new ESAP programme for Ethiopia. Meantime, the East Asian financial crisis was in full spate, and many analysts were saying that premature opening of the capital account by the East Asian countries was an important proximate cause of the crisis. The Fund was coming in for strong criticism for insisting that some of the crisis-affected countries open their capital account even further as a condition of Fund emergency financing. So in the new round of negotiations with the Ethiopians the Fund did not press the capital account issue. The Fund agreed to release the next tranche in April 1998, but even though the government met the Fund's conditions to a high degree relative to other African countries in the ESAP programme, the Fund refused to extend Ethiopia's ESAP status in 1999. It was not until 2001 that the Fund's Board agreed a new programme for what was by then called the Poverty Reduction and Growth Facility (PRGF).

It is not clear just how much the Fund was driven to insist on Ethiopia opening the capital account (before the Asian crisis) for the sake of the country's own development, for the sake of the world economy, in antipathy to a self-declared 'Marxist' regime, or because as agents of the American bank and the US Treasury the Fund was seeking a pretext to make life difficult for the government. World Bank officials involved in the events are in no doubt that while the US Treasury may have stiffened the Fund's resolve on account of the anger of the American bank, both the Treasury and the Fund really did want to make Ethiopia an example to show that all African countries were expected to open their capital accounts and could be cut off from concessional funding if they balked.[7]

11.2 Financialization

'Private property enclosure' means that 'enclosed' assets become commensurable against each other according to their relative market value, so one can compare the market value of 1000 hectares in the Amazon with the market value of a patent on a semi-conductor process in the United Kingdom. The implication is that finance becomes more and more the universal unit of account, the finance sector grows relative to the 'real' economy, and a rising share of national income goes to capital, a falling share to labour. This is the process of 'financialization of the economy' (FOE). Throughout the OECD world FOE rose sharply through the 1980s and 1990s (Wade, 2006).

We see it, for example, in the increase in total credit outstanding as a percentage of GDP in the United States, from 168 per cent in 1980 to 275 per cent in 1999. The figures for the 1990s are the highest in US history. We see it in the rapidly rising share of the financial sector in total credit, from 25 per cent of the total in 1989 to 55 per cent in 1999. This implies that the rapidly rising volume of financial transactions in the US economy is being supported by even more rapidly rising volumes of borrowings. Never before in US history have financial institutions borrowed more than they lend to non-financial customers. We also see it in the growing importance of institutional investors (pension funds, insurance companies, mutual funds, and trust funds) relative to banks and other depository institutions, as savers have switched from the latter to the former. Finally, we see the sharp increase in FOE in the way that consumer credit has become almost as readily available on demand as water from the tap, thanks to the growth in sub-prime credit, no-money-down mortgages, and home equity lines of credit. As a result, a much higher proportion of US consumption is supported by credit than ever before, making for an unprecedentedly high marginal propensity to consume of 111 per cent since the US expansion began in 1991. This is almost 20 percentage points above the 1946–90 average (Henwood, 2001). As of 2005, US household-debt service payments are at an all-time high of 14 per cent of disposable incomes, despite modest interest rates.

But FOE is more than the rising share of finance. It is the growing dominance of finance over the rest of the economy which has altered the system-ness of the economy, especially in the United States. Financial dominance over the rest of the economy is achieved through mechanisms of institutional interlock and normative congruence, each reinforcing the other.

11.2.1 Institutional interlock

Institutional interlock means that other economic institutions, such as corporations, households and pension firms, come to organize themselves around financial markets, with the stock market becoming the economy's pivotal institution (Dore, 2000). In the corporate sector institutional interlock with finance comes through the transformation of managers' financial incentives and their perceptions of their responsibilities. Their remuneration increasingly takes the form of stock options rather than salaries; and at senior levels they are recruited from the external labour market rather than promoted from within. Both things together promote the notion that maximization of shareholder value is their sole legitimate objective. They raise or lower budgets, buy or sell bits of companies, with the objective of raising the share price, not only because they gain directly from stock options but also because the higher share price reduces the chances of hostile takeover – and their ouster. The same forces affect who become CEOs: they come increasingly from a financial background rather than engineering or marketing. Furthermore, the substance of 'corporate strategy' is increasingly focused on buying and selling companies, going with the rising incidence of mergers and acquisitions.

In the United States, the average remuneration of the top 100 CEOs rose from 39 times the pay of the average worker in 1970 to over a 1000 times higher in 1999 (Krugman, 2002). Maybe they did add two or three times more value to their corporations, but 25 times more in

29 years seems very unlikely. In 2000, chief executive remuneration in the United States climbed 16 per cent, giving the average company head a total pay of $10.9 million, a new world record. Meanwhile, in the United Kingdom, the retailer Marks and Spencer recruited an executive chairman in 2000 who received nearly US$3 million in shares. The Marks and Spencer compensation committee then awarded him a US$1.2 million bonus at the end of the year. But in response to critical press comment and anger from shareholders and staff that the bonus came at a time when the company was doing badly, the chief executive waived his bonus. However, while announcing his waiver the management announced it would grant him US$500,000 in shares the next year and an equivalent cash sum if he met specific targets (Skapinker, 2001).

The other side of this transformation of top managerial incentives is the shredding of the old social contract between employers and workers. Work-life is characterized by more frequent job changes, more freelancing, more homeworking, more opportunity, and more uncertainty. The average 32-year-old American has already worked for nine different firms (*The Economist,* 2000). For those with scarce skills, opportunity dominates; for those without scarce skills, the new labour market allows companies and governments to play 'beggar-thy-labor' (Kapstein, 1999). In the United States, median wages for male workers are lower in real terms than they were in the 1970s. In 1979, the earnings of the average American college graduate were 38 per cent more than the earnings of the average high-school graduate; in 1999 the gap was almost double that, at 71 per cent. Lay-offs (job-cut announcements) in 1998–2000 were higher than at any time before 1989 despite nearly a decade of uninterrupted economic expansion. Polls show that Americans, particularly older males with long tenure, were more frightened than ever of losing their jobs even while the long boom continued. As the old social contract is shredded or fades, the shape of a new and defensible social contract is still unclear.

In the household sector institutional interlock has been achieved by financial markets becoming the pacesetters of consumption markets through the wealth effect, amplifying economic cycles. Those in the top 10 per cent or so of the US wealth distribution now typically have so many of their assets in the form of stocks that they are as concerned about the movements of financial markets as they are about house prices. In 1998, the top 10 per cent of the US wealth distribution held 63 per cent of US assets, and only 30 per cent of liabilities. On the other hand, the bottom two-thirds of the wealth distribution had few assets apart from their houses and pensions.

In the pensions sector the move away from 'pay-as-you-go' (PAYG) pensions (in which today's pensions are paid out of today's taxes on the incomes of those currently in work) towards 'defined contribution' pensions (in which the individual's pension depends on the performance of their pension fund's investments in the stock market) has given most citizens some stake in stock market performance. This, it may be presumed, tends to shift the centre of gravity of class interest away from the defence of labour incomes (on which taxes are paid) and towards the defence of capital incomes (from which individuals' pensions are increasingly paid). The shift in the financing of pensions, in other words, tends to consolidate a political common interest across the richest third or so of the electorate in favour of capital. Financialization of the economy has the fortunate consequence for the beneficiaries of capital income that finance becomes too important in the functioning of the economy and the polity to be allowed to fail. Various public policy ratchets are put in place to socialize private losses of financial institutions while doing little to curb their enclosing of private profits.

11.2.2 Normative congruence

Norms adjust, too. It is now taken for granted, more forcefully than before, that the criteria for judging economic performance should relate mainly to the returns to capital rather than to labour productivity. 'Efficiency' is normally used to mean efficiency in the use of capital. The quality of corporate management is judged by its success in capital markets, not by its success in labour markets or by the employees' dedication to the firm and the firm's ties to its employees. The share price is accepted as the best composite index of company performance.

The OECD report *Corporate Governance: Improving Competitiveness and Access to Capital in Global Markets*, known as the Millstein Report (April 1998), is a telling illustration of how deeply rooted these norms are (Dore, 2000: 89). It was written by a committee of people who are not all disciples of the American way. It adopted a studied neutrality between what it called the Anglo-Saxon model and the Rheinish model. Countries can and should have different social or employee-favouring objectives, it said; what matters is that the objectives and the ways of achieving them be 'transparent'. But be transparent with respect, implicitly, to potential investors, not to potential employees. The subtitle says it all: the problem of corporate governance is defined to be largely about access to capital.

Norms of public sector organization have shifted in a 'financialization' direction too. As private corporations have remodelled themselves in the pursuit of shareholder value, so the public sector has come to take private corporate models as models for how public sector organizations should be restructured. In this way the public sector is also reshaped around the stock market through the adoption of private corporate models that are themselves oriented to the stock market, even though public managers are not yet paid in line with the performance of the national stock market. 'New public management' (NPM) sought to shrink the public sector and introduce surrogate markets in that which remained. Much activity has been privatized, or if not privatized, then 'corporatized': put into autonomous public corporations. Within what remains of the public sector, much activity has been outsourced to private suppliers, who are less subject to public sector rules and public sector union power, and public sector employment has become more subject to market relations. Lifetime employment contracts have been replaced with task-based contracts in the name of 'flexibility', and recruitment takes place not mainly at the bottom but at all levels of the hierarchy, breaking the Weberian notion of a public service 'career'. At the top, the elected minister sets the policy, writes a performance contract for the head of department (the CEO), gives him a freer hand than before to secure the minister's objectives, and rewards him according to performance ('performance-related pay'). There is no need for the CEO or other public managers to have prior civil service experience. 'Management is management is management' is the mantra. Ministries of finance, applying market principles, have removed the core grants of public research institutes, which now have to compete for funds against each other by submitting specific research programmes to foundations, companies or government agencies.

11.2.3 Income distribution between capital and labour

Two sets of statistics illustrate the precipitate of financialization in OECD-type economies. First, the profits of financial corporations as a percentage of the profits of all American corporations rose from 20 per cent in 1970 to 42 per cent in 2002 (US National Accounts, Table 6.16). Second, for the OECD countries as a group, the share of labour remuneration in business revenue hovered around 70 per cent for decades after the Second World War, increased to around 72 per cent by 1980, and then, with Reagan and Thatcher setting the roll-back policy, fell steadily to about 64 per cent today. Conversely, the share of profits went up by eight percentage points between 1980 and 2003, a very satisfactory outcome for shareholders (Bennhold, 2005).

11.2.4 Financialization and dollarization in developing countries

In developing countries, financialization is occurring with a damaging twist. Over the 1990s they have experienced a strong trend towards 'dollarization', that is to holding wealth in foreign currencies, mainly the US dollar and the Euro. ('Dollarization' does not refer only to dollars.) For example, average foreign currency deposits to total deposits in South America (excluding Mexico) rose from 46 per cent to 56 per cent in just five years, from 1996 to 2001; in Africa, from 28 per cent to 33 per cent; and in the 'transitional' economies, from 37 per cent to 48 per cent (Nicolo *et al.*, 2003).

These figures reflect the declining competitiveness of national currencies in developing countries relative to the US dollar and the Euro. Why? Average inflation rates are still much higher in developing countries (six per cent) compared to developed countries (two per cent), even though they have fallen substantially. The risks of currency devaluation are significant. Hence private wealth holders try to move out of the national currency into one that will better hold value.[8]

The result of currency competition of this kind is a global hierarchy of currencies: those at the top fulfil both domestic and international functions; those in the middle fulfil domestic but not international functions; those at the bottom (the majority) fulfil neither domestic nor international functions.[9]

No central bank can ignore the non-acceptance of its currency, which means that the domestic currency is not fulfilling basic (domestic) functions. The costs of non-acceptance (or 'dollarization') include the limited effectiveness of monetary policy, and amplified impacts of currency changes. Central banks supervising uncompetitive currencies (most developing countries) therefore try to keep interest rates high in order to induce people to hold the domestic currency. High real interest rates (eight per cent or more) restrict dynamic economic growth. Few investment projects can earn a rate of return above the cost of borrowed money. This 'competition between currencies' helps to explain slow economic growth in most developing regions and widening world income inequality (Wade, 2008).

11.3 The move towards an anchorless economy

The upshot of private property enclosure and financialization is that the current global economic architecture is 'anchorless' as compared to the Bretton Woods architecture. Of course, if one assumes from the start that 'the market economy is a stable system', the absence of (non-market) anchors or stabilizers is not so important. If one assumes that the market economy is inherently unstable, the absence of anchors is damaging, and public policy should aim to reinsert some.

11.3.1 Erosion of the wage anchor

Throughout the OECD, governments have removed earlier-established non-market wage-determination mechanisms, and insisted that wage determination occur through the free market. They assume, wrongly, that labour market deregulation is the only route to labour market flexibility. One problem with the emphasis on deregulation is that, as Keynesian economists would emphasize, a market-driven mechanism for wage determination will not ensure that hourly wages increase in line with productivity and an inflation target. If wages rise by less, there is a danger that the price level, anchored mainly by nominal wages, will fall and the economy will slip into wage deflation. The German government should be especially concerned about this mechanism, because Germany, among several other major economies, has been close to deflation.

11.3.2 Erosion of financial asset anchors

The post–Bretton Woods adoption of floating exchange rates between the major currencies, combined with largely free capital mobility, made the world economy subject to the inherent volatility of financial asset markets – inherent in the sense that there is no anchor or 'gravitational centre' for stock prices or currency prices akin to the cost-of-production anchor for goods prices. Especially when the ratio of short-term 'speculators' to long-term 'investors' in stock markets and currency markets is high, prices of assets are propelled by flimsy expectations, giving rise to high volatility.

This volatility of financial asset prices spills out of financial markets into the 'real' economy through the balance sheets of firms, banks, households, and governments. Ironically, one of the main innovations designed to reduce volatility at the level of individual speculators and investors, the Over-the-Counter (OTC) derivative, has become a major source of systemic risk at the level of the world economy. It has this effect partly through the power of the OTC derivative to make just about all enclosed (propertied) assets commensurate with each other.

The mushrooming growth of derivatives markets has constituted one of the biggest institutional innovations in global finance since the early 1990s. The markets purport to be about spreading risk, but there are good reasons to think derivatives markets have become a major source of financial instability and crisis. As one global finance analyst remarked, 'I have long warned, only half jokingly, that derivatives could be the end of Western civilization as we know it' (Richard Duncan, personal communication).

The reason is that derivatives markets and contracts, or the large and very profitable OTC subset, are largely unregulated. One financial firm, JP Morgan Chase (JPMC), is estimated to be involved as the hedging counterparty in about one in four of derivative trades transacted globally. Typically JPMC designs and sells a contract, makes itself the counterparty to this contract, then makes another off-setting contract with another dealer; meanwhile this other dealer has JPMC as the off-setting counterparty for many of its own contracts. This is why JPMC is the biggest derivatives player in the world, by far. It might be thought that the extraordinarily high degree of concentration in the derivatives 'industry' would have a stabilizing effect, since JPMC would be in a position to have 'encompassing' knowledge about the whole market. In practice, this possibility is overwhelmed by the negative effects.

One of these negative effects is that JPMC itself is very vulnerable, because its exposure is massive and it is not able to hedge against itself because it constitutes such a large part of the total market – it faces a shortage of hedging counterparties. In other words, the high degree of concentration creates a potential liquidity problem. If market conditions suddenly change, JPMC may want to unwind some of its positions quickly, but cannot do so because there are too few parties willing to take the other side of the trades.

A second negative effect is that the dominance of one firm introduces a pro-cyclical, therefore destabilizing impetus to the market, because other firms tend to treat the dominant firm's trades as a signal to do the same trades, on the assumption that the dominant firm must have better information than themselves. So if it becomes known that JPMC is selling certain kinds of trades, others will also want to sell, making a self-fulfilling prophecy and causing more volatility than otherwise.

There are many other problems in the OTC derivatives market that suggest that this market could be the source of major financial instability worldwide.

The following story illustrates the reaction when the US regulatory body most directly responsible for regulating the more traditional derivatives, like commodity futures, floated the idea that it might have a regulatory role in OTC derivatives too, even if just by way of requiring more disclosure of the terms of the contracts. The regulatory body is the

Commodities Futures Trading Commission. During the second Clinton administration the head of the agency, Brooksley Born, proposed in a discussion paper that her agency might take a role in regulating the OTC market, just as it already regulated more traditional types of derivatives. The financial community got so angry that Federal Reserve Chairman Alan Greenspan, Treasury Secretary Robert Rubin, and Chair of the Securities and Exchange Commission Arthur Levitt came together to persuade President Clinton to approve her firing. She officially 'resigned' in 1999. It is not that these gentlemen wished the powers of regulation to be vested in some other agency, perhaps their own, but that they did not wish OTC derivatives to be regulated at all by any public body (Barboza, 1999). They and other critics of derivatives regulation invoked several arguments, including the trump card that 'it can't be done' (Wade, 2000).

11.4 Interaction between financial and real economy instabilities

In 1989, in a lecture on 'Recent developments in international finance', a famous Carnegie Mellon Professor of International Finance talked excitedly and at length about the new technologies of finance, the new instruments like derivatives, and how these were revolutionizing the whole sector. At the end he was asked from the audience, 'Could you give some idea of how these developments in finance might impact on the 'real' economy – on things like economic growth and income distribution?' He looked surprised, hesitated, and then said, 'That's a really good question! I asked my assistant [he gestured towards a woman in the front row] to bring a tape recorder so that we can record good questions like that and think about them later.' He unwittingly illustrated the danger of focusing on 'finance': one can easily lose touch with the interactions between finance and the 'real' economy.

In the end, the stability of the international financial system is a function of the stability of real economy exchanges between countries. We know from the work of cumulative causation theorists like Mydral, Kaldor, Hirschman, Krugman, Brett, and many economic geographers that spatial polarization into economically strong centres and economically weak peripheries is an endogenous feature of market systems. The tendencies towards 'uneven' development dominate the tendencies towards 'even' development in the presence of increasing returns to scale, scope, and agglomeration. As a corollary, real economy exchanges between countries tend towards persistent deficits in some countries and persistent surpluses in others.

A trading system in which some countries run persistent payments deficits and others, persistent surpluses will tend to have unstable financial relations, as in persistent pressures towards exchange rate changes. But, *pace* Milton Friedman, the changes are likely to be abrupt and to overshoot, because the price of currency in the shorter run does not have a strong anchor in the real economy, especially when the volume of finance crossing exchanges for purposes of speculation is high relative to the volume crossing for investment purposes.

If 'uneven' development (in the real economy sense) generates financial instability, so also monetary instability can have damaging effects on the real economy. The president of Sony once said that dealing with currency fluctuations 'is like changing the handicap in golf at every hole. Wouldn't you lose interest in playing golf eventually? If the money scale expands or shrinks every day in different currencies, how can we make up our minds to invest?' (cited in Wade, 2004b: 347).

Moreover, deficit economies face pressure to become more 'flexible' so that resources can flow more readily into activities whose expansion will help them out of deficit. But with changing currency values they may 'adjust' in response to signals that turn out to be short term, at great cost to people's lives and the environment. This is the downside of 'flexibility', a word that carries strongly positive connotations in neoliberal thinking. Yet think of the costs to the American economy of the dot.com boom and bust in the late 1990s and early 2000s, where flexible capital markets functioned like drunken air-traffic controllers.

The international financial system is currently in an extremely unstable state, with the United States running the second biggest current account deficit in relation to GDP ever recorded by a major economy: 5.7 per cent in 2004.[10] The US White House and Treasury is demanding that the Chinese revalue the renminbi by a large amount, blaming the Chinese for the United State's gigantic current account deficit. Framed in this way, it will be the fault of the Chinese if the dollar crashes: another instance of the US government externalizing responsibility for the problems it causes.

The even more remarkable thing is that the dollar overhang and its hazards have been the staple of media worries for the past 30 years and more. It would be chastening to trace media coverage of the US current account deficit over the past 30 years and note the repeated invocation of Herbert Stein's law, 'If something cannot go on forever, it will stop.' Guess the year of the following statement: '... the enormous and mounting US deficits abroad... flooded the world monetary system, doubling world reserves from the end of... to the end of... i.e. increasing them by as much in this short span of three years as in all previous centuries in recorded history'. It was Robert Triffin in 1978–79, referring to the period 1969–1972 (Triffin, 1978–79).

Weighing up the risks of major disruption is like putting ourselves in the position of the geologist who knows only too well that the 600-mile-long Cascade fault off the Northwest coast of North America is, by extrapolation from the geological record and from current stress measurements, due to break any year now; and that when it does it will make a 'megaquake' that will release many times more energy than the one off Sumatra that caused the Boxing Day 2004 tsunami. The geologist knows we are on a cliff perched precariously above the rocks and waves, but recognizes that prediction of timing is so imprecise that we cannot live like that: we have to live as though we are down on the beach on a gentle slope of sand (Galbraith, 1997).

11.5 What is to be done?

In crisis conditions things become possible that were not before, and remaking institutions after the crisis depends on the magnitude and causes of the crisis and on the ideas on the margins of good currency at the time. The Great Depression from 1929 caused an existential crisis of the US system that was overcome, thanks in part to New Deal policies; but the intellectual underpinnings of New Deal policies had been formulated in marginal progressive circles over the previous several decades. This is the justification for 'wasting breath' on public policy ideas that at the moment may look implausible.

11.5.1 Regulate derivatives

It has often been said that OTC derivatives are beyond the reach of regulation except by the counterparties themselves, and that they should regulate themselves. In fact, it should be quite feasible to regulate derivatives transactions, at least to the point of improving the information about contract characteristics in the hands of a regulatory body. The counterparties to derivatives contracts often find themselves in court arguing over the interpretation of the fine print of the Amendments to the standard contract. Why not have a law that only derivatives contracts that are registered, including all of the Amendments, can be enforced in a court of law? If a contract is broken by one of the parties, the other counterparties shall receive no legal protection if the entire contract has not been registered. This should be incentive enough to ensure registration of most contracts. Once registered, they or the organizations doing them can be subject to at least minimal forms of regulation.[11] There is no doubt, though, that introducing derivatives regulation now, when the market is so deep and finance so politically strong, would be difficult.

11.5.2 'Utilitize' the banks

In unstable times we need to think about not only regulating derivatives markets, but also semi-nationalizing the banks and treating them like (public or private) utilities. The government promises it will not let them go under, but also subjects them to restrictions and monitoring, as it does electricity utilities. This would make it easier to subject their derivatives trading to prudential rules that are conservative enough to protect the stability of the financial system. At the same time, the government should pass legislation to ensure that the bank regulators are not drawn mainly from finance.

Short of semi-nationalization, it is difficult for governments to ensure that bank regulators themselves are not captured by the spiral of 'good news to euphoria and back to good news', so that they too act pro-cyclically rather than counter-cyclically.

11.5.3 Permit capital controls

Foreign portfolio investment can certainly be useful for financing long-term investments in developing countries, and developing-country governments should encourage it. The trick is to get it without the pro-cyclical boom and bust characteristics that go with it, which can wreak havoc on recipient economies through sharp fluctuations in prices and exchange rates. Capital controls can help. They may take the form of quantitative restrictions or an increase in the cost of capital flows so as better to reflect risk.

Capital controls are a second-best option. It is better to rely on more 'market-friendly' solutions, like more transparency and tighter regulation and supervision. But we know from the financial instability that has plagued industrial countries that not even their level of competence in regulation and supervision wards off crises. Still less will more transparency and tighter regulation and supervision ward off crises in emerging markets (Akyuz, 2000).

The many analysts of emerging market crises who call for open capital accounts plus 'sound' regulatory institutions ignore the point that it is difficult to distinguish between 'sound' and 'susceptible' regulatory institutions in advance of a crisis. Consider the World Bank publication *Private Capital Flows to Developing Countries* published in April 1997, just a few months before the onset of the East Asian financial crisis in July 1997. It identified which developing countries had financial regulatory frameworks robust enough to be fully integrated into the world financial system. They were 'Korea, Malaysia, and Thailand, with Indonesia and the Philippines not far behind' and 'Chile and Mexico, with Brazil also ranking well' (World Bank, 1997: 59). Most of the countries it identified were badly affected by the crisis.

If we do not have good measures of the robustness of regulatory frameworks in advance of a crisis, we should err on the side of caution in opening the capital account. The World Bank and the Fund should help countries to improve the functioning of capital controls, rather than press for their removal. In particular, the recent establishment of the Continuous Linked Settlement (CLS) Bank provides a new means by which a national government or group of national governments could levy a currency transactions tax on their currency or currencies. The tax could be two-tier, with a very low base tax for revenue purposes and an additional variable tax on capital inflows and capital outflows when the government(s) decides the flows are excessive. Far from being 'distortionary' the tax could reduce the existing 'encephaliticization' of global financial markets that results from the taxing of other financial transactions and the untaxing of international currency transactions (Schmidt, 2001).[12] Furthermore, it has no need for global coordination; it could be implemented unilaterally or by a 'coalition of the willing'.

11.5.4 Create a public international closed-end mutual fund for developing countries

Capital surges in and out can be reduced by means of a public closed-end mutual fund for developing countries (D'Arista, 1999). The fund would tap funds of private institutional investors, and invest them in the shares and bonds of private enterprises and public agencies across a spectrum of developing countries. It would issue a limited number of shares to be bought and sold on the market. But as a closed-end fund the underlying assets (the shares and bonds in its invested enterprises and agencies) would not be bought and sold. The prices of the shares would fluctuate without triggering destabilizing sales or purchases of the underlying assets. This is a step towards replacing the present private-sector-dominated international financial system with a mixed public–private one. A country that chose to accept foreign portfolio investment only through this vehicle would be less vulnerable to capital surges and have less recourse to capital controls. The World Bank is a possible operating agency for such a fund.

11.5.5 Revise WTO agreements to permit preference for domestic over foreign firms

As noted, WTO agreements, including TRIMS and GATS, require equal (or better) treatment of foreign firms relative to domestic firms. As a blanket rule this is a mistake in terms of development. Companies rooted in their country of ownership are more likely to make the country's problems their own and deploy resources and influence to reduce them. They are more likely to invest in better infrastructure and other public goods, from roads to universities to national branding campaigns. The Indian software giant Infosys is more likely to press for a world-class airport in Bangalore, its headquarters, than IBM, which also has a big office in Bangalore (Khanna, 2006).

With the international agreements changed to permit differential treatment, the trick is to design public policy in such a way as to promote these 'domestic ownership' effects without conferring protection on unresponsive domestic firms. This is a step towards a larger industrial policy to accelerate industrial upgrading, which can help to support more robust financial systems.[13] For the past 25 years industrial policy has dared not speak its name; this has to change.

11.5.6 Establish an international clearing agency

Finally, we should be thinking of how to design an arrangement that breaks the link between a country's borrowing from abroad (which is often desirable for development) and the imperative of exporting in order to earn hard currency with which to service the debt (which has many negatives for development when the economy is 'adjusted' to maximize exports). With this link broken, developing countries could service their external debt from wealth generated through domestic economic activity in domestic currency. There would be no foreign exchange markets in the normal sense, and the private sector would be removed from international foreign exchange transactions.

Rather, central banks would undertake transactions among themselves through an international clearing agency (D'Arista, 2000: 44, 82; Wade, 2000). The clearing agency would clear payments between countries internally, between one account and another, without the payments having to go through an open foreign exchange market. The internal exchange rates would be adjusted periodically in response to changes in the levels of reserves held at the clearing agency. Countries running persistent surpluses would face an appreciation and countries running deficits would face a depreciation, the changes reflecting shifts in relative costs of production, not speculation on future movements. The European Payments Union of the 1950s might be taken as a prototype, with Keynes and Albert Hirschman as patron saints.[14]

The ratio of 'finance' to 'real economy' would have to fall hugely before such an idea became feasible, and that would require a world crisis. But the idea of a multilateral clearing agency replacing private foreign exchange markets does help to stretch the mind beyond the marginal changes to bond contracts and the like that are the limit of the current mainstream. It goes without saying that progress on any of the more international of these policy ideas is unlikely without some of the major developing countries mobilizing a coalition to press for them against the likely resistance of the major industrial states.

In the end we have to come back to the enormous costs inflicted on much of the world's population by the present arrangements. As the most respectable of bodies, the Bank for International Settlements, remarks:

> In many emerging markets, financial cycles have been particularly pronounced...typically being reinforced by large swings in the flow of international capital. The cost of these cycles has been high, with the direct cost of resolving bank crises often exceeding 10 per cent of gross domestic product and the indirect costs in terms of lost output higher still.
>
> (Wolf, 2001)

It cannot be beyond our wit to design something that consigns such severe cycles to history. Yet the challenge remains to weave the various policy proposals into one or more coherent alternatives to the neoliberal agenda. With only bits and pieces of alternatives, real-world policymaking is likely to continue to take the coherent neoliberal agenda as its centre of gravity.

Notes

1. Sales of bottled water run to about $22 billion per year, and consumption is increasing around the world: at 15 per cent a year in Asia and 10 per cent in North America. The industry caters to insecurity about the public supply. The danger is that the increasing popularity of bottled water could weaken pressure to improve the public supply (Olson, 2001).

2. This refers specifically to the Diamond (after Peter Diamond) ranking. It puts no non-mainstream journals in the top tier. In the United Kingdom the ranking of Economics Departments for the Research Assessment Exercise depends heavily on publications in the Diamond top-tier journals, and the ranking makes a big difference to the amount of public funding. In the United States, assistant professors who score a hit with an article in the top-ranked journals, like the *American Economic Review* and *Econometrica*, may even be advised not to list in their CV articles published in non–top-tier journals, on the grounds that the hit may be regarded as a fluke of a too-prolific author, rather than as a confirmation of top-flight talent.
3. Davidson relates another story: 'In 1979, I was encouraged by someone at the National Science Foundation to put in a grant proposal request for a project to generalize THE GENERAL THEORY for an open economy. The NSF sent copies of my proposal to a group of "outside" examiners and to the usual group of "inside" peers which evaluates all proposals. (The outside peer evaluators were supposedly chosen because they were experts in the specific field of the proposal.) These peer examiners are requested to grade various aspects of the proposal on a scale of one to ten, with ten being the highest. After the NSF makes a decision it sends the peer evaluations back to the proposal submitter. Each evaluation peer report is identified only as either from an outside or inside peer evaluator. I received top grades (nine or ten) from all the outside peers but only one, two, or three from the inside peers. Each peer had a place to write anything he wished besides providing numbered evaluations. One of the "inside" peers wrote: "Davidson may have had considerable success in his past record of publications, but he marches to a different drummer and hence he should get his own money and not try to get some of ours." ' (A copy of these evaluators' reports, along with other Davidson papers and correspondence over the years, has been deposited at the Duke University Library Archives of papers of economists.) (Davidson, personal communication, 15 May 2005).
4. From a participant who requested anonymity.
5. From a participant who requested anonymity.
6. The ESAP was later renamed the Poverty Reduction and Growth Facility (PRGF).
7. At a social gathering I chatted one-to-one to the IMF's Ethiopia country director in Addis Ababa in August 2004, and asked him about the grounds on which the Fund had pressed the government to open the capital account. He became indignant, denied that the Fund had ever so pressed the government, and demanded, 'Show me a document, show me a document.'
8. In many 'emerging markets' the business community and some academics promote official dollarization as a means of reaching a key medium-term objective, namely to tie the government's hands in monetary policy, limit the scope of national economic autonomy, and hard-wire a neoliberal policy stance.
9. An interesting question is, how is the current sharp fall in the US dollar against the Euro, and the pressure on East Asian surplus countries to revalue, affecting this hierarchy of currencies?

10. The worst current account deficit of any major economy was Italy's 7.7 per cent in 1924, the year before Mussolini seized power (that is, in January 1925).
11. Michael Pettis warns, 'I am not sure that either UK or NY law, under which most agreements are written, could tolerate a statement that a contract is only enforceable if it is registered. The enforceability of all contracts is a cornerstone of the law' (personal communication, 24 October 2001).
12. See also proposals from the NGO, Stamp Out Poverty.
13. This is only a small part of the changes needed in the world trade and investment regime. The proliferation of Bilateral Investment Treaties (BITs) should also be resisted, especially those (the majority) which use an ICSID (International Center for the Settlement of Investment Disputes) arbitration clause to remove treaty disputes from national jurisdiction. Most countries are sleepwalking into signing on to this clause. The arbitration panels are comprised of lawyers who, in other cases, represent large firms before other panels. In the tiny world of arbitration lawyers, conflicts of interest abound. The spread of this type of dispute settlement aligns international investment law with that of the United States, the United Kingdom, and the European Union, tipping the structure of power in favour of large firms and against developing-country governments; and it pre-empts the content of a future *multilateral* agreement on investment (Wade, 2003b: 621–44).
14. Keynes' proposals for the Bretton Woods conference of 1944 contained the idea of an international clearing agency. Hirschman helped to design and implement the European Payments Union (EPU) in 1949–52. The EPU was an extraordinarily successful institutional innovation; one of the main architects of the Marshall Plan described it, long after it had ceased to exist, as 'in some ways the supreme organizational achievement of the Marshall Plan' (Richard Bissell, quoted in Hirschman, 2001: 41). The US Treasury, the Federal Reserve, and the IMF, however, were 'highly critical', in Hirschman's phrase, of the EPU. The Europeans went ahead, despite this opposition, because Paul Hoffman among others managed to make the idea of the EPU the central symbol for 'European integration', momentum for which was already beginning to grow by 1949.

References

Akyuz, Y. 'The Debate on the International Financial Architecture: Reforming the Reformers'. UNCTAD Discussion Paper No. 148 (April 2000).

Baker, G. 'The Keynesian Genie is Recalled from the Bottle', *Financial Times*, 3 May 2001.

Barboza, D. 'Chief Regulator of Futures to Step Down', *New York Times*, 20 January 1999.

Bennhold, K. 'Richer Companies, Poorer Workers', *International Herald Tribune*, 10 April 2005.

Business Week, 'Containment, Nineties Style', *Business Week*, 17 January 1994: 52.

D'Arista, J. 'Building the Financial Infrastructure for Middle Class Emerging Economies', Paper for the Council on Foreign Relations Project on Development, Trade and International Finance (December 1999) http://www.cfr.org/content/publications/attachments/DArista_FinInfra_Paper.pdf.

D'Arista, J. 'Reforming International Financial Architecture', *Challenge*, 43 (3) (2000): 44–82; reprinted in M. Della Giusta, U. Kambhampati, and R. H. Wade (eds), *Critical Perspectives on Globalization* (Cheltenham: Edward Elgar, 2006).

Dore, R. *Stock Market Capitalism: Welfare Capitalism: Japan and Germany versus the Anglo-Saxons* (Oxford: Oxford University Press, 2000).

The Economist, 'The Future of Work', *The Economist*, 29 January 2000.

Galbraith, J. 'Can't We Grow Faster?', *The American Prospect* (1997).

Henwood, D. 'An Eye-Popping Propensity to Consume', Letters, *Financial Times*, 1 May 2001.

Hirschmann, A. *Crossing Boundaries* (New York: Zone Books, 2001).

Kapstein, E. *Sharing the Wealth: Workers and the World Economy* (New York: W. W. Norton, 1999).

Khanna, T. 'At Home, it's Not Just Profits that Matter', *International Herald Tribune*, 21 February 2006.

Krugman, P. 'For Richer', *New York Times*, 20 October 2002.

Lipschutz, R. 'From Place to Planet: Local Knowledge and Global Environmental Governance', *Global Governance*, 3 (1997): 83–102.

Nicolo, G. de, Honohan, P., and Ize, A. 'Dollarization of the Banking System: Good or Bad?', International Monetary Fund, Working Paper No. 03/146 (2003).

Olson, E. 'Environmental Group's Latest Message: Drink Tap Water', *International Herald Tribune*, 3 May 2001.

Reddy, S. G. and Minoiu, C. 'Real Income Stagnation of Countries, 1960–2001' (1 May 2006) http://ssrn.com/abstract = 799824.

Reinert, E. 'Globalisation in the Periphery as a Morgenthau Plan: The Underdevelopment of Mongolia in the 1990s', in E. Reinert (ed.), *Globalization, Economic Development and Inequality: An Alternative Perspective* (Cheltenham: Edward Elgar, 2004): 157–214.

Schmidt, R. 'Efficient Capital Controls', *Asian Exchange*, 17 (1) (2001): 88–103.

Skapinker, M. 'Rough Justice in the Talent Market', *Financial Times*, 4 May 2001.

Stein, H. 'Herb Stein's Unfamiliar Quotations: On Money, Madness and Making Mistakes' (16 May 1997) http://www.slate.com/id/2561/.

Triffin, R. 'The International Role and Fate of the Dollar', *Foreign Affairs* (Winter 1978–79):

Wade, R. H. 'Out of the Box: Rethinking the Governance of International Financial Markets', *Journal of Human Development*, 1 (1) (2000): 145–58.

Wade, R. H. 'Capital and Revenge: Ethiopia and the IMF', *Challenge* (September/October 2001): 67–75.

Wade, R. H. 'US Hegemony and the World Bank: The Fight over People and Ideas', *Review of International Political Economy*, 9 (2) (2002): 201–29.

Wade, R. H. 'The Invisible Hand of the American Empire', *Ethics and International Affairs*, 17 (2) (November 2003a): 77–88.

Wade, R. H. 'What Strategies are Viable for Developing Countries Today? The WTO and the Shrinking of "Development Space" ', *Review of International Political Economy*, 10 (4) (2003b): 621–44.

Wade, R. H. 'Is Globalization Reducing Poverty and Inequality?', *World Development*, 32 (4) (2004a): 567–89.

Wade, R. H. *Governing the Market* (Princeton: Princeton University Press, 2004b).
Wade, R. H. 'Choking the South', *New Left Review* 38 (March/April 2006): 115–27.
Wade, R. H. ' Globalization, Growth, Poverty, Inequality, Resentment and Imperialism', in J. Ravenhill (ed.), *Global Political Economy*, second edition (Oxford University Press, 2008).
Wolf, M. 'The Age of Instability', *Financial Times*, 12 June 2001.
World Bank, 'Private Capital Flows to Developing Countries', *World Bank Policy Research Report* (April 1997).

12
The Democratic Peace and Substitutability During International Crises: Institutionalized Democracy and Foreign Policy Choices

Karl DeRouen Jr and Shaun Goldfinch

12.1 Introduction

Most and Starr (1984, 1987) argue that states are not constrained to one foreign policy option when dealing with any particular problems, and that particular policy instruments can be used in a number of different contexts and in response to different internal and external stimuli. Similar causes can lead to the use of different instruments; different stimuli can lead to the use of similar instruments. As such, studies that examine single causes and single effects are likely to produce weak and inconclusive results and provide a limited understanding of the complexities of international politics. Despite encouraging a growing body of literature focused on policy substitutability, empirical evidence for policy substitution remains mixed at best.

In this chapter we build on both the substitutability literature and the literature on the democratic peace. We provide a greater understanding of why some policy solutions may be substituted rather than others. In particular, contrary to realist or rational choice models of policy substitution, we theorize that humans select from a limited range of policy instruments, constrained and limited by the institutions within which that human being is socially constructed. In particular, the institutions of democracy socially construct leaders and actors within democracies to favour the use of non-violent means of dispute resolution during international crises, and to be reluctant to escalate from negotiation to non-violent coercion, and from this to violent measures of dispute resolution. We derive a number of hypotheses from this model, and drawing on Brecher and Wilkenfeld's (2000) International Crisis Behavior (ICB) data set of international crisis actors from 1918 to 1994, we test and find strong support for our hypotheses. We show that substitution occurs, and give a better theoretical understanding of why this substitution occurs. We show how the democratic peace relies on substitution processes and show the temporal dynamics of this process. When democracies find themselves in international crises, in a few cases they may initially react violently but over time there is a sorting-out process, and democracies substitute towards conciliatory conflict management techniques. In many cases, democracies are reluctant to substitute away from negotiation in international crises.

12.2 Substitution in foreign policy

As Most and Starr (1984, 1987) note, policy instruments can have several potential causes, and each particular policy decision or instrument can lead to different outcomes. Different policy decisions and processes may lead to similar outcomes. The substitutability literature has encouraged a growing body of international relations research that posits that individuals, leaders and states substitute different foreign policy instruments depending on the particular conditions, domestic and otherwise, that they face at any given time (Bennet and Nordstrom, 2000; Clark, 2001; Enterline and Gleditsch, 2000; McGinnis, 2000; Morgan and Palmer, 2000, 2003). Issues examined have included diversion (Gelpi, 1997; Bennett and Nordstrom, 2000), humanitarian emergencies (McGinnis, 2000) and US interventions (Regan, 2000) among others. In particular, numerous studies have focused on substitution between alliances and defence spending with results somewhat inconclusive, sometimes finding, contrary to expectations, a positive relationship between arms spending and alliances (Gates and Terasawa, 1992; Palmer and Souchet, 1994; Palmer and Bhandari, 2000). Despite initial promise, however, substitutability studies have 'produced exceedingly weak results' (Morgan and Palmer, 2003: 180). To some extent, as we argue below, this is because of the weak theoretical underpinnings of the literature.

Studies have generally focused on realist interpretations of foreign policy whereby a unitary state aims to maximize its security, or alternatively rational choice models where individuals, leaders and/or a unitary state attempt to maximize utility, variously defined as vote maximization for leaders or maximization of various types of goods/benefits for a unitary state (see Morgan and Palmer, 2000, 2003: 180; Regan, 2000; see also Bennett and Nordstrom, 2000). Policy leaders and states are generally seen to have the relevant information (although not, in all cases, perfect information). Foreign policy is goal-directed with clear aims in mind, and there is the ability to substitute one policy for another to achieve their ends (Morgan and Palmer, 2003). As Regan (2000: 94) notes:

> analysis of substitutability must work from the premise that policy substitution involves choices made by decision makers and that specific choices are re-evaluated across time. Decision makers evaluate the costs, benefits, and expectations about outcomes over a range of options. A decision rule that can guide our understanding of the choice is that of utility maximisation.

Despite its claims to better model the complexities of foreign policy-making, the substitutability literature has a number of flaws. Policy substitution models often use 'rational' models of foreign policy decision-making (see Regan, 2000). However, the assumption that policy-makers are able to marshal the relevant information in any manageable way and compare the myriad alternative policies, and costs and benefits of these policy decisions, has long been questioned for its accordance with the not unlimited capabilities of human beings (Lindblom, 1959). Indeed, truly rational policy decision-making is largely impossible due to the informational overload in examining myriad policy instruments, solutions and the prediction of outcomes this involves. To some extent, proponents of rational choice in substitutability studies are hoisted by their own petard: if an individual leader or the super-individual-like unitary state is a rational optimizer, with access to more-or-less perfect information, and assuming there is not one policy instrument that can be chosen in any given situation, then myriad policy instruments and solutions could be chosen, with myriad (and uncertain) policy outcomes. The informational overload involved in examining and comparing these myriad policy instruments, solutions and predicted outcomes would mean that to make any policy choices at all, individuals would have to limit themselves to a few standard choices or be paralysed into inaction. This would only be compounded by the fact that foreign policy decision-making is often carried out under conditions of urgency and crisis. That is, to actually make policy choices, policy-makers would have to act, at best, as if they were bounded rational individuals, or in some cases, as a-rational or non-rational individuals, making choices through habit, ideology, tradition and so on (*cf.* March and Olsen, 1996).

Partly in response to limitation in 'rational' models of policy decision-making, the concept of 'bounded rationality' (Simon, 1986) is often invoked, where policy-makers actively seek policy solutions, but the search is biased by particular cognitive shortcuts such as looking at what is close, choosing the first option that adequately meets goals, and limiting the number of changes when implementing models borrowed from elsewhere. As Mossberger (2000: 160) notes, both rational models show:

> a logical sequence of steps, beginning with problem definition, proceeding to the definition of goals, then to a search of alternatives, the evaluation of alternatives, and the selection of an alternative. Both... depict goal-driven processes, with problem-focused search.

To characterize policy decision-making as rational even in the limited sense of bounded rationality, however, or as directed at problem-solving or identifiable aims may act to mask actual policy-making processes and provide a post-hoc order where it may not have existed (Cohen, March and Olsen, 1972; 't Hart, 1994). Rather than the compartmentalization of policy where policy is a technical task (the 'means') carried out by experts – and 'politics' (the 'values') is something that concerns politicians – policy is inherently political, value-ridden and ideologically driven (Lindblom, 1959; Goldfinch, 2000). Indeed, policy may be about political advantage and jostling for power, with appeals to aims, 'solutions' and 'problems',–if there are any at all,–simply another technique in this game (Goldfinch, 2006). It may be an activity that is simply self-perpetuating, habitual, non-rational or make-work, with no clear aim, problems or solution in mind. On the other hand, 'sociological interpretations of the process of change emphasise a group's norms rather than individual rationality' (Levi-Faur and Vigoda-Gardot, 2004: 6), and much sociological policy decision-making literature focuses on the apparent spread of norms rather than an assumption of problem-solving-directed policy (Knill and Lenschow, 2005: 121). Nor does the assumption of a unitary state, treated as a super-individual, accord with many studies of policy that find the state highly divided amongst itself, with different parts of the state having different and competing policy aims, policy processes and beliefs (Goldfinch, 2000).

On the other hand, if there is an acceptance that there are myriad policy causes and policy instruments, the policy substitutability literature cannot then go ahead and act as if there are only a few, or in some cases two, policy options, without a very good reason to do so. Indeed, much of the literature says one thing and does another. An edifying example is given by Bennett and Nordstrom (2000: 38), who note, 'leaders confronted with bad economic times choose from a number of policy options in trying to reach the desired goals'. However, despite the recognition of different policy options, Bennett and Nordstrom limit themselves to just 'one of two possible actions: a leader may distract the public from its economic woes via an aggressive foreign policy manoeuvre (externalisation) or a leader may seek to devote more resources directly to the domestic economy'. There are of course a large number of other policy options that could have been examined, as the substitutability literature and other studies of diversion suggest (DeRouen and Goldfinch, 2005b). Morgan and Palmer's (2003) model of a two good theory of foreign policy of *maintenance* and *change* is of such generality that it provides little guidance as to which policy option might be chosen. And as Morgan and Palmer (2000) earlier pointed out, simple either/or models of policies substitution where resources devoted to one policy instrument imply less resources devoted to another may miss complementary relationships between different policy options where an increase in one is related to an increase in another (the example they give is the link between alliances and increased defence spending), and whether there may be multiple aims for foreign policy.

The problem of under-identification of policy substitution options still remains (Palmer and Bhandari, 2000). If there are numerous policy options and instruments, numerous reasons for the adoption of these options and numerous possible policy outcomes, to specify policy substitution studies adequately remains a Herculean task. To not do so renders empirical results inconclusive. At present, policy substitutability literature tells us little other than that some policies can be substituted for other policies, and may be, depending on the situation, with outcomes uncertain, although in some cases policies are complementary. This is not a surprising finding, unless one believes the foreign policy universe is a mono-causal and determinant one and that similar conditions must determine similar results, actions and behaviour. Instead, in a complex and uncertain world, causes are many and over-determined; policy aims, beliefs, values, instruments, decisions, strategies and tactics are many, varied and contingent and sometimes contradictory, as are the reasons given (if there are any) for their adoption; and outcomes are uncertain and often unpredictable. The more interesting question for us is if and how the choice of options is constrained and limited, and if some pattern in these choices can be discovered across states.

If, on the other hand, leaders are not the rational optimizing individuals of rational choice but instead choose policy responses from a limited range of options, then the policy substitutability literature has greater heuristic value. This is the argument of this chapter. Drawing on new institutional literature, we argue for largely socially constructed individuals rather than the rational optimizer found in many substitutability studies or a simple realist model of foreign policy. Such individuals choose policy solutions and make policy decisions from a toolbox that is itself constrained and provided by the institutions within a particular society. The behaviour and beliefs of policy actors and the responses and expectations of the wider political community to their policy rhetoric and actions are highly contingent, socially constructed and constrained by the institutions of that culture and society (Goodin, 1996; March and Olsen, 1996). In the face of limited cognitive and material resources, limited time and sometimes ideological inclination (conditions that abound in international crises), policy-makers engage in cognitive shortcuts: they often choose policy instruments, patterns, slogans and ideas that have common currency or that are ready at hand (Lindblom, 1959). This is not simply a restatement of bounded rationality, however. There are certain things that usually can and cannot be done without great difficulty and certain 'logics of appropriateness' (March and Olsen, 1996). In many cases, there are certain things that are not usually discussed as part of a policy agenda (Kingdon, 1984) and possibly certain things that may not even be thought (Lukes, 1974; Foucault, 1980). As summarized by Lodge (2003: 174), '...instead of following a "rational evaluation" of all policy options, the institutional allocation and distribution biases the selection of [certain] policy options rather than others by making them appear more legitimate and appropriate'. As such, there is some predictability of policy options as there is a narrowing of the choices available. In particular, we argue that the institutions of democracy socially construct individuals, and constrain and limit foreign policy actions to a reasonably narrow range of options, or at least a strong preference for a range of options. This range of options in international crises is a preference for non-violent methods of dispute resolution. We link our argument with a large body of research examining the so-called 'democratic peace'.

12.3 Escalation and policy substitution

A novel contribution of this study of policy substitution is that we are actually tapping into the dynamics of substitution. The first policy choice we look at is cooperative statecraft. The use of negotiated settlement or mediation by joint democracies described, *inter alia*, by Dixon (1993, 1994) has direct relevance to the democratic peace theory. We use the negotiation outcome to describe a basket of cooperative behaviours including negotiation, mediation, arbitration and adjudication.

The next form of statecraft on our continuum is non-violent coercion. We expand on the negotiation/military escalation policy options described by Huth and Allee (2002) to include the use of non-violent coercive statecraft. Coercive statecraft describes those actions between negotiation and violence. It can include sanctions, withholding aid, and threats of violence. For example, military and economic aid can be used as a reward or inducement by donor countries. Krause (1991: 314) asserts that the United States has used military aid as a vital form of foreign policy statecraft since the Second World War. The use of incentives, such as tied aid, in conflict prevention has increased (Cortright and Carnegie Commission on Preventing Deadly Conflict, 1997). Providing a loan or granting aid vital to saving an economy or a population only if certain conditions are met is, to all intents and purposes, a coercive action. Explicitly coercive measures such as sanctions can include trade embargoes or arms bans. These include bans on travel for leaders, their families and associates, the freezing of leaders' or elites' funds in foreign bank accounts, and expulsion from such international organizations as the Commonwealth (George, 1999).

The final form of statecraft is the use of violence. This form of crisis management involves combat, casualties, military operations and in some cases war (Hewitt and Wilkenfeld, 1996: 129). The realist perspective portrays the use of violence as an extreme though acceptable form of statecraft. The diversionary force literature also suggests that the force option is more likely during social unrest (Levy, 1989).

12.4 Democracy and dispute resolution[1]

There are typically two explanations for the widely noted, although not universally accepted, democratic peace. First, democracies provide institutional constraints on governmental action (Huth and Allee, 2002). It is assumed that the consent of citizens is required for democracies to go to war. Drawing on Kant, it is also assumed that citizens will resist war because it is they who will bear the burden of casualties, paying for the military, suffering economic disruption and rebuilding after war (Russett and Oneal, 2001). Democracies have competitive elections, separation of powers, upper houses, 'loyal oppositions', constitutional limits on government power, public expression of preferences, and competing and overlapping interest groups, amongst other things. These provide constraints on government and, reflecting the will of citizens to some extent, limit the ability of governments to engage in military adventurism. Governments can be removed if they do not fulfil voters' preference for peace, and democratic leaders (assuming they want to be re-elected) thus avoid wars, particularly those they might lose. Democratic institutions also limit the speed and increase the transparency of the policy-making process so that issues of mobilization of troops or allocation of resources to military spending can be monitored by those inside and outside the state, and are therefore better responded to and constrained (Enterline and Sobek, 2001), although there are examples of democracies engaging in subterfuge and misinformation regarding their military intentions (Rosato, 2003). Non-violent measures of dispute resolution can be better appraised as such in the face of this transparency. Such openness also decreases the likelihood of policy moves being misinterpreted as potentially violent, and responded to, possibly pre-emptively, with seemingly appropriate levels of force. Opponents will also be aware that democratic constraints will also make it less likely that the state in question will engage in violent activity, and are thus less likely to fear attack, again reducing the likelihood of pre-emptive strikes.

Second, it is argued that democracies embrace a series of norms and behaviours that facilitate the peaceful resolution of conflicts and disputes. According to Rummel (1995: 4), democracies encourage an environment where social conflicts that may become violent are resolved by 'voting, negotiation, compromise and mediation'. Political leaders are accustomed to using these non-violent measures to achieve their aims. Indeed, democratic politics often rewards those better able to manage and convince constituencies, political opponents and colleagues without resorting to aggressive or belligerent behaviour (Dixon, 1994). At the same time it socializes leaders to use these methods (Rousseau *et al.*, 1996). Political leaders unable to use these non-violent methods to resolve disputes may be seen as lacking the requisite statecraft and therefore suffer in elections (Geva *et al.*, 1993). Leaders of democracies facing other democracies in a dispute will be aware that other democratic leaders share the same conception of 'bounded competition' or 'rules-of the-game' that privileges non-violent methods of dispute resolution and thus respond in kind (Dixon, 1994).

However, a strong distinction between institutional (or structural) constraints, and norms and behaviours (or cultural constraints) is difficult to maintain. Instead, behaviours and norms are constrained and to some extent formed within and by formal and informal institutions and institutional structures. Existing cultural norms and beliefs might foster the development of certain formal institutions. This is the argument of 'new institutionalism' (*cf.* March and Olsen, 1996). For Goodin (1996: 19–20), 'individual agents and groups pursue their respective problems in a context that is collectively constrained'. These constraints include institutions, which are 'organised patterns of socially constructed norms and roles and socially prescribed behaviours expected of occupants of those roles which are created and recreated over time'. These constraints have historical roots as 'residuals of past actions and choices' and 'also shape the desire, preferences and motives' of agents. They 'embody, impart and preserve' different power relations and resources. However, individuals and groups are not the near-automatons of structuralist approaches. Individual and group activity, socially constrained as it may be, 'is the engine that drives social life'. Distinguished here are the concepts of organization and institution. As Brennan and Castles (2002: 5) note, 'an institution is to be viewed as some amalgam of norms, practices, structures and organizations, an organization like a university or a large corporation can only be understood "institutionally" when all the norms and habits and structures governing the actual relationship of players within the organization are filled in'.

In sum, democratic institutions constrain, channel, influence and to some extent form preferences, values and behaviour. While there may be a formal element to democratic institutions – either organizational structures, laws or written rules – these become 'institutionalized' when the accompanying norms and behaviours become embedded and routinized. We argue that different sorts of people arise in democracies. Rather than the asocial, ahistorical, rationally optimizing agent of more extreme rational actor models, or the simple realist assumptions made regarding state behaviour, individuals and leaders in democracies are influenced, constrained and to some extent socially constructed within and by institutions to behave and think in certain ways. These norms and behaviours are to a considerable extent internalized, and even to some extent become automatic. In democracies these norms and behaviours include a preference towards non-violent means of conflict resolution, and particularly towards the accommodation and negotiation of settlements. As Dixon (1994: 16) argues, democracies foster 'the internalization of norms for regulating and reconciling different interests and values in public affairs in ways that are neither violent nor coercive'. Moreover, democratic leaders facing other democratic leaders in a crisis are aware that these institutionalized constraints against the use of violence are shared. In his study of conflict during 1945–79, Dixon (1994: 29) finds that the 'democratic states embroiled in disputes will be more likely than others to achieve peaceful settlements'. As Dixon concludes elsewhere, 'the more democratic a state the more likely its political leadership will maintain conciliatory norms of dispute resolution, and leaders with conciliatory norms are more likely than others to adopt or at least accede to conflict management efforts' (1993: 46).

This discussion leads to our first hypothesis based on joint democracy:

Hypothesis 1: Democracies are less likely to substitute/escalate from negotiation to coercion and violence if the opponent is a democracy, but are likely to de-escalate from initial violent crisis management techniques to non-violent ones.

12.5 Monadic democracy

While it seems clear that democracies are less inclined to use violence against other democracies, it is argued that they do not engage in war any less often than non-democracies (Dixon, 1993; Rousseau *et al.*, 1996). A non-democracy might see the constraints on democratic states' war-making ability as giving an opportunity to force concessions or capitulations, although Huth and Allee (2002) found little evidence to support this. On the other hand, democracies are likely to respond vigorously if attacked, as history shows. If losing a war or facing capitulation is seen to have greater electoral costs than fighting a war, there may be incentives for democracies to engage in pre-emptive strikes (Bueno de Mesquita and Lalman, 1992), although there are few cases of pre-emptive strikes starting wars (Reiter, 1995). Due to the greater transparency of support (or dissent) within populations or within political and governmental actors for military action, and the greater availability of information on the intent and ability of democratic governments to engage in war, opponents are better able to gauge whether threats of military force are credible or whether such threats will be undermined and constrained by possible lack of electoral and/or political support (Fearon, 1994; Schultz, 2001; Huth and Allee, 2002). Correspondingly, democratic governments are less able to 'bluff' by threatening violence in international disputes and crises, but threats of force are given reluctantly and can be taken more seriously, and so can be effective deterrents.

On the other hand, as Schultz (2001) argues, once democratic governments commit to engaging in violence to settle an international crisis, particularly in the face of widespread electoral and political support for such a stance, there are considerable incentives not to back down. This is due to the possibility of being seen as indecisive and weak and the consequent diplomatic, status, electoral and other costs that may be faced (*cf.* Fearon, 1994; Schultz, 2001). Consequently, as Fearon (1994: 586) theorizes, 'democratic leaders have a structural incentive to pursue more escalatory, committing strategies when they face authoritarians than when they face fellow democrats, and this can generate a greater overall chance of war'. However, as Huth and Allee (2002: 281) found in military disputes between democracies and non-democracies, non-democracies were more likely to initiate and escalate military threats and 'military conflict generally resulted from the more aggressive policies [and norms] of non-democratic leaders'.

Bueno de Mesquita *et al.* (1999) theorize that due to the demands of electoral politics that will more immediately punish leaders for their losses, democracies are more likely to shift extra resources to fighting wars and will therefore be more successful in their execution. Assuming that non-democratic leaders are more-or-less rational actors and will suffer to some extent by losing a war, if this widely held (Bueno de Mesquita *et al.* 1999; Reiter and Stam, 2003;) but disputed (Desch, 2002) belief that democracies are better at winning wars is correct, this should dissuade attacks by non-democracies upon democracies, *ceteris paribus*. On the other hand, as Bueno de Mesquita *et al.* (1999) theorize, due to the electoral costs to democratic leaders for lost wars, democracies are less likely to initiate wars they do not expect to win, and will be aware that fighting other democracies provides a greater possibility of this occurring. At the same time, however, the possibility of defeat for democracies is not as great in the case of non-democratic opponents, *ceteris paribus*, and so there are lower disincentives in initiating wars against non-democracies. As Bueno de Mesquita *et al.* (1999) argue, the democratic peace is explained by a combination of these incentives and disincentives, and democracies are not by nature any less war-like.

In a different vein, Dixon (1994: 17–18) argues that the proposition that shared norms between democracies leads to less war between democracies does not imply that democracies are any less war-like. Instead, his democratic norms model only holds when both parties to a dispute share norms of peaceful settlement and 'bounded competition', that is the rules of the game. To this extent, his normative model contains realist assumptions regarding non-democracies whose behaviour is thought to be primarily determined by standard realist notions of anarchy and power-seeking (see also Maoz and Russett, 1993).

There may, however, be some reasons why democracies are less likely to go to war, whatever the regime of the opponent. If the institutional model provides justification for the dyadic democratic peace (that is, between two democracies), we suggest it will hold to some extent for monadic (that is, single) democracies. That is, the norms and constraints that encourage non-violent behaviour between democracies are also likely to encourage democracies and democratic leaders to seek to engage in non-violent crisis management with non-democracies. These non-violent values are seen as internalized by democratic actors. That is, rather than statecraft being a purely instrumental (or realist) selection of appropriate means in a crisis, democratic actors chose from the norms and toolbox of solutions they are socialized or institutionalized within: they have a preference for using non-violent means of dispute resolution if at all possible, even if the opponent does not share this preference and does not hold to 'the rules of the game'. We argue that such internalized preferences for non-violence may not always be entirely overridden by the exigencies of immediate electoral politics, even if there is some current electoral support for belligerence (*cf.* Schultz, 2001). Relatedly, we suggest that political actors are not simply or entirely focused on office seeking, although this will likely be a major factor in their behaviour (*cf.* Bueno de Mesquita *et al.*, 1999). Indeed, such rational choice approaches, while parsimonious, are reductionist and evidentially challenged, and we argue that our assumption of complex, somewhat conflicted, and socially constructed humans is more compelling (*cf.* March and Olsen, 1996). In any event, electoral politics in democracies will sometimes (or most often) support non-violent dispute resolution for reasons already outlined.

This preference for non-violence amongst democratic actors is not, however, a naive Panglossian view of statecraft. It will take into account opponents and their values and behaviour. Such preferences for non-violence will be subject to corrosion in the face of failure; that is, institutions, values and constraints are not immutable and may develop and change over time, particularly in the processes of policy and international disputes and electoral battles. Given the possible lack of trust in and transparency of policy processes of non-democracies, and the awareness that non-democratic states may not share norms and behaviours facilitating non-violent resolution, democracies and democratic leaders may be more circumspect in using non-violent measures when dealing with non-democracies. Moreover, if the opponent is not a democracy, this lack of shared norms of compromise means negotiation is probably less likely to be successful, and democracies will more likely use or escalate to non-violent coercive measures, and indeed violent measures, to resolve disputes. However, we argue that these new institutional constraints are such that democracies and democratic leaders will still be reluctant to resort to violence, whether or not the opponent is a democracy. This leads us to our second hypothesis:

Hypothesis 2: If a democracy faces a non-democracy, it is more likely to escalate/substitute coercion and violence than if the opponent is a democracy.

12.6 Research design[2]

12.6.1 Method and data

Brecher and Wilkenfeld's (2000) ICB data provide a wealth of information on international crises, from civil war to interstate war. In contrast, many studies focus only on interstate war or civil war, thus limiting their generalizability. Unless otherwise stated, the data below are derived from Brecher and Wilkenfeld (2000). The ICB dataset defines an international crisis as having two hallmarks:

(1) a change in type and/or an increase in intensity of *disruptive*, that is hostile verbal or physical, *interactions* between two or more states, with a heightened probability of *military hostilities*; that, in turn,
(2) destabilizes their relationship and *challenges* the *structure* of an international system.

Some of the crises escalate to violence but most do not. Most crises are less than 100 days and the longest is 1359 days. Our observations are the state actors in these crises (1918–94).[3] This data set is not explicitly dyadic in nature. In order to capture the dyadic component needed to create some of the independent variables below we turned to the ICB 'source of threat variable'. This variable identifies the state that poses the greatest threat to the values of the actor during a crisis.[4] This state is usually, but not always, the same as the triggering entity (Brecher and Wilkenfeld, 2000: 49). Hereafter we refer to the state that poses the greatest threat to the actor as the opponent.

We operationalize substitution by noting state behaviour in the immediate aftermath of the crisis (just after the trigger) and then noting the overall state response. Some states substitute policy and others do not. We expect that when democracies substitute, it will be towards the cooperative policy. We examine a number of substitution options. We look first at the initial crisis management technique, and then the primary crisis management technique to examine whether substitution occurs. This provides nine substitution possibilities; that is, no substitution from the initial crisis management technique, or escalation (such as escalation from negotiation to non-violent coercion or to violence) or de-escalation (where the initial management technique may be violence, or coercion), but substitution to negotiation or similar occurs. Figure 12.1 shows the nine crisis management technique substitution possibilities.

We employ multinomial logit to test the hypotheses. This is the appropriate method when there are multiple nominal outcomes that are not rank-ordered (see DeRouen and Sobek, 2004; DeRouen *et al.*, 2005). The three non-substitution outcomes are coded as 0, and this is used as the base category. The cooperation-to-coercion outcome is coded as 2,

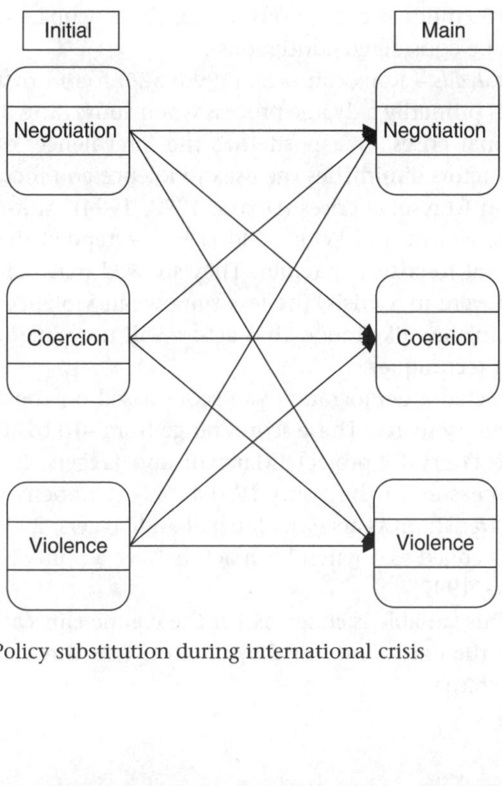

Figure 12.1 Policy substitution during international crisis

cooperation-to-violence is coded as 3, coercion-to-cooperation is coded as 4, coercion-to-violence is coded as 6, and violence-to-cooperation and violence-to-coercion are coded as 7 (outcomes 7 and 8 are combined because there are so few cases). Multinomial logit coefficients are interpreted by comparing them to the base category. Thus a positive coefficient increases the probability of the corresponding form of substitution. Since some crises have multiple actors, we estimate the model with robust standard errors adjusted for crisis.

12.6.2 Independent variables

Contiguity – Bremer (1982) showed that contiguous states are more likely to fight than non-contiguous ones. Brecher and Wilkenfeld (2000) find that contiguous dyads are more likely to use violence in resolving crises than are 'near neighbours' or dyads separated by distance. Following this line of reasoning, a shared border might increase the likelihood of the violence option. On the other hand, neighbours might share norms that more readily lend themselves to negotiated outcomes (Dixon, 1994).

We created our own contiguity variable by looking at each actor – opponent dyad and coding as 1 instances where the two are contiguous, and 0 otherwise. In cases involving separation by water, we coded states closer than 100 miles as contiguous (for example, Cuba and the United States would be considered contiguous).

Democratic dyads – Rousseau *et al.* (1996: 526) found that 'the democratic peace is primarily a dyadic process when addressing the escalation of international crises'. We posit that the 'prevalence' of democracy among crisis actors diminishes the use of violence and increases the use of negotiation to resolve crises (Dixon, 1993, 1994). More relevant for our purposes, Hewitt and Wilkenfeld (1996) extended the democratic peace argument to crisis behaviour. They showed that the more democracies there were in a crisis, the less the overall violence in the crisis and the diminished likelihood that actors will use violence as a crisis management technique.

We constructed a democratic dyad score based on the actor and its opponent's polity scores. These scores range from –10 to 10. These data are from the Polity IV project (Marshall and Jaggers, 2004). We use the polity2 measure in the Polity IV data as it compensates for interregnum and transition years (see Marshall and Jaggers, 2004 codebook). DYADDEM is coded as 1 when both actors have a polity2 score of 6 or above (Senese, 1997).

Gravity – This variable is coded as 1 if the regime elites are threatened as a result of the crisis, and 0 if they are not. This threat can be either internal or external.

Monadic democracy – There is some evidence that regime type impacts the propensity for actors to use force. Rummel (1997) and Benoit (1996), for instance, have shown that democracies are more pacific *in general*. Gelpi (1997) has shown that democracies are more likely to use diversionary force while Oneal and Tir (2006) find to the contrary. We create two measures of monadic democracy. The first is simply the polity score of the actor from the Polity IV data. The second is a dummy variable coded as 1 if the actor is a democracy and the opponent is an autocracy. These data are from Marshall and Jaggers (2004).

Social unrest – When social unrest is high, we might expect leaders to attempt to divert attention and respond more forcefully to a crisis trigger (Brecher and Wilkenfeld, 2000: 176). In other words, if an actor has domestic problems, it may be more willing to use violence and less likely to seek peaceful resolution of crises (see Bennett and Nordstrom, 2000). We use the ICB variable 'Social Unrest' to create this variable. Social unrest captures assassinations, general strikes, terrorism, demonstrations and riots. It is coded as 1 when there is evidence of unrest *prior* to the crisis, and 0 otherwise.

Capability differences – Standard realist assessments of conflict incorporate measures of the power ratio of the adversaries. Decision-makers are not expected to initiate violence against much more capable adversaries (Bueno de Mesquita, 1981). Brecher and Wilkenfeld (2000: 177) suggest that crisis behaviour based on power balance essentially follows general conflict behaviour. Russett and Oneal (2001) find that dyadic preponderance decreases the likelihood of militarized interstate disputes because strong states do not need force to achieve goals. Thus capability advantage should decrease chances of violence. However Dixon (1994) notes that stronger states should be less likely to agree to negotiated settlements. On balance, we expect states that command a greater share of capabilities than their adversary to opt for violence or coercion rather than negotiation. We create a variable that taps the ratio of actor-to-opponent capabilities.[5] The capability data are from the Correlates of War project and are based on population, urban population, military personnel, military spending, iron and steel product, and ion (Singer and Small, 1999).[6]

Rivalry – Gochman and Maoz (1984) found that rivalries account for a lion's share of the violence that occurs between nations. Diehl and Goertz (2000: 216) write that interstate rivalries obtain when two states experience at least six militarized interstate disputes (MIDs) over a 20-year period. These rivalries can be waged over territory, status or a number of other issues (Goertz and Diehl, 1993). Classic rivalries include Pakistan/India, North Korea/South Korea and USA/USSR. The behaviour of states in an enduring interstate rivalry is different from the behaviour of any random pairs of states by their continued intensity and bellicosity and reliance on coercive measures of some kind (Diehl and Goertz, 2000). Our expectation is that to the extent rivalries substitute, they will be more likely to substitute towards more coercive policies. These data are from Diehl and Goertz (2000).

Duration – We measure the amount of time between the perception of the trigger to the crisis and the termination of the actor's involvement. The expectation is that longer crisis involvement will increase the probability of some form of substitution. This is measured in days and we use the logged form because of outliers in the data. These data are from Brecher and Wilkenfeld (2000).

12.7 Findings

Our multinomial results are contained in Table 12.1. We find that if two democracies are in a crisis there is an extremely low probability of substitution from negotiation to violence. If two democracies are involved in a crisis, there is an increased chance (relative to odds of no substitution) of substitution from coercion to negotiation. This is the core finding of our analysis. That is, even if a democracy initially uses coercion or violence in response to a crisis trigger, it will tend to use negotiation as its primary management technique. The norms and values promoting negotiation in democracy are such that over time they will prevail over even initially violent situations. Similarly, non-violent coercion will tend to shift to negotiation as the main management technique, although there are only a few cases of this in our data. These findings support hypothesis 1. Further, where there is joint autocracy, there is less of a chance of substitution from coercion to negotiation. If two actors in a crisis are rivals, then substitution becomes much more likely and there is a much greater chance of moving from negotiation to coercion. This is not a surprising finding but it adds further to the literature on enduring rivalries. Duration also impacts on crisis management techniques. In longer crises, there is less chance of substitution from coercion to negotiation. When the regime is threatened, states are more likely to substitute from negotiation to coercion and from coercion to violence. These are important findings, as gravity of the crisis impacts on the policy instrument used; that is, policy substitution is highly context-specific. If a state has power preponderance over its opponent in a crisis then it is *less* likely to substitute from negotiation to violence. This suggests negotiation and

Table 12.1 Multinomial logit: Substitution and the democratic peace

variables	Outcomes				
	neg->coercion	**neg->violence**	**coercion->neg**	**coercion ->viol**	**viol->neg/coercion**
joint democracy	−0.130	−31.242	**1.532**	−0.194	**2.404**
	0.631	0.361	0.562	1.076	1.175
joint autocracy	−0.267	0.353	*−1.003*	−0.330	−0.192
	0.305	0.339	0.563	0.444	1.005
rivals	**0.614**	−0.180	0.234	−0.898	−0.313
	0.281	0.356	0.386	0.553	1.038
log duration	−0.102	0.167	**−0.346**	0.204	0.192
	0.094	0.124	0.127	0.163	0.335
contiguity	−0.061	0.333	−0.451	−0.072	0.162
	0.296	0.342	0.456	0.431	0.842
social unrest	0.266	−0.042	0.497	0.431	0.557
	0.275	0.354	0.413	0.461	0.828
gravity	**0.744**	0.598	−1.173	**1.027**	1.624
	0.332	0.361	0.782	0.456	0.875
relative capability	0.082	**−1.134**	−0.948	0.150	0.327
	0.434	0.526	0.622	0.666	1.343
constant	−1.893	−3.028	−0.786	−3.744	−6.329
	0.475	0.581	0.621	0.821	1.500
obs.	669				
Wald chi2	23373.16				
Prob>chi2	0.0000				

Note: Base category is no substitution; main entries are coefficients; robust standard errors are below coefficients; two-tailed significance tests: underlined coefficients are significant at .001, those in bold are significant at .05 level, and those in italics at .10.

arms build-up may be complementary policy options rather than policy substitutions.

Table 12.2 runs a number of simulations testing marginal effects using *CLARIFY*, which is a useful way to present multinomial results in a more meaningful way. This program allows researchers to take raw findings and calculate quantities of interest such as first differences or predicted values using Monte Carlo simulation (see Tomz *et al.*, 2001).[7] Baseline values are set at mean. At the baseline probabilities, no substitution is the main outcome. Our model predicts that for 80 per cent of cases there will be no substitution. Negotiation to coercion is the second most likely outcome. Where there is joint democracy the probability of substitution from coercion to cooperation goes up to 13 per cent. The probability of substitution from violence to coercion also increases. In joint autocracy cases, policy substitution is less likely. Where there are enduring rivalries, the probability of substitution from negotiation to coercion increases markedly. This may explain why a 'warm peace' is seldom achieved (for example, India/Pakistan). In terms of duration, substitution is more likely in short crises. We suspect, however, there is a selection effect operating. When a regime is threatened, the chance of substitution increases and substitution to violence and coercion becomes more likely. To summarize a number of possible policy substitution scenarios: in a short crisis where there is joint democracy, the probability of substitution from coercion to negotiation increases to 36 per cent. If the crisis is long, the probability of substitution from violence to negotiation increases. If rivals are contiguous, there is a greater likelihood of some substitution from negotiation to coercion, and this is also the case when the regime is threatened.

In the interest of space, we present only simulation results to show the impact of monadic democracy. In the baseline model with all variables set to mean, there is only a four per cent chance of substituting from coercion to conciliation. When we set the democracy acting towards autocracy variable to 1 we find that the probability of this type of substitution goes to six per cent. When we measure monadic democracy using the polity score of the actor and we set this value to its ninetieth percentile, the probability of substitution from coercion to conciliation rises even more to eight per cent. There appears to be a modest monadic democracy effect in the context of foreign policy substitution, thus we find evidence to support hypothesis 2. Democracies will often react to crises by adopting a policy of coercion. The impact of both joint and monadic democracy is to make a shift towards conciliation more likely than no shift at all. These results can be seen in Table 12.3.

Table 12.2 Selected probabilities and marginal effects after CLARIFY

	Outcomes					
	no substitution	**neg->coercion**	**neg->violence**	**coercion->neg**	**coercion ->viol**	**viol->neg/coercion**
Baseline (all at mean)	0.80	0.11	0.02	0.03	0.04	0.01
Joint democracy						
Set to no	0.76	0.10	0.07	0.03	0.04	0.01
Set to yes	0.66	0.10	0.00	0.13	0.04	0.07
Joint autocracy						
Set to no	0.77	0.12	0.01	0.05	0.04	0.01
Set to yes	0.82	0.10	0.02	0.02	0.03	0.01
Rivals						
Set to no	0.80	0.09	0.02	0.03	0.05	0.01
Set to yes	0.76	0.15	0.01	0.04	0.02	0.01
Log duration						
Set to min	0.69	0.15	0.01	0.12	0.02	0.01
Set to max	0.79	0.08	0.03	0.01	0.08	0.02
Contiguity						
Set to no	0.78	0.11	0.01	0.04	0.04	0.01
Set to yes	0.80	0.11	0.02	0.03	0.04	0.01
Social unrest						
Set to no	0.81	0.10	0.02	0.03	0.03	0.01
Set to yes	0.75	0.13	0.02	0.05	0.05	0.01
Gravity (threat to regime)						
Set to no	0.81	0.10	0.01	0.04	0.03	0.01
Set to yes	0.68	0.17	0.02	0.01	0.08	0.02

Table 12.2 (Continued)

	Outcomes					
	no substitution	**neg->coercion**	**neg->violence**	**coercion->neg**	**coercion ->viol**	**viol->neg/coercion**
Relative capability						
Set to min	0.78	0.11	0.03	0.05	0.04	0.01
Set to max	0.80	0.11	0.01	0.02	0.04	0.01
Scenarios:						
1) joint democracy – short crisis	0.47	0.10	0.00	0.36	0.02	0.04
2) joint democracy – long crisis	0.65	0.07	0.00	0.05	0.08	0.15
3) contiguous rivals	0.77	0.15	0.02	0.03	0.02	0.01
4) threat to regime	0.69	0.17	0.02	0.01	0.08	0.02

Note: Probabilities are based on the multinomial equation in Table 12.1; scenarios are as follows: 1) joint democracy set to 1 and log duration set to .1; 2) joint democracy set to 1 and log duration to 7; 3) rivals and contiguity set to 1; 4) gravity (threat to regime survival) set to 1; variables not manipulated are set to mean.

Table 12.3 Selected probabilities and marginal effects after CLARIFY

	Outcomes					
	no substitution	**neg->coercion**	**neg->violence**	**coercion->neg**	**coercion ->viol**	**viol->neg/coercion**
1) Baseline	0.76	0.10	0.06	0.04	0.04	0.01
2) Democracy-> autocracy = 1	0.77	0.08	0.04	0.06	0.04	0.01
3) Monadic democracy 90th ptl	0.72	0.09	0.05	0.08	0.04	0.02

Note: All variables are as in Table 12.2 with the following exceptions: in 1) and 2) democracy towards autocracy is the only polity variable, 3) monadic democracy score is the only polity variable.

12.8 Conclusion

This analysis of crisis management techniques adds to the literature on both substitutability in foreign policy and the democratic peace. We provide a better theoretical underpinning for the substitutability literature by rejecting 'rational' models of foreign policy decision-making. Instead, we theorize that foreign policy substitution takes place within a limited range of policy options, conditioned by the particular institutions of a country. We link this argument to the wider literature on the democratic peace by arguing that the institutions of democracy socially construct individuals to prefer non-violent means of dispute resolution in international crises. We show that both monadic and joint democracy enhance the likelihood that an actor will pursue a negotiated settlement to a crisis, and even in the few cases where initial crisis management techniques are violent, will tend to use negotiation as the main crisis management technique over time.

Our finding that democracies prefer to negotiate provides some support to Huth and Allee's (2002: 15) findings that democracies do not 'aggressively escalate to high levels against non-democracies', although Huth and Allee use different datasets, methods and timeframes and focus on territorial disputes. Our findings go beyond simply stating that democracies do not fight or escalate disputes. Rather than simply a realist view of statecraft or an instrumentally rational view of the motivations of democratic and other leaders, drawing on the new institutional literature, we hypothesize that the institutions of democracy socially construct individuals who prefer to use non-violent means of dispute resolution and substitute from a narrow range of policy options with a preference for non-violent crisis management – that humans are different in democracy. This institutional view accords with our finding that democracy has a positive impact on the probability of negotiation even if the adversary is not a democracy. This is counter to Dixon (1994), who argues that much of the democratic peace is explained by a shared conception of 'bounded competition' between democracies and as such does not apply to disputes between democracies and non-democracies (see also Huth and Allee, 2002).

Notes

An earlier version of the chapter was presented at the IED Symposium, Dunedin, New Zealand. We appreciate the assistance of Chris Sprecher, Michael Brecher, Joseph Wilkenfeld and Joe Hewitt in assembling the data. We also appreciate the advice of Todd Allee. Financial support for this research came from DeRouen's research grant from the University of Canterbury (R-6493).

1. This sections draws on DeRouen and Goldfinch (2005b).
2. This section draws on DeRouen and Goldfinch (2005a).
3. We deleted 178 intra-war crises. Brecher and Wilkenfeld (2000: 145; see also Gelpi, 1997; Rousseau *et al.*, 1996) argue that intra-war crises should be excluded as they 'have already escalated to violence and war and hence their inclusion would confound the results'. We also deleted two crisis actors (Hijaz and Najd from crisis number 29, Hijaz–Najd War) because of missing data. We deleted 11 cases where there were no data available for duration. We also deleted China as an actor in the China Civil War because its principal adversary was listed as China. From this we lose 70 cases due to missing data on our social unrest measure. We used the EUgene software program to locate some of the data (see Bennett and Stam, 2000).
4. There were two missing cases of the ICB 'source of greatest threat' variable. The first was Germany's greatest threat in the German reparations crisis of 1921. We therefore consulted Rousseau *et al.*'s (1996) dyadic data where the opponent was shown to be France. The second missing opponent came in the Iraqi no-fly zone crisis of 1992. As the Rousseau *et al.* data end in 1988, we could not use this source. Based on widely reported information, we coded Iraq's main adversary in the crisis to be the United States.
5. The ICB data have a variable based on 'power discrepancy' between the actors in each crisis, but there were too many missing observations for this to be useful.
6. The data are available at www.umich.edu/~cowproj/capabilities.html.
7. Specifically, the CLARIFY program 'uses stochastic simulation techniques to convert the raw output of statistical procedures into results that are of direct interest to researchers' (Tomz, Wittenberg and King, 2001: 1). After estimating an equation, CLARIFY saves 1000 (default) simulated parameters based on the model's variables. These simulations are drawn from the asymptotic sampling distribution of the variables (Tomz, Wittenberg and King, 2001: 5-6). Variables can then be manipulated and quantities of interest generated. In this case we use CLARIFY to generate the probability of each outcome. Dichotomous variables are changed from 0 to 1.

References

Bennett, D. S. and Nordstrom, T. 'Foreign Policy Substitutability and Internal Economic Problems in Enduring Rivalries', *Journal of Conflict Resolution*, 44 (2000): 33–61.

Bennett, D. S. and Stam, A. 'EUGene: A Conceptual Manual', *International Interactions*, 26 (2000): 179–204; http://eugenesoftware.org.

Benoit, K. 'Democracies Really Are More Pacific (in General): Reexamining Regime Type and War Involvement', *Journal of Conflict Resolution*, 40 (1996): 636–57.

Brecher, M. and Wilkenfeld, J. *A Study of Crisis* (Ann Arbor: University of Michigan Press, 2000).

Bremer, S. 'The Contagiousness of Coercion: The Spread of Serious International Disputes, 1900–1976', *International Interactions*, 9 (1982): 29–55.

Brennan, G. and Castles, F. 'Introduction', in G. Brennan and F. Castles (eds), *Australia Reshaped. 200 Years of Institutional Transformation* (Cambridge: Cambridge University Press, 2002): 1–24.
Bueno de Mesquita, B. *The War Trap* (New Haven, CT: Yale University Press, 1981).
Bueno de Mesquita, B. and Lalman, D. *War and Reason: Domestic and International Imperatives* (New Haven: Yale University Press, 1992).
Bueno de Mesquita, B., Morrow, J., Siverson, R. and Smith, A. 'An Institutional Explanation of the Democratic Peace', *The American Political Science Review*, 93 (1999): 791–807.
Clark, D. H. 'Trading Butter for Guns – Domestic Imperatives for Foreign Policy Substitution', *Journal of Conflict Resolution*, 45 (2001): 636–60.
Cohen, M. D., March, J. G. and Olsen, J. 'A Garbage Can Theory of Organizational Choice', *Administrative Science Quarterly*, 17 (1972): 1–25.
Cortright, D. and Carnegie Commission on Preventing Deadly Conflict. 'The Price of Peace: Incentives and International Conflict Prevention', *Carnegie Commission on Preventing Deadly Conflict* series (Lanham, MD: Rowman & Littlefield Publishers, 1997).
DeRouen, K. and Goldfinch, S. 'Putting the Numbers to Work: International Crisis Escalation and Duration and the Implications for Conflict Prevention', *Journal of Peace Research*, 42 (2005a): 27–45.
DeRouen, K. and Goldfinch, S. 'Democracies Prefer to Negotiate: Diversion, Institutionalized Democracy and Statecraft during International Crises', in B. Russett and A. Mintz (eds), *New Directions in International Relations Research* (Lanham, Maryland: Lexington, 2005b): 158–78.
DeRouen, K., Peake, J. and Ward, K. 'Presidential Mandates and the Dynamics of Senate Advice and Consent, 1885–1996' *American Politics Research*, 33 (2005): 106–31.
Desch, M. C. 'Democracy and Victory – Why Regime Type Hardly Matters', *International Security*, 27 (2002): 5–47.
Diehl, P. and Goertz, G. *War and Peace in International Rivalry* (Ann Arbor: University of Michigan Press, 2000).
Dixon, W. J. 'Democracy and the Management of International Conflict', *Journal of Conflict Resolution*, 37 (1993): 42–68.
Dixon, W. J. 'Democracy and the Peaceful Settlement of International Conflict', *American Political Science Review*, 88 (1994): 14–32.
Enterline, A. J. and Gleditsch, K. S. 'Threats, Opportunity, and Force: Repression and Diversion of Domestic Pressure, 1948–1982', *International Interactions*, 26 (2000): 21–53.
Enterline, A. J. and Sobek, D. 'Fruits of Force? Domestic and Interstate Responses to Domestic Threats and the Fate of Political Leaders', unpublished manuscript (2001).
Fearon, J. 'Domestic Political Audiences and the Escalation of International Disputes', *American Political Science Review*, 88 (1994): 577–92.
Foucault, M. *Power/Knowledge: Selected Interviews and Other Writings, 1972–1977* (first American edition) (New York: Pantheon Books 1980).
Gates, W. and Terasawa, K. 'Commitment, Threat Perceptions, and Expenditures in a Defense Alliance', *International Studies Quarterly*, 36 (1992): 101–18.
Gelpi, C. 'Democratic Diversions: Governmental Structure and the Externalization of Domestic Conflict', *Journal of Conflict Resolution*, 41 (1997): 255–82.

George, A. 'Strategies for Preventative Diplomacy and Conflict Resolution: Scholarship for Policy Making', *Cooperation and Conflict*, 34 (1999): 9–19.

Geva, N., DeRouen, K. and Mintz, A. 'The Political Incentive Explanation of "Democratic Peace": Evidence from Experimental Research', *International Interactions*, 18 (1993): 215–29.

Gochman, C. and Maoz, Z. 'Militarized Interstate Disputes, 1816–1976. Procedures, Patterns, and Insights', *Journal of Conflict Resolution*, 18 (1984): 586–615.

Goldfinch, S. *Remaking New Zealand and Australian Economic Policy. Ideas, Institutions, and Policy Communities* (Washington, D.C.: Georgetown University Press, 2000).

Goldfinch S. 'Rituals of Reform, Policy Transfer and Changing the Mechanisms of Control in the National University Corporation Reforms of Japan', *Governance*, 19 (2006): 585–604.

Goertz, G. and Diehl, P. F. 'Enduring Rivalries Theoretical Constructs and Empirical Patterns', *International Studies Quarterly*, 37 (1993): 147–71.

Goodin, B. *The Theory of Institutional Design* (Cambridge: Cambridge University Press, 1996).

Hewitt, J. and Wilkenfeld, M. 'Democracies in International Crisis', *International Interactions*, 22 (1996): 123–42.

Huth, P. K. and Allee, T. L. 'Domestic Political Accountability and the Escalation and Settlement of International Disputes', *Journal of Conflict Resolution*, 46 (2002): 754–90.

Kingdon, J. *Agendas, Alternatives and Public Policies* (Boston: Little, Brown and Company, 1984).

Knill, C. and Lenschow, A. 'Compliance, Communication and Competition: Patterns of EU Environmental Policy Making and their Impact of Policy Convergence', *European Environment*, 15 (2005): 114–28.

Krause, K. 'Military Statecraft: Power and Influence in Soviet and American Arms Transfer Relationships', *International Studies Quarterly*, 35 (1991): 313–36.

Levi-Faur, D. and Vigoda-Gardot, E. 'The International Transfer and Diffusion of Policy and Management Innovations: Some Characteristics of a New Order in the Making', in D. Levi-Faur and E. Vigoda-Gardot (eds), *International Public Policy and Management* (New York: Marcel Dekker, 2004): 1–24.

Levy, J. 'The Diversionary Theory of War: A Critique', in M. Midlarsky (ed.), *The Handbook of War* (Boston: Unwin Hyman, 1989): 259–88.

Lindblom, C. 'The Science of "Muddling Through" ', *Public Administration Review*, 19 (1959): 79–88.

Lodge, M. 'Institutional Choice and Policy Transfer: Reforming British and German Railway Regulation', *Governance*, 16 (2003): 159–78.

Lukes, S. *Power: A Radical View* (London and Basingstoke: Palgrave Macmillan, 1974).

Maoz, Z. and Russett, B. 'Normative and Structural Causes of Democratic Peace: 1946–1986', *American Political Science Review*, 87 (1993): 624–38.

March, J. G. and Olsen, J. P. 'Institutional Perspectives on Political Institutions', *Governance*, 9 (1996): 247–64.

Marshall, M. and Jaggers, K. *Polity IV Project*, codebook and data files (2004) www.bsos.umd.edu/cidcm/inscr/polity.

McGinnis, M. D. 'Policy Substitutability in Complex Humanitarian Emergencies – A Model of Individual Choice and International Response', *Journal of Conflict Resolution*, 44 (2000): 62–89.

Morgan, T. C. and Palmer, G. 'A Model of Foreign Policy Substitutability – Selecting the Right Tools for the Job(s)', *Journal of Conflict Resolution*, 44 (2000): 11–32.
Morgan, T. C. and Palmer, G. 'To Protect and to Serve – Alliances and Foreign Policy Portfolios', *Journal of Conflict Resolution*, 47 (2003): 180–203.
Mossberger, K. *The Politics of Ideas and the Spread of Enterprise Zones* (Washington D.C.: Georgetown University Press, 2000).
Most, B. A. and Starr, H. 'International-Relations Theory, Foreign-Policy Substitutability, and Nice Laws', *World Politics*, 36 (1984): 383–406.
Most, B. A. and Starr, H. *Inquiry, Logic, and International Politics*. (Columbia: University of South Carolina Press, 1987).
Oneal, J and Tir, J. 'Do Diversionary Uses of Force Threaten the Democratic Peace?', *International Studies Quarterly*, 50 (4) (2006): 755–99.
Palmer, G. and Souchet, A. 'Security, Autonomy and Defense Burdens – The Effects of Alliance Membership in the 19th and 20th Centuries', *Defence and Peace Economics*, 5 (1994): 189–204.
Palmer, G. and Bhandari, A. 'The Investigation of Substitutability in Foreign Policy', *Journal of Conflict Resolution*, 44 (2000): 3–10.
Regan, P. M. 'Substituting Policies During US Interventions in Internal Conflicts – A Little of This, a Little of That', *Journal of Conflict Resolution*, 44 (2000): 90–106.
Reiter, D. 'Exploding the Power Keg Myth: Preemptive Wars Almost Never Happen', *International Security*, 20 (1995): 5–34.
Reiter, D. and Stam, A. 'Understanding Victory: Why Political Institutions Matter', *International Security*, 28 (2003): 168–79.
Rosato, S. 'The Flawed Logic of the Democratic Peace', *American Political Science Review*, 97 (2003): 585–602.
Rousseau, D., Gelpi, C., Reiter, D. and Huth, P. 'Assessing the Dyadic Nature of the Democratic Peace', *American Political Science Review*', 90 (1996): 512–33.
Rummel, R. J. 'Democracy, Power, Genocide, and Mass Murder', *Journal of Conflict Resolution*, 39 (1995): 3–26.
Rummel, R. J. *Power Kills: Democracy as a Method of Non-violence* (New Brunswick, N.J.: Transaction, 1997).
Russett, B. and Oneal, J. *Triangulating Peace* (New York: W. W. Norton, 2001).
Schultz, K. *Democracy and Coercive Diplomacy* (Cambridge: Cambridge University Press, 2001).
Senese, P. 'Between Disputes and War: The Effect of Joint Democracy on Interstate Conflict Escalation', *Journal of Politics*, 59 (1997): 1–27.
Singer, D. and Small, M. *National Material Capabilities Codebook*. Correlates of War Project, University of Michigan (1999) http://www.umich.edu/~cowproj/capabilities.html.
't Hart, P. *Groupthink in Government: A Study of Small Groups and Policy Failure* (Baltimore: John Hopkins University Press, 1994).
Tomz, M., Wittenberg, J. and King, G. 'CLARIFY: Software for Interpreting and Presenting Statistical Results', Version 2.0. (Cambridge, MA: Harvard University, 2001).
Tomz, M., Wittenberg, J. and King, G. *CLARIFY: Software for Interpreting and Presenting Statistical Results*, Version 2.1 Stanford University, University of Wisconsin, and Harvard University, 5 January 2003 http:///gking.harvard.edu.

13

The Professions as Systems that Support Transactions Involving Knowledge: Their Contribution to Economic Development and their Response to the Growth of Global Markets

Gordon Boyce

13.1 Introduction

This chapter examines professions as systems that support transactions involving knowledge. With respect to transactions with clients, professional bodies facilitate such exchanges by validating knowledge, creating brands and establishing a price. The associations also rely on network structures to effect exchanges of knowledge and know-how among practitioners, and they operate as communicating nodes when interacting with outside constituents, including other professional groups, governments and regulatory agencies.

Historical examples are used to illustrate these propositions. The discussion examines the activities of Britain's 'ancient' professions, the new groups that arose in the nineteenth century and the wave of the social professions that emerged after 1945. These examples, and others drawn from the Australian and American experiences, reveal that the influence of individual professional organizations ebbs and flows as a result of a range of dynamic factors. The study then considers how the rapid growth in the global market for management education since the mid-1990s created an opportunity for the American Assembly of Collegiate Schools of Business (AACSB) and the European Quality Implementation System (EQUIS) to extend accreditation processes beyond national boundaries and into the international arena. They did so by using market and psychological incentives to finesse the challenge posed by the absence of any supranational entity with the power to confer and enforce the privileges of controlling entry and self-regulation. The study concludes by inviting wider consideration of how an increasingly global economy will affect the professions as systems that facilitate knowledge-based exchange.

13.2 Professions and the transmission of knowledge

The rise and proliferation of professional groups are conspicuous features of an emerging modern society characterized by growing social, political and economic complexity (Perkin, 1989, 1996). In turn, the intricacy of evolving relations, high levels of uncertainty and continuous change generated within the regions so affected posed important problems, the solution of which required the creation and application of specialized types of knowledge. People of high social position and inherited status possessed the authority to make decisions, but they lacked the in-depth expertise needed to develop informed solutions to problems afflicting those for whose welfare they were responsible. The rise and legitimization of professional status arose from growing recognition of the increasing value of specialized knowledge. By devising training programmes and instilling practitioners with vital tacit and abstract knowledge, the professions have made an important contribution to economic development, as well as social and political life, by enhancing the quality of human capital.

A profession and the association of practitioners that supports it are, acting in consort, many things: a labour organization; a social construct; and a community of practice. But this chapter explores the idea that they represent a framework that reduces the costs involved in completing notorious difficult exchanges that involve knowledge. Since the professions provide services based on specialized knowledge, the underlying transactions are affected by the Paradox of Knowledge (Arrow, 1974). This concept refers to the difficulty faced by a purchaser of knowledge who cannot assign a value to it before it has been revealed; yet for the seller prior disclosure means, in effect, that the knowledge has been divulged without receipt of payment. Market failure can only be prevented by providing some information that may or may not be related directly to the knowledge that is the object of exchange. Investment in individual reputation is one solution, but it is costly and requires considerable time. Collective advertising or group reputation-building is more cost-effective and more powerful. These advantages go far to explain the benefits of forming a professional association, or what Goodhart (1990: 57–76) calls a 'club'. Such a development, if accompanied by the installation of monitoring and policing machinery operated by the club itself or an external regulatory authority, mitigates potential free-rider problems. These difficulties arise when one practitioner behaves opportunistically and thereby debases the collective reputation of the group. Thus, professional societies play a key role in facilitating knowledge-based transactions.

Another salient insight can be derived from the work of Abbott (1988). He described the professions as systems that govern jurisdictions, which he defines as links between a profession and work. His main objective is to analyse the dynamics of these jurisdictions within many different nations, and he illustrates how a variety of internal and external factors broke, changed or facilitated the formation of these ties during the nineteenth and twentieth centuries. We develop this insight further by considering the professions as systems that support the creation and transmission of knowledge and specialized information. We consider their systemic properties explicitly and examine the underlying communicating processes. It is obvious that professional systems are not closed loops; they are open in the sense that they are connected to other constituents that may support or challenge their operations, and they interact with other institutions in the course of setting up structures to facilitate knowledge-based exchanges. Thus, from the perspective of an economy or a society as a whole, the professions represent sub-systems that are interlinked with others which govern diverse activities. However, the professions' unique role lies in gaining acceptance of the validity of a body of esoteric knowledge, protecting it, and developing constructs that enable those involved in transactions to overcome problems linked to the Paradox of Knowledge and opportunistic debasement. Without the professional sub-system, the social and economic system as a whole could be deprived of specialized knowledge, or would rely on existing institutional arrangements that might be less effective.

This is not to ignore the possibility that professional organizations in some circumstances may impede growth or innovation by using legal devices to preserve outdated or constraining routines or by causing welfare and allocative losses that stem from the exercise of monopoly power. Though sparsely documented, such outcomes have no doubt occurred, but they have arisen in particular contexts and probably should not be seen as pervasive. Nevertheless, from a broad historical perspective, the professions have provided a sophisticated system that has valuable efficiency properties.

13.3 The professional 'template'

In order to install their particular system, professional groups have employed a widely recognized template whose purpose is to facilitate the legitimization of their knowledge-based practice (Reader, 1966: 43). Reader initially observed the template in the British context, but suggested it was applied in other countries as well. Its installation involves four steps. First, emerging professional groups articulate a body of specialized knowledge that is needed to address a pressing problem in wider society. This knowledge must be clearly delineated from that of other groups and it, as well as the problem in question, must be sufficiently important to win acceptance from existing elites for the profession to provide knowledge-based services. Abbott (1988: 29) suggests that abstract knowledge has, amongst other attributes, a symbolic importance for the professions because it legitimizes their work by connecting it to cultural values. Second, the new profession must engage in 'closure'; that is, it must gain control over entry to its ranks by shaping education and accreditation processes. This goal enables the group to exclude potential opportunists, set quality standards and establish prices (potentially at the level of quasi-rents or rents) for their services, in part by controlling the number of practitioners. Third, the emergent profession enunciates ethical standards and routines to govern practitioner behaviour. The formulation of ethical standards reinforces the pursuit of quality promoted through the educational regime, and by publicizing these standards to the community at large professional organizations strengthen their case for legitimization in the eyes of the public and existing elites. The development of routines also generates a tacit dimension to the body of specialized knowledge articulated in the first part of the professionalization process. The fourth step consists of the professional organization gaining from the state the authority to self-regulate. Thus, the government or existing elites delegate to the professional organization responsibility for monitoring and sanctioning members (but see below). Matters of professional conduct are adjudicated by the profession, and the courts become involved only when criminal laws are transgressed. Working together, the four elements of the template establish a system that is largely self-organizing.[1]

Professional associations represent systems for setting standards, monitoring performance against those benchmarks and mobilizing feedback mechanisms that engage when deviations in performance occur. Standards are set through the educational systems and by articulating ethical principles. Examinations, complaint adjudication processes and informal mechanisms (see below) provide monitoring functions. Feedback is provided by structural devices and disciplinary processes that are operated by the association itself. As we have noted, the system is open in the sense that it captures information from outside constituents and projects an influence into the wider community.

The principal purpose of the professional organization is to facilitate transactions involving knowledge (and it has a number of efficiency properties that support this key function). First, professional associations articulate, delineate and codify esoteric knowledge, elements of which are tacit, abstract and embodied in people or routines. It is well known that knowledge with these characteristics poses notorious exchange- and transfer-related problems. Professional organizations mitigate some of the uncertainty surrounding exchanges of this nature by gaining recognition from existing elites that their knowledge is valid and that benefits stem from its application. This validation legitimizes the group's claim that it provides a public good-related service within a particular institutional context. In essence, this official endorsement, in addition to group advertising, serves to create a brand which, being provided by the government or the monarchy, acts as a powerful communicating device. At times, when there has been confusion regarding the worth of professional knowledge or the delineation of branches of knowledge between different groups, such branding conveyed assurances to prospective purchasers.

In addition, legislative devices employed by the state or professional organizations themselves establish a price for this knowledge and the fee may be established independently of the market and/or by manipulating supply-side factors. Thus, 'closure', that is the restriction of entry to qualified persons as defined by the professional organization, helps to determine the price level, often raising it to the level of a rent. In addition, official recognition, practitioner solidarity and the force of custom support the use of a variety of ritualized pricing practices (Reader, 1966: 37). For example, a client never pays a barrister directly, but only through a solicitor, and fees are not discussed in advance because to do so would imply that the principle of fairness would not be observed by the barrister. By custom, physicians and barristers charged fees that were denominated in guineas, rather than pounds, allowing practitioners a five per cent premium that represented the special value of their advice.

Groups that enjoyed less status than barristers or physicians devised and collectively enforced standardized pricing schedules.

13.4 Systemic links

While they facilitate transactions or applications of their knowledge on behalf of clients, professional organizations also support knowledge transfers among practitioners. They do so by enunciating ethical principles that encourage their members to share new discoveries and innovations in practice. Moreover, the various peer-rating services furnished by associations help knowledge-based exchanges in several ways. For example, recognizing leading practitioners by admitting them to the hierarchy of offices and awarding prizes to innovators reduces uncertainty and accelerates the circulation of the new discoveries they develop. Links with educational institutions also serve to ensure the rapid dissemination of improved techniques and new knowledge, and ties with other groups of allied practice may provide a similar function or may streamline applications of related knowledge across professional boundaries.

Indeed, the internal structures and the external architectures developed by professional associations support knowledge exchanges (Miranti, 1990). The organization acts as a communicating node linked to external constituents including universities and colleges, customers, government agencies, the courts and related professional groups at home and abroad. These channels support group advertising or credibility-seeking; for example, Solomon Huebner worked with the National Association of Life Underwriters (NALU) to rebuild the badly damaged reputation of insurance salesmen in the 1920s (Vande Creek, 2005).[2] A society's external conduits also provide access to a wide range of information – commercial, legislative, legal, competitive and scientific, or practice-related – that may influence transactions involving a profession's tacit or abstract knowledge. This information may reveal new opportunities for sale or application, and intelligence concerning developments that may threaten or strengthen existing patterns of transactions conducted by members.

Lipartito and Miranti (1998) highlight the ways in which American professional groups interacted with other private and public organizations for the purposes of learning and innovating. For example, they illustrate how evolving relationships between the corporate sector and the engineering, accounting and legal professions enhanced the capabilities of large-scale enterprise and stimulated the development of these groups' knowledge bases. In contrast, the arm's-length nature of the links between British companies and the highly independent body of consulting engineers in that country is thought to have reduced the rate of innovation to the detriment of its competitive advantage.

Taking a broader view of interorganizational communication ties, professional societies forged links across national boundaries from the mid-nineteenth century onwards. The Pharmaceutical Society of Australasia (PSA) created enduring ties with its counterparts in Britain and America in order to obtain information about educational programmes, legislative trends and new scientific knowledge (Boyce, 1999). Reciprocal visits, the granting of honorary positions, and exchanges of newsletters and academic journals strengthened these ties. Although a formal international body did not emerge to promote uniform practice or recognition of national qualifications that might enhance the mobility of practitioners, this informal network provided important functions in sharing information and knowledge.

The advertising business provides an unusual example of quasi-professionalization, based upon the adoption of parts of the template referred to above, and the use of a corporate hierarchy to transfer procedural knowledge across national boundaries. In the early twentieth century, the Advertising Association of America, like Huebner and the NALU, tried but failed to secure accreditation and control over educational processes. Acting independently, J. Walter Thompson Company (JWT) installed within its own organization the first three parts of the template. It articulated a body of professional knowledge, developed a comprehensive training programme for its employees and enunciated ethical standards. Inherently, it had the right to regulate the activities of its own employees. As the company expanded on the coat tails of its multinational clients during the interwar period, its practices were disseminated abroad. In addition, staff mobility between advertising agencies caused some transfers of JWT's procedures (Boyce, 2000). In these ways, a hierarchy served as a partial substitute for the network form of organization usually employed by professional societies (see Section 13.6).

In terms of linkages with practitioners within their national jurisdictions, professional organizations also operate like networks. They serve to circulate abstract and tacit knowledge among members through official publications and lectures, and they support exchanges of interpersonal knowledge through conferences and social gatherings. The former activities help to raise standards of practice and enhance the quality of service. The latter functions provide a peer-rating service and open up informal channels through which information can be transmitted. Group meetings also build member solidarity and help to socialize new entrants and practitioners-in-training by instilling behavioural patterns that encourage exchanges.

Associations also facilitate intergenerational transfers of intangible assets, including tacit knowledge, commercial connections and accumulated reputation. Apprentice and internship programmes established by these organizations, as part of the educational process through which members must pass to secure accreditation, also support transfers of knowledge directly from established practitioners to novices. In addition, the functions of these organizations in providing peer-rating services and opportunities to acquire interpersonal knowledge also smooths the way for practitioners who wish to retire to sell their practices. Indeed, some organizations, including the PSA, operated a register of practices for sale and carried advertisements in their publications alerting members of opportunities to buy into an established practice. The extended apprenticeship system itself, culminating as it usually did in journeyman status, offered a way for new entrants who lacked capital to acquire a practice by working off the purchase price. By these means, persons approaching retirement could more easily effect the potentially difficult feat of realizing the value of tangible and intangible assets they had accumulated over a lifetime of practice.

13.5 The rise of a distinctive institutional framework

Operating as nodes and networks, professional associations also reduce potentially prohibitive transaction costs in a variety of ways. They provide a framework that facilitates exchanges that could not be carried out as effectively through market mechanisms or hierarchical structures. Market failure is likely because those involved in exchanges will probably lack the specialized and contextual knowledge required to determine price and the interpersonal information or collegial assurances needed to dispel uncertainty. Hierarchies are disadvantaged because the underlying vertical communication channels cannot support free-flowing lateral exchanges. More fundamentally, hierarchies are considered by many students of institutions to be less adept and celeritous in supporting learning and innovating than networks (Williamson, 1985). In the case of professional groups, the network structure has the most suitable efficiency properties relative to available alternatives. Indeed, even though large-scale enterprise has shown a tendency to internalize some professional services, they have retained ties with independent providers in order to preserve their access to a growing supply of specialized knowledge (Lipartito and Miranti, 1998: 312–13).[3]

Throughout history, practical considerations shaped the choice regarding the most appropriate coordinating framework to employ. Delegating to a single hierarchy, the authority to provide professional services not only would have facilitated the implementation of comprehensive quality assurance programmes, but would also have conferred monopoly power to a private enterprise, and required the use of some form of regulatory machinery. While there were precedents for granting statutory monopolies, in Britain where the professions emerged early and developed characteristics employed in other countries, by the early nineteenth century these institutions faced growing criticism and strident calls for reform or abolition. An alternative would be to generate competition by permitting several organizations to provide professional services, creating an oligopoly in effect, but this option increased the likelihood that harmful variations in quality standards would result. Again, regulation would be required. The British government recognized entrenched forces that favoured minimizing state involvement and expense, and as a result finessed the regulatory conundrum by mobilizing widely recognized informal incentives.

The initial solution was to employ ethical and behaviour precepts observed by the elite to control emerging professional groups (Reader, 1966). Thus, standards of gentlemanly conduct were mobilized at the top end of the professions. Intending barristers, physicians and clerics were socialized through an Oxbridge liberal education and attendance at recognized venues where interpersonal information and the 'character' of intending practitioners could be assessed by established figures. Thus, the elite absorbed the top level of the early professions and instilled into their members a code of gentlemanly conduct that would support self-regulation.

The mid-nineteenth-century reform movement in Britain challenged this arrangement and the exclusiveness it sustained by calling for formal examination and entry by merit. Although some organizations (the Admiralty and the Foreign Office) fought rear guard actions against this movement for a time, eventually they too succumbed to the force of the new system extolled by the liberal middle-class ideology. Nevertheless, the enduring propellent of social advancement ensured that behavioural patterns characteristic of the elite were recognized by the middle ranks of professional practitioners. Indeed, gaining the legitimacy needed to implement further reforms, secure closure and win the right to self-regulate required the status of the professions to be raised. Ironically, this elevation was realized through emulating the behaviour of the elite. The aim was the social advancement of middle-class professionals to a level that, although below that of the top of society, put them at a 'comfortable sneering distance' above the lower levels (Reader, 1966: 146). This achievement also preserved an open elite, at least in terms of patterns of behaviour if not other attributes that would bring complete acceptance by the elite itself. In essence, legitimization initially entailed the lateral transfer of class-based behavioural modes across occupational groups followed by partial absorption of the middle ranks. According to Reader (1966: 183–206), this quest for social advancement, so characteristic of previous groups in Britain, distracted the attention of powerful middle-class elements towards traditional attainment and away from problems related to late-Victorian Britain's place in an increasingly competitive world. In this instance, established patterns of behaviour reduced the relevance of the second wave of professions that emerged during the nineteenth century, but the rise of the welfare state following the Second World War created a fertile environment for new occupational groups to pursue professional status (Perkin, 1989).

The pattern of professional ebb and flow observed in Britain is also evident in other countries. Professional growth and dissipation are complex phenomena involving the interaction of many variables. Some factors are internal to the professional system itself, while others are external in origin. The process of initially installing the professional template can be frustrated by numerous conditions, including an unwillingness to pursue this course (Coats, 1991). First, the knowledge claimed by the group may not be perceived by existing elites or the public as being sufficiently credible to merit professional status. Moreover, the body of knowledge claimed by a group may create jurisdictional disputes with other groups. Thus, pharmacists in Britain and Australia had to skirmish with medical doctors, dentists, veterinarians and other groups over dispensing rights. Herbalists were completely marginalized by this conflict. Second, controlling entry can be frustrated if the state withholds authority to regulate education programmes; this factor prevented the National Association of Life Underwriters and the American Advertising Association from clinching real professional stature (Schultze, 1982; Vande Creek, 2005). Third, claims that a group establishes valuable routines and strong ethical standards have to be convincing. A number of manual occupations in the United States were unable to make convincing claims of this nature (Burrage, 1990: 159). Finally, being first to secure official recognition was advantageous. When one group gained the power to self-regulate, it often undermined similar moves by other occupations that employed related knowledge.

A host of internal and external developments can affect the capacity of professional groups to support transactions involving knowledge. First, the challenges facing society can change and undermine the claim of a specific group to have exclusive access to the body of knowledge required to address these new challenges. Conversely, the proliferation of social problems after 1945 supported new professions by providing wider knowledge-based jurisdictions. Second, technological development can erode the position of groups that relied on practices involving a large content of tacit know-how. New technologies can simply sweep aside 'professions', like itinerant entertainers who were displaced by the emergence of mass media. Third, claims of legitimacy can be eroded as new knowledge becomes available. Mediums lost credibility in the post-World War era. Fourth, a variety of crises can undermine the stature of professional groups. The World Com and Enron debacles threatened the accountancy profession, while the onset of the Great Depression of the 1930s and the stagflation in the 1970s hurt the stature of economists (Coats, 1991). Fifth, institutional change may cause knowledge-based jurisdictions to shift. Accountants originally handled bankruptcy proceedings, but the spread of limited liability companies opened up a more attractive niche in providing auditing services (Abbott, 1988: 29). Sixth, broad institutional structures can evolve in ways that undermine existing associations, work sites and informal social controls. The result may be an erosion of knowledge or procedural bases. Seventh, knowledge may be commodified; the spread of do-it-yourself wills, for example, undermines the position of lawyers by generating competition from the corporate entities that provide a packaged product. Eighth, public disagreements within professional groups tend to diminish their credibility. Finally, shifts in career patterns or demographic trends can undermine a professional body. University teaching is experiencing problems arising from this source for a variety of reasons relating to funding and salary levels, status erosion and a shift in the type of knowledge society values.

Harold Perkin (1989, 1996) draws attention to a broader, more pervasive source of vulnerability. Being dependent upon the support of the state exposes professional groups to changes in the ideological climate. In Britain, professional groups that provided services linked to the welfare state became vulnerable when the free market ideology came to the fore. While this episode was particularly serious for a discrete range of professional groups, all professions are exposed to the consequences of adverse political currents. The significance of ideological change lies in the extent to which it leaves open certain groups to competition from other professions for resources controlled and allocated by the state.

More fundamentally, dependence on the state constrains the professions in extending their jurisdictions into the international arena. The usual integrated accreditation process is not applicable and instead bilateral or multilateral agreements are required. The expansion of bodies like the EU will in time provide professional groups with broader powers. Yet, the opportunity to serve global markets, some of which have experienced enormous growth recently, presents major challenges to professions that seek to install uniform codes of practice and comprehensive quality assurance systems. Nevertheless, it is possible to finesse dependence on the state.

13.6 EQUIS and AACSB

Historically, the capacity of professional organizations to transfer knowledge beyond the boundaries of their national jurisdiction has been limited in important ways. It is true that emerging associations in peripheral economies adopted the template developed by groups in Britain. Thus, the PSA imported the template and legal framework used by the Pharmaceutical Society of Great Britain, and thereby adopted the structures that facilitated transmissions of knowledge. The importation was facilitated by Quaker connections and networks that linked the colony with the mother country. Subsequently, PSA officials liaised closely with pharmaceutical organizations in the United States, Britain and other nations in order to learn about improved techniques, remedies and education programmes. National organizations therefore learned from each other, picking and choosing attractive innovations but with no intention of promoting uniformity in practice. Thus, ideas flowed fairly freely across national boundaries through informal links between allied associations, but important barriers still existed to the transmission of embodied knowledge since practitioners accredited in one country could not move and set up practice in another jurisdiction without in some way satisfying the association in their new location that their credentials were appropriate. Reciprocal recognition of accreditation was slow to emerge, even among the Australian states, in part because of concerns for limiting the supply of practitioners.

Other private transfer mechanisms were used as multinational enterprises expanded rapidly in the interwar and post-war periods of the twentieth century. Multinational advertising agency JWT transmitted procedural knowledge, which it had been unable to incorporate within a formal professional framework (see Section 13.4), to overseas locations as it set up branch offices to serve expanding multinational clients like General Motors. Management consulting firms did likewise (Kipping, 1999). Big accounting firms and legal partnerships also 'piggy-backed' on their clients and transferred knowledge abroad, but their employee practitioners had to meet the accreditation requirements of local organizations. Alternatively, they could hire local people who were already qualified.

The expansion of multinational enterprises was partially responsible for generating a backlash response among management educators. The European Foundation for Management Development (EFMD) was formed in 1971 through the merger of two European organizations, the International University Contact (founded 1952) and the European Association of Management Training Centres (1959). The enlarged entity was registered under Belgian law as an international not-for-profit organization dedicated to maintaining 'the continued competitiveness of Europe and to the promotion of Europe's global leadership in the field of management education and development' (EFMD, information supplied to the author). The new organization was a response to the spread of American and, later, Japanese management methods overseas. The EFMD believed that European management systems and approaches were also effective and that it should promulgate a different 'education model that meets the specific requirements of European companies' (EFMD, 2005, information supplied to the author). Another interpretation is that the spread of American and Japanese methods threatened European business schools with marginalization in their 'home' market. Subsequently, EFMD began to offer EQUIS accreditation to universities outside Europe. The EFMD and the AACSB, an American organization offering its own distinctive accreditation programmes, are now international organizations that set professional standards. They do not recognize national professional groups, or individual practitioners, but rather business schools.

The rivalry that has developed between EQUIS and AACSB as they have expanded overseas is reminiscent of the contests that arose in the nineteenth century between professional organizations that sought to secure recognition for specific procedural and knowledge-based frameworks. For example, border skirmishes unfolded between doctors and pharmacists over the territory of their knowledge bases and their rights to advise and prescribe; each sought to win from the government regulatory powers that would advantage their own members. However, in the case of EQUIS and AACSB there is no international authority that can approve or constrain their jurisdictions or their programmes.[4]

Indeed, the international expansion of these two bodies represents a private response to problems associated with the rapid growth of a global market for management education (Vroeijenstijn, 1999). In the absence of a transnational authority able to provide comprehensive quality assurance systems – indeed it is difficult to imagine from where one might originate–private organizations filled the void. To the extent that they provide a public good, the emergence of a private entity exercising regulatory power raises the issue of self-regulation. Moreover, how can such organizations establish their credibility without some form of support from a recognized agency?

The answer to the latter question reveals a clever use of market and psychological incentives. The overseas expansion of EQUIS and AACSB was propelled by demand from two sources. First, the rapid growth of the global market for higher education in the late 1990s was stimulated by recovery from the financial crisis of 1997 and a growing middle class in many Asian countries. However, students had little in the way of accurate information on which to judge the quality of the hundreds of institutions available to them. Internationally renowned universities, like Harvard and Stanford, could rely on their long-standing reputations to provide a proxy for quality, but most students were compelled by their previous records or financial resources to consider other institutions that lacked such stature. Their difficulties were compounded by the absence of any credible rating service (Cotton *et al.*, 1993: 18). Ranking systems provided by the business press or other groups provided some guidance, but the basis for their judgements was vague.

The second source of demand for accreditation services was generated in part by the imprecision of alternative rating frameworks. Academic pride being what it is, the universities themselves questioned the evaluations provided by these organizations and sought a more rigorously determined system of assessment. This was exactly what EQUIS and AACSB provided by means of stringent application processes, site visits which included record examination and interviews, and systematic documentation. By awarding accreditation on the basis of clearly articulated criteria, EQUIS and AACSB created an international brand that most business schools serving a global market would eagerly seek. (It remains to be seen whether these organizations will ration the use of their brand by restricting the number of accredited schools within individual countries, and it is interesting to observe that some of the foremost business schools have decided not to seek accreditation, confident that their own individual brands make it unnecessary to do so). At the same time, as we have seen, this brand also reduced the uncertainty students face when choosing where to study. By building a brand that can mediate between the two parties of a knowledge-based transaction, the accreditation bodies cleverly manipulated institutional psychology and incentives associated with an alternative governance mode, the market, to sell their services in circumstances that prevented them from installing the professional template.

What these accreditation agencies sell is first a readily identifiable brand and, more subtly, a process of continuous improvement. Cynics argue that the latter generates ongoing revenue for the organizations themselves, but more idealistically it supports serial transfers of knowledge related to academic practice, quality assurance and pedagogical technique, that is a combination of abstract, tacit and procedural knowledge. Moreover, these two accrediting organizations act as networks that provide channels for informal transfers of knowledge among the deans of accredited schools.

For all academics and schools hiring staff, the EQUIS and AACSB brands also reduce some of the uncertainty stemming from the problems of adverse selection and moral hazard that afflict recruitment processes. To some extent, the quality of new PhD graduates from accredited schools can be ascertained with greater precision, and the standing of the hiring school can be more readily determined by prospective recruits. Again, through their accreditation programmes, AACSB and EFMD facilitate knowledge transfers and reduce the attendant transaction costs.

13.7 Conclusion

This chapter extends previous work on the professions by closely exploring their systemic properties and functions within a wider economy. It argues that professional groups arose in response to the emergence of societies and economies that were becoming increasingly knowledge based. These associations acted as systems that supported difficult transactions involving abstract, procedural and embodied knowledge that was and is required to sustain growth and to solve problems afflicting communities.

As these challenges have changed over time and different problems have arisen, new professions have appeared, some have ossified and others have disappeared altogether. Further investigation is needed into the history of the professions in order to determine the full range of dynamic factors that affect the durability of specific groups of practitioners. Today, the emergence of rapidly growing markets of global dimension presents considerable difficulty in determining the scope of professional jurisdictions. The examples of EQUIS and AACSB show how challenges arising from this development can be finessed in clever ways.

Notes

1. Few academic disciplines have adopted this template and therefore raise the question whether or not they can be called 'professions.' For example, economists have deliberately chosen not to seek professional recognition, in part because they cannot ideologically defend 'closure' because of its monopolistic implications. Moreover, it is open to interpretation whether economists' knowledge is esoteric in the sense that it is inaccessible to other groups (Coats, 1991). These issues raise the possibility that there are gradients of professionalization.
2. Huebner and the Association could not install the professional template because a precedent-setting legal case barred their way. Therefore, acting informally, they developed a body of knowledge (derived largely from economics) to create a curriculum of study and set up a national body for regulating members. Huebner and his allies did not formally articulate a corpus of ethical principles to guide practitioners, they did not gain full powers of self-regulation from the government and they could not completely control entry (Vande Creek, 2005).
3. These authors also draw attention to the important mediating function that autonomous professional groups have played in shaping interactions between potentially opposing groups. For example, during the New Deal era, accountants used their knowledge to work out a 'dialectical' solution to the demands of corporations, which as suppliers of financial information sought to minimize disclosures, and the investing community, which being consumers of such data desired the fullest detail. Interposed between these two groups, the accountancy profession in effect brokered communication (Lipartito and Miranti, 1998: 311).
4. Moreover, in the 1980s, AACSB was challenged by a new group, the Association of Collegiate Business Schools and Programs (ACBSP), formed by business schools that could not obtain AACSB accreditation because they emphasized practice-based instruction more than academic research, which as we have seen has a symbolic importance for professional groups (McKenna, Cotton and Van Auken, 1997).

References

Abbott, A. *The System of the Professions* (Chicago: University of Chicago Press, 1988).

Arrow, K. *The Limits of Organisation* (New York: W. W. Norton, 1974).

Boyce, G. 'A Professional Association as Network and Communicating Node: The PSA, 1857–1918', *Australian Economic History Review*, 39 (3) (1999): 258–83.

Boyce, G. 'Contracts Based on Knowledge: The J. Walter Thompson Co.', in G. Boyce (ed.), *Co-operative Structures in Global Business* (London: Routledge, 2000): 170–87.

Burrage, M. and Torstendahl, R. (eds), *Professions in Theory and History* (London: Routledge, 1990).

Coats, A.W. 'Economics as a Profession', in D. Greenaway, M. F. Bleaney and I. Stewart (eds), *Companion to Contemporary Economic Thought* (London: Routledge, 1991): 119–142.

Cotton, C. C., McKenna, J. F., Van Auken, S. and Yeider, R. A. 'Mission Orientations and Deans' Perceptions: Implications for the New AACSB Accreditation Standards', *Journal of Organisational Change Management*, 6 (1) (1993): 17–27.

EFMD. Information provided to the author by M. Wood, 1 March 2005.

Goodhart, C. *The Evolution of Central Banks* (Cambridge, MA: The MIT Press, 1990).

Kipping, M. 'American Management Consulting Companies in Western Europe, 1920–1990', *Business History Review*, 73 (2) (1999): 190–220.

Lipartito, K. J. and Miranti, P. J. 'Profession and Organisations in Twentieth Century America', *Social Science Quarterly*, 79 (2) (1998): 301–20.

McKenna, J. E., Cotton, C. C. and Van Auken, S. 'The New AACSB Accreditation Standards: A Prospect of Tiering?', *Organisational Change Management*, 10 (6) (1997): 491–500.

Miranti, P. J. *Accountancy Comes of Age* (Chapel Hill, NC: The University of North Carolina Press, 1990).

Perkin, H. *The Rise of Professional Society* (London: Routledge, 1989).

Perkin, H. The *Third Revolution: Professional Elites in the Modern World* (London: Routledge, 1996).

Reader, W. *Professional Men* (New York: Basic Books, 1966).

Schultze, Q. J. ' "An Honourable Place": The Quest for Professional Advertising Education, 1900–17', *Business History Review*, LVI (1982): 16–32.

Vande Creek, D. 'Solomon Huebner and the Development of Life Insurance Sales Professionalism, 1905–1935', *Enterprise & Society*, 6 (4) (2005): 646–81.

Vroeijenstijn, A. I. 'The International Dimension in Quality Assessment and Quality Assurance', *Assessment & Evaluation in Higher Education*, 24 (2) (1999): 237–47.

Williamson, O. E. *The Economic Institutions of Capitalism* (London: Macmillan, 1985).

14
Communicative Transaction Benefits

S. Kesting

This chapter pursues the idea that path dependent processes which construct and change institutional arrangements not only incur cost, but also produce transaction benefits. This production of transaction benefits is based on the fundamental social institution of language. To change institutional arrangements, communicative actors evaluate speech acts which express validity claims. To derive a definition of transaction benefits, the argument starts from a critical literature review of authors working in the new and old institutional traditions of economics. A linguistic turn in the model of economic action is necessary to understand how transaction benefits may emerge from bargaining, negotiation and public discourse. Preference formation, building trust and developing routines for firms can be interpreted as transaction benefits. These benefits compensate economic actors for investing money, time, effort and energy into bargaining processes and negotiations.

14.1 Transaction costs compared to what?

Before asking what transaction benefits might possibly be, let us reflect on their counterpart, that is transaction costs. The concept was invented by Nobel laureate Ronald Coase who defined these costs thus:

> In order to carry out a market transaction it is necessary to discover who it is that one wishes to deal with, to inform people that one wishes to deal and on what terms, to conduct negotiations leading up to a bargain, to draw up the contract, to undertake the inspection needed to make sure that the terms of the contract are being observed, and so on. These operations are often extremely costly, sufficiently

> costly at any rate to prevent many transactions that would be carried out in a world in which the pricing system worked without cost.
>
> (1960: 15)

John R. Commons, who introduced and emphasized the notion of transaction for economics, wrote as follows:

> In every transaction there is a conflict of interests because each participant is trying to get as much and give as little as possible. Yet nobody can live or prosper except by dependence on what others do in managerial, bargaining, and rationing transactions. Hence, they must come to a working agreement, and, since such agreements are not always possible voluntarily, there always has been some form of collective compulsion to decide disputes.
>
> (1934: 121)

What is of relevance for the understanding of transaction benefits in this quote, and what we want to stress, is that Commons allows for and distinguishes between two different types of inducements by which an agreement or mutual understanding can be elicited: coercion and persuasion (Ramstad, 1996: 419). With persuasion or communicative action, words (as well as visual symbols, gestures and so on), and not only goods, are exchanged during a transaction. We argue that this is crucial for the emergence of transaction benefits,[1] which we define in a first approximation as the beneficial change for participants and others during a transaction which is not related to the delivered goods or services as such.

This distinction is analogous to the one between production and transaction costs, where the latter is process related and the former comparative output oriented. The level of transaction costs depends on the kind of institution involved. The questions asked in New Institutional Economics are as follows: Is it cheaper to make or buy? Are higher transaction costs involved in using a firm, a market or another kind of institutional arrangement to attain a particular good or service? We show that a number of institutional economists have argued that specific institutional arrangements are based on communicative acts and therefore also produce transaction benefits.

14.2 The neoclassical market as model of reference

The central term of new institutional economic analysis, 'transaction cost', was further developed by Oliver Williamson among others. Over the course of the theoretical debate the exact meaning of transaction costs has widened. According to Matthias Klaes, new institutional economists today '...attempt to use transaction costs as a general category to address the relative efficiency of market and non-market institutions' (Klaes, 2000a: 193). Transaction costs are used as a measure to evaluate the efficiency of different governance structures, and thus as a quasi welfare criterion (Klaes, 2000b: 588). Williamson calls it the *remediableness criterion*: 'This criterion holds that an extant mode of organization for which no superior *feasible* alternative can be described and *implemented* with expected net gains is *presumed* to be efficient' (Williamson, 2000: 601). Williamson arrives at these net gains by comparing different levels of transaction costs in comparison to the ideal neoclassical competitive market as a focus point. These higher or lower amounts of transaction costs arise depending on asset specificity and uncertainty due to bounded rationality, opportunism and idiosyncratic knowledge (Williamson, 2002: 175). The concern is not with the absolute level of transaction costs but rather with their relative differences. This 'ordinal' approach to the problem of operationalization can be criticized, however, because in most of the studies perfect competition serves as the reference model (Frambach and Eissrich, 2002: 53). Though Williamson is aware of different methodologies and modes of explanation in the social sciences, he wants to see them applied at particular levels of analysis which do not interfere with what he regards as the core of the transaction cost approach (Williamson, 2000: 597). Hence, from his point of view there is only limited need for an integration of different brands of theory to enhance explanatory power and no need to think about transaction benefits.

14.3 Olson's critique of the transaction cost approach

The arguments in Olson's book *Power and Prosperity* (2000) are helpful in understanding why the notion of *transaction benefits* might enhance the explanatory power of institutional economics. Olson criticizes the transaction cost approach for its 'Panglossian implications' (Olson, 2000: 57), because (at least in Williamson's approach) it tells us: '...we are automatically in the most efficient of all possible worlds' (Olson, 2000: 55). He describes the new institutional approach as follows:

> Some advocates of the transaction cost approach then go on to argue that individuals and firms in society will make all of those trades that, after taking account of the transactions costs that fall upon

> each party, are mutually advantageous. When the transactions costs of the trade exceed the gains it would bring, the parties do not make the trade, and that too is as it should be. Thus, any status quo resulting from the market is efficient. If there had been an outcome that, after taking account of the transactions costs, was better for the participants in the economy, they would have made the deals that generated that better outcome.
>
> (Olson, 2000: 55)

A similar argument is outlined in Olson (1996). Hence, there is no room for an explanation why some institutional arrangements are actually not efficient or advantageous for its participants. If a careful evaluation of costs *and* benefits arising during a transaction were done, however, case studies could be undertaken that could show either a positive or a negative balance of an analysis of actual institutional arrangements, assuming a way could be found actually to measure or evaluate those costs and benefits.

Thus, if transaction benefits were considered, Olson's critique could be turned into a fruitful development for New Institutional Economics. However, that is not what he himself had in mind. In the aforementioned book he offers his ideas on power and coercion as an alternative to the transaction cost explanation, what he terms the 'dark side of the force' (Olson, 2000: 60). From our vantage point this is one-sided as a transaction cost approach since it does not take benefits into account. Olson decides to focus only on coercion and ignores persuasion as a means of solving conflicts.

A large part of the problem stems from Olson's self-determination to work within a neoclassical human actor model. He acknowledges:

> As I see it, human beings rarely act out of unmixed motives. There is not only self-interest but also a benevolent element – and even a malevolent streak – in human nature. Historical outcomes surely depend not only on the incentives and self-interest of those in power but also on their morals and temperaments.
>
> (Olson, 2000: 3)

Nevertheless he decides, '…I start with a focus on the incentives and inducements to rational and self-interested action that face those with power' (Olson, 2000: 3). Olson is well aware of the limitations of such narrow assumptions and also of the dangers that come with them (Olson, 2000: 46). However, he never gets to the point in his analysis where he systematically manages to integrate the full, or at least a wider, range of human motivations. Hence, Schmid concludes his critical review of Olson's work: 'While Olson does not deny a possible role for what he calls non-economic behaviours, one gets the impression from Olson's overall work that these behaviours are marginalized' (Schmid, 1996: 223). To use Olson's Hollywood-inspired metaphor, one might ask, Where is the return of the Jedi (that is, the bright side of the force)?[2]

Nevertheless, Olson does implicitly relax standard neoclassical assumptions when he arrives at his explanation of why small groups have the ability to act collectively. He writes:

> When a potential beneficiary of a collective good knows that another will match its provision or share the costs of provision, that reduces the cost of each unit of the public good to each party and increases the likelihood that some amount of the good will be provided.
>
> (Olson, 2000: 73)

However, how should the beneficiary know? Some kind of interaction or exchange of information has to take place before such certainty or trust can arise. Thus Olson introduces communicative action at the level of small groups (Olson 2000: 91), without being explicit about this change in his model of behaviour. Olson may succeed in explaining free riding, but he does not expand our understanding of cooperation (Schmid, 1996: 224).

This methodological switch is also apparent when we look at his discussion of the Prisoner's Dilemma. Olson observes:

> A driving force in the two-person Prisoner's Dilemma is that an almost universal feature of any interaction of two individuals with a common problem – communication about how to obtain the outcome that is a collective good for both of them – is prevented by some exceptionally special circumstances.
>
> (Olson, 2000: 75)

He seems to suggest here that communication alone can be sufficient to ensure mutually beneficiary agreements. He is correct if we consider the evidence from game theoretic experiments which claim that not even binding commitments but merely a casual chat for a few minutes is enough to raise the cooperation rate considerably (*cf.* Dawes *et al.*, 1990; Bohnet and Frey 1994; Frey and Bohnet, 1995, 1997). However, this shows that the rational actor model is insufficient to explain behaviour even in laboratory settings based on assumptions of strategic action. In a world of neoclassical or of new institutional (opportunistic) standard assumptions, 'talk is cheap' (Farrell, 1995). However, in the real world, so it seems, it is not!

Because of his reluctance to extend his behavioural model of explanation, Olson has to claim 'lucky circumstances' (Olson, 2000: 91) to come to grips with the superior capacity of a working democracy to ensure long-run property rights, and thus even greater economic benefits than stable autocracies (see also Olson, 1993). If communicative rationality is taken into consideration, as is demonstrated for instance by Jon Elster's study of constitutional assemblies of France and the United States (Elster, 1998), peaceful order, voluntary social contracts and consensus can be explained even for large groups (Olson, 2000: 90).[3] Schmid's remarks on Olson's thinking in general are pertinent: 'Could it be that it contains an implicit argument that political reform depends more on ideology and emotion than on rational calculation?' (Schmid, 1996: 234).

14.4 Comparing institutional arrangements with distinct path histories

Douglass North tries to explain the efficiency of institutions without referring to the neoclassical ideal-type market: 'Institutions everywhere are a 'mixed bag' of those that lower the costs and those that raise them' (North, 1993: 251). Real-world markets are no exception to this rule. Whether they are efficient in solving economic coordination problems depends on their history (path dependence). North tries to compare transaction costs of particular institutional arrangements. This leads him to look much closer at negotiation and bargaining processes which determine and construct the most suitable governance structure. With the afore-exercised critical inspection of Olson's work in mind, his statement that '[a] self-conscious incorporation of institutions into economic theory will force economists to question the behavioural models that underlie the discipline' rings very true (North, 1993: 258). North seems to imply that the broadening of the economic actor model has to go into the direction of communicative action: 'It is easier to be convinced of the genetic aptitude of human beings for language – a subject in which there is a lot of interesting research – than to be similarly convinced of the genetic aptitude for cooperation' (North, 1998: 505). However, is it sufficient to conceptualize communication as a one-way, simply receptive relationship? North seems to imply just this in writing: 'Interactive learning is a two-stage affair in which we first receive a social signal that tells us how to behave, and then test the behaviour against our preferences to see whether we wish to follow its recommendation' (North, 1998: 505). In acknowledging the role of shared mental models, Denzau and North point to the role of possible transaction benefits during bargaining and negotiation processes (Denzau and North, 1994).

14.5 Shared mental models: A linear, unilateral form of interaction

Williamson views bargaining (that is, communication) as only transaction costly, that is without any transaction cost–saving effect (Williamson, 1991). [4] Denzau and North, however, have come to the conclusion that communicated and hence shared mental models have a transaction cost–saving effect: 'Some types of mental models are shared intersubjectively. If different individuals have similar models they are able to better communicate and share their learning. Ideologies and institutions can then be viewed as classes of shared mental models' (Denzau and North, 1994: 4). If we take a close look at Denzau and North's definition of shared mental models and related terms, it becomes clear that a certain mode of interaction is required to arrive at them. 'Ideologies are the shared framework of mental models that groups of individuals possess that provide both an interpretation of the environment and a prescription as to how that environment should be structured ... [I]nstitutions are the rules of the game of a society and consist of formal and informal constraints constructed to order interpersonal relationships. The mental models are the internal representations that individual cognitive systems create to interpret the environment; the institutions are the external (to the mind) mechanisms individuals create to structure and order the environment' (Denzau and North, 1994: 4). The influence of institutions on individuals and vice versa does not seem to work smoothly due to the stated internal versus external dualism. Mental models seem to be imposed on the actor from outside and are not an integrated part of the person. Moreover, shared mental models ease human interaction. However, it is not quite clear how they are produced and reproduced. In other words, for Denzau and North the explanation is causal linear from institution to individual. In addition, Denzau and North stress the constraining aspect of institutions compared to their enabling aspect which is overlooked.

In Denzau and North's view, every individual is faced with uncertainty (Denzau and North, 1994: 9) and begins to deal with it while relying primarily on his or her own limited experiences:

> The world is too complex for a single individual to learn directly how it all works. The entire structure of the mental models is derived from the experiences of each individual – experiences that are specific to the local physical environment and the socio-cultural linguistic environment.
>
> (Denzau and North, 1994: 14)

Moreover, the behavioural disposition of individuals in Denzau and North's approach is not only goal-oriented (Denzau and North, 1994: 13), but even individual benefit–oriented (Denzau and North, 1994: 8), and thus learning and communication as a precondition of human action (Denzau and North, 1994: 14–15) is mixed with the assumption of learning and communication as a matter of pure self-interest.[5] Denzau and North acknowledge that some kind of transaction benefit does occur: 'Mental models are shared by communication, and communication allows the creation of ideologies and institutions in a co-evolutionary process. The creation of ideologies and institutions is important for economic performance, as there exist gains from trade and production that require coordination' (Denzau and North, 1994: 20). The individualistic, gain-oriented perspective explains why communication is seen as a one-way exchange model (Denzau and North, 1994: 19). Denzau and North are aware of the theoretical weakness of this self-interested kind of methodological individualism to account for the effects of communication: 'This approach works at the level of the individual chooser. But many of the changes we wish to understand are social, such as changes in informal institutions or ideologies' (Denzau and North, 1994: 23, footnote 11).

To sum up, we agree with Rutherford's interpretation of North's work and its relation to American Original Institutionalism. He states that '... the differences between the old and the new [institutionalism] can, on closer examination, be revealed as less sharp than usually supposed' (Rutherford, 1995: 444), but '[t]o incorporate ideology will require much more extensive modifications to the neoclassical model than North has contemplated to date' (Rutherford, 1995: 450). If we compare Denzau and North's shared mental models to Boulding's public images, the two important modifications required are to integrate an empathic or other-regarding kind of rationality,[6] and to allow for a truly interactive relationship between individual and institution which includes an influence that works in both directions.

14.6 The image as explanation for transaction benefits

The following arguments draw on Kenneth Boulding's image as a major theoretical building block for the conception of transaction benefits arising from an inclusive social process.[7] A short, and at the same time inclusive, definition of the image is provided by Medema and Samuels:

> The fundamental role of the image is to define the world. The image is the basic, final, fundamental, controlling element in all perception and thought. It largely governs our definition of reality, substantively and normatively, in part as to what is actual and what is possible.
>
> (Medema and Samuels, 1997: 311)

Hence, the image carried in our heads largely governs our behaviour. As Boulding puts it, 'The behavior is response to an image, not a response to a stimulus, and without the concept of an image the behavior cannot possibly be understood' (Boulding, 1997 [1956]: 43). Quite a number of economic transactions are embedded in a process of 'imagination' which incorporates value judgements: 'The image of value is concerned with the *rating* of the various parts of our image of the world, according to some scale of betterness or worseness. We, all of us, possess one or more of these scales. It is what the economists call a welfare function' (Boulding, 1997 [1956]: 11).

It is open to argument as to whether the image remains stable or changes depending on the experiences of the individual and the influence of outside messages on it: 'The image is part of – and changes within – an ongoing process in which experience and image and selective perception coevolve' (Medema and Samuels, 1997: 312). How does one's image, containing our value judgements, preferences and welfare perception, change, and how do others influence that process? Boulding insists that human beings communicate with each other via symbols (that is, communication that can become independent of the communicator) as well as face-to-face (Boulding, 1997 [1956]: 88) and that communication constitutes and changes our images: 'It is this symbolic image and the communications which establish it and which change it which constitutes the peculiar quality of human society, a quality which no animal society shares' (Boulding, 1997 [1956]: 44). Samuels highlights the linguistic character of the image: 'Images are linguistic phenomena for mankind. Language is the material of images. Having an image, reducing it to words, talking about it – all this involves the use of language' (Medema and Samuels, 1997: 317).

Image and language alike are at the same time intra- and inter-individual and their change takes place via correspondence of these levels:

> The basic bond of any society, culture, subculture or organization is a 'public image', that is, an image the essential characteristics of which are shared by the individuals participating in the group... Indeed, every public image begins in the mind of some single individual and only becomes public as it is transmitted and shared.
>
> (Boulding, 1997 [1956]: 64)

It is not only true for the images of individuals, however, but also for shared images, '...that there is not a single public image, but there are many public images, as many indeed as there are cultures and subcultures within the great frame of the human race' (Boulding, 1997 [1956]: 132). In fact, a subculture can be defined as a group of people sharing a certain public image. What does this microtheory of behaviour, guided by individual and public images which are stabilized or changed through communication, contribute to the development of an alternative approach to understanding economic transactions?

What we regard as good for us is a value-laden public welfare image by which we try to evaluate economic processes and their outcomes. Our image also helps us on the individual level to deal with uncertainty, which is done via the interplay of the image with habits and routines of behaviour:

> In the course of the repetition of habitual activities changes occur in the value structure, that is, in the value image of what we are doing. As we contemplate in good, rational manner the alternatives which are presumably open to us today the likelihood that we will select something else than the habitual pattern depends, of course, upon our satisfaction with this pattern. If we were miserable yesterday we are much more likely to assess the nonhabitual alternative favorably than if we were happy. At some point the misery in the contemplation of

> the habitual behavior overcomes the uncertainty involved in contemplating any other kind of behavior and we make a reorganization.
> (Boulding, 1997 [1956]: 87)

On the collective level, gains from transactions are not a summation of individual preference functions, but defined and attained by a

> process of the mutual modification of images both relational and evaluational in the course of mutual communication, discussion, and discourse. The course of the discussion is punctuated by decisions which are essentially temporary in nature in the sense that they do not close the discussion, although they do, of course, have the effect of modifying it. In one sense, in a successful political process all decisions are interim. We live in a perpetual state of unresolved conflict. A decision is partial resolution of conflict. It should never be a complete resolution.
> (Boulding, 1997 [1956]: 103)

The explanatory advantage of such an image/communication-based theory of economic transactions is not only that it includes changing preferences and interdependence of individuals, but also that it allows for welfare-enhancing effects through social learning. Transactions within the firm or in the market involve communication which potentially creates images, that is new ideas and solutions, and thus transaction benefits.

How does Boulding's image explain how transaction benefits are created? Images may differ from individual to individual. They are, however, also connected via integrative power which is based on emotional bonds and communication: 'Integrative power within such a network may be a gradual process of a person gathering respect from the other people in the network through communication and the formation of images of that person in the minds of the other network members' (Boulding, 1990: 114). Via integrative power (for networks, compare Granovetter, 2005) inter-subjective public images (shared mental models in Denzau and North's terminology) of welfare are formed and changed. Hence, during transactions, institutions and ideologies are emerging, are rebuilt and are transformed. Because it is very likely that individual images and public images of subcultures are in conflict with each other, some form of conflict resolution (mediation) is necessary to facilitate and legitimate this process and organize it in a peaceful way.[8]

14.7 The role of democratic participation in the modern welfare state: Virtuous and vicious cumulative circular causation based on public discussions

The way Myrdal (1968) conceptualizes 'democratic planning' is very similar to Boulding's formation of public images through integrative power. He explains his discursive conception of human action in Appendix 1 'A Methodological Note on Valuations and Beliefs' of his book *The American Dilemma*. Myrdal starts from the concept of an individual whose actions are determined by his or her value judgements.[9] These judgements may not only be in conflict from person to person, but also be intra-personal: 'In this treatise, therefore, behavior is conceived of as being typically the outcome of a moral compromise of heterogeneous valuations, operating on various planes of generality and rising in varying degrees and at different occasions to the level of consciousness' (Myrdal, 1972 [1944]: 1028).

People do not just become aware of intra- and interpersonal conflicts coincidentally. It happens instead while communicating with others:

> The individual or the group whose behavior we are studying, moreover, does not act in moral isolation. He is not left alone to manage his rationalizations as he pleases, without interference from outside. His valuations will, instead, be questioned and disputed. Democracy is a 'government by discussion', and so, in fact, are other forms of government, though to a lesser degree.
>
> (Myrdal, 1972 [1944]: 1028)[10]

This exchange and critique of each other's arguments as an attempt to persuade and convince takes place on the background of a life-world, which is at least partly shared by participants in discourse:

> When discussion takes the form of moral criticism by one person or group or another, it is not that the one claims to have certain valuations that the other does not have. It is rather an appeal to valuations which the other keeps in the shadow of inattention, but which are assumed, nevertheless, to be actually held in common.
>
> (Myrdal, 1972 [1944]: 1028)

This rational argumentative exchange of validity claims based on some common normative ground[11] leads to a common ground which might turn latent conflicts into open ones (*cf.* Lukes, 1974).

> By this democratic process of open discussion there is started a tendency which constantly forces a larger and larger part of the valuation sphere into conscious attention ... A need will be felt by the person or group, whose inconsistencies in valuations are publicly exposed, to find a means of reconciling the inconsistencies. This can be accomplished by adjusting one of the conflicting pairs of valuations.
>
> (Myrdal, 1972 [1944]: 1029)

Myrdal's conception sounds familiar to someone acquainted with Habermas' discourse ethics. This urge to clarify inconsistencies through adjustment and modification is what Habermas sees as the forceless force of the better argument (*cf.* Habermas, 1995; Biesecker, 1997; Ulrich, 1997). Though Myrdal is aware of a tendency to neglect and deny the existence of value conflicts,[12] he is relying on the fascination of new ideas which will bring about a trajectory towards an open and rational public discourse: 'The direction in a normal and peaceful process of popular education is toward decreasing inconsistency' (Myrdal, 1972 [1944]: 1033).

To sum up, Myrdal stresses the importance of participation in democratic discourse processes in solving value conflicts and directing economic development. We interpret the value changes and peaceful conflict solutions as transaction benefits.

14.8 The original institutional approach

As we have seen, scholars working in the tradition of old or American institutionalism developed a range of notions of transaction benefits. Boulding calls these gains from cooperation *public images*: They are the basic bond shared by any society, culture, subculture or organization (Boulding, 1997 [1956]: 64). Myrdal also stresses the transaction benefits of clarifying and sharing one's interests and preferences in public discourse. Contemporary American institutionalist authors who elaborate the transaction benefits of clarifying and solving conflicts of interests and values are Schmid, Samuels and Medema, as well as Dolfsma and Nooteboom (Samuels *et al.*, 1997; Nooteboom 2002; Dolfsma, 2004; Schmid, 2004).

Though quite a theoretical gap still has to be overcome to link transaction costs in Williamson's sense of make or buy decisions with a notion of transaction benefits derived from shared images in communicative democratic processes as proposed by Boulding and Myrdal, some political scientists have tried to build such conceptual bridges. One scholar who started out as a new institutional economist and whose views about conflict resolution frameworks come close to such a perspective on transaction benefits is Jack Knight, who writes as follows:

> Institutions make life easier; in a world of social interdependence, they provide a means of living and working together. They allow social actors to produce, by acting with others, benefits that they would fail to achieve by acting alone. In some contexts, these benefits are called *gains from trade*; in others, *gains from cooperation*; in still others, *advantages of coordination*. The stability of these institutions and the knowledge of that stability shared by the members of a group or community enable the types of behavior necessary to achieve these benefits. It is not surprising that these collective benefits form the basis of an answer to the question of what difference social institutions make.
>
> (Knight, 1992: 25; see also Knight, 2001; Knight and Johnson, 1999)

14.9 Theory of communicative action: Habermas' discourse ethics

The productivity of speech that brings about a specific kind of rationality and thus allows the creation of benefits during a transaction can further be clarified by drawing on Habermas' theory of communicative action. Though Habermas is not an economist and his behavioural pattern of communicative action is not directed to the economic realm, his theory is nonetheless quite similar to Boulding's and Myrdal's attitudinal and procedural concepts of communicative action.

Communicative action in Habermas' sense is not only oriented to success, efficiency or personal goals. It aims also to reach an understanding among the participants of a discourse and is coordinated 'through cooperative achievements of understanding among participants. In communicative action, participants are not oriented primarily to their own success, but to the realization of an agreement which is the condition under which all participants in the interaction may pursue their own plans' (Habermas, 1995: 541; Biesecker, 1997: 220). Communicative action is based on language and operates in the process of discussion. This procedural exchange of arguments during which participants learn to understand each other's motivations, underlying norms and opinions is called *discourse* by Habermas. In discourse, participants have the chance to learn from each other and to change their own attitudes towards the world in general or towards certain problems occurring within it.[13]

Habermas' concept of *communicative action* or *discourse* is similar to the integrative process of public image formation described by Boulding. What Habermas adds is a certain procedural *communicative rationality*[14] that helps to differentiate three basic types of arguments (speech acts) which can be criticized or defended, grounded in their specific rationality. Habermas argues that communicative rationality occurs inevitably during discourse, which is evident if we thoroughly consider the intersubjective meaning of illocutions (*cf.* Austin, 1969). If we try to persuade during discourse, we suppose that the other person can be convinced by our arguments and will accordingly change his or her mind. When we do this, however, we implicitly concede that exactly the same might happen to us but in the opposite direction. That is to say, we are ready to admit the superiority of others' arguments and change our minds.[15]

What follows is that participants in a dialogue logically have to allow for mutual understanding to occur or they will commit a 'performative contradiction'. Apel (1992) and Habermas argue that if you want to influence through persuasion (that is, exchange of arguments) any assumption of opportunism or strategic behaviour in dialogue[16] would lead to such 'performative contradiction'. What is true for persuasion in one direction of influence will in turn also be true for learning in the other direction. If you try to receive information (useful ideology or mental models for instance) from a person, you assume that people are capable of learning. Vice versa you should assume that the other will also be able to learn from whatever information you provide in the process of communication. This crucial interactive element of discourse is missing in Denzau and North's concept of shared mental models, but included in Boulding's and Myrdal's approaches.

The communicative rationality of speech acts is not merely instrumental, like the utilitarian rationality of economic man. As Biesecker puts it (quoting and translating Habermas):

> The [speech acts] are not simply grounded in knowledge of the object world (as in empirical thinking), but also in the norms of the society in which the discourse is taking place (Habermas's social world) and the values of the partners in the discourse (Habermas's subject world). Communicative rationality, therefore, has three dimensions: An action [or a statement] is rational if it is objectively true, socially right and subjectively sincere.
>
> (Habermas, 1995: 149, translated in Biesecker, 1997: 220)

The participants of a discourse use their shared experiences (made in their life-world) as background and reservoir to test the validity of arguments along such dimensions of rationality. In a certain discourse situation, the discussants recur to their shared experiences, which contain all opinions and world views taken for granted to begin a cooperative process of interpretation. During this process, some elements of their experiences will remain untouched or stable, while others will become a matter of doubt and may change. Because discourse, as a form of social coordination, is linked to the social and subjective worlds, it has the capacity to integrate values other than those occurring during a neoclassical transaction or in an Austrian market process (*cf.* v. Hayek, 1969, 1978; Buchanan and Vanberg, 1991), which is merely based on instrumental rationality and where values have to be reflected monetarily in supply or demand to influence the outcome.

For the development of creative solutions for social problems or conflicts discussed in a discourse, following communicative rationality, Habermas and social economists[17] rely on all the persons participating in discourse. This establishes the special productivity of the discursive process; in other words, the potential for transaction benefits.

Philosophically, a strong Kantian, *a priori* emphasis on reason is apparent in discourse ethic. This bright-side-of-the-force view of discourse is probably as one-sided as the dark-side view of interpreting it as solely strategic (*cf.* Kesting, 1998, 2005). Empirically both opportunistic behaviour (manipulation, betrayal, false and broken promises, and so on) and mutually rewarding cooperation are possible and indeed observable in actual transactions. It depends on the specific actual conditions whether transaction benefits or costs prevail.

14.10 Conclusion

Our conclusion is that transaction benefits are derived from the collective communicative processes which accompany and embed economic transactions. These discourses invent and change ideas in the minds of participants, which leads to construction and transformation of reassuring and stabilizing institutions.

Because of the existence of transaction costs, Coase himself (Coase, 1960) amongst other institutional economists (Samuels, 1997) does not believe in the analytical value of the *Coase Theorem* in explaining economic development in the real world. However, if we consider the contribution of transaction benefits to the actual economy, the notion that individuals have an incentive to bargain and negotiate in the market place, within organizations and in public arenas, until they have maximized their joint gains becomes more appealing. If transaction benefits level out transaction costs, the chances for mutually beneficial negotiations grow and the *Coase Theorem*, theoretically enriched by a communicative actor model, becomes surprisingly true. To accept this conclusion we require a change in the assumptions underlying the motives of economic actors and a general progression in theory from a rational choice towards a pragmatic and discursive conception of human action. Whether this can be done by integrating both approaches or rather by a parallel and comparative use of a set of research methods has yet to be determined.

The arguments presented here, however, demonstrate how the approaches of old and new institutionalism can be combined to conceptualize a fruitful notion of transaction benefits. This theoretical contribution is meant to enable institutional economics to develop a fully elaborated cost–benefit analysis of existing institutional arrangements and their change over time.

Notes

1. Albert O. Hirschman pioneered such a theoretical perspective in economics (Hirschman, 1970, 1995).
2. See the movies *Star Wars*, directed by George Lucas. In these science fiction movies there are two collectives of 'knights' constantly battling each other. The good guys are telepathically connected to the 'bright side of the force'; the bad guys are spiritually linked to the 'dark side of the force'.
3. Moreover, this does as well render reference to veils of either ignorance (Rawls, 1971) or uncertainty (Buchanan, 1975) obsolete.
4. Though in his most recent programmatic article in *JEL* Williamson shows some awareness of Jon Elster's arguments on 'arguing and bargaining' (Elster, 1998) and Mark Granovetter's network approach (Granovetter, 2005), which are related to the communicative transaction benefit theory developed in this chapter, such concepts are confined to what he regards as level 1 of an economics of institutions which has not much to do with level 3, that is the realm of transaction cost economics (Williamson, 2000).
5. Quite the same critique is raised by Geoff Hodgson: 'Neoclassical economics has great difficulty accommodating the notion of learning because the very idea of 'rational learning' is problematic' (Hodgson, 2000: 327).
6. Be it communicative, procedural or expressive rationality (*cf.* Hargreaves Heap, 1989; Simon, 1997; Habermas, 1995).
7. Boulding's works on integrative power (1990, 1992), conflict resolution (1962, 1974a, 1974b) as well as on altruistic motivation (1973, 1981) are also based on a concept of communicative action which allows him to construct an alternative approach to welfare (*cf.* his critique of the conventional theory in Boulding, 1972 [1952]).

8. See Boulding's works on integrative power (1990, 1992) and conflict resolution (1962, 1974a, 1974b).
9. This strong emphasis on the importance of value judgements for human activities, whether scientific or mundane, goes back to his earlier analysis of their role in the history of economic thought (Myrdal, 1963 [1932]).
10. See my critique of methodological inconsistencies in Olson's analysis of democracy earlier in this chapter.
11. See Martha Nussbaum's aristotelean argument for a vague catalogue of universal human needs (Nussbaum, 2000).
12. An observation true not only for public discourse, but also for certain strands of economic theory like NIE. See the emphasis on values in Dolfsma, 2004.
13. The open attitude towards arguments of the other, which is implied here as a precondition, was called *democratic ethos* by one of Habermas' critics: 'The time has come for Habermas to acknowledge what pragmatists – especially Dewey and Mead – emphasized long ago: there is no democracy – in *theory* or in *practice – without a democratic ethos*' (Bernstein, 1996: 1146).
14. To develop this type of rationality, Habermas drew on George Herbert Mead and two generations of ordinary language philosophy including the speech act theory of John L. Austin (1969) and John R. Searle (2005).
15. The discourse concept developed by Bill Waller and Linda Robertson shows some similarities to Habermas' (Waller and Robertson, 1991: 1035).
16. As Denzau and North do in their approach to mental models.
17. We are indebted to Biesecker and Ulrich, who developed an economic theory based on Habermas' work, which they termed *Practical Social Economics* (Biesecker, 1997; Ulrich, 1987, 1997).

References

Apel, K. O. 'Diskursethik als Verantwortungsethik und das Problem der ökonomischen Rationalität', in B. Biervert, M. Held, and J. Wieland (eds), *Sozialphilosophische Grundlagen des ökonomischen Handelns* (Frankfurt a. M.: Suhrkamp, 1992): 121–54.

Austin, J. L. *How to Do Things with Words* (Cambridge, MA: Harvard University Press, 1969).

Bernstein, R. J. 'The Retrieval of the Democratic Ethos', *Cardozo Law Review*, 17 (1996): 1127–46.

Biesecker, A. 'The Market as an Instituted Realm of Action', *Journal of Socio-Economics*, 26 (1997): 215–41.

Bohnet, I. and Frey, B. S. 'Direct-Democratic Rules – The Role of Discussion', *Kyklos*, 47 (1994): 341–54.

Boulding, K. E. 'Einführung in die Wohlfahrtsökonomik', in G. Gäfgen (ed.), *Grundlagen der Wirtschaftspolitik* (Köln: Kiepenheuer & Witsch): 77–109. In English as: 'Welfare Economics', in B. F. Haley (ed.), *A Survey of Contemporary Economics* Vol. II (Homewood, Ill.: R. D. Irwin for the American Economics Association, 1952): 1–34.

Boulding, K. E. *Conflict and Defense: A General Theory* (Lanham: University Press of America, 1962).

Boulding, K. E. *The Economy of Love and Fear: A Preface to Grants Economics* (Wadsworth: Belmont, 1973).

Boulding, K. E. (ed.), 'The Communication of Legitimacy', *Collected Papers: Toward a General Social Science* Vol. IV (Boulder: Colorado Associated University Press, 1974a): 239–43.

Boulding, K. E. (ed.), 'The Role of Legitimacy in the Dynamics of Society', *Collected Papers: Toward a General Social Science* Vol. IV (Boulder: Colorado Associated University Press, 1974b): 511–23.

Boulding, K. E. *A Preface to Grants Economics: The Economy of Love and Fear* (New York: Praeger, 1981).

Boulding, K. E. *Three Faces of Power* (Newbury Park: Sage, 1990).

Boulding, K. E. (ed.), 'The Role of Conflict in the Dynamics of Society', *Towards a New Economics: Critical Essays on Ecology, Distribution, and Other Themes* (Hants: Edward Elgar, 1992): 190–97.

Boulding, K. E. *The Image: Knowledge in Life and Society* (Ann Arbor: University of Michigan Press, 1997 [1956]).

Buchanan, J. M. *The Limits of Liberty* (Chicago: University of Chicago Press, 1975).

Buchanan, J. M. and Vanberg, V. J. 'The Market as a Creative Process', *Economics and Philosophy*, 7 (1991): 167–86.

Coase, R. H. 'The Problem of Social Cost', *The Journal of Law & Economics*, 3 (1960): 1–44.

Commons, J. J. *Institutional Economics – Its Place in Political Economy* (New York: MacMillan, 1934).

Dawes, R. M., van de Kragt, J. C. A. and Orbell, J. M. 'Cooperation for the Benefit of Us – Not Me, or My Conscience', in J. J. Mansbridge (ed.), *Beyond Self-Interest* (Chicago and London: University of Chicago Press, 1990): 97–110.

Denzau, A. T. and North, D. C. 'Shared Mental Models: Ideologies and Institutions', *Kyklos*, 47 (1994): 3–31.

Dolfsma, W. *Institutional Economics and the Formation of Preferences – The Advent of Pop Music* (Cheltenham and Northampton: Edward Elgar, 2004).

Elster, J. 'Deliberation and Constitution Making', in J. Elster (ed.), *Deliberative Democracy* (Cambridge: Cambridge University Press, 1998): 97–122.

Farrell, J. 'Talk is Cheap', *American Economic Review (Papers and Proceedings)*, 85 (1995): 186–90.

Frambach, H. and Eissrich, D. 'Transaktionskosten – konzeptionelle Überlegungen zu einem fundamentalen und kontrovers diskutierten Ansatz der Neuen Institutionenökonomik', in D. Ipsen and H. Peukert (eds), *Institutional Economics: Theoretical Approaches and Empirical Applications* (Frankfurt a. M.: Haag + Herchen, 2002): 43–66.

Frey, B. S. and Bohnet, I. 'Institutions Affect Fairness – Experimental Investigations', *Journal of Institutional and Theoretical Economics (JITE), Zeitschrift für die gesamte Staatswissenschaft*, 151 (1995): 286–303.

Frey, B. S. and Bohnet, I. 'Identification in Democratic Society', *Journal of Socio-Economics*, 26 (1997): 25–38.

Granovetter, M. 'The Impact of Social Structure on Economic Outcomes', *Journal of Economic Perspectives*, 19 (2005): 33–50.

Habermas, J. *Theorie des Kommunikativen Handelns* 2 Vols (Frankfurt a. M.: Suhrkamp, 1995 [1982]).

Hargreaves Heap, S. *Rationality in Economics* (Oxford and New York: Basil Blackwell, 1989).

Hayek, F. v. 'Der Wettbewerb als Entdeckungsverfahren', in F. v. Hayek (ed.), *Freiburger Studien gesammelte Aufsätze* (Tübingen: J. C. B. Mohr (Paul Siebeck),

1969). English translation: Hayek, F. v. (ed.) 'Competition as a Discovery Process', *New Studies in Philosophy, Politics, Economics and the History of Ideas* (Chicago: University of Chicago Press, 1978): 179–90.

Hirschman, A. O. *Exit, Voice and Loyalty: Responses to Decline in Firms, Organizations, and States* (Cambridge, MA: Harvard University Press, 1970).

Hirschman, A. O. 'Exit, Voice, and the Fate of the German Democratic Republic', in A. O. Hirschman (ed.), *A Propensity to Self-subversion* (Cambridge, MA: Harvard University Press, 1995): 9–44.

Hodgson, G. M. 'What is the Essence of Institutional Economics?', *Journal of Economic Issues*, XXXIV (2) (2000): 317–29.

Kesting, S. 'A Potential for Understanding and the Interference of Power: Discourse as an Economic Mechanism of Coordination', *Journal of Economic Issues*, XXXII (4) (1998): 1053–78.

Kesting, S. 'Countervailing, Conditioned and Contingent – the Power Theory of John Kenneth Galbraith', *Journal of Post-Keynesian Economics*, 28 (2005): 3–24.

Klaes, M. 'The History of the Concept of Transaction Costs: Neglected Aspects', *Journal of the History of Economic Thought*, 22 (2000a): 191–216.

Klaes, M. 'The Birth of the Concept of Transaction Costs: Issues and Controversies', *Industrial and Corporate Change*, 9 (2000b): 567–93.

Knight, J. *Institutional and Social Conflict* (Cambridge: Cambridge University Press, 1992).

Knight, J. 'Explaining the Rise of Neoliberalism – The Mechanisms of Institutional Change', in J. L. Campbell and O. K. Petersen (eds), *The Rise of Neoliberalism and Institutional Analysis* (Princeton: Princeton University Press, 2001): 27–50.

Knight, J. and Johnson, J. 'Inquiry into Democracy: What Might a Pragmatist Make of Rational Choice Theories?', *American Journal of Political Science*, 43 (1999): 566–89.

Lukes, S. *Power – A Radical View* (Houndsmills and London: Macmillan, 1974).

Medema, S. G. and Samuels, W. J. 'Kenneth Boulding's The Image and Contemporary Discourse Analysis', in W. J. Samuels *et al.* (eds), *The Economy as a Process of Valuation* (Cheltenham: Edward Elgar, 1997): 299–327.

Myrdal, G. *Das politische Element in der nationalökonomischen Doktrinbildung* (Hannover: Verlag für Literatur und Zeitgeschehen, 1963 [1932]).

Myrdal, G. *Beyond the Welfare State: Economic Planning and Its International Implications* (New Haven: Yale University Press, 1968 [1958]).

Myrdal, G. *An American Dilemma: The Negro Problem and Modern Democracy* (New York: Pantheon Books, 1972 [1944]).

North, D. C. 'Institutions and Economic Performance', in U. Mäki, B. Gustafsson and C. Knudsen (eds), *Rationality, Institutions, and Economic Methodology* (London and New York: Routledge, 1993): 242–61.

North, D. C. 'Where have we been and where are we going?', in A. Ben-Ner and L. Putterman (eds), *Economics, Values, and Organisation* (Cambridge: Cambridge University Press, 1998): 491–508.

Nooteboom, B. *Trust – Forms, Foundations, Functions, Failures and Figures* (Cheltenham: Edward Elgar, 2002).

Nussbaum, M. C. *Women and Human Development – The Capabilities Approach* (Cambridge: Cambridge University Press, 2000).

Olson, M. 'Dictatorship, Democracy, and Development', *American Political Science Review*, 87 (1993): 567–76.

Olson, M. 'Big Bills Left on the Sidewalk: Why some Nations Are Rich and Others Are Poor', *Journal of Economic Perspectives*, 10 (1996): 3–24.
Olson, M. *Power and Prosperity: Outgrowing Communist and Capitalist Dictatorships* (New York: Basic Books, 2000).
Ramstad, Y. 'Is a Transaction a Transaction?', *Journal of Economic Issues*, 30 (1996): 413–25.
Rawls, J. *A Theory of Justice* (Cambridge: Belknap Press of Harvard University, 1971).
Rutherford, M. 'The Old and the New Institutionalism: Can Bridges Be Built?', *Journal of Economic Issues*, XXIX (2) (1995): 443–51.
Samuels, W. J. 'Ronald Coase and Coasean Economics: Some Questions, Conjectures and Implications', in W. J. Samuels *et al.* (eds), *The Economy as a Process of Valuation* (Cheltenham: Edward Elgar, 1997): 72–128.
Samuels, W. J., Medema, S. G. and Schmid, A. A. *The Economy as a Process of Valuation* (Cheltenham: Edward Elgar, 1997).
Schmid, A. A. 'Mancur Olson, Jr', in W. J. Samuels (ed.), *American Economists of the Late Twentieth Century* (Cheltenham: Edward Elgar, 1996): 216–37.
Schmid, A. A. *Conflict and Cooperation – Institutional and Behavioral Economics* (Oxford: Blackwell, 2004).
Searle, J. R. 'What is an institution?', *Journal of Institutional Economics*, 1 (2005): 1–22.
Simon, H. A. 'Rationality in Decision Making', in H. A. Simon (ed.), *An Empirically Based Microeconomics* (Cambridge: Cambridge University Press, 1997): 3–31.
Ulrich, P. *Intergrative Wirtschaftsethik: Grundlagen einer lebensdienlichen Ökonomie* (Bern: Paul Haupt, 1997).
Ulrich, P. *Transformation der ökonomischen Vernunft: Fortschrittsperspektiven der modernen Industriegesellschaft* (Bern: Paul Haupt, 1987).
Waller, W. T. and Robertson, L. R. 'Valuation as Discourse and Process: Or, How We Got Out of a Methodological Quagmire On Our Way to Purposeful Institutional Analysis', *Journal of Economic Issues*, XXV (4) (1991): 1029–48.
Williamson, O. E. 'Comparative Economic Organization: The Analysis of Discrete Structural Alternatives', *Administrative Science Quarterly*, 36 (1991): 269–96.
Williamson, O. E. 'The New Institutional Economics: Taking Stock, Looking Ahead', *Journal of Economic Literature*, 38 (2000): 595–613.
Williamson, O. E. 'The Theory of the Firm as Governance Structure: From Choice to Contract', *Journal of Economic Perspectives*, 16 (2002): 171–95.

Index